QDA B

D0550632

LANGAN

Radical Social Work Today

Radical Social Work Today

edited by

Mary Langan & Phil Lee

London
UNWIN HYMAN
Boston   Sydney   Wellington

Published by the Academic Division of
Unwin Hyman Ltd
15/17 Broadwick Street, London W1V 1FP, UK

Unwin Hyman, Inc.
8 Winchester Place, Winchester, Mass. 01890, USA

Allen & Unwin (Australia) Ltd,
8 Napier Street, North Sydney, NSW 2060, Australia

Allen & Unwin (New Zealand) Ltd in association with the
Port Nicholson Press Ltd,
Compusales Building, 75 Ghuznee Street, Wellington 1, New Zealand

First published in 1989

British Library Cataloguing in Publication Data

Radical social work today.
  1. Great Britain. Welfare work
  I. Langan, Mary   II. Lee, Phil
  361.3′0941

  ISBN 0–04–445368–X
  ISBN 0–04–445321–3   Pbk

Library of Congress Cataloging in Publication Data

Radical social work today / edited by Mary Langan & Phil Lee.
    p.   cm. — (The State of welfare)
  Bibliography: p.
  Includes index.
  ISBN 0–04–445368–X. — ISBN 0–04–445321–3 (soft)
  1. Social service.   2. Social service—Great Britain.   I. Langan,
Mary.   II. Lee, Phil.   III. Series.
HV37.R336   1989
361′.941—dc20   89–34003
                                                                 CIP

Typeset in 10 on 11 point Bembo by Nene Phototypesetters Ltd,
and printed in Great Britain by Billing and Sons, London and Worcester

Contents

List of Contributors

Peter Beresford is a worker with the Open Services Project and co-organizer of Battersea Community Action. He has previously been a Lecturer in Social Administration at Lancaster University and a Research Fellow, Sussex University. He has worked in the Social Services and Community Action Research Project. He has a number of publications and is co-author of *A Say in the Future* (Battersea Community Action), *Schools for All*, *Whose Welfare?* (Lewis Cohen Urban Studies Centre), *In Care in North Battersea* (University of Surrey). His joint interests with Suzy Croft are citizen involvement and empowerment in local life and services.

Suzy Croft is a worker with the Open Services Project and co-organizer at Battersea Community Action. She has been a Robert Kennedy Fellow and has worked in the Social Services and Community Action Research Project. She is a qualified social worker and a bereavement counsellor. Suzy has a number of publications and is co-author of *A Say in the Future*, and *Whose Welfare?*. Her joint interests with Peter Beresford are citizen involvement and empowerment in local life and services.

Yvonne Dhooge is a member of an EEC research programme on neighbourhoods and social and economic change. She is based at the Community Projects Foundation. She previously led a training initiative on the implications of unemployment for health and social services – an area she has researched. She is the author of *Ethnic Difference and Industrial Conflicts* (SSRC/RUER, University of Aston, 1981), and one of the co-authors of *Living in South London* (Gower, 1982), *Unemployment and Health; What Role for Health and Social Services* (Health Education Council, 1986) and *Working with Poverty and Unemployment* (South Bank Polytechnic, 1988).

Nick Frost is a Development Officer with a local authority social services department. He has formerly been a social worker and a Lecturer in Social Work. He is author of various articles on social work and social policy, and is co-author, with Mike Stein, of *The Politics of Child Welfare* (Wheatsheaf, 1989).

Annie Hudson is Lecturer in Social Work in the Department of

Social Policy and Social Work, University of Manchester. She previously worked in a local authority social services department and in a voluntary organization. Many of the ideas expressed in her article derive from her particular interest in social work practice with young women in trouble and from her involvement in a women's support group for incest survivors. She is currently working on a book *Troublesome Girls: Adolescence, Femininity and the State* (to be published by Macmillan).

Michael Hutchinson-Reis is presently employed as Head of the police committee support unit at the London Borough of Lambeth. He has previously worked as a community social worker on the Broadwater Farm Estate, Tottenham. He has also worked as a hospital-based psychiatric social worker and as a social worker on an intake team in East London. He has been a lecturer and a tutor on the degree in Sociology and CQSW courses at the Polytechnic of North London. He has also been a trade union official. He is currently a member of the editorial collective of *Critical Social Policy*.

Mary Langan is Lecturer in Social Policy at the Open University. She has many years experience of social work and social work education. She has worked as a local authority social worker and teamleader in Wiltshire and the London Borough of Tower Hamlets. For a number of years she was a social work tutor and Senior Lecturer in Applied Social Studies. Her research interests focus on the relationship between state, social policy and social work. Her publications include *Crises in the British State 1880–1930* (edited with B. Schwarz, Hutchinson, 1985) and *State Social Work, Race and Gender* (edited with L. Day, Unwin Hyman, 1989). She is General Editor of Unwin Hyman's social policy series *The State of Welfare*.

Phil Lee has recently been appointed to a lectureship in social work and social policy in the School of Social Work at Leicester University. Prior to that he had been a Senior Lecturer in Applied Social Studies at Sheffield City Polytechnic for ten years. He is a founder member of the Critical Social Policy Collective and his interests and writings largely focus on the relationship between politics, social theory and welfare. He is a qualified youth and community worker and teacher, and has practised in various settings as a social, youth and community worker. His publications include *Welfare Theory and Social Policy* (Sage 1988; co-authored with Colin Raban); *Theory and Practice in Social Work* (Basil Blackwell, 1982; with Roy Bailey). He is presently working on a project to do with young men, masculinity and gender awareness.

Nigel Parton is Principal Lecturer in Social Work at Huddersfield Polytechnic and has worked as a local authority social worker. His previous publications include *The Politics of Child Abuse* (Macmillan, 1985) and *The Political Dimensions of Social Work* (edited with Bill Jordan, Blackwell, 1983). He is also a member of The Politics of Child Abuse Study Group whose book, *Taking Child Abuse Seriously*, is shortly to be published in *The State of Welfare* series by Unwin Hyman.

Geoffrey Pearson is Professor of Social Work at Middlesex Polytechnic, London. He taught previously at University College, Cardiff and at the University of Bradford where he was Reader in Applied Social Studies. His published work includes *The Deviant Imagination* (Macmillan, 1975), *Working Class Youth Culture* (Routledge, 1976), *Hooligan: A History of Respectable Fears* (Macmillan, 1983), *Young People and Heroin* (Health Education Council & Gower, 1986), *The New Heroin Users* (Blackwell, 1987) and *Social Work and the Legacy of Freud* (Macmillan, 1988).

Chris Phillipson is Professor of Applied Social Studies and Social Gerontology at the University of Keele. He has conducted a number of research projects in the field of old age. His particular areas of concern include retirement issues, health education and the political economy of ageing. His most recent publications include *Drugs, Ageing and Society* (co-authored with B. Burns, Croom Helm, 1986) and *The Sociology of Old Age* (co-authored with G. Fennell and H. Evers, Open University Press, 1988).

Jennie Popay is a Senior Researcher at the Thomas Coram Research Unit based at the University of London Institute of Education. She is presently conducting research into patterns of health and health care in households with dependent children. Her research interests are broad ranging but include a focus on social class and gender-linked inequalities in health and on the implications for health of changing employment patterns, household structures and familial relationships. She is author of 'Women, Unemployment and the Family' in *Family and Economy in Modern Society* (Macmillan, 1986), and 'Women Workers and Health Hazards' in *Health Struggles and Community Action* (Pluto, 1985). She is co-author of *Employment Trends and the Family* (Study Commission on the Family, 1982) and *One Parent Families and Social Policy* (Study Commission on the Family, 1983).

Bruce Senior is the Manager of a Resource Centre for Young People in Avon. Until 1988 he was Senior Lecturer in Applied Social Studies at Sheffield City Polytechnic (where this chapter was written). His main interests as a lecturer and social work tutor were in the areas of anti-racist social work, policy development and organizational change in the public sector, and residential care. Prior to working in higher education he had extensive experience of social work in inner London, for the most part based in a local authority children's home.

Paul Senior holds a joint appointment as a Senior Lecturer in Social Work at Sheffield City Polytechnic and a Senior Probation Officer (Training) with South Yorkshire Probation Service. Prior to this appointment he worked for six years as a probation officer. His publications include 'Probation Order: A Vehicle of Social Work or Social Control', *Probation Journal* (June 1984), 'Group Work with Offenders' in *Working with Offenders* (BASW/ Macmillan, 1985) and 'Community Probation Initiatives: Exploring the Wider Issues' in *Enquiries into Community Probation Work* (Cranfield Press, 1988). He was chair of the national Probation Practice Committee of the National Association of Probation Officers from 1983 to 1986 and is currently a council member of the Central Council for Education and Training in Social Work (CCETSW).

Naseem Shah is Senior Lecturer in Social Work at the West London Institute of Higher Education. She was previously a Senior Lecturer and the only black staff member in the Department of Social Work and Social Policy at Newcastle upon Tyne Polytechnic. Prior to this she was a social worker at Newcastle Social Services department, where she was also the only black worker. She has been a race development officer and she is currently a member of the Critical Social Policy Collective. She has published in the areas of education and racism and social work and racism.

Mike Simpkin has been in local authority social work since 1968. He has worked in child care, generic teams, and a psychiatric hospital, and most recently was attached to a politically oriented general medical practice in Sheffield. He now works for the Leeds City Council Health Unit. He is the author of *Trapped within Welfare* (2nd edn, Macmillan, 1983).

John Winston Small is Assistant Director of Social Services with the London Borough of Hackney. He worked in several London Boroughs as a social worker and with the Jamaican Government for four years. He established the New Black Families Unit which has attempted to transform adoption and fostering from a Euro-centric approach to a much more racially and sensitive professional activity. He is the founder and first President of the Association of Black Social Workers and Allied Professions. He is a council member of CCETSW where he is serving on the Course Approval Committee and is Chairperson of its Black Perspectives Commit-tee. He has written extensively on the transcultural mode of social work in professional journals. His most recent publication is *Social Work with Black Children and their Families* (jointly written with S. Ahmed and J. Cheetham, Batsford, 1985).

Neil Small is Lecturer in Social Work at the School of Applied Social Studies, Bradford University. He previously worked as a social worker in the London Borough of Wandsworth and at the Henderson Hospital, Sutton, Surrey. His research interests include planning and policy making in the welfare state. His recent publications include work on violence in social work in *Critical Social Policy* and in *Community Care* and inter-occupational re-lationships in the health service (*British Journal of Social Work*).

Ian Smith left school to study architecture but dropped out well before qualifying and joined the UN Association as workcamper and, later, workcamp organizer. He was then employed as a community development worker by the Bakgatla Tribe in Bots-wana. This was followed by two years as a community work student at Goldsmiths' College in southeast London. He then worked in Sunderland for ten years – three years in the town hall as social work manager and apprentice bureaucrat then seven years as community worker/advice worker employed by local management committee. Since 1983 he has been principal community worker with Sheffield City Council.

Mike Stein is a Lecturer and Dr Barnados Research Fellow in Applied Social Studies in the School of Continuing Education, University of Leeds. He is co-author with Kate Carey of *Leaving Care* (Blackwell, 1986) and has contributed to several books and journals on young people in care. Forthcoming publications in-clude *The Politics of Child Welfare* (with Nick Frost, Wheatsheaf, 1989) and *Leaving Care Projects* (First Key, 1988) based upon ongoing research.

The State of Welfare: Editor's Preface

Over the past decade the postwar consensus on the welfare state has been undermined by economic crisis and the growing appeal of right-wing social policies. In all Western countries public debate has focused on the burden of public spending, particularly on welfare, and on the measures necessary to reduce it. Austerity policies have squeezed welfare provision under governments of the right in Britain, West Germany and the USA, and under socialist governments in France and Spain.

In Britain, all sides are dissatisfied with the old system of welfare. The new right denounces the profligacy and inefficiency of public services while feminists and the left insist that social welfare provision must be transformed to establish new democratic forms of socialized welfare provision. After forty years of consensus, the debate about welfare has entered a new phase.

In practice, the attempts by governments in Britain and abroad to restructure welfare services have encountered difficulties. Welfare professionals, trade unions and substantial bodies of public opinion have opposed drastic cuts in welfare services. In general resistance has been most effective in relation to health provision, where established facilities tend to enjoy considerable public popularity, and least effective in social security and council housing, where unpopular state services have been the targets of hostile media comment and political propaganda.

However, despite some successful delaying tactics, the general trend towards retrenchment and piecemeal privatization is unmistakable. The increasingly defensive position of the welfare agencies and their supporters, and the growing reliance of welfare on charitable and voluntary initiatives, large and small, reflects the growing success of government pressure in transferring the cost of caring away from the state. The 1989 White Paper on the National Health Service signalled a major extension of market principles into the area of welfare provision which had most successfully resisted the pressure of Thatcherite austerity over the previous decade. Meanwhile the Conservative government's social security 're-forms' threaten to deepen and widen the scale of poverty in Britain.

The attempts by government to restructure welfare and the continuing resistance to austerity policies have provoked widespread debate. Some consider that capitalist counter-crisis strategies will necessitate a major rationalization of welfare and that the appeal of anti-welfare prejudices can create a new consensus of support for such a policy. Others argue that the economic and political consequences of dismantling the welfare state infrastructure would be too great for any Western democracy to face.

The attack on welfare and debate about the future of welfare services provide the context for a new series of books. *The State of Welfare* will include books on the different aspects of the welfare state, analysing new and emerging trends in the organization and delivery of services and the economic and political determinants of welfare policy. They will also examine alternatives to current welfare services. The second book in this series – *Radical Social Work Today*, edited by myself and Phil Lee – examines the difficulties facing social work and outlines the way forward for a radical social work practice.

Mary Langan

Foreword

Radical Social Work was first published in the UK in 1975 and in the USA and Sweden within two years. From the responses to that publication, we could reasonably assume that the essays included in that 'original' reader had made a significant impact on social work education and hopefully, on practice. There followed a number of volumes on a similar theme from distinguished authors. During the next fifteen years or so, I had the good fortune to visit a considerable number of Departments of Social Work in the UK and elsewhere, including the USA and Canada. In all cases *Radical Social Work* was clearly becoming a 'standard text'. Social Work curricula even had sections on 'radical social work'. Although I was never wholly convinced of such a section, it at least demonstrated an impact. To introduce a discrete section within a syllabus was likely to separate the framework from the substance of the studies.

In recent years invitations to talk to both staff and students have tended to be invitations to answer the question: 'Whatever happened to radical social work?'. The social and political landscape has changed very considerably since 1975! What was once radical is now, in some senses, commonplace. It is less easy today to blame unemployment on the unemployed, or indeed poverty on the poor. Considerable evidence exists to expose the fallacy of such views. Skilled and unskilled workers along with many professionals, are aware of the seemingly fragile nature of their 'security'. Whether we are teachers, social workers, shipbuilders or coal miners, the changes taking place in our economic and political surroundings impinge upon, and it seems threaten, us all. The critiques the radical authors of the 1970s were developing were I believe, offered from a commitment at the very least, to 'humanize' social work provision and welfare development. The criticisms, I read and hear in the 1980s, all too often, seem to be offered as a reason to inhibit social work and dismantle welfare provision.

This volume, *Radical Social Work Today*, is a timely consideration of the framework the earlier books had sought to develop. In some cases looking afresh at similar issues (community work), in others, introducing new issues (a feminist and a black perspective). The essays are challenging and stimulating. Without wishing to sound patronizing, I would urge social work educators and social work practitioners to consider these essays and take the debate forward together. If ever there was a need for the sharing of experience in teaching, research and practice, it is now. Professional education and training courses are demanding closer collaboration between practitioners and 'theorists'. Social Work education and training must, in my view, be 'practice led'. If it isn't I fear it will be 'employer led' and that will be to the detriment of educator, student, practitioner and 'client' alike. The concerns of this volume should inform future development of social work if we are to avoid a retreat into discrete areas and lose sight of a social structure and an institutional configuration which conditions and creates the problems with which social workers must deal. This volume supports those who seek to oppose the stigma and stereotyping of the recipients of social work, and who resist authoritarian attempts by the state to undermine their dignity.

Roy Bailey
Sheffield City Polytechnic
November 1988

1 Whatever happened to radical social work?

MARY LANGAN and PHIL LEE

During the late 1960s and early 1970s social work in Britain was subjected to a fierce critique from a loose coalition of welfare activists, social workers, consumers, students and academics. Its sources of inspiration, both theoretical and practical, were so diverse as to be contradictory. The emphasis on the subjective experience of the consumer derived from deviancy theory and phenomenology did not rest easily with some of the more structurally derived Marxist analyses of the role of state welfare. Nor did the latter blend comfortably with some of the pluralist-inspired direct action strategies of the community activists. The feminist critique of social work theory and practice developed after the first flowering of the movement and added another influential and often discordant trend. Nevertheless, this internally explosive mixture of activists inspired by Marx, Freire, Alinsky, Illich, Neil, de Beauvoir, Becker, Goffman and Gramsci, among others, made a highly significant impact on the study and practice of social work.[1]

The themes of the early radical social work movement in Britain were brought together in the influential *Radical Social Work*, edited by Mike Brake and Roy Bailey in 1975, and in the follow-up collection, *Radical Social Work and Practice*, published in 1980. The activist dimension of the movement was best represented by the duplicated periodical *Case Con*, self-styled as 'a revolutionary magazine for social workers', which ran through twenty-five lively and provocative issues between 1970 and 1977. Throughout the 1970s the National Deviancy Conference provided a forum within which many of the theoretical disputes and political difficulties encountered by the radical social work movement were thrashed out.

Many commentators have consistently registered a negative verdict on the impact of radical social work.[2] For others, including the present authors, it was a significant moment in the development of social work in Britain. While some of the excesses of the early period – such as the idea of 'client refusal'[3] – now seem embarrassing, it is impossible not to be struck by the energy and commitment of the radical social work movement. Only recently we were reading through local authority case notes from the early 1960s and were struck by their naive and apolitical content, permeated by an aloof, middle-class judgementalism. Many contemporary social workers are, of course, still middle class and they certainly have their prejudices, especially regarding racism and sexism. However, as a result of the impact of radical social work, their case notes and their working attitudes are likely to be informed by a sharper political awareness about the realities of their clients' lives and the restricted options available to them.

The radical social work movement widened the scope of modern social work. It challenged the narrow preoccupation of traditional social work with the individual, introduced a wider set of issues and put politics on the agenda. However, the events of the past ten or fifteen years have fundamentally changed the context within which social work operates. While many of the attitudes and values of the radical movement entered mainstream practice, social work now faces new challenges which demand a rethinking of the radical project. We can broadly identify four factors in the new climate affecting social work.

First, fifteen years of economic recession and a decade of Conservative government have dramatically increased the work load of social workers. Permanent mass unemployment and the deepening impoverishment of an ageing population have forced more and more people to seek social work assistance. Government legislation in the fields of social security and housing pushes a heavier burden onto welfare workers.[4] Lawrence estimates that since 1972 some sixty-two Acts of parliament have been passed that have implications for the practice of social work.[5]

The impact of austerity policies in promoting 'community care' of the mentally ill and handicapped and the chronically sick and disabled has increased demands on social work agencies in the community as well as pressures on women in the home. National panics about child abuse and crime have resulted in a heavier burden of work for social workers, probation officers and other specialist workers. All these demands have hit local authority social services departments at a time when local government services have been a focus of political conflict as well as a target for spending cuts and privatization policies.

Second, social workers in general – and radical social workers in particular – have come under an unprecedented barrage of public criticism and condemnation. A number of highly publicized inquiries into cases of child abuse have scapegoated social workers for the failures of the system of supervision of 'at risk' families. As part of the wider Thatcherite campaign against 'sixties' permissiveness', the radical social worker became a personification of the liberal trends in welfare which the government sought to replace with a return to the values of the Poor Law. The caricature of 'Damien the social worker' – a 'wimp' talking in a mixture of left-wing slogans and sociological jargon – who was a featured guest for a period in the mid-1980s on the popular radio show 'Steve Wright in the afternoon', summed up the prevailing prejudices.

The demonization of the radical social worker has played a key part in the third significant shift – the drive to press social workers into assuming a more coercive and interventionist role in policing deviant families in Thatcher's Britain. The child abuse scare in particular has led to concerted pressure for social workers to work more closely with the police and the courts and to make full use of statutory powers to remove children from their families. Local authority social workers, as well as probation officers, find that their traditional caring functions have been squeezed out by new responsibilities in enforcing state controls, especially in relation to child care and juvenile delinquency. Paradoxically the controversy over child sexual abuse which raged around cases in Cleveland in 1987 and 1988 produced a marked, though not favourable, shift in the public image of the social worker. No longer the ineffectual liberal, the radical social worker was now a zealot, endowed by legislation with extensive coercive powers, and not reluctant to use them against respectable and god-fearing parents.

Fourth, radical social work has come under growing criticism from representatives of the oppressed both within social work and in the wider radical movement. While early radical social work shared the male dominance characteristic of the traditional left, it later took up some of the issues raised by the women's movement in the 1970s. However, feminists have continued to expose the limited progress made in challenging patriarchal structures and relationships in the provision of welfare services. Black activists have pointed to the 'race blindness' of much of the early radical social work literature. They have also criticized the often tokenistic character of the equal opportunities policies and 'racial awareness training' procedures adopted by many local authorities and voluntary agencies in the early 1980s. Black women have made known their concern with the continuing effects of sexism and racism in the world of social work. Activists concerned with disability and older people have also expressed concern that their interests have not been adequately articulated by the radical movement.

Given the scale of the challenge radical social work now faces, it is surprising that there has been little attempt to take forward the approach pioneered by the movement of the 1970s. This may be partly attributable to a degree of complacency that surrounded the early movement following its initial impact. For example, Jeffrey Galper, a leading contributor to radical social work theory in the USA, echoed the prevailing mood of optimism in 1975 when he wrote: 'I firmly believe, as many on the left do, that the ability of the liberal–conservative positions to contain the debate, and surely the utility of that containment for all of us, is passing.'[6]

How wrong we were! Far from declining, liberal–conservative thought enjoyed a remarkable renaissance and in the era of Reagan, Thatcher and Kohl it became a major influence on social policy. There is clearly a need to reassess radical social work from the perspective of today. We also need to ask to what extent it is still relevant to our needs and which aspects should be modified or even rejected in the light of experience. This is the project we have set ourselves in *Radical Social Work Today*.

Radical Social Work revisited

On looking back, the striking features of the *Radical Social Work* text are the clarity and simplicity of its basic themes. It chastises conventional social work for its failure to develop a critical self-awareness and argues the need for a critical professional literature. It challenges social work's preoccupation with individualistic explanations of social problems. Such notions are condemned for pathologizing the poor/deviant/victim and devaluing the role of collective political action and self-help in the attainment of humane welfare provision. *Radical Social Work* insists that social workers need to become much less judgemental of minority lifestyles and cultivate cultural diversity and acceptance of gay people, criminals, etc. It urges social workers to get involved in socialist political action as much in their own interests as in the interests of those who depend on their services.

In their useful account of the radical social work movement, Clark and Asquith have summed up the characteristic features of its activists.[7] They noted that social workers attracted to the movement tended to be committed to some form of socialism, 'from mild social reformism to revolutionary Marxism'. Radical social workers typically related social problems to 'their specific societal context rather than to the failings of individuals'; it was the social system that required change, not the people who suffered the results of defective social arrangements.

Radicals were mistrustful of the way the state used social workers to control sections of the population. They were also suspicious of professionalism among social workers, arguing that 'authentic personal relationships between client and worker' were preferable to 'relationships of instrumental authority'. Radical social workers shared a 'commitment to participatory styles of decision-making within and between agencies as between social worker and client'. They often regarded their own agencies as just as big a problem as external factors. Finally, there was a common 'disaffection with the nuclear family as the basic social unit, and an aspiration to other forms of social living such as the collective or the community'.

Some of the absences in the early work are immediately apparent. There was little analysis of the role of women as the large majority of both social work clients and practitioners. Consideration of racism or of forms of anti-racist practice was minimal; there was no discussion about how to practise with the unemployed; older people and the non-able bodied were ignored. We have attempted to correct the gender and race blindness of the early texts. We include Annie Hudson's assessment of the feminist contribution to radical social work (Chapter 4) and Naseem Shah's essay on the oppression of black women in social work (Chapter 9). The collection also carries contributions by black social workers John Small (Chapter 14) and Michael Hutchinson-Reis (Chapter 8). Our other contributors have paid particular attention to the ways that sexism and racism operate in their areas of concern.

Geoffrey Pearson (Chapter 3) and Jennie Popay and Yvonne Dhooge (Chapter 7) discuss the impact of unemployment on social work. We also include a piece by Chris Phillipson (Chapter 10), who has previously criticized the radical movement for its neglect of older people. He insists that 'old age is less of a biological and psychological problem, more of a problem for a society characterised by major social inequalities in the distribution of power, income and property'.[8] Let's look at some of the themes of radical social work more closely and evaluate their relevance to the theory and practice of social work into the 1990s.

Radical critique

One of the most positive features of the radical social work movement from the start was that it put forward a CRITIQUE of

existing patterns of social provision. This meant relating developments in welfare to the wider social and political context as well as
assessing the practical consequences of social work interventions.
While radical social work has been much criticized for failing to
move much beyond a critical mode, there has been a considerable
underestimation of how necessary this critique was and of the
constructive role it has played.

The pioneering work of the early radical social work movement
has been followed up by contributions examining, among other
things, the naivety of some of the moral prescriptions underlying[9]
social work intervention;[9] the deskilling of the social work task;[10]
and the failure to develop proper yardsticks by which to measure
the effectiveness of social work intervention.[11] Others have
appraised the pressures upon social workers to work in individualistic ways that reinforce a stigmatized client status;[12] others
still have advanced a swingeing critique of the disease model as
applied to the problem of child abuse.[13] There have also been
attempts to locate the crisis of social work in a wider political
context,[14] and recent feminist and anti-racist contributions have
advanced a wide-ranging critique of traditional social work
methods.[15]

In this collection, we make no apology for continuing in a critical
vein. All the contributors critically examine developments in their
specific areas of concern. For example, Suzy Croft and Peter
Beresford (Chapter 5) advance a detailed assessment of the fashionable concern with community social work and patch system
delivery which is affecting all aspects of personal social service
provision. Nick Frost and Mike Stein (Chapter 2) provide an
overview of what has been happening in social services departments over the past few years. Paul Senior (Chapter 15) does the
same for the probation service and Ian Smith (Chapter 13) for
community work.

Radical social work has been criticized from both left and right
for its allegedly abstract critique of conventional social work and
for the supposed impracticality of its proposals for work in the
field. For example, Rein, from a left-wing standpoint, dismissed
the whole project of radical social work with the claim that 'social
work, *by itself*, has almost nothing to contribute to the reduction
of the interrelated problems of unemployment, poverty and
dependency'.[16] He went on to suggest that radical social workers
were effectively reinterpreting 'social work as *radical social policy*
. . . [and] then it ceases to be social work'.

From inside the profession, Pinker,[17] Halmos [18] and Butrym
have taken a similarly negative view of the radical movement. As

Butrym has written, 'there are no special grounds for social work to claim a sense of special overall responsibility for such massive national social problems as those of homelessness, poverty and unemployment'.[19] Of course, in a literal sense both Butrym and Rein are right. But nobody has ever suggested that social work should take on such an *overall* responsibility. The consequence of these arguments is to relegate social work merely to offering 'band aid' solutions to social problems.

Proponents of conventional social work restate the familiar criticism that the real job of the profession should be to deal with supposedly perennial social casualties such as the disabled, neglected children, the psychologically disturbed and older people. Clarke, for example, repeats the old allegation that 'the danger of radicalism is that it denies that fundamental helplessness exists'.[20] This is patent nonsense. One of the major achievements of the original radical social work movement was that it questioned conventional practice in terms that pushed the interests of the client to the fore, and as such *made sense to practitioners*. It pointed out, for example, just how frequently conventional practice militated against client empowerment as well as against progressive social change.

For the most part the critics of radical social work have ignored the extent to which radical social workers *are* steeped in practice. Many have been attracted to radical theory because they found conventional theory *inappropriate* for practice in the real world. Too often such theory is remote from reality, denying for example the impact of racism or the extent to which government legislation, particularly in the sphere of income maintenance, is making social workers agents of punitive and repressive policies. Radical social work texts have been widely read by practitioners, and practitioners have made important contributions to radical theory. More than half the contributions to this collection come from people who are currently practising social workers and all have substantial practical experience. Most of the contributors make extensive proposals for practice in their particular field of social or community work.

John Small's contribution to this collection (Chapter 14) exposes the extent to which conventional social work employs a 'deficit' and racist concept of black family life, regarding it as inherently unstable. Using psychological concepts in a radical and original way, he illustrates how social workers might develop a more sensitive and anti-racist practice. Bruce Senior (Chapter 12) argues that organizational theory holds the key to the development of progressive residential practice. He argues that it is more often than

not conventional residential practice that fails to translate its theory
into practice. Similarly, Mike Simpkin (Chapter 11) argues that
social workers are much better placed than they think to promote
democratic health care within their authorities and trade unions.

Micropolitics

The radical social work movement has always emphasized the
importance of what Statham has called 'micropolitics'.[21] This means
making small practical changes in methods of day-to-day working
that may have significant consequences both for relationships with
clients and for developing more effective modes of participative
practice. Given the restricted scope for more dramatic styles of
radical practice in today's conditions, this is an approach that has
considerable relevance for modern radical social work. In their
article on unemployment, for example, Popay and Dhooge (Chapter 7) show the potential for a micropolitical approach. They show
how monitoring the effects of unemployment in a local area can be
used for propaganda purposes; they emphasize how cultivating
channels of information both among staff and between staff and
clients can improve take-up and increase awareness. They also
discuss take-up campaigns, mobile welfare rights offices,
claimants' unions and food co-ops – all practical initiatives that can
transform the experience of the unemployed and change the nature
of work with claimants.

Micropolitics also implies what Hugman has called 'integrity on
the job' and the need for attention to apparently trivial but really
important issues in the workplace – like office layout, the wording
and style of notices, the conduct of reception staff and the
atmosphere of waiting areas.[22] It means too that workers must
always be aware that they possess access, or potential access, to a
great deal of information that is unavailable to the users of their
services. This information can make a useful contribution to
political campaigns for more responsive welfare services. In a
number of significant ways, working at a number of different
levels, social workers can resist the process through which clients
become dependent on arbitrary officialdom. In small ways,
perhaps, they can employ strategies that *empower* rather than
control the consumer.

Micropolitics also involves recognizing how broader political
processes operate at the level of the individual and personal
relationships, among social workers and at the interface between
social workers and clients. For the early radical social workers this

meant being attentive to the dangers of adopting paternalistic or repressive attitudes towards clients. Today the wider recognition of the forces of racism and sexism in society and social work imposes a responsibility on radical workers to confront these powerful influences, among social workers themselves as well as in their work with clients.

Some have always argued that progressive work can only be done *outside* official agencies – in what Rolston and Smyth describe as 'the spaces between cases'.[23] Others, such as Pearson, are less pessimistic and more flexible about the ways in which workers can support progressive change, even to the extent of openly advocating forms of industrial deviance.[24] Different social workers will choose different ways of fighting back; there has never been a monolithic radical social work. One of the lasting strengths of the radical social work movement, and the main reason why it has been able to adapt to the demands of women and black people, is its openness to debate and the willingness of its activists to undertake diverse forms of resistance.

Class, gender and race

The early radical social work movement was acutely aware of the ways in which the practice of social work reinforced the chronic dependence of sections of the working class on paternalistic welfare services. The radical movement emphasized the necessity of transforming the relationship between the provider and the user of services. Activists attempted to break down barriers by democratizing services, involving consumers in decision-making and in the day-to-day running of the institutions in which they lived.

The key concept that evolved out of the radical movement was the *empowerment* of the consumer. Radical social work sought to generate a wider awareness of the power that social workers had by virtue of their access to information and resources that were not readily available to service users. 'Empowerment' was the process of transferring this power into the hands of the people who were systematically denied it within the framework of the welfare state.

While radical social workers were highly perceptive of the class inequalities reinforced by the operation of the postwar welfare system, they failed to recognize the systematic denial of power and resources to women and black people. The sexist and racist motives underlying the foundation of welfare services in Britain have only been slowly recognized.[25] For today's radical social work movement, considerations of gender and race have severely disrupted the early movement's simple preoccupation with class.

A wider recognition of the complex ways in which the state and social work are implicated in oppression has forced radical social workers to reappraise their concepts and analytic tools. This process has involved more than a theoretical review of the role of conventional social work institutions and practices in mediating sexism and racism. It has also meant recognizing that the radical social work movement has itself reproduced sexist and racist practices. This awareness was the result of the growing criticism of radical social work by representatives of the oppressed themselves. Male radical social workers have experienced the full force of women's anger, complacent white liberals have been blasted by black activists, heterosexuals by lesbians and gay men.

The attack on radical social work from the movements of the oppressed has forced left-wing social workers to take note of their concerns. White people and men have attempted to 'listen' to black people and women and have tried to change their attitudes and behaviour in the light of criticism. Because the cleavages of gender and race divide the radical movement itself, this has often proved a traumatic process. Although there has never been a monolithic radical social work movement, past controversies mostly arose from differences over questions of theory or strategy. The conflicts over gender and race, however, involve the articulation of distinct and antagonistic interests *within* the movement itself.

It would be disingenuous to ignore the difficulties involved in trying to make the radical social work movement truly representative of and accountable to all sections of the oppressed. Feminist and black activists have experienced intense frustration at the slowness of even the most radical social workers to recognize the scale of the problems and to begin to change their outlook and methods. On the other hand, many male and white radicals who feel that they have made genuine attempts to transform their practice towards women and black people find themselves the object of continuing reproaches for their sexism and racism. Some results are mounting anger and hostility on the side of the oppressed and silent recrimination and paralysing guilt among social work radicals. There is a danger that these tensions may lead to the increasing fragmentation and perhaps even the ultimate disintegration of the radical movement.

If we are to preserve the positive potential of the radical movement it is vital that we forge some common ground among the diverse forces now engaged in the world of social work. The radical movement cannot carry on in the old way, merely as an extension of the traditional white, labour movement-oriented, left. Nor can it become a movement that loses sight of fundamental class divisions in society or that elevates any particular issue of oppression above others. It must be an *alliance* of social forces, representing diverse social interests but with common political goals: it must be a unity that embodies and respects difference. It is not yet clear how to achieve strategic or tactical alliances that can enable the movement to confront systematicaly all forms of oppression. These can only be worked out in practice, through a willingness of all those involved to listen to one another and to work constructively together.

It has become increasingly apparent that the institutions and practices of the labour movement are deeply imbued with the sexist and racist prejudices of British society. For radical social work today it is vital to challenge the restricted vision of the traditional labour movement in its approach to questions of welfare. For example, British unions have always put sectional wage struggles above considerations about collective child care and they have marginalized the concerns of women and black workers.

Since the early 1980s a number of Labour-controlled local authorities have attempted to overcome the legacy of neglect of gender and race issues by promoting equal opportunity policies and setting up equal opportunity units and advisers. Some have campaigned against sexual harassment and discrimination and others have run special courses to alert workers to problems of racism and racial prejudice. Much of this activity is undoubtedly tokenistic, and some has already been abandoned under pressure from the right and the media. Yet some discussion is now opening up about how to practise in an anti-sexist and anti-racist way. In this book, Annie Hudson (Chapter 4) assesses the potential of equal opportunities policies in the sphere of gender inequality in local government.

Michael Hutchinson-Reis and Naseem Shah (Chapters 8 and 9) are sceptical of the sudden discovery by the local state of the need for equal opportunities and race-sensitive social work. Hutchinson-Reis writes that 'despite these efforts, there appears to be no fundamental change in the underlying racist nature of social work'. Naseem Shah analyses the specificity of black women's oppression and argues that it is exacerbated by the manner in which white feminist theory has tended to exclude or appropriate the experience of black women. Nevertheless, she believes that it is possible for black and white women to work together, but insists that this requires 'genuine effort on the part of white people to listen to what black people are saying'.

The labour movement connection

Radical social workers have always emphasized their identification
as workers, as members of trade unions and the wider labour
movement, rather than as members of organizations aspiring to
professional status and prestige. In the past this meant playing an
active role in radical movements in the unions – the Nalgo Action
Group in the late 1970s was closely associated with radical social
work. It also meant a broader engagement in the struggles of the
labour movement – against the anti-trade union legislation of the
early 1970s and the incomes policies of the Wilson and Callaghan
governments. Another key project was providing solidarity with
workers in struggle, from the miners' strikes of the early 1970s to
the Grunwick dispute and the public service 'winter of discontent'
towards the end of the decade of radicalism. Like much else, the
role of radical social workers in the labour movement has become
much more complicated since the advent of Thatcherism.

On the one hand, the Thatcher years have strengthened basic
trade unionism among social workers. Social workers have shared
in the wider proletarianization of white-collar workers, especially
those working in the public service sector. While pay levels have
stagnated, work loads have increased and working conditions have
deteriorated, particularly as a result of chronic staff shortages in
areas where pressures are greatest. At the same time, the politicization of local government has had the effect of encouraging trade
unionism among threatened council workers. This is a result of the
emergence of radical Labour councils and the corresponding Tory
counter-attack. The imposition of central government cuts and
restrictive legislation, notably the abolition of the Greater London
Council and the metropolitan councils, provoked widespread
protest in the mid-1970s. The subsequent abolition of the Inner
London Education Authority, the section 28/29 attack on lesbian
and gay rights, the imposition of the poll tax and the advance of
privatization broadened the scope of political unrest even further.

While union membership has been decimated in private manu-
facturing, it has remained fairly steady in public services. The result
is that a union such as Nalgo, to which the vast majority of social
workers belong, has become one of the most powerful in the TUC.
Social workers therefore are now more inclined to recognize their
interests as workers and to take their place in a trade union that
appears to have retained its organizational strength when others,
such as the miners, have been drastically weakened.

On the other hand, however, the government attack on the
public services within which radical social workers are employed

has created major tactical difficulties. Since 1979 they have increasingly been forced to defend the very services that they had previously condemned as parsimonious, hierarchical and paternalistic.

Until recently most Marxist-inspired analyses regarded welfare services as either functioning on behalf of capitalism or as the product of working-class struggle. Gough's attempt to resolve this conundrum by adopting a compromise position that took account of the economic context and the balance of class forces was only partially successful.[26] It failed to explain sufficiently how different capitalist societies have different forms of state welfare provision. Another way of putting this problem is to say that ten years ago the left was so critical and dismissive of the reactionary aspects of state welfare that in the 1980s it found itself ill-prepared to defend its progressive features. Since the early 1980s radical social policy analysts have belatedly attempted to construct a more sensitive set of concepts to guide practice in this complex area.[27]

A number of related problems have followed. Radicals had argued that social workers and probation officers were employed by the state as agents of social control; but now their jobs have come under threat they are obliged to defend them as fellow trade unionists. Radical social workers in local authority departments found themselves, in campaigns against rate-capping and other central government cuts, making tactical alliances with councillors and council managers whom they had previously identified as 'the bosses'. When these same council officials voted to implement programmes of cuts, the anti-cuts alliances foundered in acrimony and in some councils the resulting conflicts even erupted in industrial disputes. In their position on the front line between the local state and the most volatile sections of the community, social services departments have often been the centres of trade union militancy and political agitation around issues of cuts in jobs and services.

The politics of radical social work

The central weakness of the early radical social work movement was an underdeveloped political strategy. It is possible to be simultaneously committed to a particular set of socialist principles and to helping people as a social worker. What is much less clear is *how* it is possible to connect the two in a manner that allows them to merge into forms of feasible practice in the here and now. The early radical social work movement contained three different, and not always mutually exclusive, approaches to political strategy.

First, there was a distinctively *revolutionary* approach, which emphasised both the controlling elements of social work and the need for dramatic social change for the realization of a socialist society. The identification of the state as an oppressive force made the translation of this political position into everyday social work practice difficult. Second, there was the *reformist* approach to welfare, which was prepared to defend what were regarded as the gains of the welfare state, while promoting socialist strategies to alter the form of welfare services. Third, there was the *prefigurative* strategy, which was heavily influenced by feminism and the slogan 'the personal is the political'. Prefigurative social workers claimed that socialists who promised 'jam tomorrow' neglected oppressive features of everyday life (sexism, racism, hierarchy, etc.) – features that could be altered in the here and now. They favoured changes that prefigured the future and transformed present relationships of dependency. In the words of the title of the most widely read prefigurative text, they favoured working both *In and against the State*.[28]

Economic crisis and the changing balance of political forces over the past decade have created a defensive climate and there are now few exponents of the old revolutionary politics, at least in the world of radical social work. There is still much support for the prefigurative approach, articulated most explicitly in this collection by Croft and Beresford (Chapter 5), who are deeply sceptical about Labour Party politics, social work professionalism and the social services bureaucracy. Their work constantly poses difficult questions about how services can be democratized so that they match people's needs and come under the control of service users, workers and local people.

Many radical social workers now adopt what has been characterized as a *realist* perspective. This perspective is based on the conviction, more or less explicitly acknowledged, that in a period of sustained reaction it is unrealistic to expect that a dramatic transformation of society can be achieved in the short term. The objective now is to defend existing services and to attempt to preserve the best possible conditions for social workers and their clients. Radical social workers recognize the increasingly repressive character of the state, yet argue that its contradictory nature still allows some scope for radical intervention. There is a growing impatience with those left-wingers who repudiate state intervention wholesale. Frost and Stein (Chapter 2), for example, accuse some left-wing social workers of 'workerism' and an inability to 'make a fundamental distinction between working for the state and working for capital'. They propose alliances around limited defensive objectives between council employers, workers and service users.

The future of radical social work

The early radical social work movement was a jolt to the complacency of a profession that was beginning to insulate itself from the essentially political nature of its basic tasks. Where mainstream practice wanted to close issues off and wrap them up in a technical and professional blanket, radical social workers asked awkward questions. These questions were not posed in any systematic fashion, and certainly they were not answered with any programmatic coherence. But the very fact that they were asked caused discomfiture in the burgeoning professional bureaucracies.

Radical social work threw up a range of moral and political dilemmas for social work and social work education. Some of these questions had already been posed by the 'rediscovery' of poverty in the early 1960s. Yet it was left to the radical social work movement to tackle head on the implications of the failure of the postwar welfare reforms. What role should social workers have in relation to ever-worsening poverty? How much discretion should they be allowed in dealing with clients? How many of their clients assumed client status only because of chronic destitution? Were there ways of working with people in extreme poverty that enhanced their independence rather than reinforced their dependency? The wider role of social workers in enforcing social security regulations has only intensified the dilemmas that were originally encountered in the field of welfare rights.

How should radical social work respond to the now worsening problems of poverty and state repression? Becker and MacPherson's excellent *Public Issues and Private Pain – Poverty, Social Work and Social Policy*, published in April 1988 just as the new social security regulations took effect, implies that the only way forward is to strive to make social work a more *adversarial* activity.[29]

One of the most useful things radicals can do is to resist new attempts by the authorities to promote the idea that poverty is a problem of personal failure, rather than a social problem. As Jordan puts it, 'decisions about relieving poverty are disguised as something else – as professional judgments about whether a person or family is helpable by the provision of cash or services'.[30]

Another priority for radical social workers today must be to resist the spread of reactionary ideologies and punitive methods. This point is echoed and amplified here by Parton and Small (Chapter 6), who identify the trend towards mounting state repression in response to the increase in violent tensions in society. As they point out, the trend in child care work is all in the direction of statutory powers and orders at the expense of the 'voluntary, participatory' kind of social work.

The social worker – radical or conventional – is left with the anger, loss and misery of people suffering economic devastation. This is particularly true of workers with people suffering the effects of long-term unemployment. Pearson (Chapter 3) is right that one of the oversights of the original radical social work movement was its failure to develop a psychology of personal troubles. Consequently, few practical strategies were developed about how to work with the emotional needs of poor people. For radical social work, tackling such issues inevitably meant 'cooling people out' or 'conning' them. In an article that may well anger some radicals, Pearson suggests that it is misconceived to see the debate about how to work with the poor or unemployed in terms of either 'adapting' or 'fighting'. Pearson argues that neither social workers nor the unemployed have the power to raise the level of benefits, any more than they can spirit away the dole queues. In addition, Popay and Dhooge point out that in material terms social workers know that they are powerless to do anything other than provide temporary relief. For Pearson, radical social workers have to reject the abstract 'adapt/fight' counterposition and think instead in terms of 'attack/defend'. Defensive strategies must be developed within the cultural traditions of the working class – around issues such as literacy, health and diet – if they are to be relevant.

Popay and Dhooge's research (Chapter 7) reveals that few social workers have given any serious consideration to the implications of unemployment for their practice. They also note how most professional social work and theoretical treatments of the issue still tend to see it as a white man's problem. They accept some of Pearson's argument that the radical social work critiques of individual-oriented social work had gone too far, but also point out the dangers of merely concentrating on defensive work. They emphasize that 'radical social work responses to unemployment must recognize both the structural roots of individual and family problems and the personal pain involved' (as well as identify the basic elements of radical social work with the unemployed). These two pieces on unemployment remind us that at root all radical practice must involve an attitude of mind that seeks to alleviate distress while constantly seeking out ways of transforming the client's position.

All the contributors to this collection are concerned with the development of radical social work practice. As the spaces and the resources become smaller, the need for such practice becomes greater. Times are hard for many people, particularly users of personal social services. Social, community and probation workers have to try to tackle the human misery that results from economic recession and political reaction. It is particularly important that social workers think and respond to these events in political terms. Never has it been more important for social workers to act in ways that minimize the worst effects of current state policies and maximize the potential for resistance of the underclass. We hope this collection will stimulate serious and creative thinking about social work theory and practice today.

Notes and reference

1 See R. Bailey and M. Brake (eds), *Radical Social Work* (Edward Arnold, 1975); M. Brake and R. Bailey (eds), *Radical Social Work and Practice* (Edward Arnold 1980); N. Parry, M. Rustin and C. Satymurti (eds), *Social Work, Welfare and the State* (Edward Arnold, 1979); P. Corrigan and P. Leonard, *Social Work Practice under Capitalism – a Marxist Approach* (Macmillan, 1978); J. H. Galper *Social Work Practice – a Radical Perspective* (Prentice Hall, 1980).

2 See P. Halmos, *The Personal and the Political* (Hutchinson, 1978); S. Taylor, 'Where fantasy radicalism leads us', *Community Care*, 10 May 1978; N. Tilley, 'No Marx for clients', *Community Care*, 2 March 1977.

3 I. Taylor, 'Client refusal: a political strategy for social work', *Case Con*, 7 April 1972.

4 P. Alcock and P. Lee (eds), *Into the Third Term: Thatcherism and the Future of Welfare* (Social and Urban Policy Papers, Sheffield City Polytechnic, November 1988).

5 J. Lawrence, 'Wanted: a super social worker', *New Society*, 15 April 1988.

6 J. H. Galper, *The Politics of Social Services* (Prentice Hall, 1975), p. 4.

7 C. L. Clark and S. Asquith, *Social Work and Social Philosophy* (Routledge & Kegan Paul, 1975), pp. 105–6.

8 C. Phillipson, *Capitalism and the Construction of Old Age* (Macmillan, 1982), p. 1.

9 G. Pearson, 'Social workers and political action', in H. Jones (ed.), *Towards a New Social Work* (Routledge & Kegan Paul, 1975), pp. 45–68.

10 P. Lee, 'Some contemporary and perennial problems of relating theory to practice in social work', in R. Bailey and P. Lee (eds),

Theory and Practice in Social Work (Basil Blackwell, 1982), pp. 15–46; and S. Bolger, P. Corrigan, J. Docking and N. Frost, *Towards Socialist Welfare Work* (Macmillan, 1981); C. Jones, *State Social Work and the Working Class* (Macmillan, 1983).

11 S. Rees and A. Wallace, *Verdicts on Social Work* (Edward Arnold, 1982).
12 C. Satyamurti, *Occupational Survival* (Basil Blackwell, 1981).
13 N. Parton, *The Politics of Child Abuse* (Macmillan, 1985).
14 J. Clarke, M. Langan and P. Lee, 'Social Work: the Conditions of Crisis', in P. Carlen and M. Collison (eds), *Radical Issues in Criminology* (Martin Robertson, 1980).
15 M. Langan, 'The unitary approach: a feminist critique', in E. Brook and A. Davis (eds), *Women, the Family and Social Work* (Tavistock, 1985); A. Hudson, 'Feminism and social work: resistance or dialogue', *British Journal of Social Work*, vol. 15, no. 6 (1985); C. Husband, 'Culture, context and practice: racism in social work', in R. Bailey and M. Brake (eds), *Radical Social Work and Practice* (Edward Arnold, 1980); V. Coombe and A. Little (eds), *Race and Social Work – A Guide to Training* (Tavistock, 1986).
16 M. Rein, 'Social work in search of a radical profession', *Social Work*, vol., 15, no. 2 (April 1970), pp. 13–28.
17 R. Pinker, 'Address to Conference on the Barclay Report', *Community Care*, 13 May 1982.
18 Halmos, op. cit. (n. 2).
19 Z. T. Butrym, *The Nature of Social Work* (Macmillan, 1976),
20 M. Clarke, 'The limits of radical social work', *British Journal of Social Work*, vol. 6, no. 4, 1976, pp. 501–6.
21 D. Statham, *Radicals in Social Work* (Routlege & Kegan Paul, 1978).
22 B. Hugman, 'Radical practice in probation', in Brake and Bailey (eds), op. cit. (n. 1), pop. 123–55.
23 B. Rolston and M. Smyth, 'The spaces between cases: radical social work in Northern Ireland', in Bailey and Lee (eds), op. cit. (n. 9), pp. 201–28.
24 G. Pearson, 'Making social workers: bad promises and bad omens', in Bailey and Brake (eds), op. cit. (n. 1), pp. 13–45.
25 For a useful overview, see F. Williams, *Social Policy: A Critical Introduction* (Polity Press, 1989).
26 I. Gough, *The Political Economy of the Welfare State* (Macmillan, 1979).
27 For a fuller discussion of this, see P. Lee and C. Raban, *Welfare Theory and Social Policy – Reform or Revolution* (Sage, 1988), Part 2.
28 London/Edinburgh, Weekend Return Group, *In and against the State* (Pluto Press, 1980).
29 S. Becker and S. MacPherson, *Public Issues and Private Pain – Poverty, Social Work and Social Policy* (Social Services Insight Books, 1988).
30 B. Jordan, 'Poverty, social work and the state', in Becker and MacPherson, op. cit. (n. 28), p. 347.

2 What's happening in social services departments?

NICK FROST and MIKE STEIN

Our discussion begins with a brief analysis of the disintegration of the postwar social democratic consensus and the consequent growth in the influence of the new right. This analysis will provide the political framework for making sense of the major policy developments in the personal social services, including state expenditure and the organizational, legislative and training arenas, since 1979. We go on to propose a framework for the development of progressive, oppositional forms of practice.

The decline of social democracy and the rise of the new right to dominance was the result of a number of factors, which have been discussed by others[1] in more detail than is possible here, but they can be summarized as follows. First, economic crisis compounded by rising oil prices in the early 1970s made a commitment to Keynesian policies increasingly difficult. The 1974–79 Labour government, at the behest of the International Monetary Fund, opted for a monetarist response to the crisis and introduced policies which shifted the burden of the crisis on to working people: public expenditure cuts, cash limits and wage controls followed. Whereas these measures caused bitterness, confusion and disorganization on the left, they provided the launching pad for a right-wing Conservative revival. Margaret Thatcher and her mentors firmly rejected a return to social democracy and its 'inflationary' consequences.

Second, the Tories seized upon the way the Labour government had demonized the militants who resisted its austerity policies during the 1978–9 'winter of discontent'. They whipped up a coherent populist sentiment against 'trade union power'. With enthusiastic media support, the Tories promoted the menace of trade union militants, and soon extended the same approach to a range of perceived threats to traditional values and institutions. Muggers, hooligans, extremists, feminists – even social workers –

joined 'mindless militants' in the Thatcherite rogues gallery. All were identified as undermining law and order, the family and the nation. As unemployment and poverty grew, welfare 'scroungers' were blamed for defrauding the system and undermining the economy. As the 1979 election approached, Thatcher added an explicitly racist theme to Tory propaganda: 'People are really afraid that this country might be rather swamped by people with a different culture. People are going to react and become rather hostile to those coming in . . .' (Mrs Thatcher, 30 January 1979).

Finally, the Tories developed a powerful critique of Labour's welfare statism, focusing upon people's contradictory experience of public service bureaucracies. The new right promoted the cause of 'freedom from the state' – freedom from paternalistic, remote, inefficient welfare agencies which, it was argued, *controlled* peoples lives. In the late 1970s Conservatives in opposition benefited from working–class disillusionment with Labour's wage controls and public spending cuts and built upon the failure of Labour's vision of the welfare state. For those living in inner-city areas or on large, desolate council estates it was difficult to be committed to the idea of 'defending *our* welfare state'.

However, it would be an oversimplification to represent the emergence of an effective new right critique, in the form of 'Thatcherism', solely as a skilful and opportunistic critique of a failed social democracy. The political philosophy of the new right was a distinct break with postwar conservatism and had its roots in nineteenth-century *laissez-faire* politics. As Stuart Hall and others have pointed out, it was a new gospel of 'authoritarian populism' connecting traditional conservative values of the family, law and order and the nation to the main tenets of an aggressive *laissez-faire* economic policy – competition, market values, minimal state intervention and individualism.

The new right identified the economic problems of the 1970s as the result of too much state intervention, too heavy taxation, 'irresponsible' trade union power and 'overburdening' state welfare. The consequences were lack of enterprise, inefficient industry, overpricing of labour, lack of individual initiative and the decline of traditional caring networks, especially the family and the voluntary network. The new right aimed to strengthen the 'free market mechanism,' in the spirit of Hayek's 'methodological individualism'. The new right argued that the state's legitimate role should be restricted to two functions. It should have a *residual* role in protecting and extending free enterprise through macroeconomic policies. It also had to undertake an *authoritarian* role in defence, law and order and social control.

The Thatcherite agenda in the sphere of personal social services can be briefly summarized:

- reduced expenditure
- less state intervention
- more privatization of welfare
- more family-based care
- increased voluntarism
- a more punitive law'n'order approach
- increasing managerialism
- increasing central control of local services.

In the next section we go on to assess the degree to which these goals have been achieved by Thatcherism in power since 1979.

1. Personal social services and policy development

Child care policy

The centrality of the family to Thatcherite policy has ensured that child care issues have had a high profile throughout the 1980s. The issue of child abuse has become a particular focus of political and media attention.

The high profile on child abuse has been maintained through the focus on a small number of cases where children, known to the social services, have been subjected to violence and neglect by their parents. The nature of the attention paid to child abuse has very much reflected the political imperatives of the period. Parton has illustrated how the reaction to the Maria Colwell case in the mid–1970s reinforced the contemporary theory of 'the cycle of deprivation'.[2] More recently, the reaction to the death of Jasmine Beckford in 1985 has reflected dominant modes of explanation of child abuse. The 'disease' model of child abuse was dominant in the Beckford Report.[3] This approach isolates child abuse from its social context. It is seen as a phenomenon that can be predicted by using a 'checklist' of indicators. It follows, then, that if social workers were only aware of these indicators they could prevent child abuse.

Whereas the physical abuse of children was an issue throughout the 1970s, the sexual abuse of children only really developed as an issue in the 1980s. There is no reason whatsoever to suspect that the *incidence* of child sexual abuse has increased; rather, what has happened is that the *awareness* of child sexual abuse has increased. The NSPCC has noted, for example, an increase of 137 per cent between 1985 and 1986 in the number of children registered with local authorities as victims of sexual abuse. This gives a projected figure of 6,330 children in England and Wales.[4] It is now a commonplace to argue that such figures are merely the tip of an iceberg.[5]

The conditions for the 'discovery' of child sexual abuse, we would argue, were developed by the women's movement. Throughout the 1970s women's groups were meeting and finding out that many women had been sexually abused within the family as children. This led to the establishment of Incest Survivors' Groups, telephone counselling schemes and campaigning work. This put child sexual abuse firmly on the agenda for welfare professionals.[6] The inquiry of Justice Butler-Sloss into events in Cleveland relates to this issue; will the inquiry help us to address sexual abuse as a major issue or will sexual abuse be pushed back into the closet? We fear that the latter is more likely to be the case.

The analysis of child sexual abuse has centred on a model that isolates it from its political and specific gender context. The dominant mode of analysis has been to focus on 'the dysfunctional family' rather than on the power relations between men and women or between adults and children.

The focus on child abuse has had a fundamental impact on social services policy. As a high profile issue child abuse work has attracted resources. The problem with this is that such work tends to be reactive and is in danger of moving resources away from preventative styles of intervention.

The drift towards more authoritarian modes of intervention in the child care field is the most immediate consequence of the child abuse panic. This is reflected in the increasing proportion of children in care, subject to court orders or parental rights resolutions, rather than under voluntary arrangements.[7] There has been an increasing emphasis on 'planning for permanency'. Permanence planning emphasizes the centrality of ensuring that a child is living on a permanent basis if possible with their natural parents, or, if this is not felt to be possible, with long-term foster or, preferably, adoptive parents:

> Increasingly . . . departments assume a stark choice must be made between full parental responsibility or full state responsibility. Either families fulfil their responsibilities for their children or departments take over their responsibilities in a more official way and draw upon their statutory powers to carry them out.[8]

'Planning for permanency' is in part a positive response to the negative aspects of state care. While it may be appropriate in particular cases, it should go hand-in-hand with a more developed preventative model. This should mean developing a continuum of services, including the provision of 'shared care', that is, the availability of periods in care by mutual agreement between parents and the local authority without the parents necessarily losing parental rights. This offers a more flexible service and could halt the drift to an absolutist policy, which in a divided and unequal society tends to act as a market that transfers children to dominant class and racial groups. We welcome the recognition of shared care in the *Review of Child Care Law* and the subsequent White Paper.[9]

Juvenile justice policy

In his analysis of Tory 'law'n'order' policy, written at the time of the 1983 election, Joe Sim wrote:

> After four years in office the Tories' early plans for a strong state apparatus have crystallised and assumed a recognisable and authoritarian form. In a whole range of areas relating to the administration, policies and practices of the criminal justice system there has been a marked shift in the direction of greater repression.[10]

There was a significant rise in spending on law and order between 1979 and 1985. The main beneficiaries of this were the police and the prison system, a situation likely to continue given current policy changes and projections. How has this affected juvenile justice?

First, as early as 1979 the then Minister of State at the Home Office, William Whitelaw, announced the introduction of the 'short, sharp shock' regimes at four detention centres. According to Whitelaw, these regimes would put the emphasis upon 'hard and constructive activities, on discipline and tidiness, on self-respect and respect for those in authority'. These tougher regimes have been extended to more detention centres despite official recognition of their failure as a deterrent. (Home Office figures suggest that as many as 75 per cent of those admitted to detention centres are reconvicted within two years, and the new regimes fare little better in this sense.) More disturbing, however, is the impact of the new regimes on the young people concerned. At one institution alone, the Glenochil Centre in Scotland, seven young people have committed suicide. A working party headed by a consultant psychiatrist made no less than sixty-three recommendations for improvements in the standard of inmate care which were necessary to bring the regime into line with contemporary notions of psychiatric care.

The government put yet another nail in the coffin of any welfare approach to juvenile justice when it introduced the Criminal Justice Act, 1982. This legislation represents a logical progression from Conservative hostility toward the Children and Young Persons Act, 1969. In the early 1970s, the Heath government blocked the implementation of key welfare sections of that Act. The 1982 Act empowers juvenile courts to add a 'charge and control' condition to a care order made in criminal proceedings. This provision, which can be used when additional offences have been committed, hands back to magistrates the power to determine where a young person will be resident. It restricts the local authority's power to allow parents, guardians, relatives or friends to care for a young person for periods of up to six months. Such powers were originally proposed in the mid-1970s but were rejected by the Home Office on the grounds that they would 'undermine the concept of the Care Order and limit the local authorities' responsibility for determining and providing the proper treatment of young people placed in their care'.

Thus, the introduction of the 'charge and control' condition is a victory for the 'law and order' lobby. It ignores research evidence that children made subject to care orders in criminal proceedings are already being placed in institutions and many further offences occur while they are resident, or absconding from those institutions. Furthermore, additional appearances before the court, sometimes for trivial offences, result in what is in effect a custodial sentence. For many children in care this may still be only a second court appearance.

Whilst the 1982 Act increased the opportunities for the court to give shorter, and therefore more readily available, custodial sentences, the use of 'short, sharp shocks' has been discredited to such a degree that the government has now been forced to drop the distinction between youth custody and detention centres as such (a remarkable 'U' turn). The 1988 Criminal Justice Act introduced a unified disposal of 'detention in a young offender institution'.

In 1983 the government issued a circular, LAC 83 (3), which laid down arrangements for alternatives to custody schemes. It provided £15 million to fund locally managed schemes for three years. At the end of this period it envisaged the local authorities would fund the schemes.

These arrangements reflect a contradictory development in government policy. Together with the law'n'order, 'short, sharp shock' policy, it has promoted 'community-based' alternatives.

While these alternatives have been described as the equivalent of 'custody in the community',[11] such criticism fails to grasp the nature of state policies. There are pressures on the state to develop non-custodial alternatives – economic and ideological.

By 1986, 110 projects had developed in sixty-two different local authority areas. The 'success' of these projects in preventing recidivism is difficult to evaluate, and varies from project to project. However, the most recent evaluation suggests that there has been a reduction in the use of custody in areas where schemes operate.[12]

These alternatives seem to indicate a counter-tendency to the 'law'n'order' drift of government. Such alternatives and the growth of Intermediate Treatment offer opportunities for social services to develop progressive practice in a difficult environment.[13]

Older people

The most successful attempt at implementing a Thatcherite economic dogma has taken place in the care of the elderly.

Social services departments have faced increasing demand from the growing proportion of older people in the population. As a result of budget limitations, they have been unable to meet demand for both residential and 'community-based' care for older people. This had led to a significant increase in private provision of residential homes for the elderly.[14]

The boom in private homes for the older people has been accelerated by the Health and Social Services and Social Security Adjudications Act, 1983, which allowed central government to assume financial responsibility for the elderly (and handicapped) in private residential homes, where no local authority places are available. The ideological commitment to privatization in these provisions is evident at a time when local authority budgets are under considerable pressure.

Central to this boom in private provision have been the questions of regulation and control. There are fundamental problems with the administration of the Registered Homes Act 1984 and the associated code of practice. Not least of these problems is that local authorities have not been given adequate resources to implement the provisions. The result is that, beyond the minimum legal requirements, the expansion of private homes is largely unregulated. This is likely to have detrimental consequences for standards within the homes and the quality of life for both residents and the, usually non-unionized, staff.

However, the impact of new right policies is not restricted to residential care. 'Community care' of the elderly, promoted by the government's *Growing Older* (1981) is grossly underfunded. For example, a survey of over 1,000 elderly people and their carers, over 80 per cent of whom were women, concluded:

> As with previous findings the data provides no support for the view that families are neglecting their elderly dependents. On the contrary it appears that carers (mainly women) are supporting their relatives at enormous cost to themselves. It seems that the notions of Community Care have limited application. In the majority of situations the burden of care fell heavily on one individual (mainly women) with very little support from other family members or community services particularly if they were resident carers.[15]

Perhaps the key sentence from the report is as follows:

> Carers are faced with a stark choice of looking after their dependents with minimal support at great cost to themselves or of putting them into residental accommodation permanently where the Government would provide up to £140 per week.[16]

The parallel with child welfare 'permanence' policies is striking. The intention is to mobilize the state to oblige families to provide care with minimal support; the alternative is that the state, in this case in partnership with the private sector, will take over.

Community care

It is clear from our discussion of policy toward the elderly that the Conservative government sees 'community care' as a policy that reduces the role of the state and depends on unpaid, mainly female, labour. This is how former Social Services Secretary Patrick Jenkin put it: 'Each and everyone of us has a personal responsibility to the community . . . and it is through our families, our neighbourhoods and our voluntary bodies that we can best express that responsibility'. This ideology applies also to policies toward the mentally ill, the mentally and physically handicapped.

It was something of a surprise when, in 1981, the government issued *Care in the Community* (LAC (81) 5), which not only addressed the problem of the long-stay hospital population but also revealed some recognition of the financial implications and consequences of community care. The document put forward seven propositions to hasten the discharge of long-stay patients into the community:

(i) joint financed projects (ii) lump-sum sponsorship arrangements (iii) capital transfers, including transfers of freeholds of hospital sites (iv) collaborative pooling of funds (v) and (vi) central transfer of funds and adjustment to rate support grants and, finally, (vii) organisational changes.

The document received a generally warm welcome: MIND called it 'far-reaching' and 'far-sighted', whilst the Association of Metropolitan Authorities saw it as a 'positive initiative'. However, the enthusiasm was to be short-lived as the follow-up circular (LAC (83) 5) announced only a small increase in joint funding allocation. The only new initiative was a statutory amendment enabling district health authorities to offer lump-sum payments or recurrent grants to local authorities or voluntary organizations. This enabled them to accept responsibility for discharged patients, 'pending a central transfer of resources'. This second circular in effect rejected the more innovative elements of *Care in the Community* and has prevented the anticipated progress. Some pilot projects have been developed but it is unlikely that, in the absence of a comprehensive statutory framework, such local initiatives can bring about a major shift of resources to community care. As the Association of County Councils has pointed out, 'the new money available through joint finance has proved to be of marginal importance'. Indeed, in 1985 about a fifth of authorities were refusing to initiate projects with long-term revenue implications.

The House of Commons Social Services Committee Report on Community Care (1985) pointed out the problems facing authorities attempting to plan a comprehensive policy for the mentally ill and handicapped. The Committee called for an increase in resources to develop community services *prior* to institutional closures. To achieve this it suggested the creation of a 'central bridging fund' to switch capital resources and to redeploy and train staff.

It is clear that current government policy is moving even further away from progressive initiatives in community care. Government policy is placing more demand on the voluntary and private sectors, and is increasingly dependent on unpaid care in the home. Provision for the mentally ill and for handicapped people is, in keeping with that for the elderly, becoming increasingly privatized in circumstances where local authorities lack sufficient resources to monitor standards.

While the government has introduced major statutes in most

areas of social welfare, it has not put forward legislation on the needs of disabled people. This is evidently largely because any legislation would involve a major allocation of resources. The government's response to Tom Clarke's Disabled Persons Act, 1986 – a Private Member's Bill which attempted to strengthen the rights of disabled people – revealed its parsimonious attitude to welfare reform.[17] Tory ministers and local government leaders pointed out that Clarke's proposal to introduce a statutory right to the disabled to a full assessment of their needs for support in the community had major resource implications. Despite the government's misgivings, the bill received substantial support both within and outside the Houses of Parliament.

Government policies on 'community care' for the mentally ill, mentally handicapped and physically handicapped rest on a similar ideological basis to their policy for care of the elderly. These policies encourage the private and voluntary sector, and ultimately depend on care mainly by women, in the home.

While the government maintains a rhetorical commitment to community care, its policies are in disarray. Because any serious policy would mean spending more money, no comprehensive strategy has emerged. The Audit Commission has been particularly critical of the lack of a coordinated strategy and the consequent waste of resources. This has left Social Services departments in the position of trying to build coherent policies without adequate central support.

This disarray is illustrated at the time of writing by the lack of a coherent government response to Sir Roy Griffiths' recommendations on community care. These recommendations illustrate two of our major points. First, the Griffiths' package would, initially at least, strengthen the role of local government; this explains the absence of government support for a person whose recommendations they are usually willing to follow. Secondly, and somewhat paradoxically, the Griffiths' package is eminently suitable for privatization, thus fitting well with one of the main themes of government policy.

Decentralization

One of the major elements of personal social service development since the early 1980s has been the decentralization of service delivery – often referred to as 'neighbourhood' social work or 'community' social work.

The Barclay Report *Social Workers – Their Roles and Tasks* is often identified as a key document in the shift towards decentralized social work. Yet, while the Barclay report advocated 'community social work', it merely reflected a trend that was already taking effect and, for reasons internal and external to social work, was set to continue. Neither the pace nor the style of decentralization has been significantly shifted by Barclay.

There are a number of reasons why the Barclay Report lacked impact. First, the committee had an unclear status: its formation was inspired by the government, but it was formally sponsored by a voluntary organization – the National Institute of Social Work. Second, while the report was welcomed by the government, it did not lead to a flurry of administrative or legislative action. Third, divisions in the committee, which resulted in the publication of dissentient minority reports, and the reluctance of the majority report to provide a 'blueprint', lessened its impact.

Decentralization, however, has continued apace. Why should this be? A major factor is that, for different reasons, decentralization has received support from both left and right. Conservative victory in the 1979 election led some Labour politicians to re-think their commitment to traditional forms of state intervention in industry and services, which, it seemed, could no longer command mass support. An influential section of Labour MPs, councillors and constituency activists began to argue for modes of service delivery that were more responsive and more accountable to local people. The move away from 'Town Hall socialism' toward 'neighbourhood office socialism' affected a whole range of local services, including the personal social services.

However, decentralization also had an impact in authorities other than those under Labour control. For the right, decentralization was a device for encouraging self-help and voluntary effort. Social service 'patch teams' could relate to 'voluntary care networks' and encourage people to 'care for their own'. In practice, this amounts to 'encouraging' and 'supporting' women as unpaid carers. Hence, decentralized social services can be seen as encouraging voluntarist and sexist modes of caring and facilitating the 'rolling back of the state'.

The move towards decentralization in social services is not amenable to any overall theory. Any specific decentralization policy must be evaluated in terms of its dispersal of power and resources, its democratic control and the way it challenges sexist and racist practices. We are convinced, however, that decentralization can form an effective part of a socialist welfare strategy.

Expenditure on personal social services

Ever since James Callaghan declared in 1976 that 'the party is over' local government has been a prime target for financial control. The Rate Support Grant (i.e. the central contribution to local expenditure) fell from 61 per cent in 1979/80 to less than 50 per cent in 1987. Local government expenditure has declined as a proportion of total government expenditure, and public expenditure has declined as a proportion of Gross National Product. How have personal social services coped during this difficult period?

The Thatcher government's first White Paper on public expenditure proposed cuts of 4.7 per cent in 1979/80 and 6.7 per cent in 1980/1. Personal social services had previously been offered a degree of protection in the form of a 2 per cent growth allocation to reflect increased demand as a result of demographic change. However, as local government acted to protect personal social services, government projections were not achieved. The out-turn spending figures illustrate a growth of around 10 per cent for personal social services from 1980/1 until 1984/5.[18] The latest government figures project a declining percentage growth for personal social services expenditure so that by the end of the 1980s growth will be around 2 per cent in cash terms.[19]

The overall figures conceal significant authority-to-authority variations. The House of Commons Select Committee points out that in 1984/5 three authorities spent less in real terms on personal social services than they had in 1979/80. This reflects the nature of local struggles and debates over personal social services expenditure.

It is also signficant that capital expenditure has been significantly reduced in real terms in every financial year throughout the 1980s, a trend that is projected to continue until the end of the decade. Every year local authority capital bids greatly outstrip the capital allocation and this trend is also expected to continue.

Social services are also facing increasing demand due to a variety of factors, including the increasing proportion of older people, legislative changes, increased unemployment and a greater awareness of child abuse, to name but a few. It is doubtful whether even the recommended 2 per cent per annum growth would be enough to meet these factors.

The extent of localized commitment to social services is reflected in the variations between government projections and out-turns. This commitment reflects the political difficulties in cutting personal social services on the ground. It is indeed significant that some Labour councils have made increased expenditure on social services central to their political programme. This has been difficult in the face of a central government programme that has emphasized 'welfare pluralism' and that has made service planning into a cost limitation exercise.

Education and training

The Thatcherite project has affected social work education in a number of crucial ways.

First, the Central Council for Education and Training in Social Work (CCETSW), a body not noted for its radicalism, was restructured as a result of the Health and Social Services and Social Security Adjudicating Act, 1983. Its membership was reduced from sixty-five to twenty-five, but more importantly the concept of nomination by educational, employer and professional associations (including trade unions and students) was replaced by appointment by the minister, 'after suitable consultation'. The broadly representative character of CCETSW has therefore been significantly diluted.

Second, throughout the 1980s CCETSW debated the reorganization of social work education.[20] The main proposals to emerge were that social work education should be extended, that the Certificate of Qualification of Social Work (CQSW) and the Certificate of Social Service (CSS) be unified to become a single qualifying award, and that employers should play an enhanced role in social work training. We do not have the space to evaluate these proposals, which were partially accepted in 1989, but the enhanced employer role in the new qualification merits comment.[21]

The proposal that employers should play a more active part in social work training fits into the wider drift towards increasingly authoritarian modes of practice. This tendency is in part the result of pressures from senior local government managers who want courses to produce social workers who are 'trained' to carry out agency expectations efficiently, effectively and unquestioningly. It is not surprising that employers are demanding more control over social work education. The influence of the Association of Directors of Social Services lobby is apparent throughout the debate. The CSS offered a model that was cheaper and more 'effective' than the CQSW. While there is a legitimate place for management in social work education, there is a danger that the drift to managerialism has gone too far in the new unified qualification. It is essential that a healthy tension between social work education and social work practice is preserved. This tension should allow space for a critical response from education, rather than a simple rubber-stamping of existing modes of practice.

The Heads of CQSW courses position paper put it thus:

Practice takes place as the Barclay Report illustrates
– within a plurality of perspectives on social problems, clients' needs and demands and social work purposes
– within a range of social structures, social processes and social policies
– at other sensitive points of power-interest-and-value contacts; and
– in relation to human behaviours involving moral and ethical choices and issues.[22]

The responsibility of social work practice cannot be confined to 'on the job' matters. The 'client service' ethic of a profession understood in this way demands that practice experience is used to evaluate critically the structures, processes and policies impinging on clients. Where these factors impinge to the detriment of clients, practice should be directed at change, including interventions that take issues into wider arenas of discussion, influence and decision-making.

The government seems to want more highly qualified social workers without being prepared to finance the extra training required. In 1988 it refused to provide a modest £40 million to fund the proposed extension of social work education. The significance of this decision was that, despite the fact that the reforms fitted with the dominant ideology of 'vocationalism' and came at a time of concern over the competence of social workers in such areas as child abuse, the present government was not willing to go along with an increased professionalism for social workers. It seems to us that this reflects their deep contempt for social workers and their clients and a wish to promote the 'Victorian values' of a return to philanthropy.

Summary

Policy developments in the personal social services reflect the political goals of the Thatcher government. Parton has summarized these developments in terms of the 'social market economy', which

stresses the importance of individual responsibility, choice and freedom, supports the discipline of the market against the interference of the state urging reductions in taxation and public expenditure. However while it argues for a much reduced state it also calls for a strong state to establish certain modes of family life and discipline.[23]

It is clear that this is not simply an economic policy; it is also a manifestly ideological strategy that places the role of the family at the centre of the stage. This is why personal social service policies are vital to an understanding of Thatcherism.

While Thatcherism has had some success in personal social services, we do not see this in any way as a monolithic policy that can be imposed without generating struggle and dispute. Let's look at the political opportunities opening up in personal social services.

2. Opposing the new right: the development of an oppositional practice

One significant spin-off of Conservative policy on personal social services has been the increasing politicization of personal social services issues. Topics such as child abuse, fostering policy and care for older people have become arenas of political debate. This has been partly as a result of the increased conflict between central and local state, but it is also due to the demands made by women, ethnic minorities and other disadvantaged groups upon personal social services. One result of this process of politicization is the growing trend of challenging the view that social service policy is a 'technical' matter to be dealt with by 'experts'. As a consequence, it is now easier to raise political issues in the context of personal social services and for social workers to identify themselves as having a political role.

Many of our proposals as outlined below may be rejected by some on the left as being merely 'reformist'. It will become clear from our analysis that we do not regard the reform/revolution dichotomy as relevant or useful in helping us to develop forms of oppositional practice. The aim of our proposals is to open up arenas of contestation, which then provide the *possibility* of progressive gains that strengthen the position of workers and clients alike in opposition to the new right.

The impact of feminism

Central to any strategy for a progressive social work practice must be an understanding of the signficance of feminist theory and practice. Much of our analysis has illustrated how recent developments in the personal social services have attempted to exploit the double oppression of women – as low-paid workers and as carers in the home.

As workers, women form the vast majority of social services personnel. They are to be found concentrated at the bottom end of the hierarchy both in terms of the social services workforce as a whole, and also among professional social workers. Women are most likely to be home helps and basic grade social workers and less likely to be area managers or directors.[24] While social services departments are dominated by men, social work practice is dominated by transactions between women workers and women clients.

In the home, women also carry the main burden of being carers. The Equal Opportunities Commission study *Carers and Services* found that 59 per cent of all carers for dependent adults were female. This study also illustrated that male carers are more likely to receive support from statutory services. The EOC,[25] and other research evidence, suggests that increased emphasis upon community care and 'informal caring networks' in practice means increasing dependence upon unpaid, female carers in the home.

Early radical social work literature was mainly written by men and did not adequately analyse the position of women. However, in recent years literature has emerged that is committed to feminist social work practice.[26] This literature makes a clear link between a feminist analysis and feminist practice within the welfare state.

It is of course one thing to criticize from a feminist perspective and quite another to change social work practice along these lines, but our experience as social work educators suggest that significant numbers of feminist social workers are now entering the profession. It seems unlikely that they are going to be simply incorporated by patriarchal social services departments. They form a major source of change within social work. Feminist social work practice has challenged dominant forms of practice around domestic violence and work with adolescent girls in particular. The potential exists for this challenge to be extended to all those areas of practice where patriarchal ideas are currently predominant.

It is also significant that trade unions are addressing their female members as women workers. This applies to the main social work union (Nalgo) and also the unions organizing home helps and residential care workers (Nupe, GMBATU). Hence women trade unionists are campaigning vigorously around issues that have been seen as marginal, or even irrelevant, by male-dominated unions. These include issues such as sexual harassment, job-sharing and child care.

The role of anti-racism

An oppositional social work practice must also be anti-racist. The recognition of racist practices within social services departments has played a key role in the politicization of social work.

Black social workers, councillors and pressure groups have raised issues such as trans-racial adoption and fostering, ethno-centric social work practice, the employment of ethnic minority social workers and the delivery of services to ethnic minority groups.

Throughout the 1960s and 1970s there was a tendency for social work to strive for a 'colour-blind' practice, which sought to overcome racial discrimination by ignoring race as an issue. This approach was reflected in the active encouragement of trans-racial adoption, which in practice meant the adoption of black children by white families, which was felt to be a contribution to a multi-racial, integrated society. The problem was that the transfer of black children (to usually professional, middle-class) white families led to the black children losing an identification with their own colour and culture.

In the 1980s, many social workers have rejected 'colour-blind' practice in favour of an anti-racist perspective. Some social services departments have adopted anti-racist employment practices and methods of service delivery. In some departments these new policies are being energetically pursued and are being backed up by adequate resources. Elsewhere, however, equal opportunities policies remain paper policies, while recruitment of black workers, often with the assistance of central funding through Section II of the 1966 Local Government Act, sometimes amounts to the recruitment of 'low-status' workers to deal with 'low-status' clients. Much remains to be done to tackle racist employment practices and social work methods. Many of these issues have been taken up by black social worker groups and by black trade unionists.[27]

White social workers need to commit themselves explicitly to anti-racist policies, and to argue for these policies in their teams, communities and unions.

The role of trade unionism

We have written elsewhere[28] of the importance of trade unionism in social work. It seems to us that the development of trade unionism in social work has a particular significance given the professional aspirations of social work. Why should a group of aspiring professionals choose to join a trade union? The fact that social workers are now overwhelmingly union members has important implications for understanding what is happening in social services departments.

The possibility of trade union interest in social services policy has been well illustrated by Leeds Social Workers' Action Group, which has produced, and campaigned around, detailed policy documents.[29] Trade unions can begin to act as a link between the traditional labour movement and the community-based groups with which social workers are in day-to-day contact. This style of campaigning has been all too rare, although the Greater London Council, prior to its abolition, was beginning to build these sort of alliances.

It is not always easy to build campaigns around personal social services issues, not least because of the bureaucratic and patriarchal organization of many services. However, Beresford and Croft have argued in a range of publications that people are interested in social services and would welcome the chance to participate.[30] This is increasingly true as social services issues assume a higher political profile.

Social work trade unionism should be redefined as a bridge between the people the unions have traditionally ignored (youth, single parents and older people, for example) and the labour movement. Such a coalition of interests could help to defend welfare services, while popularizing them and winning wider support for expansion. This will involve social work trade unionists in the active development of policy on a local and national basis.

Some criticisms of current modes of social work trade unionism are appropriate. There is a real, if not very widespread, problem of *workerism* among some social work trade unionists. This contains two related elements: first, a simplistic transfer of trade union ideology from the private sector to the public sector and, second, an over-reliance on all-out industrial action.

The transfer of modes of organization and struggle from the private sector fails to make the fundamental distinction between 'working for capital' and 'working for the state'. In the state sector, a clear worker/boss opposition does not always exist. Local management cannot be seen simply as the 'enemy'. The attack on the local state by central government lays the basis for tactical alliances between unions and management, in particular in the defence of services from the effects of rate-capping and privatization. Yet such ideas are anathema to some social work trade unionists.

An extract from the Nalgo Action Group (NAG) Bulletin illustrates the workerist overemphasis on all-out industrial action: 'we'll only win our demands if we back them with action . . . not selective action, which can only divide and confuse the membership, but an all out strike'.[31] This rhetoric is frequently heard regardless of whether the dispute is a national pay claim, a local dispute over staffing or an individual grievance. Yet the call for strike action fails to recognize the distinctive position of public sector workers. When they take all-out industrial action, public sector workers are withdrawing the very services they are committed to defending. Limited industrial action, in contrast, can be used to harm management without harming users or even positively benefiting them, e.g. by non-cooperation in completing financial assessment forms. Of course, such limited action may provoke management to suspend people and this could lead to all-out action. However, in this situation the blame can be clearly placed on management.

Trade unions have a crucial role in progressive struggles in social services departments. They should take on a more positive role in policy formation, based on a clear analysis of the contradictory position of social workers within the local state.

Working within the Labour Party

As well as becoming trade union activists, many social service workers have become involved in political parties as a way of attempting to fight for the services that they work in. There is, of course, nothing particularly new about this development, and over the years many local authority workers have become councillors in authorities other than those in which they work. In recent years an increasing number of District Labour Parties have established 'working groups' that 'shadow' council committees in areas such as Social Services, Housing, Leisure Services, etc. The terms of reference of these groups include the formulation of new policies, the preparation of manifesto statements and the monitoring of existing policy. The working groups usually consist of members elected by the District Party and councillors from the relevant committee. Policies generated by these groups, if approved by the District Party, then become local policy. The experience of many members of these groups is that they offer genuine opportunities for policy development beyond the tokenism of 'advisory groups'. In some areas this arrangement has developed to establish a shadow working group for the key Policy and Resources Committee. The working group consists of the chairs of the other working groups, the council committees and the Leader of the Council, who is chair of the Policy and Resources Committee, and the chair of the District Labour Party.

Labour's 'working groups' do not offer a total solution to the problems of participation and democracy in social services. The Labour Party in many local authorities still offers a patronizing, 'top-down' approach to local government, which needs to be challenged. However, we do see this party political activity as part of a continuum for radical intervention in personal social services.

Alliances – possibilities and practicalities

The politicization of personal social services delivery and practice has had two crucial effects: first, an increase in politicians' awareness of personal social services issues, notably around race and gender; and, second, the continued growth of pressure groups in relation to social services.

Both developments have consequences for social work practice. Significant conflicts have developed between councillors and social service managers and also between councillors and social service workers. These conflicts have numerous causes, and such conflict is no doubt endemic in local state structures. However, there are important possibilities for alliances between workers, managers and councillors in specified conditions. There should be no principled objection to such alliances from social workers. Alliances can be constructed particularly around attacks from central government or around policy issues such as equal opportunities, access to information, child care provision, etc.

For such alliances to become more widespread, changes in attitude are required on both sides. First, social service workers need to accept that councillors are the nearest we have to popular control of social services departments. Hence, attitudes such as 'why are they interfering?' or 'what has it got to do with them?' are not very helpful. Such attitudes risk lapsing into a defensive professionalism committed to protecting our areas of expertise. Equally, it is not helpful for councillors to caricature social workers as 'middle-class colonialists' or 'parasitic do-gooders' – prejudices that appear to be prevalent among some left councillors. Social workers are working under considerable pressure in large bureaucracies for salaries around or below the national average income, and they have become increasingly radicalized over the past decade. It is not good enough to conceptualize them simply as 'professionals' or 'middle class'. Rather we should emphasize the possibilities for alliances with councillors, state employees and local people in defence of their common interests.

The second strand of the politicization has been the growth of pressure groups such as the Family Rights Group, the National Association of Young People in Care, Parents against Injustice, and many others. These groups are taking an interest in such day-to-day practices as arrangements for parental access to children, the rights of young people in care or the guidelines for child abuse investigations. Many groups hold a deep-felt mistrust of social workers. There is no doubt that social work has lost much of its public credibility.[32] It is crucial that social workers take steps to work with such groups in an open way that will challenge much social work practice. Such groups are calling for more open and more accountable forms of social work practice.

Social workers are often said to feel under siege from all sides – the state, the media, councillors and clients. However, if social work is to protect itself, it cannot stand alone. For this reason we see alliances – whether they are within Nalgo, with management and councillors or with pressure groups – as central to the future of social work.

An oppositional social work practice?

We do not see social workers as simply 'agents of social control'; nor do we see practice as determined in some monolithic way by the state. We have identified the impact that new right principles have had on welfare policy, but it is important to recognize that this process is happening in a way that is challenged and contested. Social work can develop a form of practice that can oppose the policies of Thatcherism.

This point can be illustrated in relation to child care practice. Although recent child care policy has developed toward a controlling and authoritarian mode, it does not follow that *all* social work practice must follow these prescriptions. By making this point we are not arguing that social work practice is a totally autonomous process that exists independently of ideological, economic and structural constraints. However, social work decision-making does have a significant degree of independence. In child care work, key decisions are taken at basic grade level and management approval is often little more than rubber-stamping. Hence, social workers can be committed to a concept of shared care, open decision-making and parent and child participation in meetings, for example, and thereby contribute something to resisting the pressure of the new right.

Similar styles of work can be adopted in all areas of social work practice. In such a way social work can make a modest contribution to resisting the dominance of the new right.

Notes and references

1   S. Hall, 'The great moving right show', *Marxism Today* (January 1979); A. Walker, 'Why we need a social strategy', *Marxism Today* (September 1982); A. Walker *et al.*, 'Conservative Economic Policy: the social consequences', in D. Bull and P. Wilding (eds), *Thatcherism and the Poor* (CPAG, 1983).

2   N. Parton, *The Politics of Child Abuse* (Macmillan, 1985).

3   *A Child in Trust: The Report of the Panel of Inquiry into the circumstances surrounding the death of Jasmine Beckford* (London Borough of Brent, 1985); N. Parton, 'The Beckford Report, a critical appraisal', *British Journal of Social Work*, vol. 16 (1986).

4   NSPCC figures, published June 1987.

5   D. Finklehor *et al.*, *A Sourcebook on Child Sexual Abuse* (Sage, 1986).

6   L. Domenilli, 'Father–daughter incest: patriarchy's shameful secret', *Critical Social Policy*, no. 16 (summer 1986).

7   N. Parton, 'Children in care: recent changes and debates', *Critical Social Policy*, no. 13 (summer 1985).

8   ibid., p. 114.

9   See: HMSO, *Review of Child Care Law* (1985); *The Law on Child Care and Family Services* (Cmnd 62). The points in this section are pursued in N. Frost and M. Stein, *The Politics of Child Welfare* (Wheatsheaf, 1989).

10 J. Sim, 'Law and Order' in P. Lee (ed.) 'Banishing dark divisive clouds: Welfare and the Conservative government 1979–83', *Critical Social Policy*, no. 8 (autumn 1983), p. 16.

11 This criticism has been applied to schemes involving 'tracking' of young offenders in particular.

12 JOT/NACRO, *Findings from the Second Census of Projects Funded Under the DHSS IT. Initiative July 1st–December 31st 1985* (August, 1986); *Diverting Juveniles from Custody* (JOT/NACRO, 1987).

13 See, for example, B. Featherstone, *There is an Alternative* (Prison Reform Trust, 1987).

14 See chapters by Chris Phillipson and Bruce Senior in this volume (Chapters 10 and 12).

15 D. Jones, 'A carer's work is never done', *Community Care*, 4 July 1985, p. 22.

16 ibid., p. 23.

17 E. Blyth and J. Milner, 'An end to an end', *Insight*, 26 June 1987.

18 A. Walker, 'More ebbs than flows', *Insight*, vol, 1, no. 3 (1986).

19 HMSO *Government Expenditure Plans 1987–88 to 1989–90 Volume II* (CM 56 – II).

20 See various CCETSW papers 20.1 to 20.8.

21 N. Frost and M. Stein, 'The political education of social workers', in R. Fieldhouse (ed.), *The Education of Servants of the State* (MUP, 1988).

22 Standing Conference of Heads of CQSW courses, *CCETSW Review of Training Policies* (n.d.).

23 N. Parton, op. cit. (n 7), p. 115.

24 D. Howe, 'The segregation of women and their work in the personal social services', *Critical Social Policy*, no. 15 (spring 1986).

25 Equal Opportunities Commission, *Caring for the Elderly and Handicapped: Community Care Policies and Women's Lives* (1982).

26 See, for example, J. Hale, 'Feminism and social work practice', in B. Jordan and N. Parton (eds), *The Political Dimensions of Social Work* (Blackwell, 1983); A. Hudson, 'Feminism and social work: resistance or dialogue', *British Journal of Social Work*, vol. 15, no. 6 (1985); E. Brook and A. Davis (eds), *Women, the Family and Social Work* (Tavistock, 1985).

27 See, for example, S. Ahmed *et al.* (eds), *Social Work with Black Children and Their Families* (Batsford, 1986); P. Stubbs 'The employment of Black Social Workers: from "ethnic sensitivity" to anti-racism?', *Critical Social Policy*, no. 12 (spring 1985).

28 N. Frost, 'More than your jobs to lose', *Community Care* (January 1983).

29 Leeds Social Workers' Action Group chapter in B. Jordan and N. Parton (eds), *The Political Dimensions of Social Work* (Blackwell, 1983).

30 P. Beresford and S. Croft, *Community Control of Social Services Departments: discussion paper* (Battersea Community Action, 1981).

31 Nalgo Action Group, *End Low Pay Now* (n.d.).

32 J. Seabrook, 'The fall of the caring classes', *New Society*, 9 August 1985.

3 Social work and unemployment

GEOFFREY PEARSON

Modern social work ideas and practices were shaped during the postwar era of full employment. This applies equally to conventional casework and to the 'radicalism' that emerged during the late 1960s and early 1970s. Now, with the return of mass unemployment, the 'postwar era' has come to an end, and it becomes necessary to question past assumptions in social work and to attempt a reconstruction.

The postwar era was characterized by a 'social democratic' consensus between Labour and Conservative Parties around the principles of the 'welfare state' and a 'full employment' policy. Other basic assumptions of this era, which were particularly important in the development of social work defined the limits of normal family life and the place of women in the home and emphasized the virtues of 'community care' compared with institutional containment. There was a widespread conviction that poverty was being eliminated within a general movement towards a 'classless' society.[1] There were, of course, conflicting themes within this consensus – the increasing involvement of women within the labour market, the 'rediscovery' of poverty in the 1960s, the failure of 'community care' and the emerging politics of race. Even so, the consensus remained more or less intact throughout the postwar years.

Where we came in: Work, family, leisure

We can take as an emblem of this era and its contradictions the late 1950s' film of the British new realist cinema, *Saturday Night, Sunday Morning*. The film's central character was a young man who worked at a hard, boring job – but took home a decent wage and enjoyed an excess of beer-drinking and other thrills at the weekend: 'What I'm out for is a good time, all the rest is propaganda.' Arthur

Seaton was in rebellion against conventional values, personified by an older stable workmate. One of the ways in which his rebellion was expressed was in having an affair with the older man's wife. Having sown his wild oats, the hero was nevertheless quick to settle down with a nice girl. As the film came to a close and the young couple walked hand in hand into their own family future, new houses were being built in the background . . . the future was just about secure. Even so, there was a residual feeling that perhaps the hero had been trapped by conventional values.

Saturday Night, Sunday Morning raised the characteristic question of the era. Should Arthur's progress be regarded as a successful graduation into maturity (the conventional judgement)? Or should it be seen as a collapse of justified rebellion into conformity (the radical judgement)? For many people today mass unemployment, which hangs over towns and cities like a shroud, has closed off these options: the question of whether they represent graduation or acquiescence is simply irrelevant.

This change offers in microcosm a version of the dilemma that confronts social work in its response to the new era of mass unemployment. How can personal success or failure be measured when all the available measuring-sticks have been taken away? The older, received forms of judgement – whether radical or conventional – no longer work. It is time to take stock and view the awfulness of what is around us. In a part of the world where people have grown used to comfortable lifestyles, technological power has curtailed drastically the need for human labour. The consequence is unemployment at local rates and levels which are as devastating as those suffered in the interwar slump. In some ways unemployment today is even more devastating: whereas in the Depression the National Unemployed Workers' Movement mobilized mass resistance to dole cuts and other attacks on the unemployed, our own era has produced little enthusiasm for marching for jobs or any other form of effective political opposition.[2]

Yet our concern here is neither with political economy, nor with macropolitics. Rather, we are interested in the smaller, human scale of this devastation: the sense of loss, anger, fear and despair that now visit so many people's lives. These sentiments upset the expectations of a generation, interrupt the vital props to self-esteem and identity, and gnaw at the bones of those who were already poor in the 'affluent' society. Mass unemployment inspires on the one hand such a pessimism that a return to full employment now seems unthinkable. On the other hand it inspires rage that regularly sets our cities ablaze. Let's begin by looking at the doomed prophecies of the welfare state and social work's role within it.

The 'rehabilitative ideal': Counting 'success' and the problem of gender

The return of mass unemployment has thrown the accustomed assumptions of what counts as 'success' in social work into disarray. Postwar social work ideology assumed full employment. People did not become the clients of social workers unless they were regarded as in some way troublesome. One important form of trouble was a person's inability to be self-reliant, which often implied their capacity to maintain at least a foothold in the labour market. Of course, this approach did not apply to all areas of social work. It did not, for example, apply to marital work, or necessarily to child care work, or to all psychiatric social work. Nevertheless, even in those areas of social work not immediately defined as being concerned with employment (and very little social work was strictly defined in relation to employment), the ability to return clients to the labour market was commonly either an explicit or an implicit goal. The successful rehabilitation of mental patients, for example, could often be most easily tested against whether they were able to sustain a job. Sometimes, through a combination of social work intervention and 'occupational therapy', the problem and the therapeutic objective were explicitly defined in labour market terms.[3] Social work with disabled people also commonly centred around such assumptions, or involved the provision of a variety of 'sheltered' employment schemes. In what was defined as 'child care' work, too, the problem underlying a family's fragility was often either actual family poverty, or the problem might be defined by social workers as one occasioned by haphazard work disciplines.

The test was never more sure, though, than in work directed towards the 'resettlement' of offenders. Here, a 'steady job' was a guarantee of removal from the temptation to commit further crime. The notion that 'the devil makes work for idle hands', and the place of enforced labour as an instrument of penal discipline and reform (whether in the form of useful work or the symbolic rigours of the treadwheel and hand-crank) played a highly significant role in the development of the modern penitentiary system in the course of the eighteenth and nineteenth centuries.[4] The probation service developed out of the mission to save souls and rescue people from drink, towards an emphasis on the reintegration of the offender into the labour market. This required the probationer to 'lead an industrious life' through 'suitable and regular employment'.[5] Across a whole range of philanthropic and social work activities the notion that the client should regain a 'steady' employment record could be regarded as a test of social work success, as well as a major justification for social work itself. The return of mass unemployment has made these easy assumptions redundant.

Another assumption in the traditional social work discourse was that the client was a man. It was also assumed that men were the sole breadwinners in families, or, in the case of single men, that they would be self-supporting. In 1942, at a time when women were playing a critical role in the battle for production on the home front, Beveridge still expected that women would again become economically dependent upon men on the resumption of normality. Beveridge regarded man and wife 'as a team' for insurance purposes,[6] anticipating quite wrongly as it turned out, that women would return to a minimal role in the labour market. 'During marriage most women will not be gainfully employed', he predicted, and such paid work that they might undertake would be 'intermittent'. Furthermore, Beveridge insisted, the 'attitude of the housewife to gainful employment outside the home is not and should not be the same as that of the single woman. She has other duties . . .'[7]

As for 'single women', with or without children, they were defined as problems by their very status. They were 'problem mums' or 'neurotic spinsters', women who had never quite been able to adjust to the wholesome rigours of marriage.[8] Girls who became pregnant too early in their lives, when not blessed by marriage status, could only be labelled as guilty of 'moral insanity', and be openly chastised for their promiscuity. And it was not only the status of women as single and unmarried that was subject to regulation, but also their relationship to the external world of work. In the unusual circumstances of war, it had been grudgingly accepted that women must be a major part of the workforce. But on return to normality it was assumed that they would once again preside over the family and home – which Christopher Lasch has described as the 'haven from a heartless world'.[9] Just as the early Victorians condemned the working mother as 'an unnatural arrangement' and 'a stigma upon the social state', working mothers in postwar Britain were blamed for the rampage of delinquent 'latch-key kids', truants, vandals and 'Teddy Boys'.[10] The proper relationship between a woman, work and the family for a working-class woman was precisely defined. On leaving school she should immediately gain employment in some menial job such as shop-assistant, 'mucky buffer' in a cutlery factory, or 'anode welder' in one of the new 'light industries', or in any one of the other jobs reserved for girls commonly known and disparaged as 'scrubbers'. She should then, after an interval of time long enough to assuage social anxieties about early marriage, 'settle down' through courtship and marriage into a respectable family life with a proper quotient of children. When these were sufficiently grown up, she might return to one of the menial jobs reserved for more mature working-class women – such as a cleaning woman in an office or factory, working behind a market food-stall, or rather more daringly as a 'clippie' on the buses, etc.

Organized as they were around the world of work, social work's rehabilitative assumptions were upset by the return of mass unemployment. Yet even in their heyday they were particularly ill-suited to much of social work activity, which involved working with women in a variety of caring roles. The accepted aim of social work rehabilitation was to enable the client to achieve economic independence in the labour market. For women, however, independence was not valued and the status of marriage was paramount. The fact that marriage and employment were regarded as mutually exclusive categories exposed the contradictions inherent in the whole framework of assumptions underlying postwar social work.

The central aim of this paper is not, however, to redress these grievous gender confusions in welfare discourses on employment and unemployment. This is for the simple reason that they run so deep that, in spite of some recent attention to gender divisions,[11] women's work tends to remain 'invisible'. Even less is known about the impact of unemployment on women than is known about its effect on men. Rather, my aim is first to examine the ways in which social work ideology has been undermined by the return of mass unemployment, and how these developments unsettle not only the traditional concerns of casework ideology and the 'rehabilitative ideal' but more particularly some of the basic assumptions of social work's 'radical' hour in the 1970s. We can then attempt to reconstruct a social work response to unemployment and to unemployed people. In doing this I am concerned not so much with macropolitical concerns or the economic consequences of unemployment, but rather with the 'social psychology' of unemployment and how social workers might help to minimize the damage that unemployment can cause in the personal sphere.

This emphasis might be misinterpreted as implying either that political action against the structural roots of unemployment is unimportant, or that the financial consequences of unemployment are somehow less significant than its impact on a person's self-esteem and personal identity. I am prepared to take this risk, however, because it seems to me that not only do social workers not enjoy any kind of privileged leverage through which they might hope to influence the political economy of structural unemployment, but they can also do little to relieve the financial impact of unemployment. What they can do, however, is to work in such a way as to ameliorate the damaging effects that poverty and unemployment can have on people's health, diet, social relationships and self-esteem.

The inheritance of 'radical' social work

Whatever its shortcomings, the 'rehabilitative ideal' in social work offered taken-for-granted goals and measures of success. If it now lies in ruins, what goals can social workers put in its place? In the early 1970s radical social work put forward its own critique of the rehabilitative ideal. Casework ideology has tended to see poverty and unemployment as a consequence of some kind of personal inadequacy, sometimes explicitly identified as the problem of the 'work-shy' person who was unemployed because of emotional difficulties.[12] 'Radical social work' diagnosed this (often quite appropriately) as a deflection from the structural roots of unemployment and poverty – although, under conditions of 'full employment', the ranks of the unemployed would on any reckoning have included substantial proportions of people who were marginal to the labour force by virtue of personal or physical handicap.[13] Even so, the revelation by Abel-Smith and Townsend[14] that one-third of people at or near poverty levels were in full-time employment showed up the irrelevance of the notion of 'inadequacy' in explaining family poverty.

However, the 'rediscovery of poverty' in the 1960s was only one of the inspirations for the subsequent radical emphasis on the structural basis of poverty. The radical critique went on to argue that all attempts to ameliorate the effects of poverty – such as casework or counselling, the encouragement of steady employment routines, attention to the management of scarce family finances, etc. – were to be judged as a 'cool out' and a 'con', as attempts to adjust the client to the system. Such techniques were a means by which working-class anger was 'bought off' and 'defused'. The welfare state was a 'safety-valve' that functioned in such a way as to avert protest and the eventually inevitable revolution, which would come about if and only if the working class and the poor were cast adrift on the free-market seas to feel their pain and to recognize their true class position. The social system functioned in Herbert Marcuse's evocative phrase through 'repressive tolerance', and social workers were the 'soft cops' who serviced this tolerant version of repression. Viewed from the radical perspective, social care was in fact a form of social control. Casework, in this analysis, was just what the Charity Organisation Society had said it was in the 1920s: the final bastion against Bolshevism.

The Charity Organisation Society had its own reasons for promoting this rather grandiose view of social work's functional capacities in maintaining capitalism. However, I am more concerned here to examine the equally dramatic emphasis of radical social work in the 1970s. The radical critique, as I have suggested elsewhere, worked by a series of reversals.[15] If conventional casework emphasized individualized personal troubles, then radical social work stressed structural inequalities. Where the emphasis had been placed on the emotions and feelings, radicalism proposed an attention to material inadequacies. Where the traditional emphasis had been placed upon the failure of the individual, radicalism identified a failure of society. And, under the influence of the profound romanticism of such diverse influences as Laingian anti-psychiatry and the counter-culture, where certain individuals and lifestyles had been diagnosed as 'deviant' aberrations from the norm, the new radicalism defined these same individuals and lifestyles as successful escape attempts from the yoke of conformity.[16] The stage was set for the idea of the deviant as hero, someone who by breaking the rules of the social order had managed to slip the noose of our disastrous civilization. This romanticism was by no means new to European and North American civilization, of course, and had been reproduced in a variety of forms, most notably the heroic outlaw.[17] The idea of madness as grace also came from a long tradition, and had been starkly registered in Samuel Beckett's novel *Murphy*, first published in the 1930s. Murphy had been brought into contact with a variety of deviant conduct through his work as a mental nurse at the 'Magdalen Mental Mercyseat', where his experiences 'obliged him to call sanctuary what the psychiatrists called exile and to think of the patients not as banished from a system of benefits but as escaped from a colossal fiasco'.[18]

Within the context of a full employment policy and a postwar improvement of living standards, Murphy's judgement was revived in the late 1960s and early 1970s within the new radicalism, which embraced not only social work but also anti-psychiatry and the 'misfit sociologies' of deviancy theory. It was a radicalism that found the sources of its inspiration primarily in a variety of North American libertarian assumptions that had little to do with the socialist tradition in Britain – and that were indeed sometimes overtly hostile to the socialist tradition. This radicalism directed attention towards questions of personal liberty and freedom of expression, rather than to problems of inequality and poverty. It was conformity to the prevailing order of consumerism that was seen as oppressive. Freedom was to be seen only where people failed or refused to conform, within a political scenario that owed some kind of vague debt to Herbert Marcuse and an even vaguer debt to the work of Wilhelm Reich and his politicized psycho-analysis. It is important to remember that feminism had hardly made any impact on these currents of thought in the early 1970s, and that the politics of race and ethnicity, which are now such a dominant preoccupation, were quite unknown – at least in Britain. This was a quite different politics, born out of a different age, and it was supremely confident.

Radical social work was also characterized by a healthy and confident criticism of a welfare state that had not only failed to deliver the goods, but acted as a subtly constraining force against human liberty and the possibilities of emancipation. Living in an essentially well-fed world, radical social workers knew that the world they criticized was not about to collapse as a result of their criticism. What this radicalism did not count on, however, was the election of a British government fired with its own fresh-air libertarian philosophizing about the stifling influences of the 'nanny' state and social provision. After the emergence of Mrs Thatcher, the world of radical social work did begin to collapse. Radicals could now be counted in vast numbers rushing to the defence of what they had criticized and condemned in such round terms merely a decade ago. When history tries to repeat itself, in Marx's joke, tragedy turns into farce. But when the libertarian right stole the clothes of the libertarian left, counter-cultural farce turned into monetarist tragedy.

The radicalism of the late 1960s and early 1970s was not entirely a lost cause. Its enduring strengths were evident in the revitalized environmentalist and ecological politics, the politics of cultural diversity, and in the social movements that championed a variety of 'underdog' causes from handicapped people to homosexual rights. The development of more assertive self-help networks and the emergent power of the new feminism were all real gains.[19] The eagerness with which the left has turned its back on everything connected with what it calls 'the sixties' reflects partly an ignorance of recent history, if not the enveloping growth of authoritarianism of the 1980s.

Nevertheless, there were some blind-spots and inadequacies. One of the emerging problems that radical social work did not foresee, except in its own weird way, was unemployment. And its own weird way was exemplified by Fred Davis's 'Why all of us may be hippies some day',[20] in which the hippie refusal of work was proclaimed as an essential cultural preparation for the enforced idleness which would result from the revolutions in production technology and computers. Many radicals shared the same vision of a workless future in the 'leisure society' foreseen since the 1950s by theorists of the 'end-of-ideology' and 'post-industrial' society such as Daniel Bell. Davis's more combative thesis formed part of a wider set of values which defined conformity to a distorted society as the dominant social pathology. Because this conformity was guaranteed and reproduced principally through wage labour, unemployment involved an exemption from the means by which conformity was reproduced, experienced and enacted. Unemployment might even be welcomed as release from social control. Fred Davis's justification for the hippie refusal coincided with the vaguely anarchist tradition which defined the 'refusal of work' as a mode of crypto-political opposition to the dominant system and as a manifestation of a tendency towards an alternative kind of society.[21]

Apart from its more surreal, knockabout attempts at a reversal of the dominant order assumptions, the counter-culture asserted an important truth. It was correct in its recognition that the future of the West was a workless future, at least in terms of the conventional understandings of 'work' and 'employment'. It also offered a potential recognition of the personal and subjective dimensions of the politics of employment and unemployment. Means would indeed have to be found of living viable lives without employment, and of fashioning viable identities outside the work ethic.

But having said that, there was always a danger, because of the specific ways in which these currents made themselves felt within the 'radical hour' of British social work, that these responses would dehumanize both social work and its clientele. The utter rejection within this 'radicalism' of any notion of a psychology of personal troubles, coupled with the radical demonology which defined attempts to ameliorate the effects of poverty as a 'cool-out' and a 'con', left radical social work high and dry. It failed to put forward any acceptable practical strategies other than gestures – 'community action' and the short-lived politics of the claimants' unions.[22] The politics of radical social work were essentially libertarian, voluntaristic and subjectivist. Starting out without any sense of a psychology, it also lacked a coherent politics of the social structure.

The welfare rights movement was a focus of social work radicalism, although even here the refusal of a complementary psychology of human need risked the possibility that 'the client in "radical social work" has become a wooden, dehumanised figure at the bargain basement of a welfare-rights stall'.[23] When recession began to threaten in the mid-1970s, the prospect of a more depersonalized social work loomed large: 'Radical bandwagons such as "welfare rights" might even be a premonition of things to come . . . helping clients to get their rights when they have no rights'.[24]

It is not that it is a bad thing to help people to obtain their rights. The point is that this should not be seen as the sole basis for practical action in the lives of the poor. Social security payments have always been an inadequate response to family poverty, and as they have become even more inadequate so the 'welfare rights' movement has become an increasingly threadbare defence. So how should social workers respond to families and whole communities who face a possibly workless future in the era of mass unemployment? A return to the rehabilitative ideal, even if it were desirable, is clearly not on the agenda. Indeed, in a recent study of social work responses to unemployment, the inadequacies of both the rehabilitative ideal and the radical solution emerged as major difficulties facing practising social workers.[25]

Social workers are in fact well placed to offer certain forms of guidance and counselling to the poor and the unemployed. They can help people to fashion an effective identity and to minimize the effects of unemployment that threaten to wreak havoc on their lives. These, of course, were the sort of social work responses to problems of emotion, identity and so on that were rejected as a 'con' by early radical social work. In the context of mass unemployment, this faulty analysis must itself be rejected as nothing more than a luxury, which could be afforded in a time of relative affluence but which has now become as redundant as the rehabilitative ideal itself. Rather, there is an obligation on those whose work brings them into routine contact with the unemployed to offer what help they can give. This may mean offering counselling, solace, or even courtesy to people who often experience a bewildering mixture of emotions (despair, anger, loss, fear) as well as the material difficulties of poverty. As a preparation for such a programme of action, let's look in a little more detail at what is known about the personal effects of unemployment.

The social psychology of unemployment

To reconstruct the social work agenda in response to the problems of unemployment, we must first ask 'What is life like on the

dole?' There is a considerable literature not only from the current
recession but also from the 1930s which addresses the social
psychology of unemployment and its accompanying lifestyles.[26] It
points to recurrent patterns in the 'cycle of adjustment' to the fact
of losing one's job and to the major difficulty unemployed people
experience when their habitual time-structures are thrown into
disarray. The available research also hints at the different pressures
bearing upon the unemployed, whether they are young workers,
mature workers, or older workers nearing retirement. It suggests
that we need to study the different impacts of unemployment on
women and men, as well as on family members other than the
unemployed individual. As a body of literature, it is a somewhat
depressing read. But it is an essential resource if we are to evaluate
and transform social work practice, so that it can become an
effective response to the needs of the unemployed.

In policy discussions the social psychology of unemployment is
invariably subordinated to questions of income maintenance.
Where a social psychology is implied, in fact, it tends to be the
context of the debate on public disorder. A great deal of rhetoric by
politicians repeatedly suggests that unless something is done about
mass unemployment, and in particular youth unemployment, then
there will be more inner-city 'riots', more youthful hooliganism,
more vandalism, and more crime. While this may be true, the more
obvious fact about the actual lives and experiences of the unemployed is not that unemployment produces restlessness and riot,
but that it leads to apathy and despair. This was the experience of
the Great Slump of the 1930s, just as it is today. This is not to deny
that there were serious riots among the unemployed in Britain in
the 1920s and 1930s, because there were.[27] Even so, a typical 'day in
the life' of an unemployed person in Britain today involves not
rising at the crack of dawn to plot the overthrow of the state, but
staying in bed until late in the day and then mooching around the
house until it is a respectable time to go out and meet your friends.
This respectable hour is often dictated by a residual shame of being
out of work so that many unemployed people do not like to be seen
around the streets during the day. It feels better to emerge only in
the evening when it is possible to 'role-play' the leisure hours of
those actually employed. Others take the different option of
hanging around shopping precincts and other public locations, in
the manner of a proletarian *flaneur*, where it is possible to merge
imperceptibly with the cash nexus and to 'role-play' consumerism
and to 'shop for images'.[28]

A listless apathy characterizes the lives of the unemployed, who
know that they have been rejected as useless by a society in which

identity and status are largely determined by job. This is particularly so among the male- working class where the skills of a bricklayer, the manly strength of a labourer, the resourcefulness of a car mechanic, are highly prized social attributes. This is not to say that unemployment does not have a demoralizing effect on women. Brown and Harris's study *The Social Origins of Depression*[29] showed that a lack of employment outside the home was one of the factors that made it more likely that a woman would suffer from depression. Yet far less is known about the specific effects of unemployment on women. Researchers have a tendency to operate with a male norm into which they then attempt to force the experiences of women, with some predictably strange results. Griffin[30] has recently argued in a discussion of feminist approaches to youth unemployment that the idea that unemployment can be equated with 'worklessness' for young women is wide of the mark. Unemployment for women invariably means that they are thrust back into a variety of unpaid domestic labour. Although there are some indications that unemployed men make a larger contribution to household chores than when they are in work, the division of labour between women and men within the home remains essentially intact. Hilary Graham offers a compact account of what is involved: 'While unemployed men take on more chores, they do not necessarily share responsibility. They help out and lend a hand, but the job remains the woman's'.[31]

Research on the impact of unemployment during the interwar slump confirmed the general picture of its demoralizing effects. Paid employment brings a variety of benefits other than financial reward, so that unemployed workers suffered not only from financial hardship but also from the subtle social psychology of unemployment.[32] The importance of non-financial rewards undoubtedly goes a long way to explaining why significant proportions of unemployed people are prepared to return to the labour market, even though this means that they suffer a loss in real income.[33]

With a number of minor shifts of emphasis, most researchers agree that the unemployed pass through an identifiable 'cycle of adjustment' to the fact of being without employment. In one study from the interwar years, Jahoda *et al.*[34] from Austria described how shock and surprise were the most common reactions when a person was laid off for the first time. Housewives typically panicked about whether they would be able to cope with household management. Panic was followed by a period of recovery when people learned that they could manage on decreased resources. This did not always last, however, as increasing economic hardship threatened even this adaptive pattern of lowered expectations. A similar pattern of adaptation was described from Warsaw by Zawadski and Lazarsfeld,[35] who noted how initial feelings of fear and distress were followed by numbness and apathy, which itself gave way to a period of relative adaptation when the unemployed person would begin a search for work. As this search for work became more obviously futile, hope would once more begin to drain away, as the unemployed person became resigned to his or her position, accepting this lot with an air of fatalism.

The limitations of research that addresses only the experience of male unemployment nevertheless reflect accurately patriarchal household arrangements. Indeed, in one study of the 'cycle of adjustment', which explored how family tensions sometimes lead to the break-up of the family unit, there was a major preoccupation with the way in which any attempts by a man's wife to improve the family's economic position by securing paid work was experienced as a threat to the man's assumed identity as 'the' breadwinner.[36] This will no doubt remain a real problem in a household steeped in the ideology of the independent male breadwinner. However, it is likely that it would assume far less significance now that the involvement of women in the labour market is much more widely accepted. According to one recent estimate, households with a lone male breadwinner, non-employed wife and two children comprise only 8 per cent of the male labour force between 16 and 64 years of age. Households with the same division of labour and three or more children represented 4 per cent of the male labour force.[37] Nevertheless, the ideological assumption of the 'male breadwinner' as the bedrock of the domestic economy remains largely intact, and can be assumed to be an area of difficult negotiation within many unemployed households.

One of the enduring strengths of the tradition of research on the 'cycle of adjustment' is that it alerts us to the varieties of experience – and the often dramatic shifts of experience – which are all too commonly just lumped together as 'being on the dole'. A wide range of social and personal consequences flow from the social psychology of unemployment. People lose status and identity and the variety of social contacts that come through engagement with the workplace. They lose not only companionship, but also the experience of being part of a collectivity (the firm, the union) with its own structure of loyalties and oppositions ('Us' and 'Them', 'the bosses' and 'the shopfloor', the 'works canteen' as against the 'staff dining-room'). Workplace social contacts involve more or less direct engagement with the many-sided experience of contradictory relationships of solidarity and satisfaction, exploitation and antagonism. The workplace provides an informed political education[38] and, correspondingly, there is a tendency for the unemployed to lose interest more generally in external affairs. For young people who have never known paid employment, except in the most marginal sense, this implies a vast shrinking of their social horizons which no amount of 'street wisdom' can remedy.

In one major study of the 1930s, Marie Jahoda's analysis of the impact of the Slump on the Austrian cotton town of Marienthal, a surprisingly wide variety of knock-on effects from unemployment were identified, even down to the fact that people walked more slowly when going about their business.[39] The enforced leisure of unemployment proved to be a 'tragic gift', so that unemployed men also had a significantly shorter waking life. Jahoda also noted a large number of deleterious effects of unemployment on relationships, activities and health. At first, the health of adults actually improved in Marienthal because they were no longer subjected to daily inhalations of dust in the cotton mills. Nevertheless, diet and health subsequently deteriorated. A large body of evidence now indicates a clear relationship between unemployment and a variety of physical and mental ill health, as well as the increased likelihood of suicide.[40] Among other effects noted in Marienthal were that unemployment resulted in a sharp decrease in the likelihood that someone would read a newspaper or use a library, even though these were facilities being made available to the unemployed at reduced cost. There was a corresponding decline in involvement in political organizations and clubs.

A more subtle effect which emerged in the Marienthal study was the impact of unemployment on the experience of the passage of time. Unemployment seemed to have the effect of destroying the habitual time-structures by which people order everyday life. Those fortunate enough to be in work often curse these same time-structures – the need to get up every morning at the same time, to catch the same bus or train, to clock in and clock out at certain hours, to work to the strict timetable of the factory or the office. But if these routine time-structures are suddenly removed, through unemployment or retirement, then people are often left feeling bewildered and rudderless.

One of the findings of the Marienthal study was that for unemployed men everything seemed to take twice as long as it did when they were in work. Simple household chores that previously would have occupied only a few minutes would now consume a whole morning. Although these men had so much time on their hands they seemed quite unable to meet deadlines effectively, and their wives would complain that they persistently failed to turn up punctually at meal times. 'Nowadays we are always having rows at lunchtime', said one woman, 'because my husband can never be in on time, although he was as regular as clockwork before'.[41] It was as if, without a routine time-structure to break up the day, time and the passage of time became quite meaningless.

This is not, of course, some kind of natural phenomenon. It is an aspect of an urban-industrial culture in which time has become dominated by the requirements of factory and office routines and time-clocked work.[42] Whereas in the pre-industrial world the most significant passages of time were those dictated by the seasons and the natural rhythms of the sun, moon and tides, we have now become so accustomed and socialized into the time-structures demanded by capitalist production that these now appear to be natural and we find it difficult to cope without them.

It is not that unemployed people lack the 'inner resources' to cope with unstructured time. Nor is it that they lack sufficient personal interests or hobbies that might fill the day. Jahoda suggested that the 'heavy psychological burden' resulting from 'the destruction of a culturally imposed time structure' should be understood as a universal phenomenon in a society such as our own, although one that might bear down most heavily upon the poor and underprivileged:

> Now there is, of course, no external obstacle that prevents the unemployed from establishing their own time structure for engaging in hobbies and other types of meaningful work outside the contractual arrangements of employment. Indeed, in Marienthal some functionaries of political parties managed to do so. But these were rare exceptions . . . To blame the unemployed for their inability to use their time in a more satisfactory way is pointless; it would amount to asking that they singlehandedly overthrow the compelling social norms under which we all live and which provide a supportive frame within which individuals shape their individual lives . . . Even with all their material and educational advantages some academics, freed for a year from their regular time structure, flounder and feel lost.[43]

The experience of the dislocation of routine time-structures undoubtedly differs appreciably for people who have been involved in different kinds of employment, from different social classes, and also between men and women. Among other important occupational and regional variations revealed by detailed study of daily routines of activity structure and time allocation, gender differences are undoubtedly central.[44] Women who are engaged in full-time work as housewives and child-carers, for example, are less affected by the removal of the time-structures imposed by external employment. This was the experience in Marienthal, which is worth referring to as a rare moment of gender-specificity in unemployment studies:

> Time in Marienthal has a dual nature; it is different for men and women. For the men, the division of days into hours has long since lost all meaning . . . Getting up, the midday meal, going to bed, are the only remaining points of reference. In between, time elapses without anyone really knowing what has taken place . . . Everything that occurs happens as if it were unintentional . . .
>
> The term 'unemployed' applies in the strict sense only to the men, for the women are merely unpaid, not really unemployed. They have the household to run, which fully occupies their day. Their work has a definite purpose, with numerous fixed tasks, functions, and duties that make for regularity . . . They cook and scrub, stitch, take care of the children, fret over the accounts, and are allowed little leisure by the housework that becomes, if anything, more difficult at a time when resources shrink . . .[45]

What Jahoda and her colleagues found particularly astonishing was that, before the onset of the Slump, women in Marienthal had also been employed in the mills:

> Watching the women at their work, it is hard to believe that they used to do all this on top of an eight-hour day in the factory. Although housekeeping has become more difficult and time consuming for them, the purely physical effort involved before was nevertheless much greater. The women know this and remark on it. Nearly all the accounts of their lives mention the fact that their housework used to keep them up late into the night after a day at the factory. But nearly all of these accounts also contain a sentence such as this: 'If only we could get back to work.' This wish would be understandable enough on purely financial grounds but it is repeatedly qualified by the disclaimer that it is not merely because of the money . . . The factory widened their sphere of existence and provided them with social contacts they now miss. But there is no evidence that the women's sense of time has been disrupted in the way it happened with the men.[46]

This amply confirms Griffin's observation that unemployment

merely thrusts women back into unpaid household chores.[47] Nevertheless, this should not be allowed to mask the varying impacts of unemployment on men and women, which were revealed by the Marienthal study as more complex than she implies. Griffin is certainly right to mock the remark by Parker[48] in his study of leisure that housewives (along with prisoners, the unemployed and the idle rich) have 'nothing but free time' on their hands. Even so, the major sex difference in the impact of unemployment is that for men it appears that the disruption of routine time-structures is much more devastating. This is not only the result of the fact that for women unemployment does not mean that they are 'workless'. The organization of a woman's time within domestic labour is already less structured than formal factory or office routines, so that women are perhaps better equipped by their experience and socialization to cope with 'unstructured' time. This is not to say that there are oceans of 'free' time available within the busy round of shopping, cooking and cleaning, or that there are not familiar landmarks such as getting children off to school, getting breakfast and lunch ready for the younger ones, preparing an evening meal, etc. But within those externally determined landmarks, other forms of routine time-structure are essentially self-imposed, because there is nothing objective in saying that shopping should be done before washing dishes, or that the launderette should be visited before or after lunch, or that beds should be made before the hoovering is done, etc. The fact that sometimes women will devise quite rigid routines by which to order the day simply indicates how important it is for people to have their day guided by supporting time-structures.

Because of their wider experience of dealing with unstructured time, women are often better prepared to cope with unemployment than men. Indeed, these kinds of considerations might help to explain something of why the psychological damage caused by unemployment varies in its severity for different classes of workers. For example, the evidence suggests that the psychological impact is greater for men than for women; greater for older men than for younger men; greater for married men than for single men; but greater for non-married women than for married women.[49] The stress is also found to be greatest for men aged between 45 and 54 years, and least for those under 25 years of age or over 55 years of age. One explanation for these differences is that the severity of psychological effects is related to the attachment of the person to employment status as a central focus of their personal identity. It is worth noting in passing that these results do not confirm the common view that unemployment has the most demoralizing effect on young people. Another explanation, however, might be that these different effects depend on the extent to which a person is embedded in the routine time-structures afforded by different kinds of work – both paid and unpaid. Nor should the financial consequences of unemployment be ignored in this context, in that different statuses imply different levels of financial responsibility and different levels of financial commitments. Indeed, at every point it is necessary to bear in mind the intricate and interlocking relationships of the effects of unemployment on the domestic economy, social relationships and psychological well-being.

It should be clear by now that 'work' has more than an economic function. Moreover, any analysis that understands work only as 'exploitation' or 'alienation' simply cannot address the actualities of the experiences of the unemployed. Some may stubbornly insist that these experiences are merely 'false consciousness' resulting from an over-involvement with the ideology of the work ethic and a failure to see that unemployment is in fact a liberation from the destructive embrace of alienation. This would then make it easy to explain away evidence that young people, for example, can actually benefit in terms of psychological well-being from being involved in a Youth Opportunities Programme.[50] For the radical conscience if it is not 'real' work, it must be 'false' consciousness. While consciousness can be a fickle thing and some of the alternative 'employment' schemes have undoubtedly been a grim charade, these would be poor excuses for failing to recognize and engage with the actual experiences of the unemployed.

The argument comes back again to whether it is right to encourage people to adapt to unemployment and poverty. But this is a confused argument. The opposite to 'adapt' is to 'fight'. But how is it possible to fight unemployment at the level of everyday life where both social workers and the unemployed themselves confront it? Neither group has the power to raise the level of benefits, any more than they can spirit away the dole queues. At the material level, as practising social workers know from their experience, they are powerless.[51] All they can do is tinker around with limited amounts of Section 1 money, acting as the occasional stop-gap in a crisis. This is not unimportant, but there are other possible strategies – although to find these one must abandon the 'adapt/fight' duality and think instead of 'attack/defend' as more appropriate. Unemployment is attacking families and whole communities, and threatening their viability. What we must look to, then, are strategies of defence.

Defensive action: From counselling to cookery

This brief discussion by no means exhausts the range of difficulties experienced by unemployed people, although it does begin to suggest some of the subtlety and complexity. We talk about people being 'thrown on the scrap-heap', implying quite rightly the way in which being unemployed imputes worthlessness. But how often do we reach beyond that glib formula to try and understand the precise workings of the damage to self-respect and self-esteem? In trying to devise strategies of defensive action, various options suggest themselves as possibilities that might be usefully developed for social work with unemployed people.

In discussing the difficulties faced by unemployed people I emphasized time and time-structures because this is an issue that seems both most important, and also most neglected. Perhaps this is because it is a less obvious effect than impairments of self-esteem, isolation or boredom. However, the problem of the management of time is so central that it might well often be the key to these other areas of difficulty. For someone who has been 'released' into the 'free time' of unemployment, the ensuing experience of bewildered incapacity might easily reinforce their sense of worthlessness. Effective responses to such difficulties might then include counselling that retains a primary emphasis that such experiences of incapacity are not an indication of some individual failing, together with appropriate forms of group work or assertiveness-training. The impact of unemployment might also be experienced as a profound sense of 'loss', suggesting an analogy with bereavement, so that an appropriate adaptation of 'bereavement counselling' could offer an initial focus.

These responses are not, of course, to be regarded as an end in themselves for unemployed people. However, the recovery of self-esteem and self-respect, together with the development of strategies of 'time management', can provide a start from which people might more effectively engage in local forms of organization such as tenants' associations, mother-and-toddler groups, political activities, or informal systems of neighbourhood care. And these, in turn, might lead to tangible improvements in people's social and material circumstances – whether by mobilizing for improved resources, or by means of self-provision within a neighbourhood. Although it can be argued that the Barclay Report's recommendations of 'community social work' were in many senses lightweight and ill-judged,[52] it nevertheless remains true that a neighbourhood focus will often be vitally important. Unemployment does not cast its shadow evenly across even a single town or city, or even across a single housing estate. Rather, poverty and unemployment tend-to dwell in small huddles of a few streets.[53] Indeed, these problems are often most densely concentrated in localities that are experiencing multiple difficulties such as wretched housing and other deficient public amenities, with significant proportions of single-parent households, extensive criminal victimization, high levels of 'fear of crime', and so on.[54] Moreover, areas experiencing high levels of social deprivation also seem most likely to be visited by serious problems of heroin misuse.[55]

In response to such accumulations of multiple deprivation, one vigorous form of practical response has been suggested by the work of NACRO's Safe Neighbourhoods Unit on 'difficult to let' housing estates. This aims for a concerted multi-agency strategy directed towards a variety of problems in consultation with local residents.[56] The work of the Department of Environment's Priority Estates Project has also suggested ways of working with tenants and official agencies to improve life in impoverished neighbourhoods – including a significant record of achievement on the Broadwater Farm Estate between 1981 and 1985 when the estate suddenly achieved notoriety in the Tottenham 'riot'. Social work interventions have not been significantly placed within these initiatives, and multi-agency work is not without its own difficulties.[57] Nevertheless, in terms of the future development of such strategies it is important that social workers begin to devise effective systems of collaboration. This is especially important where vulnerable groups of people are identified who might otherwise be marginal to a neighbourhood's concerns.

Another practical direction, this time combining counselling and therapeutic interventions within a neighbourhood focus, is suggested by Sue Holland's work with depressed women on a so-called 'problem estate' in inner London.[58] The initial focus here was to enable women who had become dependent on medically prescribed tranquillizers to redefine their difficulties in such a way that they could reassert more control over their own lives. Through limited psychotherapeutic interventions as a second phase of work, the women were subsequently involved in group activities that combined a therapeutic and an educational function. For example, they might study the history of colonialism to gain a better understanding of the difficulties that many experienced in 'mixed-race' relationships and marriages, by recognizing the intrapsychic damage and self-hatred that can flow from the internalization of the structures of colonialism.[59] For some women, individual or group therapy will be all that they required or desired, although these interventions have also led to forms of collective action and self-help through which women act directly on a variety of their life problems, such as housing difficulties, child care, or domestic violence. Although beginning within a conventional counselling or therapeutic framework, this overall strategy can become a process of political empowerment for some women.

In attempting to reconstruct social work practices so that they become relevant to both the personal as well as the material circumstances of the unemployed, other resources might include Wilhelm Reich's attempt to develop a politicized psychoanalysis in Germany in the 1930s. Reich's 'sex-pol' programme, in particular, combined action on the housing question with therapeutic interventions and sex education for young people. This programme was crucial to Reich's understanding of sexual repression as a basis of authoritarianism and support for fascism.[60] Reich's work, which excited a spasmodic interest among libertarians and anarchists in the mid-1970s, should now be reread in a different climate. Although Reich's psychoanalytical theory suffered from a reductionist biological emphasis on the primacy of orgasm, and eventually culminated in the full-blown lunacy of the 'orgone box', he was nevertheless a prolific and pioneering theorist who foresaw the basis of authoritarianism as a 'fear of freedom', which was subsequently to become more widely known through the writings of Erich Fromm.[61]

It is mistaken to think of this kind of work as simply encouraging people to adapt to unemployment and to accept their lot. The long-term unemployed will in any case adapt themselves soon enough, with or without any help from social workers, through the predictable slide into apathetic resignation. The aim of social work should be to provide forms of defence for the poor and unemployed against these injuries of the self. Demoralized and incapacitated people are not well equipped either to deal with the external world and what it has to offer (even if it does not offer them very much) or to deal with the 'internal worlds' of their families, friends and lovers.

One of the incapacities sometimes associated with poverty and unemployment is a marginal hold on literacy – itself a likely product of inadequate education, or a young person's lack of commitment to educational opportunity because of what they correctly foresee as the discouraging prospects of the job market. The difficulty is likely to be compounded, moreover, for ethnic minorities, perhaps especially for people from Afro-Caribbean backgrounds, owing to the stubborn incapacity of the British educational system to understand that Afro-Caribbean dialects ('creoles' and 'pidgins') are linguistically distinct entities and not merely forms of 'broken English'.[62] Social workers themselves are not equipped to teach literacy, of course, although it might be appropriate to refer someone to an adult literacy centre. Once again, adult literacy is not simply an end in itself. Learning to read, as Paulo Freire put it, is not merely a question of learning the A B C. Rather, it involves a new and specific form of engagement – 'a difficult apprenticeship in naming the world'.[63]

The impact of unemployment on health and diet is a further question that demands a more effective consideration by social workers.[64] The responsibility for health care is one that invariably falls on mothers, and, as Hilary Graham has noted,[65] the various measures that have been adopted by health education policy-makers to encourage health-promoting lifestyles are often inappropriate to the realities of family life and household manage-ment. The constraints bearing on poor families, the unemployed and single-parent households limit their health choices even more:

> On a day-to-day level, where the struggle to establish a healthier lifestyle begins, the evidence suggests there is little flexibility in the routines of many families. Poverty limits a parent's com-mand over, and thus choice about, the family's lifestyle. A diet high in fresh fruit may be preferred, but cannot be chosen, unless the mother reneges on equally vital health obligations; the rent and fuel bills, for example. Similarly, single parents, constrained by their childcare responsibilities as well as by their income, have little opportunity to choose the more labour-intensive methods of promoting health, like walking and jogging.[66]

Some advances have been made in relation to health care and health education through local initiatives by women's groups and other forms of self-help. However, such developments are very uneven and probably do not reach into the poorest localities and families. The question of diet, meanwhile, remains intractable for many poor families. Indeed, in a context where diseases of mal-nutrition become a real possibility again in unemployed Britain, it might even be that we will have to rescue from the clutches of Victorian philanthropy the human virtues of teaching more effec-tive domestic skills such as cookery. Both the practice and ideology of this late nineteenth-century tradition were informed by assump-tions concerning the responsibilities of motherhood in rearing a 'virile' imperial race.[67] Classes were often organized around cheer-less sermons on how many mouths could be fed by a cheap cut of meat, or, in the case of the indefatigable Mrs Helen Bosanquet, straightforward moral bullying:

Begin with the girls in school, and give them systematic and compulsory instruction in the elementary laws of health and feeding, and care of children, and the wise spending of money. Go on with the young women in evening classes and girls' clubs; and continue with the mothers wherever you can get at them . . . It has been possible to awaken an intelligent interest in window gardening in the very poorest quarters of our towns, and it ought not to be impossible to awaken a similar intelligent pride in the care of children . . . What we want is a reform which will provide suitable food and care for the children from the first day of their lives, and continue to provide it throughout manhood and old age; and there is no way of securing that except through the mothers and wives.[68]

We should not take this document, one of the more hysterical reports to the 1904 Inter-Departmental Committee on Physical Deterioration,[69] as a model for future action. Nevertheless, it was not always quite as bad as this. One remarkable surviving document from early in the century, for example, is *The Pudding Lady: A New Departure in Social Work*, which described the work of the St Pancras School for Mothers in the Somers Town district of London, and in particular the approach adopted by 'The Pudding Lady' herself, Miss Florence Petty, to teach domestic skills and cookery. Her approach involved working alongside people in their own homes and with their own kitchen utensils, thus avoiding the pitfall of school-based schemes which often used elaborate forms of kitchen equipment not available in working-class homes and therefore more suited to training for domestic service than to their own family needs.[70] Not only does the account of Florence Petty and her colleagues indicate a more sensitive approach to work among the poor than the aloof Mrs Bosanquet was ever capable of imagining, but in the preface to a new edition of the book it was even hoped that the teaching of domestic skills in schools and continuation classes should be 'made obligatory for boys as well as girls'.[71]

The problem of diet, as a defence against the injuries of unemployment and poverty, has undoubtedly been exacerbated in our own time by the acceleration of the 'commodity form' of food, which renders access to cheap and health-promoting forms of food preparation much more difficult. The 'cheap and wholesome' cuts of meat so beloved by Victorian philanthropists are often simply not available. And when they are, they prove to be more expensive than fish-fingers and 'fast food'.[72] This makes it all the more imperative that ways and means are devised to offer poor families effective means of culinary defence. Even so, these strategies (which again, as with adult literacy, are not the domain of social workers but must be developed in collaboration with those with appropriate skills in 'domestic science' and 'home economics') must be devised within the cultural preferences of working-class people if they are to be relevant. For social workers or others to go around preaching to the poor on the virtues of high-fibre diets, pulses to replace animal protein, and other versions of middle-class vegetarianism would simply be to reproduce the worst features of high-minded Victorian philanthropy in a modern guise.

These are necessarily only broad brush-stroke indications of what we might aim to achieve in work with the unemployed. Social work hardly seems to have begun to wake up to the problem of mass unemployment, possibly because social workers have traditionally worked among sections of the population who were marginal to the labour market even in times of 'full employment'. But other equally important reasons for this neglect flow from the inheritance of the form of radical social work that turned its face against anything that might smack of 'adapting' people to their condition. That earlier 'radicalism' was a response to its own historical moment, locked in opposition to forms of conventional response such as the 'rehabilitative ideal'. Each of these responses now seems equally irrelevant. It is time to reconstruct social work's aims and responses, and in particular to give a central importance to questions of employment and unemployment, together with a redefinition of what constitutes 'work'. To do otherwise might be to lend some legitimacy to the wider, public acquiescence to the intolerable length of the dole queues, while at the same time the invisible realms of 'work' – the unpaid work of the home, and the dodgy hustles of the street – continue to reproduce the divisions of our already deeply divided society.

Notes and references

1   See G. Pearson, 'Welfare on the move, 1945–1975', in *Introduction to Welfare: Iron Fist and Velvet Glove*, Block I Course DE 206, 'Social Work, Community Work and Society' (Open University, 1978).
2   See W. Hannington, *Unemployed Struggles 1919–1936* (EP Publishing, 1973); J. Stevenson and C. Cook, *The Slump* (Quartet, 1979).
3   E. Heimler, *Mental Illness and Social Work* (Penguin, 1967); National Association for Mental Health, *The Place of Work in the Treatment of Disorder: Proceedings of a Conference* (NAMH, 1959).
4   See M. Ignatieff, *A Just Measure of Pain* (Macmillan, 1978);

M. Foucault, *Discipline and Punish* (Allen Lane, 1977); G. Rusche and O. Kirchheimer, .*Punishment and the Social Structure* (Russell & Russell, 1939); J. Bentham, *Panopticon, or the Inspection House* (1791), in *The Works of Jeremy Bentham*, ed. J. Bowring, vol. 3 (Wm Tait, 1838).

5   See W. McWilliams, 'The mission to the English police courts 1876–1936', *Howard Journal*, vol. 22, no. 3 (1983); W. McWilliams, 'The mission transformed: Professionalisation of probation between the wars', *Howard Journal of Criminal Justice*, vol. 24, no. 4 (1985); H. Walker and B. Beaumont, *Probation Work: Critical Theory and Social Practice* (Blackwell, 1981); Home Office, *Probation of Offenders: The Probation Rules* (HMSO, 1965).

6   W. Beveridge, *Report on the Social Insurance and Allied Services*, Cmnd 6404 (HMSO, 1942), pp. 49–50.

7   ibid., p. 52; E. Wilson, *Women and the Welfare State* (Tavistock, 1977), pp. 149–54.

8   See S. Jeffreys, *The Spinster and her Enemies* (Pandora, 1985).

9   See D. Riley, 'War in the nursery', *Feminist Review*, no. 2 (1979); D. Riley, 'The free mothers: Pronatalism and working women in industry at the end of the last war in Britain', *History Workshop*, no. 11 (1981).

10 See G. Pearson, *Hooligan: A History of Respectable Fears* (Macmillan, 1983); M. Hill, *Juvenile Delinquency* (Smith, Elder & Co., 1853), p. 39.

11 See R. E. Pahl, *Divisions of Labour* (Blackwell, 1984); H. Graham, *Women, Health and the Family* (Harvester, 1984); C. Griffin, 'Turning the tables: Feminist analysis of youth unemployment', *Youth and Policy*, no. 14 (1985).

12 Heimler, op. cit. (n3).

13 C. Hakim, 'The social consequences of high unemployment', *Journal of Social Policy*, vol. 11, no. 4 (1982).

14 B. Abel-Smith and P. Townsend, *The Poor and the Poorest* (Bell, 1967).

15 G. Pearson, *The Deviant Imagination* (Macmillan, 1975).

16 See S. Cohen and L. Taylor, *Escape Attempts* (Allen Lane, 1976).

17 See K. L. Steckmesser, *Western Outlaws: The 'Good Badman' in Fact, Film and Folklore* (Regina Books, 1983).

18 S. Beckett, *Murphy* (Picador, 1973), p. 101.

19 See R. Williams, *Towards 2000* (Chatto & Windus, 1984); Pearson, op. cit. (n15).

20 F. Davis, 'Why all of us may be hippies some day', *Transaction*, vol. 5, no. 2 (1967).

21 Echanges et Mouvement, *The Refusal of Work* (Echanges et Mouvement, 1979). A Gorz, *Farewell the Working Class* (Pluto, 1982); A. Gorz, *Paths to Paradise: On the Liberation from Work* (Pluto, 1985).

22 See H. Rose, 'Up against the welfare state: The claimants unions', in R. Miliband and J. Saville (eds), *Socialist Register 1973* (Merlin, 1974).

23 Pearson, op. cit. (n15), p. 135.

24 G. Pearson, 'Making social workers', in R. Bailey and M. Brake (eds), *Radical Social Work* (Arnold, 1976), p. 44.

25 See J. Popay, Y. Dhooge and C. Shipman, *Unemployment and Health: What Role for the.Health Services?* Research Report No. 3 (Health Education Council, 1986), pp. 33–4, 55.

26 See M. Jahoda, *Employment and Unemployment: A Social-Psychological Analysis* (Cambridge University Press, 1982); A. Sinfield, *What Unemployment Means* (Martin Robertson, 1981).

27 See Pearson, op. cit. (n10); G. Pearson, 'Short memories: Street violence in the past and in the present', in E. Moonman (ed.), *The Violent Society* (Frank Cass, 1987); Hannington op. cit. (n2).

28 See P. Willis, 'Youth unemployment: Thinking the unthinkable', *Youth and Policy*, vol. 2, no. 4 (1984).

29 G. W. Brown and T. Harris, *The Social Origins of Depression* (Tavistock, 1978).

30 Griffin, op. cit. (n11).

31 Graham, op. cit. (n11), p. 61.

32 Jahoda, op. cit. (n26); E. W. Bakke, *The Unemployed Worker* (Nisbet, 1933); B. Zawadski and P. F. Lazarsfeld, 'The psychological consequences of unemployment', *Journal of Social Psychology*, vol. 6 (1935).

33 See Hakim, op. cit. (n13).

34 M. Jahoda, P. F. Lazarsfeld and H. Zeisel, *Marienthal: The Sociography of an Unemployed Community* (Tavistock, 1972).

35 Zawadski and Lazarsfeld, op. cit. (n32).

36 E. W. Bakke, 'The cycle of adjustment to unemployment', in N. W. Bell and E. F. Vogel (eds), *A Modern Introduction to the Family* (Free Press, 1960).

37 Hakim, op. cit. (n13).

38 See R. Sennett and J. Cobb, *The Hidden Injuries of Class* (Knoft, 1972).

39 Jahoda *et al.*, op. cit. (n34), p. 67.

40 See Hakim, op. cit. (n13); Popay *et al.*, op. cit. (n25).

41 Jahoda *et al.*, op. cit. (n34), p. 76.

42 See E. P. Thompson, 'Time, work discipline and industrial capitalism', *Past and Present*, no. 38 (1967); G. Simmel, 'The metropolis and mental life', in K. H. Wolff (ed.), *The Sociology of Georg Simmel* (Free Press, 1950); D. A. Reid, 'The decline of Saint Monday, 1776–1876', *Past and Present*, no. 71 (1976).

43 Jahoda, op. cit. (n26), p. 23.

44 See D. Parkes and W. D. Wallis, 'Graph theory and the study of activity structures', in T. Carlstein, D. Parkes and N. Thrift (eds), *Human Activity and Time Geography* (Arnold, 1978), pp. 83–7.

45 Jahoda *et al.*, op. cit. (n34), pp. 67–75.

46 ibid., pp. 76–7.

47 Griffin, op. cit. (n11).

48 S. Parker, *The Future of Work and Leisure* (Longman, 1971).

49 See Hakim, op. cit. (n13).

50 See E. M. Stafford, 'The impact of the Youth Opportunities Programme on young people's employment prospects and psychological well-being', *British Journal of Guidance and Counselling*, vol. 10, no. 1 (1982).

51 See Popay *et al.*, op. cit. (n25).
52 See G. Pearson, 'The Barclay Report and community social work', *Critical Social Policy*, vol. 2, no. 3 (1982).
53 See G. Pearson, 'Developing a local research strategy', in P. Wedge (ed.), *Social Work: Research into Practice* (BASW, 1986).
54 See A. Power, *Priority Estates Project: Improving Problem Council Estates. A Summary of Aims and Progress* (Department of the Environment, 1982); A. Power, *Local Housing Management: A Priority Estates Project Survey* (Department of the Environment, 1984); F. Reynolds, *The Problem Housing Estate* (Gower, 1985); M. Hough and P. Mayhew, *Taking Account of Crime: Key Findings from the 1984 British Crime Survey*, Home Office Research Study no. 85 (HMSO, 1985); M. G. Maxfield, *Fear of Crime in England and Wales*, Home Office Research Study no. 78 (HMSO, 1984).
55 See H. J. Parker, K. Bakx and R. Newcombe, *Drug Misuse in Wirral: A Study of Eighteen Hundred Problem Drug Users* (University of Liverpool, 1986); G. Pearson, M. Gilman and S. McIver, *Young People and Heroin: An Examination of Heroin Use in the North of England* (Health Education Council & Gower, 1986); G. Pearson, 'Heroin and unemployment', in N. Dorn and N. South (eds), *Drugs and Social Policy* (Macmillan, 1987); G. Pearson, *The New Heroin Users* (Blackwell, 1987).
56 J. Bright and G. Petterson, *The Safe Neighbourhoods Unit* (NACRO, 1984).
57 See Lord Gifford, *The Broadwater Farm Inquiry* (London Borough of Haringey 1986). Power, op. cit. (n54).
58 See S. Holland, 'The second Pam Smith Memorial Lecture', Polytechnic of North London (1984); S. Holland and R. Holland, 'Depressed women: Outposts of empire and castles of skin', in B. Richards (ed.), *Capitalism and Infancy: Essays on Psychoanalysis and Politics* (Free Associations, 1984).
59 See F. Fanon, *Black Skins, White Masks* (MacGibbon & Kee, 1968); R. Littlewood and M. Lipsedge, *Aliens and Alienists: Ethnic Minorities and Psychiatry* (Penguin, 1982).
60 W. Reich, *The Mass Psychology of Fascism* (Souvenir Press, 1970); W. Reich, *Listen, Little Man!* (Souvenir Press, 1972); W. Reich, *The Sexual Struggle of Youth* (Socialist Reproduction, 1973); W. Reich and K. Teschitz, *Selected Sex-Pol Essays 1934–37* (Socialist Reproduction, 1973); M. Brinton, *The Irrational in Politics*, Solidarity Pamphlet no. 33 (1975); P. A. Robinson, *The Sexual Radicals* (Paladin, 1972).
61 See R. Jacoby, *Social Amnesia: A Critique of Conformist Psychology from Adler to Laing* (Beacon, 1975); E. Fromm, *Fear of Freedom* (Routledge & Kegan Paul, 1942).
62 See L. Todd, *Modern Englishes: Pidgins and Creoles* (Blackwell, 1984).
63 See P. Freire, *Pedagogy of the Oppressed* (Penguin, 1972); P. Freire, *Cultural Action for Freedom* (Penguin, 1972).
64 See Popay *et al.*, op. cit. (n25).
65 Graham, op. cit. (n11), pp. 145ff.

66 ibid., p. 187.
67 See A. Davin, 'Imperialism and motherhood', *History Workshop*, no. 5 (1978).
68 H. Bosanquet, 'Physical degeneration and the poverty line', *Contemporary Review* (January 1904), p. 73.
69 See Pearson, op. cit. (n10), pp. 55–6, 70.
70 See Davin, op. cit. (n68), p. 27.
71 M. E. Bibby, E. G. Colles, F. Petty and (the late) J. F. J. Sykes, *The Pudding Lady: A New Departure in Social Work* (National Food Reform Association, 1916), p. xiv.
72 See B. Campbell, *Wigan Pier Revisited: Poverty and Politics in the Eighties* (Virago, 1984), pp. 69–71.

4 Changing perspectives: feminism, gender and social work

ANNIE HUDSON

When the concept of 'radical social work' first entered our occupational vocabulary in the late 1960s, contemporary British feminism was at an early stage of development. Since then, feminist knowledge and practice have expanded considerably; not least, there is now a more explicit consciousness of the differences as well as the similarities between women. Moreover, the experience of challenging the sexist structures of our social institutions has emphasized the enormity of the task of transforming gender relations.

The attempts by successive Conservative governments since 1979 to roll back the welfare state have clearly exacerbated the oppressive circumstances faced by many women. The 'feminization' of poverty has myriad representations: women's unemployment, for example, is rising faster than that of men; the rate for black women, moreover, is twice that for white women.[1]

The Thatcher administration's continuous assault on the role and expenditure patterns of local authorities has added to the pressures faced by all women, particularly working-class and black women. In the late 1970s there was widespread confidence that local government initiatives would extend opportunities for women to gain a fairer share of society's resources. It is clear, however, that the reality has been precisely the opposite. The demand, for example, for universal free pre-school provision is now much further away from being realized than it was in the mid-1970s.

A paper about gender and social work practice in the late 1980s must consequently begin by acknowledging the depressing experiences of the past decade. It is important, however, to maintain a degree of optimism about the possibility of developing social work's more progressive facets. To do otherwise is to collude with the status quo. By comparison with the limited understanding of the relationship between gender and social work that prevailed in the 1970s, there is now much wider recognition of the way in which gender shapes the lives of consumers and social work's organizational responses.[2]

One trend that gives grounds for a degree of optimism is the fact that recruits to social work in the late 1980s are more likely than their counterparts ten or fifteen years earlier to have been influenced by feminism. Many women now entering social work organizations have themselves had direct experience of involvement in groups such as Women's Aid and rape crisis centres or in informal 'consciousness-raising' activities at college, in the workplace or in their local communities. Consequently their perceptions of social work are likely to be influenced by a critical understanding of the relationship between gender relations and the state.

However, it is also clear that social work has been slow to take active account of the accumulated wisdom of the contemporary women's liberation movement. The reasons for such resistance are manifold and have been detailed elsewhere.[3] Gender has certainly become an issue of concern for an increasingly large number of practitioners; but whether or not there has been a corresponding change in the approach of social work agencies is open to dispute. My own experience of acting as a consultant to a number of agencies in their provision of services for 'troublesome' young women suggests that a few committed practitioners are still given the dubious honour of carrying the organization's 'anti-sexist' banner. While there may be departmental support for organizing the occasional day workshop and so on, when it comes to putting resources into overhauling service provision, organizational backing is usually singularly absent.

The purpose of this chapter is not, however, to concentrate merely on the inadequacies of the status quo; the broad aim here is rather to evaluate feminist critiques of social work. There is a conscious focus on gender relations rather than on specific issues facing women. For one of the limitations of feminist and anti-sexist perspectives has been the tendency to reduce issues about gender to work with women. A thorough scrutiny of the influence of assumptions about 'normal' masculinity on the organization and practice of social work is a key prerequisite of 'radical' perspectives: to ignore men is to ignore the heart of the problem. This paper looks first at issues concerning the values of feminist social work; it then examines developments in feminist approaches to direct work with clients and, finally, some contemporary themes in the relationship between social work organizations and gender.

Feminist values and principles in practice

Feminism in the 1970s was able to evolve in a general political climate that, whilst certainly not favourable to social minority groups such as black people and women, was none the less conducive to a degree of optimism. Today, however, feminist perspectives must take account of the deepening recession and the general shift to the right. Not least, it is clear that social work's policing functions have been considerably advanced.

One striking feature of the new right's promotion of 'normal' family life is its implicit distinction between 'abnormal' and supposedly 'healthy' families. Of particular concern to social workers is the way in which such language is increasingly finding its way into professional discourses. This is clearly evidenced in the child protection field where the idea of the 'dangerousness' of particular families is becoming increasingly purveyed by some practitioners.[4] The state, it seems, is prepared to offer support to women only when they have been defined by professionals as 'less than adequate' parents. Such trends further undermine the potential of social work to become a positive resource for women.

Working-class and black women who are unable to resist state interference are particularly susceptible to negative labels from social workers. Female-headed Afro-Caribbean families in receipt of social work services may, for example, be liable to the charge that their children's 'troubles' are a function of 'inappropriate' forms of parenting. Such attitudes were revealed in my study of decision-making concerning adolescent young women 'in trouble'. As one social worker commented:

> 'You have the whole morality of the Church . . . her mother is trying to force it upon her . . . I think that J felt that every time she went out, her mother . . . would sort of point out and say "ah there is a bad girl" . . . the Church had taken over from her father as being the major influence in her mother's life.'[5]

In this situation it is clear that the social worker concerned viewed the mother's membership of the Church as a pathological response to single parenthood which, in its turn, was seen as creating problems for the young woman. Women who, either through choice or because of social and economic circumstances, do not conform to the notion of 'proper' parents are possibly more vulnerable to the watchful gaze of welfare professionals than ever before.

But what of political changes that have occurred within feminism? My own acquaintance with both feminism and social work occurred concurrently when I was a social work student in the early 1970s. I recall a great sense of relief when I 'discovered' feminism; not only did it provide a framework for understanding much of my own experience but it also provided me with a survival mechanism for coping with many of the contradictions of doing (and subsequently teaching) state-sponsored social work. Feminism, more than any other political credo (notably Marxism), demonstrated some of the practical possibilities of working towards change in the 'here and now'. It clearly affirmed the politics of personal relations; its values and modes of organizing also seemed more conducive to participation and organizational change.[6] Such values were clearly of potential utility for the tasks of social work, even if putting them into practice has always been more difficult.

Since I first 'discovered' feminism in the early 1970s the terrain of political debate and practice has, however, evolved new contours. Feminism has always had as many meanings as it does adherents but today it has changed beyond recognition. Lynne Segal's comprehensive and provocative account of contemporary feminism[7] provides a useful starting point for a consideration of the implications for social work of the changing shape of feminism.

Segal suggests that there is less unity among feminism's constituencies today than there was in the early 1970s. Perhaps the most significant influence in this process of fragmentation has been a greatly enhanced awareness of the significance of differences between women. Particular groups of women (for example, black women, lesbians and women with disabilities) have developed critiques of the ways in which they are dominated by other women, including feminists. Consequently, by the mid-1980s, it had become clear that feminism's presumption of 'universal sisterhood' was a conceptual and organizational barrier to addressing unequal relationships among women.

The tendency of many recent feminist critiques of social work practice (my own included) has undoubtedly been to focus on the commonalities of women's experiences at the expense of recognizing social divisions that uphold the power of some groups of women at the expense of others. Naseem Shah[8] highlights how feminist perspectives on social work have been guilty of such presumptions, thereby denying the significance of racism as a key factor in the experiences of black women as both clients and workers. It is not merely that middle-class white women are 'better off' than working-class and black women; it is also the case that the interests of the former are frequently in opposition to those of the latter.

Since the early 1970s the perspectives of many feminists have thus been considerably shaken. Challenges first from lesbian and working-class women, then from black women, have meant that white, middle-class heterosexual women have had to come to terms with the fact that we do not, cannot and should not have any kind of monopoly in defining 'feminism'. The process of acknowledging such ideas has not always been easy; sometimes we have retreated into futile apologizing or immobilized ourselves with guilt. At other times we have felt frustrated and sometimes angry that we should apparently have to shoulder the responsibilities for the legacies of our class, race and sexual identity. Such emotional mechanisms provide convenient distractions from the need to listen to the voices of women whose situations are different and more oppressive than our own.

These issues have a number of consequences for social work. First, social workers are generally middle class, predominantly white and mostly actively heterosexual. If feminism is to be a dynamic force within social work then it is vital that it is not fashioned by the experiences, values and assumptions of the majority of its workers and spokespersons. Nor should the diversification of feminist perspectives be seen as being solely concerned with ensuring that 'minority' experiences and interests are protected. Lorde's work[9] exemplifies the importance of using social differences as an instrument for 'creative change'. Black women can, for example, teach white women a great deal about ways of actively subverting the status and label of 'victims'.

Secondly, the experiences of many feminists during recent years highlight the complex and highly contradictory nature of the task of tackling gender oppression. The process of recognizing how our attitudes and behaviour are part of the dynamics of social oppression also means accepting that what we criticize in others frequently mirrors the ways in which we act in the world. The challenge to this aspect of feminism's orthodoxy has been most clearly articulated within social work's debates about racism and anti-racism. Black feminists have focused in particular on the way white feminists' presumptions about the 'intrinsic oppression' of the family have denied both the impact of racism on black families and the role of the family as a bulwark against a racist world.[10] Ahmed's work reminds us how many white feminist social workers perceive their work with young Asian women as a form of 'salvation' – aiming to rescue them from the oppressive clutches of their culture.[11] The danger of white feminists monopolizing the path to 'liberation' is very evident.

Similarly, lesbian feminists have emphasized how heterosexist assumptions must be confronted so that, for example, when working with young women 'in trouble', feminists' affirmation of their right to define their own sexuality is not narrowly defined.[12] The implementation of the section of the Local Government Act, 1988, which outlaws the 'promotion' of homosexuality, is likely, moreover, to make social workers even more hesitant about ensuring that young people are offered positive images of lesbian and gay lifestyles.

Finally, it is important to stress the importance of refusing to collude with the establishment of a hierarchy of more or less 'worthy' oppressions. Such a hierarchy enables those in power to pitch one set of political rights and demands against others. It also implies that the causes and manifestations of different forms of oppression are similar; this is clearly not the case. Racism and sexism, for example, have different historical roots; their consequences are also generally dissimilar. So, whilst black and white women may share some similar goals, for example that of combating sexual violence, there are many instances where the similarities cease and it is up to white women to acknowledge the impact of racism on black women's lives and how their own actions may contribute to the subordination of black women.

Segal's work is relevant in registering how differences in assumptions about the 'nature' of femininity have contributed to the fragmentation of the contemporary women's movement. She argues that the images of femininity presented in the work of radical feminists such as Daly and Dworkin presume that women have essential (and ultimately biologically based) qualities that make them intrinsically superior to men. Such perspectives, Segal concludes, have engendered a political philosophy that is ultimately no more than a politics of 'retreat and despair':

> A feminism which emphasises only the dangers to women from men, which insists upon the essential differences between women's and men's inner being, between women's and men's natural urges and experience of the world, leaves little or no scope for transforming the relations between men and women.[13]

Segal argues that much of what passes for feminism today assumes 'inherent' qualities and 'natural' characteristics in both women and men. She proposes a feminist strategy based on the conviction that women and men are *socially* rather than biologically determined and are hence susceptible to being changed by the conscious intervention of human beings, female or male. If we accept this then anti-sexist radical social work should repudiate the fatalism that follows from feminist essentialism and develop forms of practice that can begin to transform the seemingly 'natural' order of things.

Social work practice with young men 'in trouble' reveals the complexities of these issues. A crucial first step is to acknowledge the impact of everyday assumptions about 'appropriate' masculinity in contemporary practice.[14] Such understandings, together with those concerning other forms of oppression such as racism and class-inequalities, need to be blended creatively into a coherent value system for social work intervention. However, it is equally important that anti-discriminatory practice with young men proceeds on the premise that individual men can (and indeed might want to) alter some facets of their behaviour towards women. In so doing, it is also crucial that attention is paid to some of the potential benefits of such change for young men. Greater expressiveness about their feelings might, for example, enhance not only their self-esteem but also the quality of their relationships with other young people.

However, in many situations it is difficult to sustain much confidence in the capacity of men to alter their behaviour. In the field of child sexual abuse, for example, there is considerable evidence that the behaviour of perpetrators is very resistant to change.[15] Balancing the current realities of male violence against children and women with a belief in the potential for social relations to be different is undoubtedly a struggle that will continue to confront feminists in and out of social work for a long time to come.

The 1980s have witnessed some progress in denting the sexist edifices of social work. The 'trade' journals provide greater coverage of gender and BASW now has a working group on 'gender issues', something that would have been unheard of ten years ago. Similarly many training courses now include teaching about gender, though this is often assigned a peripheral status and is only rarely integrated into the main body of college-based teaching and practice assessment.[16] Yet there are still many ways in which social work continues to ignore the way that women's experiences are structured by oppression. The 1987 Cleveland child sexual abuse crisis starkly revealed social work's institutionalized reluctance to accept that the power dynamics within many families operate in favour of adult men. The media's constant focus on the rights of parents has avoided differentiating between mothers and fathers and so diverted attention away from the evident fact that, in the vast majority of cases, it is men who sexually abuse children. It is the 'rights' of the male abusers that would be threatened if professionals, the judiciary and politicians alike were to accept such realities. The denial of the significance of gender throughout the Cleveland 'crisis' is, as MacLeod and Saraga comment, 'quite staggering and amounts to a deceit'.[17]

There is some evidence that practice wisdom concerning child sexual abuse has affirmed the importance of believing children and emphasizing that it is not their fault in any way. However, approaches to intervention have now, quite significantly, shifted their focus onto the children's mothers; 'fathers' continue to be largely let off the hook. Such 'mother blaming' is most revealingly portrayed in the CIBA Foundation's widely circulated text entitled *Child Sexual Abuse within the Family*.[18]

Drawing upon the work of Tilman Furniss, a prominent child psychiatrist in the field, the authors make great play of the characteristics of families in which child sexual abuse occurs. Furniss hypothesizes that two 'types' of family are most 'prone' to such abuse: those he characterizes as 'conflict-regulating' and those he typifies as 'conflict-avoiding' families. The notion of attributing family pathology as the cause of child sexual abuse is bad enough, but Furniss then goes on to discuss the role of mothers in 'allowing' and 'facilitating' the abuse of their children. Little space is afforded to the behaviour of 'fathers' in perpetrating abuse. As MacLeod and Saraga have commented, the absence of the abuser in professional accounts, except in describing their responses to their female partners, is indicative of the continued adherence to the idea that male sexuality is 'driven and uncontrollable'.

> The subtext here is that it is up to women and children not only to nurture and care for their men adequately, but also to control men's sexuality, because the men cannot 'stop' themselves.[19]

Work with child sexual abuse offenders continues to be situated within traditional treatment frameworks that imply a 'cure' and that the 'disease' is suffered by a small and aberrant minority. The testimonies of survivors of child sexual abuse suggests otherwise.[20]

Contemporary developments in the sphere of child sexual abuse are certainly telling reminders of social work's continued obsession with staying on the fence and avoiding a more political role. The assumption that white middle-class forms of family life are both safe and 'natural' has repercussions for many aspects of social work practice; hence, for example, the second-rateness and presumed reactionary nature of residential care.[21] Shifting such conceptions is not only costly, it is also politically highly threatening at a time when the family as the 'front-line carer' is being promoted more strongly than ever.

Feminists in social work have constantly criticized the way in which feminist ideas had been 'added in' rather than substantially altering the practice of social work. While there is a greater consciousness of the ways in which gender affects the life experiences of women and men, issues concerning gender have in practice concentrated on women. Black people have experienced similar difficulties in ensuring that issues concerning race are perceived by white social workers as being about racism rather than problems of culture.

Feminist perspectives need to broaden out to develop approaches to work with men; otherwise anti-sexist strategies will only ever be half-hearted. Social workers constantly work with men –, as fathers, partners, single men, relatives, and so on. But although a number of writers[22] have begun to articulate the need to address sexism in work with male clients, social work unerringly retreats from taking up the challenge of developing anti-sexist strategies with male clients. Such a project will, however, only have any validity when male social workers begin to connect their own attitudes and behaviour with the endemic sexism of social work policy and practice.

In this section we have seen how the values and principles underpinning feminist perspectives on social work must develop and change. This is not only because of the need to take account of changes in the broader political climate but also because it is clear that much taken-for-granted feminist 'wisdom' has been based on very limited understanding of the needs of different groups of women.

Direct social work practice

In the early days of radical social work there was scant literature towards which feminists could turn for guidance. However, over the past decade a series of books and articles have provided a much clearer outline of a feminist approach to social work practice. Yet in many senses pursuing the goal of feminist social work practice is like chasing the end of the rainbow. The contradictions are such that the concept can never be fully realized. There is, however, considerable scope for change, as has been shown by the individual and collective projects of many women in social work.[23] In recent years some of the constraints of working according to feminist principles inside large state-sponsored bureaucracies have been revealed. But in the course of pursuing feminist perspectives we have gained much insight into the scope for changing social work practice, even within the limitations imposed by existing structures.

It is not difficult to understand why some feel very pessimistic about the possibilities of fundamentally changing either our own practice or that of social work agencies. It is one thing to state a commitment to anti-sexist values but quite another to disentangle ourselves from the inegalitarian views of the world in which we live.

The integration of feminist principles into practice is made more difficult by the fact that social work roles are frequently ill defined and often highly ambiguous. In contrast to education or health, social work tasks rarely have clear boundaries. While teachers and health staff have relatively clear objectives – to educate or to heal – social work has more diffuse responsibilities for the 'whole person'. If traditional social work is riddled with ambiguity, feminist social work is even more complex and contradictory. The limits of what is possible must be recognized at the same time as pushing forward and testing our visions of anti-discriminatory social work practice. A consideration of the work of innumerable feminist projects in social work over the past ten to fifteen years provides us with a patchwork quilt image of apparently small endeavours that none the less have some consistent threads. This section considers some of the elements that have come to characterize feminist approaches to direct social work practice.

Feminists in social work have challenged the continued influence of psychological paradigms that obscure the impact of social, cultural and political factors on the development of individual identity and personality. Traditional social work's reluctance to recognize the impact of power relationships within the family has already been commented upon. Because social work intervention (particularly in statutory agencies) has a prime focus on individuals and small groups, feminists have needed to challenge mainstream psychological thinking and to insert, in its place, alternative ways of making sense of the relationship between the social and the personal. Indeed, efforts to use social work intervention as a means of 'de-individualizing problems' whilst simultaneously affirming the specificity of individual women's experiences have been a central objective of feminist social work practice.[24]

In *The Second Sex*, Simone de Beauvoir noted that:

This humanity is male and man defines woman not in herself but as relative to him . . . she is the incidental, the inessential as opposed to the essential. He is the Subject, he is the Absolute – she is the Other.[25] .

De Beauvoir's perception has been amplified by a host of studies attesting to the differential experiences of women and men respectively.[26] Eichenbaum and Orbach[27] have highlighted how, from earliest infancy, women and men have different experiences of themselves. Through watching and identifying with their mothers, girls develop a strong and intuitive sense of the needs of others. They quickly learn that, to be approved of and loved, they must demonstrate their ability to be nurturing and emotionally giving. In contrast, boys rapidly perceive profound differences between themselves and their mothers, with the consequence that they expect women (initially their mothers and then later other women) to meet their needs for intimacy and affection. The costs of these patterns are considerable, Eichenbaum and Orbach suggest, for boys not only often develop a deep distrust of women but they also become inhibited about openly expressing emotion and affection.

The consequences of such differential experiences in infancy and early childhood are manifold. Women often develop a vague sense of emotional deprivation, a feeling that 'something is missing'. When faced with emotional stress or crisis in adolescence or adulthood, women often experience difficulties in expressing their emotional needs. Consequently they are more likely to turn their stresses 'inwards' and become depressed, make suicide attempts and generally lack self-esteem. Such processes help explain the fact that the rate of attempted suicide amongst adolescent young women is over four times higher than that of adolescent young men.[28] Men, however, because they have been schooled to have a deep resistance to expressing emotional vulnerability are much more likely to 'act out' their intra- and interpersonal conflicts, for example through physical violence.[29]

The work of the American psychologist and moral philosopher Carol Gilligan[30] is similarly of relevance for social workers in understanding the impact of gender on the development of individual identity. In a fascinating study of the development of the structures of morality in women's lives, she argues that women's inner identity revolves around the themes of affiliation, emotional openness and the assumption of responsibility for the well-being of others. Hence, whereas (white) men's behaviour is shaped by a wish for autonomy, women experience considerable conflicts in balancing their needs for relationships with their desire to assume control over their lives.

The insights of Eichenbaum, Orbach and Gilligan must, however, be used with a degree of caution. For not only do their accounts make minimal reference to the impact of race and class on women's identity, but Gilligan's ideas in particular could also be construed as implying that gender differences in the evolution of personal identity are 'natural'. In the light of Segal's arguments referred to earlier, the notion of a 'female' (or indeed 'male') personality is somewhat problematic.

That said, the contributions of a number of feminist psychologists such as Eichenbaum and Orbach have considerable relevance for social workers. For example, in work with women who are at the receiving end of male domestic violence, their ideas, along with feminist critiques of society's response to domestic violence,[31] can facilitate a clearer understanding of the contradictory emotions experienced by abused women. A critical understanding of some of the psychological processes that may make it extremely difficult for women to leave their violent partners is clearly a prerequisite of an effective challenge to the notion that some women are 'addicted' to violence. Similarly, feminist psychology can help reframe the responses of mothers who find it difficult to believe that their children have been sexually abused by their spouses. Rather than castigating them for not believing their children, it then becomes possible to understand women's responses as a product of the way in which many women equate self-worth with being in a relationship with a man.

The ways in which structural factors such as race, class and gender shape individual personality development and behaviour are considerable. It is important that these factors are acknowledged in the curriculum of social work training courses and in the assessments that social workers make of their clients. Corob's discussion of practice with women who are depressed exemplifies the importance of integrating an understanding of the impact of gender-related factors such as low self-image, vulnerability to domestic violence and low-status social roles into the ongoing process of assessment.[32] Similarly, the process of compiling social inquiry reports for courts should include a consideration of the impact of gender and sexism on the clients' circumstances. That said, the presentation of such information is not unproblematic, for it should obviously not be phrased in a way that prejudices an equitable outcome. What is clear, however, is that social work must take more meaningful account of the impact of social inequalities on the interpersonal and emotional lives of its consumers.

Social work's preoccupation with 'problems' has meant that training and general professional socialization encourages workers to concentrate on the 'weaknesses' and 'difficulties' of individuals, families and communities. The work of rape crisis centres, Women's Aid, incest survivors' groups and black women's groups confirms the necessity of basing campaigns and the provision of practical services around the presumption that women's survival strategies offer creative resistance. A constant thread of both black and white feminist social work perspectives has thus been a recognition of the capacities and strengths of women. This is clearly evidenced in Donnelly's vivid account of work with a women's group on a working-class housing estate in Leicester. Meeting together 'provided the forum for the realisation of their collective strength', with the consequence that not only did the women's self-confidence increase but they also came to realize their rights and power to challenge the opinions of those in authority.[33]

Yet social work's institutionalized resistance to establishing links with the diverse resources of the women's movement remains entrenched. Fears that the collective voice of women might undermine the status of 'expert' professionals have, moreover, been exposed in the course of public and professional debates about child sexual abuse. Neither the local rape crisis group, nor indeed any women's organization concerned with male sexual violence, was called to give evidence to the Cleveland inquiry. Campbell's account of how women's groups were silenced makes for salutary reading. She wrote in the *Guardian* in July 1988:

> The last year has been unnerving for the diverse groups which make up the women's movement in Middlesborough town: here was their community consumed by a single issue – child sexual abuse – which they themselves had tried and failed to put on the political agenda. It was *their* issue . . . [yet] while the town talked and talked about child sexual abuse, they fell silent. Or rather they felt silenced. (Her emphasis)[34]

The experience in Cleveland has been consistently repeated: feminist groups are perceived as a threat to the claims of social workers and allied professionals that they are the fount of knowledge and expertise. Feminist social practitioners may feel that they are 'between the devil and the deep blue sea'. On the one hand they cannot deny their status and authority, but on the other they may want to build bridges with women's organizations. It would be easy, for example, for individual women social workers to work with a women's group with the best of intentions and yet, sometimes quite unwittingly, perpetuate power imbalances and thereby constrain the autonomous development and strength of the group. Donnelly's work incisively describes these dilemmas; it is clear that the social workers concerned had to 'recognise and utilise their knowledge and skills' in the formative stages of the group. But there came a point when they needed to withdraw in order that the group could become more independent and explicitly political.[35]

Donnelly's paper discusses a situation where feminist social workers assume a quasi-community development role. Different issues arise in terms of the relationship between social workers and existing autonomous groups such as Women's Aid. Social workers are often extremely reluctant to draw upon the diverse resources of the women's movement because of stereotyped perceptions that feminist groups are 'men hating', 'aggressive' and 'inappropriate' for their 'vulnerable' clients. Such attitudes maintain a view of women as passive and unable to define their needs. They also deny the capacity of women's groups (for example, young lesbians and black women) to provide forms of support and advice that are neither feasible nor provided for within statutory departments. Support to women's organizations can also be given by mobilizing agency resources when (as is increasingly the case) groups such as Women's Aid are threatened with financial cuts. However, as we shall see in the final section, the ability of feminist social workers to coordinate their support is frequently constrained by the lack of a firm organizational base.

The statutory and professional power of social work is another issue with which feminists have attempted to engage. The report of the inquiry into the circumstances surrounding the death of Jasmine Beckford (1985) highlighted the potentially fatal repercussions of social workers being ambiguous about their use of authority.[36] In an evocative account of her experiences of attempting to integrate feminist thinking into social work practice, Sue Wise suggests that conventional feminist analysis has oversimplified the realities of social work practice, with the consequence that the needs of society's most vulnerable groups (for example, children) are sometimes disregarded. She comments:

> I came to believe that . . . feminist social work, as I had defined it in terms of working non-oppressively with women, was a fantasy based on a fundamental misunderstanding of what local authority social work is about. That is, I see 'social work' now as the policing of minimum standards of care for, and the protection of the rights of, the most vulnerable members of our society – some of whom are women, but most of whom are not.

Moreover, this 'policing' and 'control' function of social work is one I feel happy with. . . .[37]

Through a series of case studies, Wise details some of the complexities of local authority child care work. She argues that social workers have a moral as well as a statutory duty to ensure that the needs of small children are attended to when their mother is unable to provide basic minimum standards of child care (for example, leaving them alone at night, being rejecting, and so on). Wise points out that such complexities generally 'seem to defeat feminist analysis'.[38] She concludes that feminists should accept that some social control dimensions of 'the job' are not only inescapable, they are also essential.

Other feminist writers and practitioners have emphasized the importance of social workers using their professional and personal influence in a constructive manner. Corob reminds us that many women experience the prospect of personal change as very risky. The possibility of becoming more independent and assertive may, for example, engender resentment, jealousy and anger on the part of a male partner. Consequently women often feel ambivalent and anxious about personal change. Female clients will therefore need plenty of permission to discuss such feelings and, most importantly, to be given maximum space to 'choose to act in ways they see fit'.[39] At all times social workers need to check that they are not imposing their own ideas about 'healthy' femininity onto their clients; the danger of feminism becoming yet another dogma is never far away.

The importance of equating anti-sexist practice with work with men as much as with women has already been noted. But how can anti-sexist work with male clients assume a more prominent place in social work practice? There have been few accounts of social work with men *qua* men; there is even less evidence that social work has assimilated anti-sexist ideas into its methods of working with men.

It is apparent, for example, that work with young male offenders frequently replicates ideas about 'appropriate masculinity' that are intrinsically oppressive of women. By not challenging young men about their apparent emotional invulnerability, their 'bonding and bantering' with one another, and their approach to sexual relationships as a form of 'conquest', social workers are evading the responsibility of translating feminist perspectives into their daily practice with male clients. It is no coincidence, moreover, that a disproportionate number of practitioners working with young male offenders in Intermediate Treatment projects are men.[40]

The absence of a collective commitment by the majority of men in social work to scrutinize the influence of their own socialization as well as that of their male clients presents women with a dilemma. Should men be left to assume responsibility for taking forward this component of anti-sexist strategies? Male social workers must take the prime responsibility for evolving anti-sexist work with male clients but feminists will need to keep a close watching brief to ensure that a critical edge is maintained.

There are some areas of practice, notably work with both young and adult offenders, where the client constituency is predominantly male. In these areas, developing approaches to practice that take account of the impact of masculinity is fairly straightforward. However, in work with families where the 'problem' is often that men are positioned or place themselves at the periphery, the issues are more complex. In family situations where, for example, there is evidence of violence towards adult women, social workers (female and male) may be confronted with the dilemma of how to challenge men about their behaviour without putting their female partners further at risk. Social workers are sometimes fearful about challenging men about the conduct of their interpersonal lives. In such situations, it is important to clarify whether such avoidance is a result of internalized assumptions about the 'inappropriateness' of delving into men's private lives, or whether there is indeed a real physical threat.

Understanding the impact of other forms of oppression on the lives of clients and the ways in which welfare services are implicated creates further dilemmas. Do, for example, white middle-class men or women have a right to challenge the sexism of working-class men? Black feminist perspectives have highlighted how white feminists have consistently presumed that their experiences of sexism are the same as those of black women.[41] In Chapter 9 in this volume Naseem Shah points out some of the intrinsic difficulties involved in black and white women working together. For white women can all too easily exploit their power to maintain control and define the parameters of discussions about sexism as well as racism.

Gender and social work organizations

The commitment of many local authorities to equal opportunities policies generated a degree of optimism that gender inequalities in social work agencies might begin to be transformed. But how have

changes in organizational (and particularly management) philosophies affected the position of women in social work?

As Hale[42] has commented, it is a matter of fact rather than
controversy that the numerical representation of women in social
work is inversely related to their level of seniority. Women are
concentrated in low-power positions within social work hierarchies. They are also generally engaged in tasks demanding their
supposedly 'natural' capacities to care for dependent and vulnerable
people. In contrast, men are more likely to be in positions
warranting the use of authority and the administration of control
over other workers as well as clients.[43] In short, social work has
maintained the tradition established in the nineteenth century when
'The iconography was of a perfectly matched husband and wife
with a household and family to maintain. He was the head, and,she
the heart of the enterprise'.[44]

The professionalization of social work in the postwar years has
made it even more difficult for women to assume positions of
authority. Social work was made a more attractive career proposition for men by the extension of training opportunities and by the
creation of hierarchical agencies such as social services departments,
following the Seebohm reorganization in the early 1970s. Although
most social work students continue to be women,[45] most of these
are destined to remain in lower-paid and lower-status positions. A
number of authorities have concluded that in several key respects
the position of women has worsened in the post-Seebohm era.
There are today, for example, fewer female directors of social
services departments in England and Wales than at their inception
in 1970.[46] Why is this so?

First, women's general relationship to the labour market highlights how women workers must continuously negotiate the
perennially conflicting demands of home and work. Hence,
although women social workers may be able to 'buy in' child care
and other forms of domestic support, this does not free them from
the constant need to manage the boundary between home and
work. When children are ill, for example, women are more likely
to take time off work. It is clear that the 'new man' is more of a
media myth than a reality.[47]

For similar reasons, it may be more difficult for women with
domestic commitments to attend conferences and meetings away
from their immediate locality. Hence they constrain their opportunities for enhancing their personal confidence, professional expertise and public visibility. It is rare, moreover, that the managerial
skills and energy required to sustain work and domestic careers
simultaneously are recognized by employers. If women take time

off to look after their children when they are young, the possibilities for promotion are considerably reduced.

The reluctance of many employers to promote job-sharing schemes, together with the paucity of child care provision (especially in after-school hours and during school holidays), means that women are rarely offered a real choice about whether or not they continue working full or part time after they have children. There is little evidence that men are prepared to 'forgo' their careers and abandon full-time work when their children are growing up. No wonder then, that NAPO[48] found that, of women who achieved the grade of assistant chief probation officer, 71 per cent were single (as compared with 3 per cent of men). Even allowing for the fact that single women may have children and married women may not, the disparity is dramatic.

The fact that many social work roles replicate broader patterns of gender socialization is a second key influence on gender segregation in social work. From an early age, women are brought up to see themselves as providers of physical, social and emotional care: 'proper' women must demonstrate competence in expressive and nurturing tasks. It is not surprising, then, that so many would-be social workers are women; a more pertinent question might be why do some men enter social work? Howe's distinction between 'vertical' and 'horizontal' gender segregation in the personal social services is relevant here.[49] His survey suggests that, whereas fieldwork teams with a bias towards work with children and their families generally maintained the 'average' of 60 per cent female staff, teams specializing in work with older people had a much higher concentration of women workers (87 per cent). Similar patterns were to be found in residential establishments for children and older people.

Social work tasks that involve an explicit use of authority and control seem to be more attractive to male social workers than those involving a greater concentration on the organization of care for dependent people. The relative dominance of men in the probation service can be explained by the explicit social control focus of their work.[50] It will be interesting, moreover, to see whether work with previously low-status groups such as older people becomes more attractive to men as the professional and political profile of community care initiatives expands.

The impact of class and race on these trends is also significant, although there are few empirical data. Working-class women are concentrated in the lowest-paid positions in social work agencies (for example, as care assistants in residential establishments and as home helps). Black women are also more likely than white women to be employed in low-paid positions, for example as care and domestic assistants in residential homes.[51] It is also worth noting that the attempt of some local authorities to increase the number of black people employed in senior management positions in social services departments has in reality generally meant the employment of black men. There are still no black women directors of social services departments in England and Wales. The double oppression of black women is once more revealed.

However, socialization processes and the structure of the majority of women's lives do not fully explain the 'shutting out' of women from high-power positions in social work agencies. Equally powerful are popular stereotypes about the characteristics of a 'good manager'. The continuing cultural purchase of the idea that men are the rightful 'heads' of social work agencies means that women will often have to demonstrate, more conclusively than their male counterparts, their capacity to provide leadership, to control staff and to define and implement policies: in short, women who apply for management posts must prove that they are 'pseudo-men'.

Such injunctions place women in a double-bind. If they demonstrate assertiveness, independence and a capacity to organize they are then often condemned as being 'aggressive' or 'too emotional'. Christine Walby[52] has drawn attention to some of the subtle but pervasive ways in which women are effectively blocked from senior management positions in social work agencies. These range from their suggestions being ignored, to being patronized and humoured, to the assumption that they are 'innumerate, illogical and intuitive'. Finally the culture of most senior management groups is such that a lot of discussion about 'important matters' takes place via injokes and conversations in the pub or the men's lavatory. Social work's management culture is, in many respects, as 'macho' as that operating in organizations that are usually considered to be more conservative such as the civil service or private companies.

Women in social work are faced with a difficult choice. Many may want to continue working primarily with clients, but in taking this route women diminish their prospects of influencing policy or of increasing their salaries. Alternatively, they may seek management positions, in which case they will have to battle not only with their own lack of confidence but also with the generalized prescription that only 'exceptional women' make good managers. Once inside management posts, the battle to survive may be equally challenging: women have to continue to fight for recognition and may also be forced into styles of management with which they are less than comfortable. It is these forces that, Walby suggests, 'may push some women into becoming "one of the boys"'.[53]

Until prevailing conceptions of 'good management' alter dramatically it is unlikely that more than a handful of women will assume positions of power and status within social work agencies. However, changing such conceptions might enhance the quality of services provided to clients. Evidence from the private sector suggests that women often make 'better' managers, not least because their style is more likely to be sensitive and cooperative.[54] It is interesting to note that, in many respects, the private sector has been more active than its public equivalents in attempting to infuse its recipes for 'good management' with 'feminine' ingredients. A number of private companies have now formally recognized that women's learned capacities to be supportive, flexible and cooperative can be a vital component of a positive management style. They have realized that hard, macho styles are good neither for labour relations nor for the quality of the final product.[55]

The fact that discrimination against women in social work continues is apparent. Feminists have, however, tended to ignore a number of issues concerning social work's organizational context – notably the impact of 'value for money' philosophies and the scope of equal opportunities policies. Public service enterprises are increasingly dominated by the need to demonstrate that they provide 'value for money'. Feminists, along with many other radical welfare commentators and writers, have been slow to engage with management issues. The result is that current preoccupations with 'effectiveness, efficiency and economy' have been virtually ignored except when it comes to mounting an overall critique of the Thatcher administration assault on welfare.

The radical left has generally tended to avoid consideration of management issues, equating management with control and thus intrinsically a 'bad thing'. The problems of such an approach are manifold; not least it means that when the left has electoral power (as it continues to in a number of local authorities) there is no consensus about the qualities that are required of 'managers'. However, one has only to look through the job advertisement pages of the social work press or, more particularly, at the debates taking place within social work's management journal *Insight* to see that social work is developing, albeit haltingly, its own consensual definitions of what makes for 'effective' management. The fact that the left has largely excluded itself from these debates is potentially dangerous. Feminists and others on the left have a responsibility to enter the debate to ensure that principles such as participation are an integral component of definitions of 'effective' management.

It is easy to see why the concept of 'value for money' has been equated with Thatcherism. The concept has undoubtedly been deployed as the rationale for cutbacks in services (most obviously in the health service). Reports from the Audit Commission are having increasing influence on both the scope and level of social welfare services.[56] Similarly, the operation of the probation service, perhaps because it is more directly controlled by central government, has already been visibly affected by an emphasis on the need to demonstrate its cost effectiveness.[57] The Audit Commission's *Managing Social Work*[58] suggests that in the near future social services departments will be similarly scrutinized.

Numerous problems are of course posed when attempting to measure the effectiveness or efficiency of social work. The left is appropriately sceptical about the possibility of 'value for money' enhancing the quality of services provided to consumers.[59] However, backing off from the debate plays into the hands of the right's argument that the administration of welfare is inefficient and uneconomical. The progressive left should instead be developing its own arguments about the importance of social work being self-scrutinizing and explicit about the ends and means to which it is deploying its resources. An important first step is to open up the debate concerning the values and criteria that should underpin such evaluation.

Feminists have a particular interest in the development of alternative approaches to 'value for money'. Financial pressures, together with the gathering momentum to demonstrate 'value for money', have meant that social work management is becoming increasingly characterized by an aggressive and 'virile' style. The ability to be 'entrepreneurial, opportunistic and risk-taking' is seemingly now a quality that is revered and sought after in senior management posts.[60] Such qualities are, however, singularly unconducive to encouraging women and other social minorities from assuming formal organizational decision-making roles. Equally importantly, they will not lead to an enhancement in the quality of services provided to consumers.

The development of equal opportunities policies during the 1980s potentially heralded new departures for the functioning of social work organizations. The extent to which such policies have been effective in combating oppression and discrimination has yet to be fully documented but, in considering their impact on gender relations within social work, their negligible impact is very striking. A number of factors help explain the apparent lack of interest and commitment of politicians and senior managers in introducing equal opportunities principles into their organizations, in terms of the needs of their female consumers and staff.

First, because women are present in large numbers in the staffing structures of social work organizations (as well as in the consumer population), the problem can be viewed as of 'marginal' significance. Hence the problem is not acted upon with energy and commitment. Second, despite their relatively large revenue budgets, social services are seen as being of low status politically by many politicians (of all political hues). Social work's consumers are portrayed as 'poor unfortunates' whose difficulties are somehow outside the boundaries of 'normal' experience. Consequently many local councillors are unable and reluctant to recognize that the way in which social services are delivered reflects and intensifies broader social inequalities and problems such as racism or sexism. No wonder then that, whereas even in some of the more 'progressive' authorities political interest may be expressed in making sure, for example, that anti-sexist and anti-racist materials are used in schools, there is often no such commitment to tackle inequalities perpetuated by field, residential and day care social work services.

However, other explanations are also required. On several occasions recently, when discussing institutionalized male domination within social work management, I have encountered some contradictory reactions from male social workers. All have unhesitatingly concurred that the status quo is inequitable. But, as discussions have proceeded, some men have begun to admit that the implementation of equal opportunities policies has implications for their personal careers. An inevitable consequence of a commitment to a more equal sharing of power with women is that men may not be able to achieve all they have come to expect from work in terms of power, status and financial remuneration. Clearly some men are resentful that their personal ambitions might have to be sacrificed for 'the greater good'.

Similar issues confront white people – male and female – in relation to tackling racism. It is not surprising that, even within supposedly progressive occupational cultures such as social work, those with structural power fear the personal consequences of equal opportunities policies. If equal opportunitites policies are to have a real impact, individual members of particular social groups will either have to give up power or have it taken from them. The experience of losing power and prestige is never easy. Of course, in reality white people generally, and white men in particular, continue to have a disproportionate amount of power inside social work organizations. It is thus somewhat ironic that the subjective feelings that shape individual and collective responses to equal

opportunities policies are frequently dominated by the false perception that women and black people are getting more than 'their fair
shares'.

In such circumstances it is possibly easier for women (and black
people) to say 'Well, that's just tough', and no doubt many of us
frequently express such sentiments, both privately and publicly.
But such responses have their own limitations; most particularly
because we may unwittingly generate even more solid resistance to
women having a greater say.

To suggest that feminist perspectives might focus on how male
staff could be more emotionally committed to sharing power with
women might sound naive, consensual and accommodating; and in
many respects, of course, it is. I am not, however, suggesting that
feminists devote their energies to 'changing men' but rather that an
item entitled 'the implications for men' is inserted into the debate
about equal opportunities. It would of course be an item for which
men would take responsibility.

Finally, feminists in social work need to consider organizational
strategies to respond to contemporary political realities. For, as Segal
has suggested,[61] the feminist principle of autonomous political
development, so strongly expressed in the 1970s, may not always
be in tune with the political realities of Thatcher's Britain. Within
social work it is difficult to find a collective vision about anti-sexist
social work; there has, for example, been no continuous national
network of feminist social workers. There have been occasional
conferences, which provide valuable forums for exchanging ideas
and experiences. However, their effectiveness in ensuring that
feminist principles and ideas are translated into action has been
limited. Balancing the importance of encouraging local initiatives
with that of influencing the more general organization of social
work, including how social workers are trained, has not been easy.

Feminists could perhaps learn from the way in which black
people have attempted to get their voice heard within social work.
The existence of groups such as the Association of Black Probation
Officers has gradually created a collective black voice in social
work, which in turn has forced organizations such as CCETSW to
begin to take account of racism. The establishment of CCETSW's
Black Perspectives Committee is no guarantee of social work
transcending its racist structures but it is a small step towards that
goal. In contrast, anti-sexism remains very low on the educational
and training agenda.

But how and to what ends should feminists in social work
organize themselves? Feminists have been highly critical of the
power-mongering, organizing style characteristic not only of the

right but also of white left groups. This has engendered a healthy suspicion of the appropriateness of women assuming positions of power and status. It is obvious, moreover, that individual women achieving power by no means necessarily enhances the position of women; Margaret Thatcher is the most public embodiment of this. There are undoubtedly questions as to whether or not one individual woman assuming formal authority in a hierarchical organization such as a social services department or an academic institution can have a marked impact on the position of women more generally. What is clear, however, is that until feminists engage more fully with some of the current debates concerning the organization of social work it is even less likely that more progressive organizational models will begin to develop.

Over the past decade feminists have struggled to put social work's institutionalized sexism on the agenda. However, while feminism and the discussion of gender inequalities have had some impact, there are many areas where traditional ideas continue to dominate. It is also clear that feminists within social work must constantly scrutinize their own assumptions. The pursuit of greater gender equality has sometimes been at the expense of recognizing other oppressions, particularly those experienced by black and working-class women and by lesbians. The dynamics and effects of oppression are like a kaleidoscope where the configurations of, and relationships between, different forms of oppression are constantly moving and changing. Feminist perspectives must constantly take account of such changes; to do otherwise is to contribute to oppression rather than to challenge it.

Notes and references

1　B. Morley, 'Women, poverty and social work', in S. Becker and S. MacPherson (eds), *Public Issues and Private Pain* (Insight, 1988).

2　See, for example, E. Brook and A. Davis (eds), *Women, the Family and Social Work* (Tavistock, 1985); D. S. Burden and N. Gottlieb (eds), *The Woman Client* (Tavistock, 1987); J. Hale, 'Feminism and social work practice', in B. Jordan and N. Parton (eds), *The Political Dimensions of Social Work* (Blackwell, 1983).

3　A. Hudson, 'Feminism and social work: resistance or dialogue?', *British Journal of Social Work*, vol. 15 (1985).

4　See Nigel Parton and Neil Small in this volume (Chapter 6).

5　Research by author into social work decision-making processes concerning young women 'in trouble', in *'Troublesome Girls': Adolescence, Femininity and the State* (Macmillan, forthcoming).

6   S. Rowbotham, L. Segal and H. Wainwright, *Beyond the Fragments* (Merlin Press, 1979).
7   L. Segal, *Is the Future Female?* (Virago, 1987).
8   See Naseem Shah in this volume (Chapter 9).
9   A. Lorde, *Sister Outsider* (Crossing Press, 1984).
10 See, for example, B. Bryan, S. Dadzie and S. Scafe, *The Heart of the Race: Black Women's Lives in Britain* (Virago, 1985); H. Carby, 'White woman listen! Black feminism and the boundaries of sisterhood', in Centre for Contemporary Cultural Studies, *The Empire Strikes Back* (Hutchinson, 1982).
11 S. Ahmed, 'Cultural racism in work with Asian women and girls', in S. Ahmed, J. Cheetham and J. Small (eds), *Social Work with Black Children and their Families* (Batsford, 1986). p. 151.
12 See, for example, A. Mountain, *Womanpower: A Handbook for Women Working with Young Women at Risk and in Trouble* (National Youth Bureau, 1988).
13 Segal, op. cit. (n7), p. 37.
14 A. Hudson, 'Boys will be boys: masculinism and the juvenile justice system', *Critical Social Policy*, Issue 21 (spring 1988).
15 See M. Macleod and E. Saraga, 'Challenging the orthodoxy: towards a feminist theory and practice', *Feminist Review*, no. 28 (spring 1988).
16 Joint University Council/Social Work Education Committee: Women and Social Work Education Group, *Study Conference Report* (1987).
17 M. MacLeod and E. Saraga, 'Against orthodoxy', *New Statesman*, 1 July 1988, p. 18.
18 R. Porter (ed.), *Child Sexual Abuse within the Family* (Tavistock/CIBA Foundation, 1984).
19 MacLeod and Saraga, op. cit (n16), p. 18.
20 See, for example, E. Ward, *Father–Daughter Rape* (Women's Press, 1984).
21 See Bruce Senior in this volume (Chapter 12).
22 See, for example, R. Bowl, *Changing the Nature of Masculinity: A task for social work?* (University of East Anglia, Social Work Monograph no. 30, 1985). Also J. Harper, 'Men as workers and clients', *Community Care* (Inside), 25 June 1987.
23 See, for example, A. Donnelly, *Feminist Social Work with a Women's Group* (University of East Anglia, Social Work Monograph no. 41, 1986); A. Corob, *Working with Depressed Women* (Gower, 1987). Also Mountain, op. cit. (n12).
24 Corob, op. cit. (n23).
25 Quoted in J. Figueira-McDonough and R. C. Sarri, 'Catch-22 strategies of control and the deprivation of women's right', in J. Figueira-McDonough and R. C. Sarri (eds), *The Trapped Woman* (Sage, 1987), p. 14.
26 See, for example, E. G. Belotti, *Little Girls* (Writers and Readers Publishing Co-operative, 1975); R. Deem (ed.), *Schooling for Women's Work* (Routledge & Kegan Paul, 1978); S. Sharpe, *Just Like a Girl* (Penguin, 1976).

27 L. Eichenbaum and S. Orbach, *What Do Women Want?* (Fontana, 1984); L. Eichenbaum and S. Orbach, *Understanding Women* (Penguin, 1985).
28 M. Kerfoot, 'Deliberate self-poisoning in childhood and early adolescence', *Journal of Child Psychology and Psychiatry*, vol. 29, no. 3 (1988).
29 E. D. Rothblum and V. Franks, 'Custom-fitted straitjackets: perspectives on women's mental health', in Figueira-McDonough and Sarri, op. cit. (n25).
30 C. Gilligan, *In a Different Voice* (Harvard University Press, 1982).
31 J. Pahl (ed.), *Private Violence and Public Policy* (Routledge & Kegan Paul, 1985).
32 Corob, op. cit. (n23).
33 Donnelly, op. cit. (n23), p. 39.
34 B. Campbell, 'Silenced in court', *The Guardian*, 11 July 1988. See also, B. Campbell, *Unofficial Secrets: Child Sexual Abuse – The Cleveland Case* (Virago, 1988).
35 Donnelly, op. cit. (n23), p. 28.
36 Report of the Panel of Enquiry, *A Child in Trust* (London Borough of Brent, 1985).
37 S. Wise, 'Becoming a feminist social worker', *Studies in Sexual Politics*, no. 6 (Department of Sociology, University of Manchester, 1985), p. 2.
38 ibid., p. 69.
39 Corob, op. cit. (n23), p. 95.
40 Hudson, op. cit. (n14).
41 See, for example, B. Bryan *et al.*, op. cit. (n10).
42 Hale, op. cit. (n2).
43 D. Howe, 'The segregation of women and their work in the personal social services', *Critical Social Policy*, Issue 15 (spring 1986).
44 E. Brook and A. Davis, 'Women and social work', in E. Brook and A. Davis (eds), *Women, the Family and Social Work* (Tavistock, 1985), p. 9.
45 Central Council for Education and Training in Social Work, *Report on Applications: 1987 Intake* (CCETSW, 1988).
46 A. Fry, 'Time to give women more opportunity to be directors', *Community Care*, 6 September 1984.
47 C. Lewis and M. O'Brien (eds), *Reassessing Fatherhood* (Sage, 1987).
48 O. Wells, *Promotion and the Woman Probation Officer* (National Association of Probation Officers, 1983).
49 Howe, op. cit. (n43).
50 ibid.
51 ibid.
52 C. Walby, 'Why are so few women working in senior positions?', *Social Work Today*, 16 February 1987.
53 ibid., p. 11.
54 M. Davidson and C. Cooper, *Stress and the Woman Manager* (Martin Robertson, 1983).
55 BBC TV, *Business Matters*, 16 May 1988.

56 See, for example, Audit Commission, *Managing Social Services for the Elderly More Effectively* (HMSO, 1985); Audit Commission, *Making a Reality of Community Care* (HMSO, 1986).

57 See Paul Senior in this volume (Chapter 15).

58 Audit Commission, op. cit. (n56) *Managing Social Work More Effectively*.

59 N. Flynn, 'Performance measurement in public sector services', *Policy and Politics*, vol. 14 (1986); J. Mallaber and R. Kline, 'Counting what can't be counted', *Insight*, 13 March 1987.

60 B. Morris, 'Tough talking', *Insight*, 27 May 1988.

61 Segal, op. cit. (n7).

5 Decentralization and the personal social services

SUZY CROFT and PETER BERESFORD

Introduction

'Radical social work' has always tended to be much more a paper activity than a form of practice. That explains why those involved have more often been academics and other commentators rather than practitioners or service users. 'Patch' decentralization has been the most conspicuous organizational development in social work and social services since the first writings of radical social work appeared.

'Patch' and 'community social work' are terms used interchangeably to describe overlapping ideas. Patch is presented as an alternative approach to and method of organization for social services departments. It is based on the decentralization of services to small local units, with sub or patch offices; a move away from an individual casework approach to more group and community work methods, and the fusion of statutory work with voluntary action in the 'community'. Particular weight is placed on concepts of locality, participation, informal aid and voluntarism.

What is interesting is the often confused response to it from writers on the left,[1] and the lack of an alternative vision at a time when supporters of 'patch' have so completely staked out their ground. This chapter reflects that, since here we have the reactive task of charting the 'patching' of social services. It might have been a happier project if we had been able to pursue a more self-determining journey, but perhaps the one can lead to the other.

Experiences of our own

We want to begin with two autobiographical examples. We found these helpful in trying to understand some of the key issues around decentralization, personal social services and radical social work,

particularly the effects of short resources on the roles and relationships of social services workers.

1. Going local before patch

One of us (Peter) worked in a London welfare department before
the new era ushered in by the 1968 Seebohm Report. The old
welfare departments were responsible for meeting the needs of old
people and people with disabilities. 'Welfare officers', as we were
called, each worked their own geographical patch. There was a
consciousness of the importance of getting to know a particular
neighbourhood, its places and people. We had a good working
relationship with several committed GPs, other domiciliary health
and social services workers. Apart from me, there was only one
other graduate in my team. Most workers had much more in
common with the people they worked with than the majority of
today's CQSW course members. There was the young woman
who lived in the block of Guinness buildings and the former rent
collector who wasn't very keen on men but once mentioned how
she felt like giving old so-and-so a cuddle. People had different
skills to offer. We were all ages and mostly women. None of us
was black – this was before most of the British-born generation of
black people had left school.

We all worked together in our office. Our senior was a woman –
middle aged and upper middle class – with a strong practical grasp
of people's needs. There were regular sessions of in-service training. We also had an especially close relation with the local lunch
club and day care centre. Our office was above it and we would
take turns once a week to go down there and work with the centre
workers. If offered an opportunity for another kind of contact with
our 'clients'. The same was true of the sheltered accommodation
just next to our office. In summer, residents and day centre users
played croquet on the lawn and all year round the social worker
could keep in easy informal touch with her clients who lived there.
Bruce Beresford (no relation!), before his famous Australian film
director days, came from the BFI to show us all at the lunch club in
pre-video days how we could make a film together. Mabel, a
regular writer of letters to the local newspaper, soon let everybody
else in the area know about our film, shown with the record
player thumping out old Beatles' hits – 'Day Tripper' and 'Ticket
to Ride'.

One of my clients was a man of 81 living in an upstairs rented
flat. He was becoming frail. He had difficulty eating. He had served
for years in India. He showed me his old army literacy certificate.

I used to see him regularly to talk and see how things were going. The flat and the stairs were getting more and more difficult for him. He wanted to find somewhere more manageable to live. One day when I went he broke down and said he'd kill himself if he couldn't get anywhere else to live. He cried and pleaded with me to find him somewhere. I felt anger and disgust that this old man, with all his values of independence and respectability, was reduced to begging me to try and find him somewhere decent to live. During the time I was there, although I pushed his case with the Housing Department, there was nothing I could do for him. However, I later learned that he did get rehoused with the help of his new social worker in the sheltered housing next door to our office.

2. Rehousing and the irrelevance of patch?

In our second example of welfare services, we were on the receiving end. In autumn 1986, one of us (Suzy) had to go into hospital for a month. A social worker told us that we should now be eligible for more housing points on medical grounds. If I would fill in the necessary form, she and the doctor would write supporting letters. We live in Wandsworth where the Conservative council has belligerently pursued right-wing policies since the late 1970s. Our social worker suggested that we contact SHAC – the London Housing Aid Centre – to see if we could be 'nominated' to a housing association waiting list. The first time I phoned, I was told that I needed to speak to a housing adviser and to phone back after 2 p.m. When I did I was told to phone back the following day between 10 a.m. and 4 p.m. So I did, promptly at 10. The woman who answered told me curtly all the lines were engaged and suggested I phone back. I tried time after time, but the line was always engaged.

Fortunately, I've got my own phone and I wasn't relying on the broken phone boxes up the road. I tried phoning once and was told that no calls except emergencies were taken on that day. Finally I managed to get through to a worker. This was early in the morning at peak rate after 10 minutes waiting to be put through, hearing the phone ringing over and over again.

The woman worker asked why I'd phoned. It was clear straight away that she was trying to find out if there was any point in me going to talk to someone. She listened to what I told her about our circumstances and then explained there was very little she could do to help. There was no point in going to the office as we did not constitute an 'emergency'. She advised me to go to Wandsworth

Housing Aid, but she didn't have the phone number. She said that with three children and one proper bedroom, we were probably overcrowded, but as we lived in Wandsworth, and we weren't actually homeless, there wasn't much she could do. She couldn't give specific advice about housing associations in any particular borough like Wandsworth.

You have to make an appointment to go to Wandsworth Housing Aid. So I did, and the following week I was interviewed by a man in his early twenties. He told me (as I already knew) that there are two kinds of housing associations – the ones whose waiting lists you can get on by yourself and those for which you have to be nominated by the council. He didn't have a list of the first kind. He suggested I look in the Yellow Pages, realizing as he said it that, of course, they wouldn't say which was which. I should ring round. We didn't have enough points to be nominated; we had just over half the number needed. He couldn't understand why we had so few, given our situation – three children, medical grounds and a very small flat. He said he'd check. The interview lasted about 5 minutes. A couple of weeks later we got a letter from the Housing Department confirming the number of points we had. Over the last year, these had risen by 50 per cent. A year ago there were 89 people above us in our category. Now our waiting list card shows 290 with more points. We had previously told our social worker that SHAC hadn't been able to help and that we'd try Wandsworth Housing Aid. She didn't have their phone number. She explained that clients who'd been there had told her that they usually referred them to SHAC!

Nowadays there is very little likelihood of us, or indeed of people in much worse circumstances, getting decently rehoused. Take our next door neighbour. When she was expecting her fourth child she told us that Shelter wrote a report saying her flat was entirely unsuitable for a new born baby. The environmental health officer agreed, but said there was no point in forwarding the document to the Housing Department as they always ignored them.

It seems from these examples that there is very little that agencies like Shelter or SHAC could do. And what could our social worker be expected to offer? What difference then could decentralization be expected to make, given the regressive redistribution of housing and other resources that has taken place since 1979? Could it counter the often unequal and unhelpful relationships popularly associated with welfare and exacerbated by inadequate resources, which our own experiences reflect? These are crucial questions and ones we will keep coming back to in this discussion.

'Patch's' top-down origins

Decentralized and 'community-oriented' social services appear very much children of the 1980s. This was when the best-known books on the subject were written, notably *Going Local*, *When Social Services Are Local* and *Decentralising Social Services: A model for change*.[2] The Barclay Report, advocating community social work, with a minority report pressing for 'patch', was published in 1982.[3] Three bulletins from the Department of Social Administration at Lancaster University have charted the mushrooming of 'patch' reorganizations of local authority social services departments over the past few years. Decentralization in personal social services has mainly meant 'patch'.

The rapid development of patch decentralized social services coincides with the election of a Conservative government and the intervention of Roger Hadley, the most effective patch advocate. He and others have presented patch as a reaction to the 'over-centralized' social services departments created in the wake of the Seebohm Report. Terms like 'bureaucracy', 'professional' and 'centralization' have become code words that are invoked not only to condemn the social services departments set up in the early 1970s, but also to malign Labour and the left. What is interesting here is that such departments, like subsequent National Health Service reorganizations, owed much more to American business management philosophy and private market thinking than socialist statism. More important, while patch decentralization has been presented by its advocates as a reaction to such departments, it can more clearly be seen, as Lambert first observed, as a feature of the post-Seebohm social services department.[4] For example, several of the schemes described in *Going Local*, the overly influential first primer of patch, began in the early 1970s, and at least one in 1970, the same year as the Social Services Act which created social services departments. The Seebohm Report argued for decentralization, calling for a family- and community-based service.[5] All the rhetoric for participation and community orientation that is now associated with patch can be traced to its pages. The important distinction lies between the intentions underlying Seebohm and the Social Services Act, and the reality of social services departments in the 1970s.

The impact of Seebohm on the team in which Peter worked illustrates this point. It was absorbed into the new social services department, dominated as elsewhere by the old children's department. Its workers, we later heard, became disillusioned one by one and left. Their wide range of backgrounds and skills was replaced, in a familiar pattern, by the much narrower spectrum of experience conditioned by the expectations and academic requirements of CQSW training.

While patch decentralization has been promoted as a 'community-oriented' approach to social work and social services, the much-vaunted 'community' seems to have had little part to play in its development. We know of no case of patch schemes emanating from 'the community' in the sense that they were inspired by service users, local residents and community groups. This is hardly surprising. Social services departments just don't work like that. On the other hand we would expect user and community groups to be pressing for what they want. Yet patch has hardly figured in their demands.

If we look at some of the key issues that have concerned such organizations over the main period of patch, they include the rights and participation of children and young people in care and their families; the physical and sexual abuse of children; the desegregation of services for people with mental handicaps; same-race fostering and adoption; and proper services for carers. The demand has been for better services, greater rights and counters to racism, sexism and other discrimination, rather than for any kind of patch reorganization. Campaigns have not been conducted and issues have not been framed as if such reorganization and restructuring were seen as the way forward. Patch has clearly not been a grassroots movement.

Nor is patch a movement that has grown out of the welfare workforce. This is not to say that social services department workers have not made important advances in working locally. There was, for example, a patch project in Brighton long before East Sussex implemented its comprehensive decentralization. There are also well-known local initiatives like Essex Road in Islington[6] and the Area sub-office in Hammersmith and Fulham.[7] But, as the *Third Patch Bulletin* reported in 1984, the trend has increasingly been to larger-scale 'top-down' patch decentralization – of which East Sussex is only the best-known case. Patch advocates have been not care workers, community activists or trade unionists, but academics and senior and middle managers. They have also been almost entirely white men.

The politics of patch

When patch first became prominent in the early 1980s, it had a strong liberal–democratic flavour. It spoke to both the frustration and ideals of many social services department workers. Its advocates seemed to recognize their weariness of the constraints of conventional casework and of rigid and remote agencies. Patch sounded as though it could make possible the desire of such workers to function in more accessible and egalitarian ways. Patch may not have been inspired by welfare workers but, make no mistake, it gained the interest and support of many of them. While the candle of radical social work was guttering in the early 1980s, many workers were still looking for a way out of the impasse their social services department role left them in. Patch appeared to offer it.

For all its liberal rhetoric, in one sense at least patch has remained politically neutral. Patch decentralization has been implemented in authorities of all political colours, from right-wing Conservative Wandsworth to Labour-left Hackney. The only apparent distinction is that more general decentralization schemes have tended to be associated with politically left councils like Walsall and Islington, although Liberal Tower Hamlets is a conspicuous exception. Single social services department schemes have shown no such consistency.

At the same time, there seems to have been a conscious effort to incorporate a wide range of different developments under the patch umbrella. This first became evident in *Going Local*, where the efforts of the Essex Road team, working collectively, to develop a different relationship with users sit uncomfortably with Normanton and its growing fixation with the 'charismatic' team leader. More recently, the *Third Patch Bulletin* included in its orbit an even more diverse range of schemes with widely differing political origins and intentions. Perhaps it is inevitable when people are trying to demarcate a new movement that they emphasize unifying features while overlooking qualities that set them apart. Indeed they may forget that any project will have a whole set of characteristics and thus should not be judged or categorized merely according to some or one – like that of decentralization.[8]

There has, however, been a remarkable consistency in the principles associated with decentralization in social services. Here can be seen the close overlap between community social work and patch. We have identified five key principles or features attributed to patch by its authors. These are: localization; greater autonomy for local teams; the integration of workers, including for example home helps, social work assistants and occupational therapists; a community orientation; and participation.[9]

More important than these attributes or goals – the two often seem to be confused and they are generally ill-defined – are the cluster of ideas associated with patch. It is these we would argue that give it an inherent politics of its own. Agencies and authorities implementing patch often appear not to have thought through or reconciled the conflicts this may create between patch and their *own* ostensible politics – as we shall see.

Important in the patch approach are an increased emphasis and reliance on voluntary organizations, volunteers and 'informal helping networks'; working in closer partnership with voluntary and community organizations; and being 'preventive'. These concerns clearly follow from the ideas of 'welfare pluralism', with its commitment to the provision of welfare services from a variety of sources. Indeed they have proponents in common. However, we are not alone in regarding the emergence of such ideas with serious reservations.[10] The patch philosophy has gained ground in the context of reduced local authority expenditure and increased central government constraints. Government has not provided any additional resources to enable voluntary agencies to take on the bigger role envisaged for them. When the Greater London Council and other local authorities attempted to provide extra funds for innovative and anti-discriminatory projects, they were attacked and abused by the media and political right. The call for more volunteers has coincided with reductions in paid care workers, such as home helps, and a fall in hospital beds and places in council old people's homes. All this has taken place at a time of rising demand for welfare services from a growing number of very old people and from the destructive effects of mass unemployment. One of the most invidious developments has been the homely appeal to 'informal care', which has generated the new industry of 'neighbourhoodism'. When we spoke to people about patch in one neighbourhood in Brighton, as part of a study of East Sussex's large-scale patch reorganization, this was the focus of most objections:

> 'If people were able to [look after each other], all well and good but I see people round here who need help and obviously don't get it.'

> '. . . it sounds like window dressing and an evasion of responsibility.'[11]

There is good reason to question increased official reliance on unpaid care, especially as patterns of employment and local life have changed. There is also overwhelming evidence that informal caring and cuts in welfare jobs and services impose burdens on people, particularly on women. As Dulcie Groves and Janet Finch reported when patch first came to prominence, 'community care' essentially means more work and responsibility for *women within the family* rather than the mobilization of new neighbourhood resources.[12] Arguments for a 'mixed economy of welfare' have also tended to understate the role that commercial provision is playing in social services. It is now the most rapidly expanding area in welfare. Patch enthusiasts have failed to offer practical proposals to deal with the problems of accountability and quality control it poses.

Supporters of patch and community social work are notoriously difficult to pin down. They seem to have an amazing capacity to absorb objections and suggest they really mean something else. Their ambiguity is perhaps their most striking characteristic. For example, when we have argued that they place too much of an emphasis on informal care, patch proponents insist that they are actually concerned with 'supporting' rather than extending it.[13] But where are the alternative services for women who don't want to be primary carers, the extended under-fives' provision, the resources for better residential services? What we find in practice are low-cost schemes offering temporary respite, which themselves rely on women's low or unpaid labour.

Who wouldn't agree with patch supporters that social services departments should have a closer relationship with voluntary and community organizations? The language of 'networking' and 'interweaving' is reassuringly folksy, but it glosses over uncomfortable differences in status and power. There has been little suggestion of how to enable more equality between 'vol' and 'stat' or how to go beyond the rhetoric of 'partnership' when the dominant relationship is one of financial dependence. The category of non-statutory agencies covers a wide range of different organizations. Bodies like Age Concern, the Red Cross and WRVS may be regarded as safe partners by social services departments; the same is far from true of community action and other radical groups and projects, especially if they are seen as challenging departments and authorities.

Patch, prevention and participation

It is perhaps in the sphere of 'prevention' that the ambiguities of patch are most revealing. Patch advocates argue that a more supportive and helpful intervention in people's problems can stop the situation from deteriorating and avoid many of the emergencies that involve compulsion. It is an appealing vision with which few would want to disagree. Patch and community social work propagandists have contrasted this approach with the 'crisis-management' and 'fire-brigade' way of working with which they stereotype other social services departments. In a field already awash with jargon, they have given us even more, styling such a 'preventive' approach as 'proactive' and its conventional counterpart 'reactive'.

But patch's pre-emptive approach, going out and seeking information about people, is not only open to the criticism made by Robert Pinker that it is overambitious, invasive and threatening to civil liberties.[14] Patch prevention also raises other questions. How is a service to be preventive without the resources to overcome key problems confronting social services users, like poverty, poor housing and unemployment? It may be able to 'prevent' in the sense of trying to avoid ill-effects of its own, like labelling, stigma and arbitrary intervention. But these are not the primary hardships that bring people to the attention of welfare services in the first place. Patch prevention is also offered as a more effective way of stopping people from ascending the social services ladder or 'tariff' – receiving domiciliary instead of residential care, intermediate treatment instead of custody. But what does this mean where services are provided on the basis of need? Success here could hardly still be defined in terms of keeping people away from them.

'Proactive' working is advocated as a means of getting closer to service users and local people. Alan Stanton, however, in his discussion of collective working in a welfare team, invites us to look at it in another way. As he reminds us, if 'reactive' essentially means responding to requests from users and other agencies, what 'proactive' may in practice entail – apart from its questionable and sometimes covert intelligence-gathering role – is little different from the prevailing approach of social services departments in substantially initiating, planning and shaping the services people receive.[15] The emphasis is still very much on the agency or team *itself* deciding what local needs are and how they should be met. It is only the methods that may be different. This was not just the pattern we encountered in East Sussex. It is also the assumption underlying the National Institute for Social Work's standard text on 'needs assessment'. It is a more 'rational' rather than more democratic approach that is envisaged.[16] As a third alternative, Alan Stanton proposes an 'interactive' process in which the aim is to develop a *dialogue* between agency, service users and other local people and groups. We see such a dialogue as a crucial precondition for the participatory and more democratic services that both patch and more general decentralization schemes have emphasized.

The crucial question is to what extent social services decentralization makes such participation more possible. As we have seen, patch and community social work are not ideas with popular origins. But they might still be the means to more broad-based involvement. However, so far this does not seem to have been the case, although this conclusion can only be tentative given the limited evidence as yet available. Indeed, democratization has not yet been a major concern of much patch research – with the important exception of the Dinnington action research project.[17] It was not, for example, an issue explored with participating agencies in the three Lancaster *Patch Bulletins*. Neither the Normanton patch initiative nor the Neighbourhood Services Project in Dinnington, the two best-known research projects, were able to point to any significant transfer of say and control to service users or local people. We found the same in our East Sussex study. It is also questionable whether patch's concern with participatory management and workers' autonomy has been reflected in increased worker control, a point to which we shall be returning.

Making services more participatory and accountable is likely to be one of the aims of patch that is most difficult to achieve. This is certainly the message we have received from many workers and schemes. Two grassroots accounts by workers in London and Birmingham sum up some of the difficulties.

It is difficult to make space to develop innovatory approaches given continuing statutory responsibilities, particularly when the team is not fully staffed.[18]

A prerequisite for substantial community self help seems to be an adequate level of the necessities of life, particularly housing and income and social workers alone cannot affect these issues.[19]

What has also been striking about social services decentralization is that, once authorities have become interested in the idea, little attempt has been made to engage people more widely in the discussions. Such a lack of consultation was a characteristic not only of East Sussex's patch reorganization, but seems to be the norm. In this respect, patch has been just like other policy initiatives in welfare, from the creation of social services departments to the running down of residential services. The same pattern of narrow involvement seems to be true of more general decentralizations. Walsall's move to neighbourhood offices was very much the decision of a new guard of councillors. The consultations that the London Boroughs of Hackney and Islington organized were limited to the detail of going local. They did not address the question of whether decentralization was wanted at all. St Helens' move to a combined 'personal services department' made up of housing and social services followed from the decision of key councillors rather than the wider involvement implied by its rather tired slogans about 'putting the community first' and 'together we can succeed'.[20]

If social services decentralization is concerned with involvement and empowerment, then how far has it encouraged equal opportunities? Developments and discussions concerned with participation that do not take account of discrimination are unlikely to be helpful. The political heterogeneity of authorities implementing patch decentralization makes it difficult to generalize, but some discouraging trends are evident. Given the close association between patch and 'informal networks', unpaid care and care *by* rather than in the 'community', it is difficult to accept unsubstantiated rebuttals of the charge that it is 'bound to reinforce the traditional role of women as carers and make it more difficult to develop more equitable sharing of such work between the sexes'.[21]

Patch seems to have closed its eyes to race as well as gender. For instance, the East Sussex account of its social services decentralization ignored the issue. Yet, as Alan Farleigh has argued of Brighton, racism and anti-racism are not just issues for inner cities with large ethnic minority populations.[22] Patch has not developed the debate about how social services could combat racism, sexism and other forms of discrimination. Furthermore its key spokes*men* have so far seemed reluctant to engage in debate on these issues. Patch supporters have had little to say on the justified fears of black people about the invasion of their networks by white agencies seeking to harness their informal arrangements for providing care. Neither of the two major research projects – Dinnington and Normanton – was in an area with large ethnic populations, and neither addressed questions of race. Yet there is no reason to believe that decentralization is necessarily going to help oppressed people and groups. Setting out a series of goals for decentralization, if it were to have meaning for black people, Herman Ouseley wrote that 'many black people would argue that the localisation of area-based social services has not always made these more responsive or relevant to their needs'. On the question of consultation, he added:

Obviously it is a much easier option to consult with organised groups and 'leaders' than to attempt to involve the rest of the local black population . . . However, unless this extra effort is made these initiatives are bound to be totally discredited.[23]

What about the representation in patch of that other marginalized majority, the workforce? As we have seen, social services decentralization has been silent on race and gender; it has tended to frame people with disabilities in terms of 'care' rather than independence,[24] and been associated more with high-unemployment policies rather than a fresh social services response to unemployed people. However, it is with trade unions and trade unionists that the most conspicuous conflict has arisen. Patch's emphasis on 'flexible working', the demystification of professionalism and the importance and potential of day-to-day carers like home helps and care assistants have given it a liberal pro-working-class ring. But because the introduction of patch has coincided with cuts and job losses, in practice these ideas have often come to mean bigger workloads, substituting lower or unpaid workers (again predominantly women) and attacks on social workers' already uncertain independence.

East Sussex's director of social services noted that, while 'there were good reasons to expect difficulties from the unions in negotiating the implementation of the new structures, plans generally proceeded without interruption or significant modifications'. However his experience was unusual, especially given the fact that he headed one of the most directive patch reorganizations.[25] Union opposition has extended to multi- as well as single-department decentralizations, and left-wing as well as Conservative authorities. Well-known cases of long-term conflict like that in the London Borough of Hackney cannot be explained merely in terms of bad management. Nor is it enough to label union resistance as reactionary and defensive, although this stereotype has been widely used by patch supporters.

We would not deny that trade unions have often failed in both their process and objectives to give enough attention to the rights and involvement of women, members of ethnic minorities or indeed service users. They may have been defensive, but, at a time when council services have been under central government attack, have they not had good reason? And why should they take the new left Labour administrations on trust, remembering that local authorities are still their bosses, often with a long history of industrial conflict? The Labour Party's commitment to decentralization has also rightly been called into question.[26] It is disingenuous of councils to expect trade unions to suspend normal negotiating relationships and to 'participate' in their proposals, often on the same no-strings basis that has quickly disenchanted local residents before them.

So why patch?

Schemes for decentralizing social and other services have been promoted as a means of making them more accessible and account-able, and of changing relationships between them and their communities. Some of the limitations of decentralization in enabling more equal involvement have already been discussed. Our experi-ence in training and research and from discussions with workers involved in decentralized social services in patch and multi-departmental schemes indicates other wisespread problems. We have identified four key issues: a lack of clarity about the purpose as well as the means of 'going local'; a lack of investment in the move; a lack of direction and support from managers and politicians; and finally a general pressure on workers to 'prove that patch works', sometimes in an unrealistically short time span and without adequate yardsticks or outside encouragement.[27]

Why, given the scale of these difficulties, has the idea of patch gained such momentum? What accounts for the accelerating pace of decentralization at a time when social services departments are under particular pressure, because of both government antipathy towards them and a series of widely publicized child care tragedies? Why have so many eggs been put into the patch basket when these schemes neither correspond to popular concerns about welfare, nor begin with them?

Some reasons are immediately apparent. Patch has served academics and policy-makers concerned to advance the interests of vulnerable agencies, departments and careers by appearing to offer a way to square the circle of providing better services with reduced resources. As part of a welfare pluralist philosohy, it filled the vacuum in social services thinking created by the collapse of traditional Fabianism under the impact of Thatcherism. Most important, perhaps, patch gave a liberal gloss to attacks on paid and professional workers and public bureaucracies in welfare.

Behind all these fears, ambitions and new philosophies lie cuts in resources and expenditure. There have been cuts in training, research, research institutions (for example, the Centre for En-vironmental Studies, the Personal Social Services Council), college departments, and, most important of all, cuts in local authority and health services. The main criticism of patch and community care policies from the left and labour movement has been their connection with cuts – whether as cause or smokescreen for them.

A market-led restructuring

However, there is a further more disturbing explanation for the drive towards decentralization. A clue can be found in the key characteristic of patch schemes – they are essentially about *reorganization* and *restructuring*. People want better services, but the argument has been that these will only come through such reorganizations. One of St Helens' new assistant directors for social services, for instance, has said 'we couldn't care less about administrative structures', but this is where the change has been made.[28]

Why reorganization? The origins of the drive to reorganize are not to be found in specifically social work or social services thinking, although the same emphasis on managerialism and administrative change has been evident in social services since the 1970s. Instead the reorganization of social services echoes and imitates much wider economic changes, which have been described as 'Japanization' in industry.[29] This entails the trend to what has been called the 'core and periphery' model of market production. It involves the break-up of large factory complexes and the growth of a sub-contract and franchise economy, while retaining strong central control. A small 'core' workforce is offered advantageous conditions and rewards, while the rest are typically engaged on temporary contracts, working part time. They are low paid, weakly organized and suffer poor conditions. There are clear parallels in patch, with its switch to contracted-out services and its emphasis on non-statutory and commercial provision. The latter especially offers inferior conditions to workers, although voluntary organizations also have their own problems of insecure funding and temporary contracts.

In the statutory services themselves, we can see other similarities, both in the extension of low-paid ancillary roles for women and in the encouragement and organization of women home workers. This goes even further than the market model, as we have seen, with women expected to work for *no* rather than low pay as carers.

Patch's emphasis on teamwork is also evident in its Japanese industrial counterpart. Teamwork is the motto of Nissan's Tyne and Wear plant. The patch idea of the team, like that of Japanese manufacture, is not an egalitarian or collective one. In patch teams, team leaders have been redefined in true market style to become managers. According to the Barclay Committee, 'he' is to be an 'entrepreneurial' figure, with the key management role of reconciling local needs to managerial demands.[30]

Managerialist and market solutions are not peculiar to social services decentralization. The Griffiths reorganization of the Health Service expresses the same concern to devolve administration, but this is combined with an increased centralization of control. The general manager role not only replaces the old model of consensual management by groups with management and professional skills. More important, it represents a top–down system of accountability. The criteria of public accountability associated with it are those of close financial control, organizational performance indicators and manpower planning, all defined and controlled from the centre.[31] This corresponds *exactly* with the approach adopted in East Sussex social services.

Social services decentralization and the left

It is easy to see how patch decentralization accords with the needs of the right. But what about those of the left? The situation in left–wing Labour councils engaged in decentralization schemes is often more complex and uncertain, perhaps because they are more clearly confronted with questions of democratization. Before looking at some of the problems posed for them, it is important to remember the priority attached to decentralization on the left. It has been adopted as a key constituent of the new 'municipal socialism'. It was the main manifesto commitment of the new Labour councils elected in 1982. It has even permeated through to become an important element in national Labour Party rhetoric. But progress has been hesitant and trade union opposition has generally been strongest in left–wing authorities.

The London Borough of Islington is the Labour authority that has made most progress with decentralization. A glossy pamphlet published by the council at the beginning of 1987 proclaimed that 'decentralisation of our services is complete'.[32] In the bricks and mortar sense this might be true but, on the far more important issue of finding ways of enabling greater citizen access, involvement and control, progress has lagged far behind. Building neighbourhood offices has seemed the primary concern, while changing the relationships and distribution of power between council and people has either been assumed to follow or been given less than the attention it demands.

Islington says its neighbourhood forums 'are essential to decentralisation as a means of devolving power as well as services'. But their 'primary purpose' is a consultative one – 'to enable local people to express their views to the Council and other authorities and organisations'.[33] In local government terms, the budgets they control are tiny. Islington has tried to ensure that forums are representative – for example, by guaranteeing a minimum number of places to people 'who are not usually adequately represented in council affairs – people with disabilities, young people, black and ethnic minorities, elderly people and women with caring responsibilities'. But the scale and speed with which Islington's top-down decentralization initiative has been pursued has made it difficult, if not impossible, for broad-based local involvement to grow and bloom.

We are not raising these issues in criticism of Islington. We are simply pointing to problems inherent in any left-wing approach to decentralization that follows this kind of large-scale, quick-fire model – as indeed most have.

In February 1987, the Decentralisation Research and Information Centre at the Polytechnic of Central London organized a conference on 'Going Local: Devolving Power'. The conference was attended by 100 people, of whom only two were black and almost all were paid local government workers. No creche was provided. All the speakers but for me (Suzy) were paid workers in local government or large non-statutory agencies. Apart from me, and I was a late addition, there were no speakers from tenants, users or community groups.

In a workshop on devolving power from the users' perspective, a number of important issues were raised by participants that do not yet seem to have been adequately recognized or addressed by left proponents of decentralization.

How are people to be involved in ways which provide safeguards to ensure that their views are listened to and negotiable?

How can we ensure that the 'guidelines' or processes of participation are set by *citizens* rather than by the council?

How can we avoid community groups being played off against each other in consultation processes so that local authorities can exclude those they see as deviant or threatening, while involving only those that are safe?

Is getting involved in the council's new forums actually likely in practice to lead to *less* say than working in outside groupings like tenants associations etc., through the traditional structures of council committees, chairs and officers?

Maurice Barnes, Islington's Mr Decentralization, gave the workshop a lengthy account of developments in his borough. He spoke of the active and articulate people involved in some of the forums, people who, in his words, were 'manipulative' and could 'out-smart' a council officer or councillor 'any day'. He seemed to be describing a process by which a different set of people made the same *kind* of decisions as the officers and councillors before them. It appeared to have nothing to do with changing relationships or processes – as had been promised. The structures had changed, but everything else seemed to have stayed the same. A woman from Sheffield said she thought the issue was about 'changing ourselves'. She felt that people like her – she was a councillor – 'should be prepared to give up some power'. This begs enormous questions, which left-wing decentralists have found as difficult to deal with as those of the centre and right.

Later in the discussion, a neighbourhood officer from another left Labour authority pointed to some problems that have emerged where he works, problems that have a much wider relevance. Devolution of services into neighbourhood offices has led to fragmentation both among workers and trade unions and among local people. For example, members of ethnic minorities, instead of coming together boroughwide, are now having to link up in smaller groups at neighbourhood level to work with the council. Council committees and committee chairs have been strengthened. Chief officers whose commitment to democratic decentralization is often questionable are able to play off neighbourhood officers against each other. They frequently do this, for example, by sending contradictory instructions to local level, making it difficult for workers from different departments in neighbourhood offices to act in a concerted way.

Some time before the conference, one social worker told me that the neighbourhood forum in the patch where he worked was dominated by older white men – party faithfuls and Tenants Association hacks. They controlled the forum and did not, for intance, want money spent on child care. 'When *my* wife was young she had to look after the children herself.' I raised the problem with a decentralization consultant and researcher who came to the conference – a white, middle-aged, middle-class man. It's up to them, he said, to regain a say in the neighbourhood budget by marching down to the local office and asserting their rights. So this is the new recipe for democratizing decentralization? It sounds rather like the old 1960s' community development brand. It is equally meaningless for many women I know, who would be too worn out to waste what little energy remained on such a demanding and demoralizing routine.

Towards democratic decentralization?

So far, decentralization has been slow to advance left ideals of democratization. Sometimes in practice it is difficult to distinguish between left- and right-wing schemes. For example, social workers in left-wing authorities are encouraged to mobilize informal networks and 'community resources', just like their Conservative counterparts. In general there seems to have been a confusion between decentralization as a solution to the problems of left authorities, offering them a simple, very visible 'socialist' policy, and decentralization as a means of resolving the problems of the communities they serve, by helping to make services more accessible and accountable to people.

The left must move beyond the 'gesture' politics epitomized by the Greater London Council, bombarding us with hoardings, posters, leaflets, stickers and badges. While the GLC may have poured fortunes into the pockets of marketing men, it was from our experience apparently unable to fill Battersea Park's toddlers' paddling pool for three years, regardless of requests from local people! Decentralization has suffered from the same hype. Labour authorities have attached enormous expectations to it, from 'educating' local people to defend council services, to involving them in a process of 'popular planning'. We need to move beyond toytown images of local democracy, with people sitting in seminar circles like so many well-rehearsed Noddies and Barbies.

The question is not how to decentralize more democratically, or what democratic decentralized personal social services would look like, but *how services can be democratized* so that they match people's wants and needs more closely and come firmly under their control as service users, workers and other local people. Decentralization has unfortunately had a diversionary effect. First, it was promised that it would help make services more accountable. Now it is clear that this is not the case, the search is on for ways of democratizing decentralization. In this way decentralization, which was offered as a means to an end, has become an end in itself. This chapter reflects that, since we have been able to approach the crucial issue of increasing people's say and involvement in social services only through decentralization, instead of giving it priority in its own right.

We have tried to develop practical guidelines for making possible increased involvement and accountability in social services in our book *Whose Welfare?*.[34] While there is not the space to set them out in detail here, there are some principles for developing a strategy towards democratic social services that it may be helpful for us to headline as a basis for further discussion and development. These include:

- involving people from the start – agencies should start as they mean to go on;
- giving priority to people's *own* accounts of their wants and needs;
- setting small but attainable goals for change;
- gaining commitments and safeguards from agencies for people's involvement;
- providing the fullest possible information and making clear what is and what is not negotiable;
- finding ways of involving people that are practical, comfortable and do not have race, gender or other biases;
- developing skills and learning for involvement among *all* interested parties;
- recognizing the resource implications of increased citizen involvement in social services.

We know from our own experience, as users of services and from being on the receiving end of schemes for 'participation', just how difficult it is to make people's involvement a practical and *pleasant* reality, and how easy it is for the initiators of such schemes to gloss over these problems in their own accounts of them. Such difficulties should not be seen as an argument against involving people in social services; instead they point to the importance of doing it *properly*, building on the experience and ideas already accumulated from pioneering initiatives in social and other services.

There are many helpful lessons to be learned. For example, councils claim they are trapped by time scales. They are forced to act fast and build big because of the cycle of elections. Decentralization seems to have been another conspicuous casualty of this paper edifice approach to policy. We need to redefine what is substantial. What may seem smaller goals – for example, bringing effective and broad-based self-management to any specific service, like day nurseries or home helps – can be far greater – and more attainable – achievements.

It is important to avoid the creation of a power vacuum when developing new forms and forums for participation. This is likely to be filled by existing or incipient power elites – for example, would-be councillors at an earlier stage in their careers – or merely offer another base for already powerful voices. We must ensure that resources, support, encouragement and protection are given to ordinary uninvolved people to give them the opportunity to take part.

Whatever the aims or intentions of an authority or department, a crucial mediator – for good or ill – of its services is the practice of its workers. As we have ourselves seen in reactionary Wandsworth, the experience of workers trying to swim against the tide can be harsh and enervating. At the same time it is policy that grows from dialogue between workers, users and local people that holds the most hope. Social services department workers can play a key part in supporting more democratic services by developing their own discussions and networks with service users and local people and groups, while at the same time recognizing the need to reinforce their position and articulate its ambiguities to sustain this activity.

One thing on which decentralization has focused attention is the need to look beyond existing departmental divisions. Given its arbitrary and irrational origins, does the social services department have a future? If people have a say in services, will its framework still be a suitable one? And, given that, do single-department decentralizations make as much sense as more general ones where different services, for example health and welfare, can be readily reintegrated? Our study *Whose Welfare?* suggests the answer may be 'no' to all these questions.

Just as local government services have become interested in greater public involvement and accountability, social services have rediscovered 'the consumer'. Democratization should not be confused with the new welfare pluralist consumerism. As with systems theory in the 1970s, it is a case of social work belatedly latching on to managerialist and market ideas. The consumerist model imposed a passivity on service users that ideas of democratization based on citizenship seek to challenge. The political right has used patch decentralization to restructure and strengthen central political and managerial control. There is a lesson here for the left. If it wants democratic decentralization, then it is not just services and the workforce that must be devolved. The old local political and administrative hierarchies must also be reviewed. Without this, decentralization won't make for a redistribution of power.

Finally, discussions about decentralization have so far been narrow – on the left as elsewhere. Where people have been involved, the terms of reference have usually already been set. It is essential to find imaginative and effective ways of opening up the discussion. It is only by doing this that important issues of race, equal opportunities and accountability can be pursued in an un-mediated and unpatronizing way. Practitioners are in a crucial position to encourage this to happen, both among themselves and with their constituencies. Then, by engaging people's own experience, accounts and ideas, we may begin to see what part decentralization might have to play in bringing social services closer to people's wants and needs.

Notes and references

1 See, for example, G. Pearson, 'The Barclay Report and community social work: Samuel Smiles revisited?', *Critical Social Policy*, vol. 2, no. 3, (spring 1983), pp. 78–86.

2 R. Hadley and M. McGrath (eds), *Going Local: Neighbourhood Social Services*, NCVO Occasional Paper 1 (Bedford Square Press, 1980); R. Hadley and M. McGrath, *When Social Services Are Local: The Normanton Experience*, National Institute Social Services Library No. 48 (Allen & Unwin 1984); R. Hadley, P. Dale and P. Sills, *Decentralising Social Services: A model for change* (Bedford Square Press, 1984).

3 *Social Workers: Their role and tasks*, The Barclay Report (Bedford Square Press, 1982).

4 R. Lambert, untitled thesis on patch, presented in part fulfilment of MSW degree, Sussex University, 1982, p. 1.

5 *Report of the Committee on Local Authority and Allied Social Services* (the Seebohm Report) Cmnd 3703 (HMSO, 1968).

6 J. Joplin, 'Essex Road team – A community based team adopts a patch system', in Hadley and McGrath, (1980), op. cit. (n2), pp. 63–70.

7 B. Bennett, 'The sub-office: A team approach to local authority fieldwork practice', in M. Brake, and R. Bailey (eds), *Radical Social Work and Practice* (Edward Arnold, 1980), pp. 155–81.

8 We are indebted to Alan Stanton who first made this point.

9 For more detail of these principles, see P. Beresford and S. Croft, *Whose Welfare: Private care or public services?* (Lewis Cohen Urban Studies Centre, 1986), pp. 4–6.

10 R. Hadley and S. Hatch, *Social Welfare and the Failure of the State: Centralised social services and participatory alternatives* (Allen & Unwin, 1981): P. Beresford and S. Croft, 'Welfare pluralism: The new face of fabianism', *Critical Social Policy*, Issue 9 (spring 1984), pp. 19–39.

11 Beresford and Croft, op. cit. (n9), pp. 59–63.

12 J. Finch and D. Groves, 'Community care and the family: A case for equal opportunities?', *Journal of Social Policy*, vol. 9 (1980), pp. 486–511.

13 Hadley and McGrath (1984) op. cit. (n2).

14 R. Pinker, 'An alternative view', in the Barclay Report, op. cit. (n3), p. 255.

15 Alan Stanton, *Participatory Research on Collective Working with Newcastle Family Service Unit* (forthcoming).

16 A. Glimpson, T. Scott and D. N. Thomas, *A Guide to the Assessment of Community Needs and Resources* (National Institute For Social Work, 1982).

17 M. Bayley, P. Parker, R. Seyd, K. Simms and A. Tennant, *Neighbourhood Services Project Dinnington*, Working Papers 1–12 (Department of Sociological Studies, University of Sheffield, 1981–5).

18 K. Lyons, A. Bolger, P. Hale, R. Schaedel, L. Williamson and S. Thomson, 'Our crowd', *Social Work Today*, 13 December 1983, p. 18.

19 G. Coffin and P. Dobson, 'Finding our hidden strengths', *Social Work Today*, 12 November 1984, pp. 16–18.

20 Job advertisement, the *Guardian*, 21 January 1987.

21 Hadley and McGrath (1984), op. cit. (n2), p. 17.

22 A. Farleigh, 'Brighton blacks', *Voluntary Action*, 16 January 1987, p. II.

23 H. Ouseley, '"Treating Them All the Same" – Decentralising institutional racism', *Going Local?*, Newsletter of the Decentralisation Research and Information Centre, no. 2, Polytechnic of Central London (April 1985), p. 9.

24 S. Croft, 'Women, caring and the recasting of need – A feminist reappraisal', *Critical Social Policy*, Issue 16 (summer 1986), pp. 23–39.

25 K. Young and R. Hadley, 'Managing to go patch', *Community Care*, 29 September 1983, p. 19. Or perhaps it was *because* it was such a directive reorganization that he was able to do this.

26 K. Beuret and G. Stoker, 'The Labour Party and neighbourhood decentralisation: Flirtation or commitment?' *Critical Social Policy*, Issue 17 (autumn 1986), pp. 4–22.

27 P. Beresford and K. Lyons, 'Patch: Training focus', *Social Services Insight*, 17–24 May 1986, pp. 18–19.

28 N. Murray, 'St Helens, The Big Bang', *Social Services Insight*, 23 January 1987, p. 14.

29 R. Murray, 'Benetton Britain: A new economic order', *Marxism Today* (November 1985), pp. 28–32. See also 'Japan behind the Mask', report by John Pilger, Central TV, 13 January 1987.

30 The Barclay Report, op. cit. (n3), p. 211.

31 R. Petchey, 'The Griffiths reorganisation of the National Health Service: Fowlerism by stealth', *Critical Social Policy*, Issue 17 (autumn 1986), pp. 87–101.

32 *Going local: Decentralisation in practice* (London Borough of Islington, 1987).

33 Petchey, op. cit. (n. 31).

34 Beresford and Croft, op. cit. (n. 9).

6 Violence, social work and the emergence of dangerousness

NIGEL PARTON and NEIL SMALL

Introduction

This chapter attempts to analyse the increasing concern within social work about the issue of violence. In our view this concern expresses in the most fundamental way the changes in the central tasks, roles and responsibilities of social workers that have been evident since the mid-1970s. The increased interest in violence is directly related both to the changes perceived by social workers in their role and to the real shifts that have taken place in wider relationships among social workers, the state and society. The space occupied by social work and the definition of its legitimate sphere of activity have been reconstructed in a way that makes concerns about violence central. To explore the possibilities for social work practice today it is important to take these concerns seriously.

The discovery of violence towards social workers is linked not only to related concerns in the wider society, but also to the violence experienced in other parts of social work. We do not feel it is by chance that the highly publicized, critical reappraisal of social work around a series of cases of child abuse in recent years has coincided with the concern expressed within social work about violence to social workers. It is as though the failure of social workers to protect the vulnerable has been mirrored by a deep sense of vulnerability and uncertainty on the part of social workers themselves. Certainly, over recent months the social work press seems to have been dominated by the issue of violence, whether it is clients (particularly children) or social workers who are being assaulted. How far are these two issues connected, and how far do both relate to the changing focus and nature of social work practice? While we concentrate primarily on the issues of violence directed against social workers and child abuse, we feel that similar arguments could be examined in other areas of social work, particularly mental health, crime and delinquency and work with older people.

Dangerousness and the bifurcatory process

Two concepts are of particular use both in helping to analyse the changes in social work since the mid–1970s and in suggesting likely scenarios for the future. These are the related notions of 'dangerousness' and 'the bifurcatory process'.

Tony Bottoms[1] has outlined these two concepts and used them explicitly to understand parallel changes in the area of penal policy. He has detected a 'quickening of interest in the concept of dangerousness in British Penal Policy'. In particular, the memorandum by the Scottish Council on Crime and the Report of the Interdepartmental Committee on Mentally Abnormal Offenders (the Butler Committee), both published in 1975, explicitly defined the concept of dangerousness and argued that it was central to their proposals.[2] Interest in the idea was reinforced by the report in 1980 by the Howard League for Penal Reform and NACRO entitled *Dangerousness and Criminal Justice*.[3]

There is now an enormous literature,[4] both in Britain and North America, about the efficacy, ethics and practice applications of the idea of dangerousness in both crime and mental health policy and more recently in relation to child abuse.

The concept of dangerousness contains two major assumptions:

(1) certain individuals have a 'propensity to cause serious physical injury or lasting psychological harm' (though 'serious' and 'lasting' are open to very wide-ranging definitions),[5] and
(2) there is within society a small but important group of individuals who are violence-prone and who are potential perpetrators of serious crimes of violence.

The central premise is that we need to improve our ability to predict the risks of dangerousness in individuals in both research and practice. Such individuals must be treated or, if untreatable, confined.

For the practitioner, assessing and predicting dangerousness has become identified as a crucial task. Yet, given that this has been a part of penal and welfare policy and practice for many years, why is it now seen as of such central significance?

Bottoms offers two suggestions. The first is the decline of the rehabilitative ethic. In the 1950s, 1960s and early 1970s there was a liberal consensus in penal thought in Britain; which believed that a rational explanation could be found for all deviant behaviour, and that treatment, welfare and professional help could reduce crime, delinquency and a wide range of social problems. Traditional forms of punishment and law and order were regarded as inhumane and unproductive.

The rehabilitative ideal disintegrated in the 1970s. A series of research studies showed it did not work, and optimism about what welfare professionals could achieve was replaced by a far more pessimistic and pragmatic view. Attention switched from treatment to containment and prevention came to be defined in far narrower terms. Rather than trying to bring about general changes and improvements in families, communities and the wider society, prevention now simply concentrated on identifying the high-risk case of the dangerous individual. The crucial role for the welfare expert thus became that of identifying and managing the dangerous.

More fundamentally however, Bottoms identified what he saw as an important shift in policies concerned with social control or social regulation – what he described as the emergence of an explicit bifurcatory process.

> Put crudely, this bifurcation is between, on the one hand, the so-called 'really serious offender', for whom very tough measures are typically advocated and, on the other hand, the 'ordinary offender', for whom, it is felt, we can afford to take a much more lenient line.[6]

He showed that while the numbers of people found guilty in higher courts had increased in the postwar period, the percentage sent to prison had decreased.

> However, whilst all this has been occurring, there has been a marked increase in the use of very long prison sentences for what are regarded as very serious offenders. Long sentences have, therefore, '*increased*' in a period when there has generally been a '*decrease*' in sentence severity.[7]

In 1977, Bottoms insisted that, while bifurcation was an emerging trend in penal policy, he wanted neither to overstate the thesis nor to suggest that there was a clear-cut division between the two types. Events since, however, suggest that an approach based on the dichotomy between the 'dangerous' and the 'rest' has gathered momentum, and has been applied in areas other than penal policy.

It has been explicitly pursued not only in the mental health field but also in the areas of child care and child abuse. Policies towards the deprived, depraved and marginalized have been increasingly premised on the twin pillars of bifurcation and the assessment of dangerousness. As a consequence the roles and tasks of social workers, who are centrally concerned with implementing such policies, have been redefined.

Dangerousness and child abuse

Child abuse provides a significant illustration of the issues of dangerousness and bifurcation for two main reasons. First, while this is just one of the range of client groups for which social workers have a major responsibility, since the early 1970s a variety of public, political and professional debates about the nature and direction of social work have taken place around the issues raised by the problem of child abuse. Events since early 1985, with the furore following the tragic death of Jasmine Beckford (a child in the care of Brent Council), have confirmed this. Second, we recognize that it may be easier to establish that the twin concerns about dangerousness and the bifurcatory process have been central in mental health, crime and delinquency. However, we feel that showing the relevance of these concepts to child abuse will make the argument even more convincing.

Many have seen the Beckford Report[8] as something of a watershed in debates about child abuse and hence social work with children and families. Whether or not it marks such a major break with the past there is no doubt that the report made previous trends explicit and helped to focus debate on the issues at stake in cases of child abuse.

As one of us has argued elsewhere,[9] a major theme of the report was to emphasize the statutory responsibilities of social work. It upheld the role of the law in providing the social charter for contemporary social work. The report's insistence on the primary role of social work and the personal social services in cases of child abuse is fundamental, yet it has received very little discussion:

> Rather than indulge in a massive investment of social resources, which at the optimum can minimise only marginally the risk of injury, fatal or serious, to the child at home, and which impoverishes other areas of social services provision, society should sanction, in 'high risk' cases, the removal of such children

for an appreciable time. Such a policy, we calculate, might save many of the lives of the 40 to 50 children who die at the hands of their parents every year, and at the same time would concentrate scarce and costly resources of Social Services Departments to the 'grey areas' of cases where something more than supervision, and something less than long-term removal, is indicated. It is on those children who are at risk – but where the risk is problematical – that Social Services should concentrate their efforts.[10]

This is a clear statement of the priorities for social workers. More particularly, it also indicates how scarce resources should be allocated.

The report emphasizes the need to assess dangerousness:

All those engaged in the multi-disciplinary process of managing the child abuse system will need to assess – and regularly to reassess so as to note any improvement that would indicate a home on trial – whether the risk to a particular child in its parents' home is so great as to warrant long-term removal of the child from potential abuse at the hands of its parents. The proportion of 'high risk' cases out of all proved cases of persistent child abuse will be small, and the task of identifying them may not be easy. But the attempt to isolate such cases from the majority of child abuse cases must always be made.[11]

The crucial focus is on separating the 'high risk' from the rest, the hard from the soft, the dangerous from the not so dangerous. Social workers are urged to apply what the Beckford Report calls 'predictive techniques of dangerousness'[12] to their work.

Since the publication of the Beckford Report, the focus on dangerousness has been reflected in official statements about the problem of child abuse. Over the years the main vehicle for trying to bring about changes in policy and practice in relation to child abuse has not been legislation so much as a variety of government circulars. They both contribute to and reflect changes in thinking about the problem. It is interesting to note the changing terms in which the problem has been defined: 'battered babies' in 1970; 'non-accidental injury' in 1974; 'child abuse' in 1980. In the DHSS circular, published in April 1986,[13] in response to the Beckford Report, the problem is referred to as child abuse, but the circular puts particular emphasis on a new concept: 'child protection'. While the definition of the problem has broadened considerably, the roles and focus of the professionals, particularly social workers, are defined in a far more limited way.

We are offered a far more all-inclusive definition of child abuse as:

> Parents or carers (i.e. persons who, while not parent, have actual custody of a child) can harm children either by direct acts, or by a failure to provide proper care, or both.

This definition includes: physical injury, neglect, emotional ill-treatment, sexual abuse and potential abuse. The definition of potential abuse is particularly illuminating:

> Children in situations where they have not been abused but where social and medical assessments indicate a *high degree of risk* that they might be abused in the future, including situations where another child in the household has been harmed, or the household contains a known abuser.[14] (Emphasis added)

While it is stated that 'the aim of this document is to provide a guide to all the agencies concerned in working together to prevent child abuse',[15] it quickly becomes evident that the notion of prevention developed is a very particular one. In fact 'prevention of child abuse' is redefined as 'child protection'. This is a far more restricted definition, which relies on a view of social workers as statutory agents concerned with protecting children. Prevention becomes synonymous with protection, surveillance, monitoring and identification.

While great emphasis is placed on getting as many agencies involved and in improving inter-agency collaboration and coopera-tion, the focus is child protection. We are to have child protection reviews, child protection registers and inter-agency protection plans. These are not simply new labels for existing practices: they are something more precise. In extending the definition and hence potential awareness of child abuse, workers must make protecting children their top priority. To do this social workers need to change their focus. This means not only putting the interests of the child first but, as Norman Fowler said in his accompanying press release, 'ensuring that all staff are fully aware of the legal framework in this area and how it affects the responsibilities which they bear'. The statutory context of child protection work is underlined. Very little mention is made of treatment or change and development, and when these are emphasized they are placed within the legal framework.

But perhaps the most illuminating statement as to how we should redefine our focus in child abuse work is made in relation to training. The circular recognizes that, given the central role of social services, the training of social workers requires special attention. It proposes that 'specialist in-service training should be directed to those involved in the investigation of abuse and provision of protective services'. The knowledge and skills required are detailed as those 'related to child care law, the concept of child protection and the assessment of danger, and alternative forms of intervention'.[16]

The concept of child protection and the assessment of dangerousness thus hang together in the field of child abuse. This link becomes even clearer when we look at the Social Service Inspectorate report.[17] This report was described as an 'urgent review' of assessment by, and supervision of, social workers handling child abuse cases where a child in care had been returned home. The central message was broadly similar to that of the Beckford Report: while immediate action to protect children following reports of abuse was generally said to be satisfactory, the report identified room for improvement in planning and monitoring arrangements for their longer-term protection. The focus is much more on when, how, and by whom decisions are made about returning a child home once they have come into care for actual or suspected abuse. The report also emphasized the importance of the supervision received by social workers 'when making an assessment of and working with complex cases of child abuse'.[18] The focus is on social work assessment, but assessment within a clearly defined statutory framework which emphasized the responsibilities of the social worker to ensure the safety of the child, if necessary by long-term institutional care:

> the inspectors were concerned to find that, in the absence of a structured approach to comprehensive assessment, crucial decisions about the children's long-term care were often made without adequate and properly evaluated information. It was evident that as a result a considerable amount of social work effort and resources are being misdirected but, more seriously, children are returned home without a thorough assessment of the risks involved, and this may mean that they are inadequately protected.

Assessment has thus become *the* pre-eminent social work role. The aim of assessment is to identify the really dangerous, to allocate scarce resources of skill and time to families who need most attention.

Official priorities in child abuse have shifted on the one hand towards broadening the definition of abuse, while, on the other, giving priority to notions of child protection. The major tasks of social workers thus become those of assessing dangerousness and identifying the high-risk cases. These developments in social work are very similar to those identified by Bottoms in penal policy. Assessing dangerousness and separating out the dangerous from the not so dangerous – the bifurcatory process in policy and practice – have become central themes of modern social work.

Violence towards social workers

The preoccupation with dangerousness and a particular under-standing of prevention in the area of child abuse are part of a wider dynamic which includes concern about violence towards social workers. This is undoubtedly an area of growing anxiety within the profession which is reflected in articles in the social work press and in the number of surveys mounted, study days held and skill workshops sct-up.

The first discussion of violence as an issue requiring serious consideration was instigated in 1975 by Herschel Prins,[19] and followed up by David Webb.[20] Prins referred to a number of cases of popular concern in the early 1970s and concentrated particularly on the small number of offender patients he believed required special consideration by social workers. Prins's work was notable for its detailed concern with the factors likely to precipitate violent confrontations and for his concern to develop a way of responding to dangerousness that would minimize risk. Prins has subsequently become an occasional commentator on issues of violence – primarily in relation to the mentally abnormal offender. He is exceptional in putting forward the view that, if social workers can become sensitive to the precipitating factors of violence, they can reduce the risk of provoking it. For Prins the 'problem' of dangerousness arose out of a combination of the characteristics of the client and the practice of the social worker.

However, there was little serious discussion of the issue of violence in the social work literature for some years following 1976. Discussion of violence towards social workers was merely reactive to particular tragic incidents. It was not until mid-1985 that this occasional interest was transformed into something more sustained. This has been evident in three main areas: in the social work press – particularly *Community Care*; in the publication of research studies; and in the preoccupations of the social work organizations – employing, professional and trade union.

Community Care looked at the question of violence towards social workers in a series of six articles beginning in November 1986.[21] This series followed articles in February, May and September 1985, and an increasing attention to violence on the news pages and in editorial comment. The tragic deaths of three social workers in less than two years and the findings of newly published research studies did much to encourage a wider questioning of the problem of violence for social work practice.

The *Community Care* series reflected a wide range of concerns and approaches. It began with an investigation of risk factors[22] that depended heavily on the work of Colin Rowett, identifying high-risk factors, biographical and situational, and making practice suggestions. It is significant that the discussion retained the term 'risk' rather than 'dangerous', implying a continued commitment to working in high-risk situations. The article showed an awareness of the way a concern with violence may represent a 'code' for a profession troubled by low morale, public scorn, excessive work and meagre rewards. This commitment to work with risk remains through the series. One article presents details of a training pack in techniques – dos and don'ts, to help workers who may face violence.[23] Agency and individual responsibilities are examined and practical advice given. Another article reports on Strathclyde Social Services,[24] where a considerable amount of planning has gone on for some time into short-, and medium- and long-term responses to the risk of violence to staff. A sensitivity to the possibility that the protection of staff may appear to be anti-client appears as part of a general concern to prevent a shift to an orientation that is against service recipients, while at the same time protecting staff. It is only in an article about probation hostels that the terminology changes to dangerousness. However, the approach remains more in the risk category, in that it seeks to identify practice considerations that will minimize risk or help staff members deal with confrontational situations should they arise.[25] A further contribution to the series is made up of accounts of actual incidents of violence to staff. These identify factors in the role and in the psychology of workers that make violence or potential violence particularly problematic – not knowing what to do, feeling unable to do anything to protect yourself, feeling at fault because both the professional role and the caring role seem destroyed by the onset of violence towards social workers.

Three research studies on violence towards social workers have been published recently, written by Robert Brown and colleagues, Colin Rowett and David Crane.[26] Each has drawn on original research and each presents a complex analysis of the phenomenon and, despite their minor differences of emphasis and analysis, they prove to be mutually supportive.

Three features of the research seem to us to be of particular importance. The first is that violence towards social workers is identified as a hidden phenomenon, one that has been newly *discovered*, rather than one that has only just emerged. Rowett, for example, found that the closer you looked the more cases of violence you found. A questionnaire to social service departments resulted in an identified annual incidence of one incident for every 259 workers, a follow-up to social workers as opposed to management found that over a five-year period 112 out of every 450 workers had been assaulted, and follow-up interviews with assaulted workers themselves found that 60 workers had experienced 588 incidents.[27] Second, the studies have shown certain situations to involve greater risk. Brown *et al.* found that, in a three-year period, 22 per cent of fieldworkers, 45 per cent of residential and 50 per cent of day care workers experienced assault. For fieldworkers the major incidence of violence was related to the reception of children into care (26 per cent of incidents) and the compulsory admission of people to mental hospital (30 per cent of incidents). Residential workers identified three situations of high incidence: when a worker was giving advice, administering discipline, or intervening to protect a third party. Day care staff identified similar high-risk situations.[28] Third, and more speculatively, the research studies show the difficulties workers experience in taking effective action to avoid attack. This is partly linked with the reluctance of management to acknowledge violence as a problem and to plan accordingly by making appropriate staffing and procedural decisions to minimize risk. It also seems to arise partly from confusion around the issue of care and control. Workers feel shocked and helpless when faced with violent incidents which appear to threaten their professional identity. Rowett describes the failure of workers to identify and respond to specific behavioural cues, which often precede violent incidents. When they were abused, threatened, even when a client picked up a weapon, they did nothing – two out of three did not even attempt a verbal response. Their response was to feel that 'this should not be happening to me, if I ignore it then nothing may happen.'

Employers' organizations, professional associations and trade unions have also responded to the problem of violence. The Association of Directors of Social Services has a working party. BASW has set up a 'Project Group' and Nalgo is working on its own guidelines. Many social work departments are developing and circulating guidelines to staff concerning how they can prevent and avoid violent situations. The professional associations in particular have been working hard to get the issue taken seriously by employers and the Secretary of State. There is now some evidence to suggest that the DHSS is giving it priority. Not only was there a major conference organised by the DHSS on the topic in December 1986, but a top-level committee has been established to examine ways of safeguarding social workers, social security staff and health workers from violent clients.

However, this widespread concern within the profession has not crossed over significantly into the media and the wider public. Only recently has the idea that welfare professionals may themselves be a victim to the sort of violence experienced by some of their clients percolated into the public domain. We reviewed press reports in the *Guardian* for the last three months of 1986 and found almost no coverage specifically related to violence in social work. Two articles reported an increase in the incidence of violent attacks on NHS staff, another reported industrial action by Lewisham Nalgo following attacks on workers in the housing department. There was one report of an attack on a Southwark social worker and an announcement of Norman Fowler's intention to call a conference on violence against care staff. There was some coverage on the radio – *Woman's Hour* and *The World at One* providing some comment. On 1 December the memorial service for Frances Betteridge, who was murdered in September, was attended by 800 people, including the Secretary of State, but was not covered on TV.

The problem of violence is not peculiar to social workers but affects a variety of occupations in the health and welfare field. Indeed it appears that the problem was recognized in related occupations before it surfaced within social work. In hospitals, COHSE was reporting a concern with an increase in violence to its members in 1977,[29] the BMA noted attacks on doctors in 1978[30] and the prison officers in 1979.[31] A TUC conference with forty unions present expressed concern about a perceived, but un-documented, increase in the incidence of violence to their members, and in 1983 the London Boroughs' Training Committee reported that there was a widespread belief that violence towards staff was greater than it had been in the past.

The rising incidence of violent attacks on welfare workers of all kinds indicates that it is important to analyse the issue in the context of related debates about the nature and incidence of violence and fears about violence in society more generally.

Changing experiences of violence in society

Although people tend to believe that the past was better than the present, there is now general agreement that there really is an increase in crime. In the 1970s there was considerable disagreement that this was indeed the case, with detailed arguments presented that the change was in detection rates, recording practice, social tolerance, etc. Now, although there may be disagreement about cause, importance and remedy, there is agreement that the incidence of crime is increasing. There is also recognition that fear of crime is an area worthy of study in its own right; this realization came first from feminism and more recently from community-based studies such as the Islington Crime Survey.[32] These insights complicate observations about crime because they identify the fear of crime as being related to the damage it would cause were it to occur, rather than the likelihood of its occurrence. They suggest that simply to count numbers is not enough and that, for example, the increase in crime by strangers and the decrease in police detection rates are in themselves likely to generate the fear of living in a violent society.

It remains the case that one-third of 1 per cent of all recorded offences either are classified as offences against the person that endanger life, or are rape or armed robbery.[33]

Nevertheless a Gallup Poll in 1985[34] found that 88 per cent of the population thought violence had increased in the last five years and two-thirds thought it due to a general breakdown in respect for authority and law and order. Coupled with this was a growing loss of faith in the criminal justice system, with only 48 per cent of Gallup respondents reporting that they thought the police were efficient and did their job well. Detailed studies of particular areas further identify the extent and debilitating impact on the lives of many people of such fears. Half the women interviewed in the British Crime Survey[35] only went out after dark if accompanied, and 40 per cent said they were 'very worried' about being raped. Moreover, as with violence towards social workers, the closer the researcher looks, the higher the incidence of crime and the more prevalent the fear.

A detailed study of one area of South London[36] concentrated specifically on male violence to women. 75 per cent of incidents were not reported to the police. This particular study reported the further finding that 92 per cent of the women interviewed did not find the streets safe at night and one-third did not find them safe in the daytime.

We are therefore presented with an increase in crime and an

increase in the fear of crime. These may be related phenomena but they are not identical. There are two policy options. One is to develop policy and practice that address the reality. The other is to address the fear or the panic. The choice is between tackling crime and promoting law and order. Our argument is that a pursuit of the latter inhibits a resolution of the former.

When the police concentrate on order and tranquillity they aim to reduce non-criminal disorder on the streets – drunkenness, hooliganism, rowdy behaviour, graffiti, litter – thereby reducing the sense of felt insecurity.[37] Non-criminal disorder produces the fear of crime, it is suggested, and as such it is this that is tackled, rather than actual crime (at which the police have a very low level of success, in either prevention or apprehension). Such an approach does not help those who live in areas of high and rising crime – in some inner-city areas in Liverpool one household in every four is burgled every year; in Islington two-thirds of women under 25 have been harassed by kerb-crawlers or otherwise sexually intimidated on the street; and in some parts of London only 4 per cent of burglaries are ever cleared up.[38]

One result of the 'fear of crime policy' is that police are concerned to identify 'dangerous' people and use wide-ranging powers of stop and search to detain and harass them. This is not a means of crime detection or law enforcement but a means of enforcing what President Reagan's law and order adviser, James Wilson, called 'order on the streets and middle class values'. In Liverpool 8, 37 per cent of males under 30 had been stopped and searched by the police at least once in 1984/5. Merseyside Police report that only forty-three arrests are made per 1,000 stops.[39] This is pre-emptive or preventive policing – the identification and control of potential criminals. Potential criminals are defined by the police as young men, particularly young black men. In Islington, 32 per cent of young white males under 25 and 53 per cent of young black males are stopped by the police each year. Such pre-emptive policing, with its harassment and discrimination, produces a series of self-fulfilling prophecies: those most likely to be stopped may have been stopped before and be on a computer which, when checked, legitimizes their being stopped!

If the police emphasize the law and order approach rather than the prevention and detection of crime, the dilemma they face in high-crime areas is that their methods are seen as random and 'tougher'. Local people are less ready to cooperate and so less crime is cleared up, and the real problem is compounded. As this occurs, the police resort to yet harder methods, provoking still greater alienation and discontent.

When dangerousness rather than crime becomes the determining factor in policy, this produces a reduction in fear in some parts and an exaggeration of problems in others.

Violence, dangerousness and the state

Concern about violence to both social workers and their actual or potential clients has emerged within a political and economic context characterized by the government's commitment to rolling back the social democratic welfare state. Since 1979, the Conservative government has set about restructuring the welfare state, both in its substance and in its symbolic manifestation as a 'safety-net' for all. The aim has been to halt and reverse the rising expectations of disadvantaged groups – in particular the unemployed, the low paid, single parents – many of whom are concentrated in inner-city areas. A large minority of the population has been marginalized from the mainstream of society, creating what Glotz has called the 'two-thirds society'.[40] The nature of citizenship and the social contract between the individual and society have changed as a result.

Bill Jordan[41] has demonstrated how the market-oriented strategy to cope with the emerging economic problems has resulted in a society deeply divided between two unequal sectors, within which distribution occurs according to different principles. In the market sphere, commercial mechanisms and values dominate, creating inequalities in terms of social status, income and wealth. In the state sphere, the distribution of revenues to nationalized industries and public services is determined by bureaucratic and political considerations. In addition, public services try to shore up traditional work patterns and traditional family roles and responsibilities. The latter sphere is characterized by chronic long-term unemployment and widespread deprivation.

The role of the welfare state in attempting to maintain full employment, equal citizenship and a basic minimum standard of living for all has been aggressively questioned by the ideologues of the radical right. They have urged the government to give priority to policies that restrict the provision of state services to the most deprived and to those requiring social rehabilitation and control. Government policy has encouraged those who can participate in the market sphere to become members of the 'property-owning' democracy. Those who can afford to buy their own houses and to take advantage of privatizing share offers are granted all the freedoms that go with being an active participant in the market. Full citizens are encouraged to pay from their private earnings not just for large and small items of consumption, but also for private and occupational insurance to cover health, housing, old age and for other social needs. Commercially provided health and social services are promoted as ways of allocating resources more efficiently and of giving the consumer more choice.

State social services are thus confined to the deprived and the depraved and increasingly explicitly come to depend on notions of subsistence and social control. State services have become more selective and concentrated on the long-term unemployed, single parents and the elderly who are unable to provide for themselves. The restructuring of the state social services therefore reinforces the inequalities already evident in the labour market and widens the social gulf between workers in the market sphere and those in the secondary state sphere. As Jordan argues:

> the gradual erosion of the postwar principles of universality and adequacy in the income maintenance schemes, and the recent deliberate erosion of equality in the other major social services through expenditure cuts, along with all the other economic and social changes in British society, point to the direction of a state social services system which selects out this sector of the population.[42]

Two interrelated consequences follow. On the one hand, a sizeable minority of the population becomes increasingly alienated (and in some cases angry and rebellious) because they are denied autonomy, full citizenship and participation in the normal activities of economic and social life. Second, such a restructuring inevitably involves a strengthening of the more authoritarian and repressive elements of the state, including the curtailment of civil liberties, to maintain social order. While such changes are most evident in the strengthening of the police and criminal justice system, they clearly have implications for the changing role and priorities of social work. Not only is the potential for violence within marginalized communities heightened, but the potential for violent conflict between members of those communities and state officials is increased. Social workers are at the centre of these mounting social tensions.

We can now see why the concentration in social work on dangerousness and the bifurcatory process is of such significance, and why both have become so central since Tony Bottoms originally made his comments. Both are connected with economic changes and the restructuring of the state. They provide an explicit rationale for prioritizing the growing and changing demands made upon social work.

One reason frequently put forward for the increased emphasis on the assessment of dangerousness is simply economic. In a period of increased concern and broadening definitions of the problem, it becomes even more important for the authorities to concentrate resources where they are most needed. Faced with increased need and reduced resources, the emphasis shifts much more towards incapacitating the dangerous by removing the children, while being much softer with the remainder, i.e. by reducing social work involvement. The social work role is hence proscribed, it becomes narrower, has much clearer boundaries and is defined much more according to its statutory responsibilities. The new wisdom is that social workers should not be afraid to make tough decisions and make full use of the authority of the law.

As Stein and Frost have pointed out elsewhere in this volume (Chapter 2), there has been a shift in child care practice more generally towards a greater reliance on compulsory rather than voluntary admissions to care, with a particular growth in the use of place of safety orders.[43] As Jean Packman demonstrated in her research on decision-making and child care,[44] this approach is the one most likely to make children and families feel excluded, and to make them critical, angry and uncooperative. For some parents the social services department was synonymous with the 'SS' and social workers with 'Nazis' or the 'Gestapo'. Of course these are the very families in which social workers are most likely to experience violence. As we have seen, in the research on violence to social workers, it is most likely to occur in situations that involve depriving individuals of their liberty, particularly where place of safety orders, care proceedings and formal hospital admissions may be used.

The reason why violence to social workers has become such an issue is not because their clients are inherently more dangerous or that social workers are less able to cope, but because the number of potentially violent situations they face has increased. This increase results directly from changes in the nature of the social work task and the restructuring of the welfare state.

At the same time, the community care policy for the mentally ill has meant that social workers are increasingly dealing with clients in the community who would previously have been in hospital and who suffer enormous disadvantages and social isolation, while receiving few material and social supports. Similarly, staff in day and residential care will be encountering similar difficulties as a result of the same policies.

Conclusions

Dangerousness and bifurcation increasingly dominate thinking on crime and have led to a police policy emphasizing the control of the fear of crime for the benefit of those at least risk of actual crime and the abrogation of any commitment to prioritize the prevention of crime or its detection in high-crime areas. Similarly, in the response to child abuse, dangerousness and bifurcation increasingly dominate policy and practice. The response to violence against social workers manifests these same phenomena, in that it identifies certain aspects of social work as being high risk and is designed to reduce the fear of violence – skills training, panic buttons, better office design and higher levels of staffing on specific cases. What is missing is an analysis of the changing nature of the social work task. In an increasingly polarized society, social workers are called upon to act as agents of the state, implementing legislation, identifying dangerousness and isolating those at risk. There is no doubt that it is useful for individual social workers to develop appropriate skills for avoiding and dealing with violence, but any approach that is limited to this is avoiding the wider issues involved. These same elements – identifying the dangerous and separating them from the rest – constitute the responses to child abuse.

The context of declining resources and increased coercion reduces social workers' room to manoeuvre. The traditional ambiguity of the state, between welfare and control, is being replaced by the concept of welfare *as* control. In gaining dangerousness and losing rehabilitation as working constructs, the social worker is being given a new role in the modern state apparatus, and the scope for radical practice is consequently diminished.

However, there is still some room for manoeuvre, and it is possible to use this for the advantage of both clients and practitioners alike. We would like to finish by giving one example of how this might be achieved.

Research studies related to decision-making in child care provide some interesting clues.[45] In many respects they confirm the increasing emphasis and use of statutory orders in child care since the early 1970s. Even so, they also demonstrate that, while many practitioners may feel powerless, they are still influential in the decision about whether or not to admit a child into care. In particular, they can exert a decisive influence over the form that admission may take – especially whether it is on a statutory or voluntary basis.

It has often seemed, however, that many managers and practitioners assumed that 'care' was bad and therefore should be resisted at all costs, even if a family was clearly experiencing problems. Unfortunately, then family members may receive little support to help them overcome their problems until they reach crisis proportions and a child is admitted under a statutory order, which gives the local authority full control.

The research is full of evidence that a statutory admission often leads to bemused and resentful parents. It also frequently leads to changes of placement because of a lack of preparation, poor planning and a failure to work in a mutually trusting relationship with the children and parents alike. Much better results have been noted when a child was admitted on a voluntary basis with the agreement of the parents. Sometimes this may mean admitting the child earlier to prevent further family difficulties.

Such findings lead Jean Packman[46] to recommend that the voluntary route into care should always be the preferred method unless there are very good arguments to the contrary. Not only does voluntary admission have better outcomes for all concerned, it also reduces the risk of violence to the social worker. Working through a mutually agreed relationship where both parties – client and social worker – can negotiate the nature of the problems and what to do about them is also the way most social workers prefer to go about their task.

While it may make little impact upon the wider changes we have discussed, emphasizing such a voluntary, participatory basis of work may make a significant difference to some children and families.

Notes and references

1 A. E. Bottoms, 'Reflections on the renaissance of dangerousness' (inaugural lecture as Professor of Criminology in the University of Sheffield, 12 June 1977), *Howard Journal*, vol. 16, no. 2 (1977), pp. 70–96.

2 Scottish Council on Crime, *Crime and the Prevention of Crime* (HMSO, 1975).
  Butler Committee, *Report of the Committee on Mentally Abnormal Offenders*, Cmnd 6244 (HMSO, 1975).

3 J. Floud and W. Young, *Dangerousness and Criminal Justice* (Heinemann, 1981).

4 See, for example, J. Monahan, *Predicting Violent Behaviour: An assessment of clinical techniques* (Sage Foundation, 1981); H. Prins, *Dangerous Behaviour, the Law and Mental Disorder* (Tavistock, 1986).

5 Bottoms, op. cit. (n1), p. 73.

6 ibid., p. 88.

7   ibid.
8   Beckford Report, *A Child in Trust: The Report of the Panel of Inquiry into the circumstances surrounding the death of Jasmine Beckford*, presented to Brent Borough Council and to Brent Health Authority by members of the Panel of Inquiry (London Borough of Brent, 1985).
9   N. Parton, 'The Beckford Report: A critical appraisal', *British Journal of Social Work*, vol. 16, no. 5 (October 1986), pp. 511–30.
10 Beckford Report, op. cit. (n8), p. 289.
11 ibid., p. 288.
12 ibid., p. 289.
13 Department of Health and Social Security, *Child Abuse – Working Together: A Draft Guide to arrangements for inter-agency cooperation for the protection of children* (April 1986).
14 ibid., p. ii.
15 ibid., p. i.
16 ibid., p. 33.
17 Social Services Inspectorate, *Inspection of the Supervision of Social Workers in the Assessment and Monitoring of Cases of Child Abuse when children, subject to a court order, have been returned home* (SSI, 1986).
18 ibid., p. 6.
19 H. Prins, 'A danger to themselves and to others', *British Journal of Social Work*, vol. 5, no. 13 (1975), pp. 297–309.
20 D. Webb, 'Wise after the event', *British Journal of Social Work*, vol. 6, no. 1 (1976), pp. 91–6.
21 W. Francis, 'Under attack', *Community Care*, 13 November 1986.
22 B. Tonkin, 'Quantifying risk factors', *Community Care*, 13 November 1986, pp. 22–3.
23 R. Weiner, 'Strategies for coping', *Community Care*, 20 November 1986, pp. 22–3.
24 B. Tonkin, 'Plan for a preventative policy', *Community Care*, 11 December 1986, pp. 22–3.
25 C. Lawrie, 'Residents are not dangerous', *Community Care*, 27 November 1986.
26 R. Brown, S. Bute and P. Ford, *Social Workers at Risk* (Macmillan, 1986); C. Rowett, *Violence in Social Work* (University of Cambridge Institute of Criminology, 1986); D. Crane, *Violence on Social Workers* (University of East Anglia, 1986).
27 Rowett, op. cit. (n26).
28 Brown *et al.*, op. cit. (n26).
29 COHSE, *The Management of Violent or Potentially Violent Patients* (1977).
30 *British Medical Journal*, Leader, 13 May 1978.
31 D. Twinn, 'Violence and professionalism: an explosive mixture', *Prison Services Journal* (April 1979), pp. 1–5.
32 T. Jones, B. Maclean and J. Young, *The Islington Crime Survey* (Gower, 1986).
33 R. Walmsley, *Personal Violence*, Home Office Research Study No. 89 (HMSO, 1986).

34 Cited in S. Benton, 'The left embraces law and order', *New Statesman*, 21 November 1986, pp. 12–14.

35 M. Hough and P. Mayhew, *The British Crime Survey* (HMSO, 1985).

36 J. Radford and C. Laffy, 'Violence against women: women speak out', *Critical Social Policy*, Issue 11 (1985), pp. 111–18.

37 Hough and Mayhew, op. cit. (n35), p. 39.

38 R. Kinsey, 'Crime in the city', *Marxism Today* (May 1986), pp. 6–10, p. 7.

39 R. Kinsey, *Merseyside Crime and Police Surveys* (Merseyside County Council, 1984–5).

40 P. Glotz, 'Forward to Europe', *Dissent* (summer 1986).

41 W. O. Jordan, *The State: Authority and Autonomy* (Blackwell, 1985).

42 ibid., p. 258.

43 See N. Parton, 'Children in care: recent changes and debates', *Critical Social Policy*, Issue 13 (summer 1985), pp. 107–17.

44 J. Packman, with J. Randall and N. Jacques, *Who Needs Care? Social Work Decisions about Children* (Blackwell, 1985).

45 Department of Health and Social Security, *Social Work Decisions in Child Care: Recent Research Findings and their Implications* (HMSO, 1986).

46 Packman *et al.*, op. cit (n44).

7 Unemployment, cod's head soup and radical social work

JENNIE POPAY and YVONNE DHOOGE

During the depression years of the 1930s, cookery classes were organised for women in poor communites in an attempt to help them to provide nutritious meals for their families despite their low incomes. One particular evening a group of women were being taught how to make cod's head soup – a cheap and nourishing dish. At the end of the lesson the women were asked if they had any questions. 'Just one,' said a member of the group, 'whilst we're eating the cod's head soup, who's eating the cod?'

A powerful and amusing anecdote but what, one might ask, has it got to do with unemployment and radical social work? Quite a lot, in fact, for it raises issues that should be central to the concerns of those who wish to develop the radical perspective.

First, it points to the links between unemployment and poverty and of these experiences to the wider inequalities in access to resources and power in our society. These links are as strong today as they were in the 1930s, as much research has demonstrated.[1] Such links testify to the important role played by labour market disadvantage, of which unemployment is but a single dimension, in generating the private social, psychological and economic troubles of individuals. Whilst today's levels of unemployment are unprecedented, unemployment and other labour market disadvantages, such as low-paid and insecure employment, are not recent experiences for social workers' 'clients', drawn as they are from the most vulnerable sections of society.[2] Yet social work in general, and radical social work in particular, have so far failed to address employment or unemployment as major causal factors in their clients' difficulties. Despite constant manipulation of the figures and the creation of large numbers of insecure, low-paid jobs, the number of unemployed people is still around 2½ million – an unprecedented proportion of whom are long-term unemployed.[3]

The need for social workers to take up problems arising from unemployment has never been more urgent.

Second, the anecdote illustrates some of the dilemmas that will face radical social work, when and if it addresses such issues. How, if at all, should social workers respond? Should they provide support for individuals (through cookery classes or counselling, for example)? What role should they have in collecting and disseminating information about the unequal social distribution of resources and of the effects of these inequalities on the life chances of individuals? How should they respond to those who, like the woman in the cookery classes, already know 'who's getting the cod' and want to know what to do about it?

The anecdote raises a third set of issues that should underpin any consideration of a radical social work response to unemployment: the position of women. In much discussion, unemployment is depicted as an individual experience that is essentially visited upon men. Yet, as the story illustrates, this experience will have ripple effects on other family members, friends and even whole communities. These will be particularly severe for women, who have responsibility for managing household budgets (often without the *control* of resources) and for providing emotional support.[4] At the same time their own unemployment remains largely invisible or is considered to have much less severe social and economic consequences – a view not supported by the limited research that has been done.[5] Women therefore may be carrying a double burden, yet social workers, like the public at large, may see neither of these.

Like any good anecdote, however, the cod's head soup story has its limitations as a tool for raising issues central to the concerns of this chapter. Whilst it helps to make visible the position of women, it cannot be used to point to one final dimension of unemployment, which any social work response must recognize – the unequal burden experienced by black people in our society. Racism – both direct and indirect – works to confine a disproportionate number of black people to the ranks of the unemployed, yet social workers may not only fail to recognize the severity of the problem amongst black people, they may also fail to give due weight to the role of racism as opposed to individual characteristics.

In this chapter we look at some of the ways in which mass unemployment appears to be changing the context within which social work is practised and how social workers seem to be responding to this situation. We shall argue that these responses are limited in both their nature and scale but that there are a number of major organizational, professional and attitudinal factors operating to constrain the development of a more coherent

approach – radical or otherwise. Some of these are amenable to
change and a few examples of 'good radical practice' exist, but it
will require a major effort on the part of fieldworkers, managers
and educationalists if such change is to come about.

Much of the discussion that follows is based on a small-scale
research project undertaken by the authors in the 1980s.[6] It involved extensive interviews with fifty-six fieldwork social workers
and their managers in three areas of the country – London, the
Midlands and Scotland. In all three areas the levels of unemployment were at or above the national average, though the history of
unemployment and the groups most affected differed. The social
workers were in a variety of situations: intake teams, long-term
generic teams, probation work and hospitals. Where appropriate
we have referred to other research to support our own. Obviously
it is impossible to argue on the basis of such a small and diverse
sample that our findings are representative of what is happening in
social work generally. But they do give important insights into
what this wider picture might be.

The impact of unemployment on social work

There is now considerable evidence that the unprecedented levels of
unemployment experienced over the past decade are changing the
context within which social work is practised.[7] The impact appears
to be most directly felt in intake work and above all social workers
are conscious of a rising tide of poverty in the communities in
which they work. As two of the social workers we interviewed
succinctly put it:

> 'A lot of people are coming through the door because they can't
> make ends meet.'

> 'They simply run out of money.'

Unemployment also appears to be generating new problems at
intake, such as homelessness amongst young people and, according to some of the social workers in our study, new 'types' of
clients:

> 'People who some years ago would have associated social work
> with being bad, in trouble, are now coming in looking for
> financial help, clothing or information about organisations
> which might be of help.'

Social workers involved in long-term work, or in specialist settings such as hospitals, seem to have a somewhat more ambivalent attitude towards the impact of unemployment on the people they work with. Nevertheless, most of those we spoke to had noticed an increase in unemployment amongst their clients and many indicated that to work with people of economically active age who have paid employment is now a rare exception.

As in intake work, this appears to be leading to an increase in the incidence and severity of financial problems, which in turn, according to some social workers, means they are facing much more complex situations:

'Working with families that are unemployed is more complex. Financial difficulties, the question of debt, is always there, whatever the other problems. It's very difficult to talk to people about themselves when they have a lot of debt, or their electricity is about to be cut off . . . a lot of time has to be spent sorting out debts.'

References were also made to psychological and relationship problems associated with unemployment, suggesting that at least to some extent social workers are aware of the social psychology of unemployment discussed by Geoff Pearson in Chapter 3 above.

'It affects families in general, very devastating, no purpose in life, it affects spending, marital relationships, children's problems, everything.'

These changes in the financial, social and emotional circumstances of people receiving social work support can be expected to have a significant cumulative impact on the context within which social work is practised. However, social workers did tend to describe them as relatively minor, compared to the effect unemployment is apparently having on their ability to close cases.

There would seem to be two somewhat different dimensions to this issue. On the one hand, unemployment is creating new long-term cases where previously social work support would have been relatively short term. The following case study illustrates how this process may operate:

'Mr Adams gave up his job more than a year ago to help his wife who had been mugged. The experience made her anxious and nervous and affected her ability to deal with the children and routine household tasks. Mr Adams had intended to stay at home just for a short time to help his wife through this crisis. However, he had been unable to find another job and the family is now experiencing acute difficulties. They have serious debts and Mr Adams has started to gamble. He and his wife are having serious arguments and this is affecting the children. The social worker became involved when Mrs Adams was close to a nervous breakdown. According to the social worker, "As long as there is no chance of Mr Adams finding employment the future doesn't look very bright. They are just coping really".'

Second, social workers are increasingly aware of the limitation of the 'rehabilitative ideal' discussed earlier by Geoff Pearson, particularly in relation to young people on probation or leaving local authority care, older ex-prisoners and people with a history of mental illness. In theory, the pursuit of employment has always been central to social work strategies with these groups, though, as Geoff Pearson also notes, such strategies have been based on the assumption that a client's employment difficulties are the result of some individual inadequacy more or less in their control, rather than being structurally determined. These strategies, however, are no longer seen to be a viable option. As the comments below illustrate, this situation is felt to affect relationships with clients and to extend social work involvement:

'Unemployment does make my work more difficult. You are dealing with teenagers and if the person has no hope of work how do you deal with them? How do you speak with them if they don't see a future?'

'It all builds up really. Where before you could possibly identify short- and long-term goals, the long-term goals seem to have got longer and longer.'

How are social workers responding?

On their own admission, then, social workers are aware of a range of ways in which unemployment is affecting the people they work with, changing the volume and nature of the problems presented to them and reducing the options they feel they have available to deal with these. How are they responding to this situation.

Given that social workers appear to be most conscious of the financial difficulties that unemployment can create, it is not surprising that they should concentrate on activities designed to ameliorate these. Certainly, such activities were the most frequent re-sponse to unemployment described during our survey and, amongst these, referrals to specialist advice agencies were the most common. Many of the social workers we interviewed also indi-cated that they were spending more time dealing with financial problems themselves: negotiating with the DHSS, fuel boards and private firms on behalf of their clients. However, it was also apparent that there was considerable ambivalence about this situa-tion amongst both individual fieldworkers and their managers:

'You make all the arrangements you can for fuel direct, say, rent out essential cooking equipment, etc., until the DHSS and the fuel boards sort it out . . . I think what's happening is, and I think it's a by-product of unemployment, is that we are becoming poor-law relieving officers and I don't want to be a poor law relieving officer.'

(Senior social worker)

'So much of the work is becoming money work . . . I'm not sure social services are the right people to deal with this.'

(District manager)

Another relatively widespread social work response to clients' financial problems appears to be to resort to charities.[8] A variety of needs are being met from such sources, including clothing, furni-ture, dietary requirements, holidays and exam fees. In part the reliance on charities seems to be a result of increasing frustration with the DHSS. There also seems to be a reluctance to use Section 1 money (Section 12 in Scotland), which was described by some of the social workers we spoke to as difficult and time-consuming to obtain or simply inappropriate. As the quote illustrates, however, the use of charities is also creating difficulties for social workers:

'We tend to accept that the DHSS no longer provides certain payments. But we are then left in the position of having to give people letters to go to a voluntary agency for second-hand clothes, which is degrading both for us and for them.'

A few of the social workers in our study were developing somewhat different responses to financial problems: working with claimants' unions, for example; running advice sessions in unem-ployed workers' centres and community centres; and helping to set up food cooperatives or community businesses providing good-as-new clothes and renovated furniture. However, such activities were rare and were more frequently seen to be the preserve of community workers.

There is also considerable uncertainty about what is to replace long-term rehabilitative goals focused on obtaining stable employment. Predictably, perhaps, the most common response to the employment problems facing young people would appear to be to find places for them on the Youth Training Scheme. Some of the social workers we spoke to did mention other MSC schemes (such as the Community Programme) as an option for adults, but relatively rarely, and, in general, knowledge of MSC provision, other than YTS, appeared to be fairly poor. For people with disabilities or those with a history of mental illness, the only employment opportunities perceived to be available were sheltered workshops.

A number of other responses to the lack of employment opportunities for clients were described to us. Some social workers, for example, were helping to establish self-help groups to provide social support and reduce isolation. A few reported that they were making more referrals to or getting actively involved with community projects providing opportunities for retraining, leisure, volunteering and/or campaigning:

> 'We've had to change a lot . . . the be all and end all of work with offenders was getting them to lead an industrious life – getting them a job. If they were working at least in theory they had less time to re-offend. Now you've got to change your whole way of thinking and try and help them to look at their leisure activities. Hence the fact that we've moved into group work . . . and establishing youth clubs etc.'

However, though there appears to be a widespread view amongst social workers that community-based projects have an important role to play in relation to unemployment, knowledge of such initiatives was limited amongst those we interviewed and there was some scepticism about the value of existing provision. Additionally, the extent to which alternatives to 'real' employment or activities designed to 'use time constructively' are perceived by social workers to be legitimate options seems to depend to some extent on which client groups are being considered, an issue we return to in a later section.

As already noted, at some stage during the interview most of the social workers in our survey demonstrated an awareness of the literature on the psychological impact of unemployment described by Geoff Pearson in Chapter 3, and many likened job loss to the experience of bereavement. However, in their accounts of how they were responding to the needs of people experiencing unemployment, there were only a few examples of social workers spending time talking to people about their experience of unemployment.

One final response to unemployment identified in our study remains to be considered. Social workers are in a unique position to collect and disseminate information on the social and economic problems created by unemployment. As one of the social workers we interviewed argued, this information can be used to inform the development of services:

> 'What social workers can do is to feed back information about the effects they see in their direct contact with the unemployed and so help to get services started or to put pressure on other organisations.'

Additionally, social workers can use such information to inform the public debate about unemployment and so contribute to pressure for structural change, a role supported by Attlee nearly seventy years ago:

> The social worker must have definite views – must have formed some clear conception of what society he [sic] wishes to see produced – and I think it is a mistake for him [sic] to hold aloof from social reform movements . . . The social worker has as much right to make clear his [sic] views as anybody else . . . It is not possible for the ordinary rank and file of social workers to hope to rival skilled investigators, but each can take his [sic] part by cultivating habits of careful observation and analysis of the pieces of social machinery that come under his [sic] notice . . . Every social worker is almost certain to be also an agitator. If he or she learns social facts and believes they are due to certain causes which are beyond the power of an individual to remove, it is impossible to rest contented with the limited amount of good that can be done by following old methods.[9]

There were a few examples in our three study areas where the experience of social workers was being used to inform service development. A working party on homelessness amongst young people, for example, and a community enterprise renovating furniture had been established. Both of these initiatives grew out of social workers' recognition of a growing problem for which they felt they had at best an inadequate response, at worst none at all.

But such initiatives were exceptions and we found no evidence amongst the social workers we interviewed that information on the social and economic effects of unemployment was being recorded in a systematic way, either to inform their own practice and that of other service providers or to contribute to the wider public debate. At perhaps the most basic level the recording of the employment status of clients was patchy and inconsistent for men and virtually non-existent for women. Several other studies have reported similar findings, which ultimately means that it is difficult, if not impossible, to link the problems presented to social services with the experience of unemployment.[10]

So far we have suggested that mass unemployment is profoundly affecting the context within which social work is practised and we have described some of the ways in which social workers appear to be responding to this situation. In seeking to describe the *range* of responses we may, however, have created the impression that a great deal is happening. Such an impression would be misleading. The overwhelming impression from the interviews with social workers was that few had given serious consideration to the implications of unemployment for their practice. Over a third of the fifty-six social workers, for example, suggested that unemployment was having little or no effect on their work. Whilst to some extent such views reflected a particular work setting (a predominantly elderly case load, for instance), this was not always the explanation. Rather it would appear that, even in the years of mass unemployment, the effects are not immediately apparent. As one social worker commented:

'I'm only just becoming aware of the effects of unemployment for clients who have had long-term social work involvement.'

Where social workers are responding to unemployment it is also apparent that such responses are limited and *ad hoc*, restricted in most cases to intervening in acute crises. Given the scale of the problems and the focus of previous radical critiques of social work, it is predictable and right that a great deal of attention should be directed at ameliorating financial difficulties as far as is possible. However, our own research and that of others suggests that there is still considerable ambivalence about the legitimacy of such activities in social work.[11] Further, we found little evidence of social work responding on any scale to the psychological difficulties that unemployment can create and relatively little use was being made of the potential resource offered by the burgeoning number of community initiatives focusing on unemployment. In other words, our interview data suggest that the view criticized by Pearson – that individually oriented social work responses are to be judged as 'cool out' and a 'con' – remains a potent legacy from social work's radical hour in the 1970s.

Other possible responses, for example the 'organization of propaganda', were totally absent in our three study areas, at least in relation to unemployment. On the basis of our admittedly small-scale survey, and contrary to the belief expressed by Clement Attlee, social workers are not 'all certain to be agitators'. Nearly twenty years ago, writing in the wake of the Seebohm proposals, Adrian Sinfield argued that, by neglecting this role, social work had failed in the 1950s and 1960s to make society aware of the persistence of poverty much earlier.[12] Today things seem to have changed very little, and social work is again missing an important opportunity to illuminate the less visible social costs of the recession. If this situation is to change and a coherent – let alone a radical – social work response to unemployment is to be developed, it is important to consider what factors are presently constraining developments.

Time and tide

Public expenditure constraints, new legislative responsibilities, growing moral panics over child abuse and the social and economic consequences of recession are creating an ever-increasing tide of demand for social services at the same time as resources and person-power are severely restricted. It is not surprising therefore that social workers should be experiencing considerable pressure. Sheer lack of time, combined with the demands of statutory work, is the most frequent explanation for failure to respond to unemployment at all or for being unable to do more:

> 'We have high case loads, there's a lack of staff, a high expectation of written work, case recording has a huge priority put on it, there's various fresh demands on the service in terms of the Criminal Justices Act, it requires extra work. Social background reports will have to be more detailed and require more information, there's various edicts and policies making demands. Everything is supposed to be a priority, nobody will say that you do this or that, but there's a sort of unwritten list of priorities, like child care which takes precedence . . . unemployment hasn't a high priority, it's just an accepted fact.'

The complexity and scale of material problems may also leave little time to address other issues:

'I would like more time just to talk to people about their feelings and their frustrations and hopefully let them talk it through – we've almost got no time to think about the effects it's having on people's self-esteem, the humiliation they are experiencing. Hopefully, as we come across it we do respond and are sensitive, but it can almost get lost in the practicalities of the situation.'

But lack of time and the demands of legislative responsibilities cannot be a total explanation for the poverty of social work's response to unemployment. If the desire is there, some time can always be found. As one social worker commented:

'The framework can always be bent if one wants to; not everything we do is determined by legislation.'

So what other factors are constraining the development of responses to unemployment? At least part of the answer appears to lie in social workers' images of unemployment and the unemployed.

Who are the unemployed?

As we suggested earlier in the chapter, unemployment is not a recent phenomenon amongst social work's clients, as many of the social workers we spoke to were at pains to point out. Yet, despite the fact that the need to gain stable employment has traditionally been seen as a vital element in strategies with many clients, it is also evident that employment problems have never really been taken as seriously as such a perspective would imply. In 1978, the authors of a small-scale study of social workers' involvement with employment services wrote:

Employment problems were not generally seen as a main reason for referrals by social workers. Work was not looked at very seriously by them. As one social worker put it 'As a profession social workers put work low down on the list of priorities. Social work reports are often sketchy on work as opposed to family background information'.[13]

Since that survey was undertaken, unemployment has more than doubled in the areas in our study yet the situation is remarkably similar. Quite apart from the poor or non-existent recording of employment status and history, which we have already noted, there is also a sense from our data that employment problems are more often seen to be a result rather than a cause of clients' difficulties and that there is a qualitative difference between social work clients and the 'real' unemployed.

Some of the social workers we spoke to were beginning to be sensitive to these issues; others demonstrated a startling lack of awareness:

'It has only recently filtered through to me that unemployment can be an important factor in the lives of the people I work with. Social workers generally are not aware enough of unemployment as a specific issue. Particularly when working in a long-term team, clients have other serious problems and it is often difficult to sort out what is due to what. Unemployment is often not picked out as a major factor.'

'Social workers don't do anything because they don't really see the effects of unemployment. The unemployed only come in once every so often. You forget him and so you forget their demands.'

'People made redundant and still unemployed, the genuine unemployed, don't on the whole tend to become social work cases. They are still usually competent people. For social work cases unemployment may be an additional factor with quite important effects, but not necessarily the only major factor.'

Only three of the fifty-six social workers we interviewed explicitly stated that unemployment was the main cause of a client's problems, though some did indicate the sort of process that might be expected to militate against them reaching such a conclusion:

'Family relationship problems seem to have increased a great deal; maybe social workers get them when there is a crisis [and] don't see unemployment as a factor that led to the crisis. The initial referral is usually financial.'

Our research was not designed to allow us to explore what priority clients themselves give to employment problems, but recent research from Sweden suggests that their perceptions may be

very different from those of their social workers. In interviews
with 227 social workers and 678 of their clients the reseachers found
that, whilst less than a quarter of the social workers saw unemployment as a main cause of their clients' problems and still fewer as the
primary cause, around half of the clients indicated that they had
approached social services for economic support because they were
unemployed.[14]

In addition to the distinction that some social workers seem to
make between 'the unemployed' and 'their clients', there appear to
be other important dimensions to the images social workers have of
the unemployed. It seems, for example, that some groups are much
more visible amongst the unemployed than others. In general,
young people and unskilled workers are seen to be most severely
affected by unemployment, while women, ethnic minorities and
people with mental and physical disabilities or illness were mentioned much less frequently.

Such images can be expected to be reflected in social work
practice, and we came across one particularly stark example of this.
Many of the social workers we spoke to felt strongly that youth
unemployment was unacceptable and those who indicated that they
were spending more time helping people to find paid employment
were invariably referring to activities with young people. The
Youth Training Scheme was widely criticized, to some extent
reflecting social workers' perceptions of how young people themselves feel:

> 'Most of our kids can get on a training programme, but all we
> end up with is kids who are feeling resentful of being made mugs
> of . . . More and more are refusing to go on schemes; it's passing
> down the grapevine that it's a waste of time.'

However social workers themselves also have serious doubts about
YTS:

> 'When you work with youngsters, you can feel a sort of sense
> amongst them that there is not much point in putting any effort
> into training because there are no jobs at the end of the day. This
> makes it very hard, but it is made much tougher by the fact that I
> don't like the YTS at all. I'm not prepared to push them to take
> up a place on the Youth Training Scheme.'

In contrast, there would seem to be a greater acceptance that
people with disabilities or those with a history of mental illness will
not find jobs in the 'open' labour market.

'In this area normal people feel that there is no work available. So I have changed my attitude. I'm no longer pushing my clients towards jobs. I am afraid they will fail to get a job, which makes the situation worse.'   (Hospital social worker)

'I have close links with careers officers and spend a lot of time with youngsters, but we've just slipped into accepting that there's no work for adults.'

This 'acceptance' appears to be reflected in attitudes towards alternative forms of 'work' – though there was little enthusiasm, we heard few criticisms of community projects, voluntary work, or sheltered schemes for these groups, other than remarks concerning the shortage of provision.

Amongst the social workers we interviewed, attitudes towards the position of women were muddled and contradictory, as one might have predicted given what Geoff Pearson aptly describes as the 'grievous gender confusions in welfare discourses on employment and unemployment'. On the one hand there were those who clearly felt that the difficulties were much less acute for women:

'I think unemployment for women may not be as difficult to come to terms with in that traditionally they have a role within the home . . . they can more easily, generally speaking, use their time in housework, cooking and so on, reading, gardening, going to classes, more easily than a man. They can also be involved with relatives in a more positive way, like relatives with children they can help out, which is more difficult for a man because of cultural roles.'

Although as one social worker noted, almost as an aside, it may not simply be that women are better able to cope than men:

'Women are more resilient, more outgoing, they'll also more readily use the GP for valium.'

Alternatively, albeit less frequently amongst the social workers we spoke to, there were those who felt that women too were adversely affected by unemployment:

'There's a strand runs through all individuals – children or adults – that's the whole business of worth – self-esteem – women experience the same problems [and] there's little employment for women now.'

'Most of the women I meet would like to have jobs . . . to have
some money of their own and get out of the house . . . but over
the last year or two they are much less likely to get these jobs.'

Additionally, there was a fairly widespread view that women
could be adversely affected by the unemployment of other family
members. However, few of the comments on the effects of
unemployment on women were made spontaneously; rather they
were forthcoming only after specific probing. Moreover, whilst
many of the case studies we collected of social workers' experience
of clients' unemployment were family case studies, the overwhelming majority of them focused on the experience of men as
individuals or in families.

It would therefore appear that social workers tend to accept the
widespread view that unemployment is essentially a man's experience. Such views will inevitably be reflected in any social work
responses to unemployment, and the difficulties women undoubtedly face in relation to their own unemployment or in
handling the financial and psychological problems created by the
joblessness of others will be largely ignored. Even 'radical' social
work responses to women's position may be failing to address this
issue. In one case in our study, for example, a social worker
involved with a large women's group indicated that the issue of
unemployment had never been raised by her or anybody else
and the issue of employment only rarely. Whilst the ideology
of group work stresses that issues should arise from within the
group, it is naive in the extreme for professionals not to acknowledge that they can and do strongly influence what these issues
include.

Furthermore, it would appear that the archetypical unemployed
man for many of the social workers we spoke to was white. The
lack of reference to the particular problems faced by black people in
the labour market was undoubtedly related to the area in which
these social workers practised and therefore to the nature of their
case loads. None of the Scottish social workers, for example,
spontaneously mentioned black people as being particularly
affected by unemployment, and, when specifically asked, several
noted that they had no contact with ethnic minority groups in their
work. Similarly, the Midlands social workers based in a predominantly white area did not seem to be aware of the extent of
unemployment amongst black people. In contrast, the London
social workers were more likely to suggest that black people were
disproportionately affected, though strongly divergent views were
apparent:

'I've not really noticed a problem with black young people.'

'It's primarily blacks – they're top of the list'.

In general, however, spontaneous comments on the labour market experience of black people were conspicuous by their absence in our data and there was little discussion of the impact of discrimination. Only one social worker made direct reference to the importance of racism in the UK, though several more noted that they did have clients who 'felt' discriminated against. There was also some suggestion that some social workers, like many of the public at large, have ambiguous views about the causal mechanism involved in generating unemployment amongst black people:

'Being black and being unskilled often go together . . . blacks are also most affected because they work in small businesses and they tend to go bust first.'

It would be inappropriate to conclude from these data that the social workers in our survey were unaware of the disproportionate burden of unemployment experienced by black people in general. If they had been explicitly and extensively questioned on the topic they may well have demonstrated an awareness of the effects of racism on the labour market position of people from black ethnic minority groups. However, our findings do suggest that, for these social workers, black people were certainly not a particularly visible group amongst the unemployed, despite their being over-represented in the national figures. It is important then to ask what priority would be given to the employment difficulties experienced by black clients.

The nature of the crisis: the experience of unemployment

Whilst images of the unemployed can be expected to influence whether or not social workers respond to unemployment and on whom they focus these responses, the types of responses that are developed will in turn be influenced by social workers' perceptions of the nature of the crisis that unemployment creates.

As we have already suggested for most of the social workers we spoke to, unemployment was above all a financial crisis. For some this appeared to be the determining factor in the experience, precipitating a range of other problems:

'Some chaps are glad at first but they're not the ones to experience poverty. Once the poverty trap closes they can't do those things they wanted to do, so it's not so much unemployment as poverty.'

'Financial problems mean problems between the husband and wife and strained relationships with the children . . . this has a very negative influence on how the family functions.'

For most, however, financial problems were seen to be parallel to other difficulties rather than necessarily causing them, and there was a widespread awareness, again also referred to earlier, of the psychological difficulties associated with unemployment. However, such difficulties were seen to be almost exclusively confined to men (occasional references were made to similar effects on single women, especially professionally trained) and particularly older men:

'Traditionally older men have been the breadwinners. It's very difficult for them to move away from that. The most important effect is loss of status and the consequent stigma, the degradation of not being able to provide for your family.'

Whilst this experience was frequently likened to that of bereavement, there was also the suggestion that there are important differences:

'The initial reaction might be "it's a break", apart from the anxiety. The stages are similar to bereavement – loss, mourning, etc. In situations of loss of a person, however, there comes a stage of acceptance which is positive. However, unemployment is not acceptable so it becomes more and more destructive.'

Young people were also seen to be vulnerable to psychological difficulties as a result of unemployment, but these were described in subtly different ways from those described for older men. The idea of loss was still evident, but it was more frequently the loss of a 'future' that was felt to be important. Additionally, boredom and alienation were seen to be an important part of young people's experience of unemployment, but, rather than apathy, the longer-term consequence of this experience were likely to be described in terms of alcohol and drug abuse and crime.

These perceptions of the nature of the experience of unemployment do appear to be reflected in social work responses, though the relationship is far from straightforward. For example, the prominence social workers gave to the financial aspects of the experience and the lower priority afforded to the psychological dimensions are paralleled in the social work responses they described to us. It may well be that financial difficulties are the most immediate and obvious impact of unemployment, determining both social workers' perceptions and their responses and allowing little if any time for other interventions – though, as we have already indicated, work on financial problems appeared at times to be severely resented. However, it is also feasible that critiques of individually oriented social work approaches have, as Geoff Pearson has argued, gone 'too far' and that individual needs are being neglected to the detriment of clients.

The ambivalence towards individually oriented interventions appears to be most obvious in relation to the issue of counselling and unemployment. As the first two quotes below illustrate, some social workers are undoubtedly concerned about unemployment as a social problem and are keen to develop responses. However, there is a sense from these and other comments we recorded that many are unable or unwilling to make a link between these private social problems and the public arena of the labour market and economic policy. In contrast, as the third quote illustrates, there are those who focus on the public arena but see no role for individually oriented interventions:

'We need to help folks see that they are worth something . . . there's still a need for personal social work skills . . .'

'We should be counselling, trying to redirect, encourage, reinforce. But in order to do that we would have to have something concrete . . . it's got to be part of a planned campaign if you like . . . we should also promote the development of community responses.'

'These activities . . . counselling and volunteering . . . are signs of accepting unemployment . . . resources and energy should go into campaigning for jobs.'

Unemployment: defining a social work role

In general, our research suggests that unemployment is seen to be qualitatively different from any of the other issues social workers deal with – a situation that adds to the difficulties they have in defining a role. Whilst there was no consensus amongst the social workers we spoke to about what it was that made unemployment different, three major sets of reasons are apparent.

First, there are those who seem to feel that it is the nature of the problems linked to unemployment that sets it apart, in particular the associated stigma:

'Old age, disablement, and unemployment are the same in terms of loss of identity but unemployment is not acceptable.'

'The end results are the same. However, society and social work react differently, less sympathetically.'

Second, there are those who feel that the essential difference is that unemployment requires a different type of social work intervention. As the quotes below illustrate, implicit in many of the statements we would include under this heading is the view that individually oriented work is equivalent to casework and that this and community-based social work represent two *mutually exclusive* models for intervention:

'Social work needs to focus on unemployment as an issue in itself. The training and practice of social work are still concerned with casework. We have not yet come to terms with the changing philosophy vis-à-vis a community approach.'

'Little can be done from a traditional social work view.'

'Social workers don't tend to stand back and look at a problem; work on problems instead of individual cases is still in its infancy.'

Thirdly and finally, there are those who feel it is different because there is no appropriate social work response. Although, as the quotes below suggest, there appear to be two somewhat different dimensions to these views, the end result would seem to be that it is possible from both a 'radical' and 'non-radical' perspective to argue that unemployment is not an issue for social work.

'We have to be realistic, there are no jobs around so what can we do?'

'As an individual social worker, changing the way I'm working isn't going to make a lot of difference.'

'Social workers feel impotent . . . it's a national issue.'

'It's different in that it involves a problem for which there is a solution and for which social workers and departments have no possibility of solving . . . this isn't the same with the elderly; there's no solution for old age, though, of course, there's a political component.'

'Unemployment is a political choice . . . therefore social workers are restricted by how far it can be tackled . . . have to go against political ideals by helping people come to terms with it.'

Quotes such as these raise many important questions for those wishing to develop a radical social work role. Issues of politics and stigma appear to be at the forefront of many social workers' minds as they seek to define the implications of unemployment for their practice. Obviously, such 'sensitive' dimensions do not in fact set unemployment apart from other facets of social work. Rather, in the past, the political dimension has been 'defined' out of other aspects of social worker's case loads such as disability, mental illness, old age, etc., in order to 'allow' a social work response to these 'problems' to be developed. Defining back the political and public dimensions of social problems is what the radical social work movement has been all about. In so doing, however, radical social work must resolve the dilemmas facing some of the workers quoted above, or define out any social work response to social problems in general and unemployment in particular.

It is also important to recognize that the neglect of labour market issues as causal factors in the problems experienced by social workers' 'clients' is not confined to the 'non-radical' elements of the profession. As at least one of the quotes above illustrates, unemployment can, and is, being defined as a crucial political problem, affecting people not normally seen by social workers. Alternatively, it could and should be conceptualized as only one dimension of the labour market disadvantage that has always been a persistent feature of the lives of poor people, the low paid, the unskilled, etc. – men and women – and that has always contributed to, if not created, the problems presented to social services. A variant on the neglect of labour market issues in radical social work is exemplified in the following quote from an article on radical social work by Jeff Hearn, who is arguing for a greater focus on questions of reproduction and gender, and notes that:

> Questions of employment and unemployment are, of course, hardly irrelevant for social work, not least for social workers themselves at a time of public expenditure cuts, but they are secondary.[15]

Unemployment: developing a radical social work response

We believe that radical social work responses to unemployment must recognize and address both the structural roots of individual and family problems and the personal pain involved. In this final section we briefly describe some of the major elements in existing responses that may help to define the nature of such an approach. On the basis of the unemployment-related responses we came across, however, it needs to be said that the position of women vis-à-vis unemployment remains a major area of neglect.

To return again to cod's head soup, besides illustrating the dilemma facing many within the social services who see any potential responses from them as essentially ameliorative, the anecdote also provides a useful way of looking at the scope of possible responses. They can be considered in terms of the *effects* that they focus on – improving household finances through cookery classes or welfare rights, for instance. Similarly, the story suggests that responses can also be considered in terms of *who* they are directed at – individuals (as in the anecdote), groups or whole communities. Finally, responses can be considered in terms of who is developing them – individual social workers for instance, a group or team, a district office, or a department. These different perspectives illustrate how responses can be seen as a continuum, rather than as mutually exclusive options. Whilst one particular response may be more appropriate for one agency rather than another, all have a role to play. The most constructive way forward is to try to develop responses at a number of different levels at the same time.

So what do the more innovative, though not necessarily 'radical', responses that already exist within social services entail? We have looked at a number of 'initiatives' focusing on unemployment and from these it is possible to identify five major elements.

(1) *Monitoring the effects of unemployment* or 'organizing propaganda'. Activities designed to do this have been developed at different levels by individual workers, larger groups and whole departments. The material collected has been used to inform everyday practice and more strategic service planning. Though much more limited, such material has also been used in the political arena to agitate for change. Strathclyde Regional Council, for example, used information collected through social services in its evidence to the House of Lords inquiry into the proposed closure of the Port Glasgow Shipyards.[16]

(2) *Improving channels of information*. Again these activities have been developed at different levels and have involved closer relationships between different statutory services and between statutory and voluntary services. The objectives have included: improving referral procedures; improving the take-up of services in cash and in kind; and increasing awareness of unemployment amongst social services staff themselves. One of the most ambitious initiatives of this kind is described in the Strathclyde report on the implications of unemployment for regional services, though this has yet to be implemented.[17]

(3) *Developing new services*. These have included: services designed to make limited budgets stretch through take-up campaigns, mobile welfare rights offices, claimants' unions and food cooperatives; services designed to provide social support, such as self-help groups, neighbourhood schemes and resource centres; and services designed to provide information at times of redundancies.

(4) *Considering how existing or new services can avoid stigmatizing the recipients*. This has been attempted in a number of ways. Some services have been provided on a universal basis while positively discriminating towards those experiencing unemployment or other disadvantaged groups. The '*leisure passport*' introduced in one of our three areas is a good example of such a service, with the same 'passport' being provided for everyone, but to some at a reduced rate. Other services have been developed with the active involvement of the recipients and eventually run by them. Food cooperatives are an example of these types of service, as are 'good as new' shops to replace second-hand charities. As Pearson argues, there is also a role for counselling in relation to unemployment, but, as he suggests, considerable thought needs to be given to how such therapeutic interventions can be appropriately adapted to provide what he terms 'a start from which people might more effectively engage in local forms of organization'. Finally, there may well be a role for

cookery classes and the like, but the cod's head soup anecdote holds a powerful message here. Too often, well-meaning professionals underestimate the level of knowledge already available to the poor and the disadvantaged. Research has consistently documented the amazing budgeting ability of people on low incomes and, rather than focus on providing information people may already have (such as how to cook nutritionally on poverty incomes), the focus should be on providing the means to use such knowledge.

(5) *Developing professional training*. The objectives of such training have included: increasing awareness of the difficulties caused by unemployment and of the services and other resources available in a local area; exploring the possibility for monitoring exercises and research; and providing a forum for workers to discuss ideas and share their own anxieties.

In addition to these five major elements, the initiatives we have looked at often included two other vital components: a strong commitment to involve people experiencing unemployment, including involvement in in-service training for professional groups; and an equally strong focus on the development of better relationships between different statutory and voluntary agencies.

It is possible to identify a number of factors that have facilitated the unemployment-related initiatives that we identified, though it is important to recognize that no *one* of these is either a necessary or a sufficient condition. Obviously, the nature of unemployment in an area is a significant influence on whether or not social services respond. But it is not simply the level. Some 'types' of unemployment, such as large-scale closures for instance, are more visible and therefore will perhaps prompt a response more readily than unemployment generated by the closure or shrinkage of many small firms. The level of support from 'management' at different levels can also be important, but, even where management is actively encouraging fieldworkers to develop responses to unemployment at a strategic level, the reservations that were discussed in earlier sections can act as powerful constraints. What most of these initiatives did have in common was a single individual or group totally committed to doing something and willing to find the time to do so. Finally, organizational factors are also important. In Scotland, for example, differences in legislation and closer working contact between social workers, community workers and community education services appear to have influenced a number of developments.

Whilst management support may not be a sufficient or a

necessary condition for the development of a social work response to unemployment, it would undoubtedly be helpful. Yet our research suggested that it rarely exists. Fieldwork social workers and team leaders are more likely to respond if they receive a clear signal that unemployment is to be given priority within the context of the statutory work that they are expected to do, and if time is found to allow discussion about the responses that are possible. Furthermore, in-service training to increase awareness, to develop skills and to exchange information should be encouraged. Our own research suggests that management support for this rarely exists. Our subsequent experience of developing training initiatives around unemployment indicates that managers too require training. Though we did not collect data on managers, it is predictable that they will share to a greater or lesser extent the dilemmas and contradictions that we identified amongst fieldworkers, and managers too will need the opportunity to address these. Social work needs radical managers every bit as much as it needs radical fieldworkers.

Notes and references

1 See, for example, S. Moylan, J. Miller, and R. Davies, *For Richer for Poorer?* DHSS Cohort Study of Unemployed Men, S.R.R. No. 11 (HMSO 1984); A. Sinfield, *What Unemployment Means* (Martin Robertson, 1981), M. White, *Long Term Unemployment and Labour Markets* (PSI Research Report, 1983) no. 622.

2 S. Lonsdale, *Work and Inequality* (Longman, 1985).

3 See, for example, Unemployment Unit *Bulletin* (spring 1988); Hansard Written Answers, Col. 553–554, 2 July 1986.

4 H. Graham, *Women, Health and the Family* (Wheatsheaf, 1984); J. Pahl, 'Patterns of money management within the family', paper presented at the BSA Conference (Manchester, 1982).

5 L. McKee and C. Bell, 'Marital and family relations in times of male unemployment', in B. Roberts *et al.* (eds), *New Approaches to Economic Life* (Manchester University Press, 1985); A. Coyle, *Redundant Women* (The Women's Press, 1984).

6 The research was funded by the Health Education Council. It was completed in the summer of 1985 and the research report was published by the Health Education Council in January 1986. The researchers have successfully funded a training initiative based on their findings.

7 Strathclyde Regional Council, *Talbot Initiative Group: Report of Director of Social Work* (1983); C. Hulme, C. and S. Balloch, *Caring for the Unemployed: A Study by the AMA on the Impact of Unemployment on Demand for Personal Social Services* (Bedford Square Press, 1985); R.

Silburn, S. MacPherson and S. Becker, *Saints, Ferrets and Philosophers* (Benefit Research Unit, Department of Social Adminisitration, 1984).

8 Child Poverty Action Group, *Carrying the Can: Charities and the Welfare State* (CPAG, 1984).

9 C. Attlee, *The Social Worker* (Bell, 1920).

10 Hulme *et al.* op. cit. (n7); A. Nash, 'The long shadow of unemployment', *Community Care* (June 1983); Strathclyde Regional Council, op. cit. (n7); D. Bennet and M. Barnes, *Unemployment and the Social Services: A Dilemma for Planners*, City of Sheffield Family and Community Services Department, Research Report No. 10 (1983).

11 M. Hill and P. Laing, *Social Work and Money* (Allen & Unwin, 1979); M. Hill, 'The relationship between local authority social services and supplementary benefit since the 1980 supplementary benefit changes' (unpublished, School of Advanced Urban Studies, University of Bristol, 1985).

12 A. Sinfield, 'Which way for social work?' in *The Fifth Social Service: A critical analysis of the Seebohm proposals* (The Fabian Society, 1970).

13 B. Bridges and J. Campling, *Unemployment Problems – the Social Work Involvement* (British Association of Social Workers, 1978).

14 H. Berglind, Unemployment – a challenge for social work', paper presented to the International Conference on Social Welfare (Montreal, August 1984).

15 J. Hearn, 'Radical social work – contradictions, limitations and political possibilities', *Radical Social Policy*, vol. 2, no. 1 (1982), pp. 19–38.

16 Strathclyde Regional Council, *Scott Lithgow Investigation*, Memorandum of evidence to the Select Committee on Scottish Affairs (1984).

17 Strathclyde Regional Council, *Unemployment: Implications for Regional Services*, Consultative Report (1985).

8   'And for those of us who are black?' Black politics in social work

MICHAEL HUTCHINSON-REIS

Introduction

This chapter is written by a black social worker from a non-academic perspective. It is aimed primarily at a black readership, although it is presumed that the majority of readers will in fact be white. It is hoped that the chapter will address itself to the professional, racial and personal politics of black social workers.

In attempting to pursue these issues I have made two basic assumptions. First that the fundamental function of a Western liberal democratic state is one of control, and that, in facilitating the continuation of a capitalist and imperialistic system, racism forms a key mechanism of such a state. Institutions of the state, such as statutory and voluntary social work, are inherently ambivalent and contradictory in practice. Second, that, at their interface with society, opportunities arise to further the progressive cause, and that these opportunities can be exploited by highlighting the theoretical and practice contradictions in social work.

For the black cause in particular, progress can be achieved by confronting the welfare system with its own ineffectiveness, illogicality and underlying racism. This confrontation will involve a critical assault on popular 'liberal' and 'leftist' attitudes in social work. It will also involve an exposure of the suspect foundations of 'welfarism'. For progressive black activists, the profession will provide a base for collective organization and joint action with the broader black struggle.

'Liberalism' is held to be the theory and practice of those who acknowledge the inequalities of the state and appear committed to change of a reformist nature. They are also characterized by their underlying interest in maintaining the status quo, from which they themselves derive an advantage. 'Leftist' is understood to be the broad perspective held by the democratic and socialist consensus. This perspective views welfare as in need of reform and development as a means of redressing the inequalities of the state.

The context

An aspect of the welfare system is control. In addition, racism is a key mechanism of control and exploitation within a capitalist and imperialist society. The welfare system's response to racism must be analysed in this context.

As a consequence of the civil disorder that has occurred in the UK since 1976, the state has developed concerns around the potential for major urban insurrections. The black population has become identified with such a possibility. As a result, various initiatives have been organized by the state to minimize such a risk. These initiatives have been mounted at all levels of state organization, including nationally and locally based political parties and the education and welfare systems. Social work and the welfare system generally have targeted the black population as being in particular need of their services on the basis that to fail to provide such services could provoke or aggravate social unrest.

Many of these initiatives appear designed to appease local communities by offering greater influence and participation in the systems and institutions that govern their lives and environment. These initiatives have been manifested in local government decentralization, housing privatization and educational and policing 'reforms'. In the welfare system, these have taken the form of 'positive action' and 'equal opportunity' programmes in the recruitment of black social workers and the provision of services to the black population.

Despite these efforts there appears to be no fundamental change in the underlying racist nature of social work. In fact, it would seem that local government equal opportunity policies are in retreat. The new politics of 'realism' has undermined previous priorities given to inequalities of gender, sexuality, disability, class, culture and race.

However, the theoretical discovery of racism in social policy persists. A leftist critique of 'welfarism' has also developed to question the ability of social work to redress inequalities. Interestingly, it is often those who articulate this theory who also have an economic interest in maintaining their employment within that same system. Many black people have concluded that such critics have no intention of compromising self-interest. This type of liberalism masks an attempt to dissociate the individual's involvement from a system they themselves claim is unjust. It is this dynamic that black social workers will have to confront.

With this in mind, conclusions about the nature of social work and its relationship to the black struggle will follow:

- principally, that the objective of the black struggle within social work is the attainment of a degree of power relative to the black population's representation and contribution in all aspects of the state and society;
- that, in achieving that objective, social work in its present form and function is inadequate;
- furthermore, that the liberal promotion of relatively privileged black social workers is potentially divisive and open to reactionary manipulation.

Experience of the civil rights movement in the USA suggests that the relative condition of most blacks has deteriorated since the 1960s. Many have criticized the movement for providing a vehicle for the advancement of individual blacks at the expense of the vast majority, and for paving the way for the advancement of white women and other minorities who enjoy relative advantages over most blacks. The history of anti-colonialist struggle provides a number of examples of how black people have been manipulated and divided amongst themselves by the promotion and patronization of individuals. The general pathologizing of black disadvantage within the Western liberal democracies and the 'third' world has further served this purpose. The setting up of black individuals, professionally and politically, to fail has become a common and humiliating occurrence.

However, there is reason to believe that black social workers, through collective political organization, can effectively confront a liberal and racist system; that black social workers can aid progressive initiatives within the broader black struggle. A struggle against liberal racism within social work should be valued as much as any other.

The marginalization of race within social work

Despite the placement of black people in parliament, councils, committees, governing bodies and managerial positions, the welfare system is still based on white and middle-class assumptions.

These assumptions include suspect liberal notions of race and racism. To date, these attitudes have effectively amounted to no more than tokenistic and marginalizing gestures. Race has been liberally accommodated without compromising fundamental interests. Racism has also been subordinated to issues of gender or class or placed in competition with other disadvantaged groups within society.

The power to define racism and its relationship to social work remains in white hands. Collective black demands in social work, in common with demands made generally in this society, are often denigrated as 'unrepresentative' and merely reflecting the self-interests of the black middle class and professional 'elites'. Similar questions should be raised about political parties and individuals who never question their own validity as representatives of the working class.

Racism has only recently been acknowledged in urban areas as a reality, and has been denied as a problem in areas without visible black communities. Anthropological and assimilationist notions of cultural alienation and inter-generational conflict continue. The pathologizing of the effects of slavery and immigration rationalizes racism as a problem for black people. This rationalization absolves whites from any responsibility apart from intellectual acknowledgement.

As black social workers have discovered, the margins of liberal tolerance can be pushed only so far. When confrontations occur central to the control of key mechanisms within an institution that define its very nature (such as recruitment), reaction, covert or if necessary overt, sets in. The control of the procedure that determines recruitment and progression has become a primary focus for struggle by black social workers. In response, liberalism has raised the issue of lowering academic and professional standards, the definition of what is, and is not, racism. It has also become concerned with who is, and is not, a representative black person and the evils of 'reverse discrimination'. The final defence has often been one of the shortage of resources. Behind this lies a basic assumption that the majority are having to pay for the provision of a minority who are not perceived to pay taxes or rates. These kinds of responses undervalue and marginalize black participation and its potential contribution to social work.

Those black social workers who have gained entry to the profession are perceived as only having experience and a role in working with black clients. The 'ghettoization' of black social workers seems superficially to meet the demands of black workers and clients. It also serves the function of relieving white social workers from having to work with some difficult clients. A developing concern amongst black workers is that the welfare system not only stigmatizes black people but also disables them by creating a dependency on welfare itself. For a black client to suggest that the welfare system is involved in a conspiracy against black people could result in a compulsory admission to a psychiatric hospital. Revolutionary wealth redistribution is not seen to be achieved by giving a black single parent £25 to last over the weekend whilst waiting for a DHSS Giro to arrive.

At this point it might be useful to give some examples of social work practice:

A black psychiatric patient on discharge from hospital is not allocated rehabilitative support. This decision is made by white staff on the basis that he has suffered from 'Caribbean psychosis', a short-term condition from which recovery is immediate. Behind this assessment is an assumption that such a condition is part of a continuum of behaviour and emotional responses found in 'West Indians' under stress, which may on occasions result in 'madness'. This may sometimes be a clinical disorder that requires psychiatric treatment. This treatment may be compulsory in extreme cases. Alternatively, medical intervention may not be appropriate in cases of 'personality disorder'. In this eventuality, police involvement may be necessary.

A multi-disciplinary case conference which is exclusively white discusses an allegation of non-accidental injury to a black child living with its family. The case conference concludes that the injuries to the child were non-accidental and of a severe nature. However, the conference agrees to take no action, as the injuries were the result of chastisement consistent with patterns of parenting within West Indian culture. The unspoken assumption is that black parents normally beat their children to such an extent that severe injuries should be expected. A presumption might be that similar injuries to a white child would result in some action by the responsible authorities.

The opening sentence of a white social worker's court report states: 'Mrs A is English, the father of the children Mr B is from Barbados and their two children C and D are hence half-caste.' In one sentence a social worker asserts that everyone who is 'English' is white; that everyone who originates from Barbados is black; that individuals are designated by their presumed genetic inheritance and that this, in the case of 'half-castes', implies a problem.

A white social worker makes a home visit to a white mother with two black children. The mother tells the social worker, 'I wouldn't have all these problems if my children weren't fucking black!' The social worker returns to the office to write up the file. Of the children he writes, 'actually, they are brown'.

A white social worker writes a court report in which she describes her Afro-Caribbean client as being 'of typical West Indian appearance'. In fact, the largest single racial group in the client's country of origin is Asian. The social worker is not questioned in court as to what she meant.

A black male single parent is noted as 'Afro-Caribbean' in his file, despite the fact he is West African. Oblivious of the white social worker's assessment to the contrary, he continues to struggle to support his children at home. Social workers resist his attempts to 'manipulate his children into care' and describe him as 'demanding and aggressive'.

A white social worker, on being introduced to a black councillor on the social services committee, exclaims 'She's lovely, isn't she!' as if the councillor were a child.

Black social workers are often assumed by their white colleagues to be newly qualified, off access courses or former nurses. In addition, black workers are often perceived as clients themselves or received with disbelief by other agencies. In general they do not receive the same consideration from colleagues and others and are not attributed with the same academic and professional status as whites. Black workers seldom receive the support of their white colleagues when confronting racist clients or others. These examples may seem trivial, but are familiar to black workers year after year.

In the education and training of social workers, black perspectives have to be fought for. As an academic area of study, racism has still not established itself as an integral part of the curriculum. 'Racism' on social work and social studies courses usually takes the form of a separate option or 'special interest' essay for individual students. Options such as 'working in a multi-racial society' still conform to basic assimilationist and anthropological perspectives on racism. Black students often complain that they are marginalized by the content of teaching and patronized by expectations that they should take an interest in black subjects. They are aware that fellow white students are able to take an interest in the 'wider' academic subjects of class and gender, to the exclusion of race, without comment by their tutors. With more financial restraints colleges are pruning their teaching to the extent that black issues on courses become token.

Often, black students are not made aware of their academic strengths and weaknesses. White tutors seem reluctant to stretch able students and have difficulty in assisting those who are struggling. As a result, many students lack confidence in their work and are intimidated by the realization that more black students fail than white. Black students have problems in finding appropriate placements and when problems arise feel themselves unsupported by college tutors. Placements and fieldwork tutors seem to be a particular problem. Colleges with higher proportions of black students find that there is a corresponding decline in the institution's academic reputation. 'Access' courses may well help black students into the system, but they may also have prejudicial consequences with future employers and colleagues.

Race-awareness training in colleges and in-service training has become discredited. It appears that white workers have personalized issues that require political responses to the very structure of society. This trivializes the issue and allows cynical participants to acquire even more sophisticated skills to avoid confronting racism.

As an institution, social work is probably no more, or less, racist than other organizations within the state. However, because of its welfare image, it does have an ability to obscure its integral racism behind a progressive facade.

A black response

For most of us, the development of a black political perspective is not the major problem. Developing a consistent collective political strategy to overcome our oppression is the primary task. For black social workers this is not a 9 to 5 exercise, but something we experience 24 hours a day. In respect of black social workers, a major concern must be in maintaining the respect of our own communities whilst functioning from a position of relative advantage. If this is not achieved, we will lose all perspective of the struggle and the support of black people generally.

The number of black social workers within the profession has expanded in recent years, particularly since 1981. For many, qualification has been a milestone in their individual struggle to achieve an improved economic and social position. Some – a minority it seems – may well be temporarily or permanently seduced by white middle-class culture into believing they have finally arrived. In some situations, they may as a result feel themselves compromised in asserting their black identity.

In order to maintain the clarity and consistency of the struggle, it is essential to retain a realistic insight into the reality of our position. This will entail an honest acknowledgement of our role, who placed us there and for what purpose, and an assessment of our individual and collective rewards for being part of the system. We should be aware of the limits of our personal commitment and what we are individually prepared to risk or compromise. It would be romanticism to believe we will all play a heroic role in the struggle as black people.

In combating racism, and the liberalism that colludes with it, a degree of individual discipline and collective organization will be required. A detailed study of the structure of the system to be confronted needs to be made. Procedural inconsistencies and vulnerable mechanisms have to be identified. Once this has been achieved, political skills and collective strategies have to be adopted to bring pressure to bear. It should always be remembered that institutional reform is not the ultimate objective. The exposure of inconsistencies and reform are strategies to which liberalism by its very nature is vulnerable. However, a strength of liberalism is its ability to change its form without fundamentally changing its substance – like a sponge.

The personal pressures and costs borne by black workers cannot be underestimated. The very reformist nature of social work makes it a frustrating environment in which to work. The continual effort of having to endure two-faced liberalism is a stress factor in itself, let alone the professional pressures of social work. Many of us have experienced the encouragement of black workers to take a stand on an issue, only to suffer the isolation of failure alone at the last hurdle; or the way in which anti-racist initiatives have been used to enhance the career prospects of white workers, leaving black colleagues behind. It would be self-deception not to question one's own commitment when life could be a lot less difficult. It is a credit to the determination and resilience of black workers that they still stick with it.

In establishing any group of black workers, discussion should be broad enough to allow the identification of agreed objectives. A definition of 'black' has to be agreed. Any such agreed definition should allow for the recognition of separate black cultures and, if numbers allow, permit the existence of various groupings to reflect this fact. Black workers may participate in alliances with other groups on issues of gender and sexuality. A consensus based on an agreed and shared perspective cannot exclude differences of opinion on interests and tactics. Valuable lessons can be learnt from past struggles and it would be arrogant to ignore the experience of others that could in turn assist our cause. Ignorance causes vulnerability; there will be a constant need to develop an awareness and understanding of the wider issues involved.

It appears that the relative ratio of black women social workers to black men is higher than that between white women social workers and white men. This implies certain questions about conditions within the black population and the attitudes of those responsible for the recruitment of social work students and practitioners. The position of black women in social work has to be acknowledged. Any collective of black workers should have this issue on the agenda if it is to consider itself genuinely representative and progressive. The separate interests of black workers have to be accepted. Automatic assumptions about the common interest and solidarity between black workers cannot be made. These divisions, if not openly resolved, will undermine any initiative. Groups need to develop the maturity and collective responsibility for addressing such issues in order to agree a joint strategy. Such collective initiatives by groups of black workers need to be resolved separately. This has to be done to avoid the introduction of divisive issues from outside and to maintain the primacy of an autonomous black perspective. This process can be educative in itself, improving the resilience and effectiveness of the group.

Organization, strategy and tactics

Any group of black workers needs to exist primarily in the interests of black workers, clients and community. To do so it needs to be autonomous, functioning independently of any other professional, trade union or political grouping. This autonomy would not prevent joint initiatives with other groups. This should be done on the basis of previous agreement on aims and objectives. Without such fundamental solidarity, black interests will be undermined and compromised, if not ignored.

One of the initial difficulties in organizing black workers in social work has been the resistance to them meeting separately from white workers in the workplace. Despite this, it appears increasingly difficult for employers, management and trade unions to prevent black workers from doing so. Even casual meetings of black workers are met with suspicion and even overt hostility, whilst similar groups of exclusively white workers are never questioned.

To attempt overtly to stop black workers meeting would invite accusations of racism. Isolated black staff, however, particularly women and clerical workers, still find themselves experiencing intimidation and obstruction from management and colleagues. This limits the full participation of all sections of the black workforce and encourages inequalities and divisive attitudes amongst black workers. A priority for any black collective must be the inclusion and fostering of working links with other sections of black workers.

Within the workplace, office politics are unavoidable. Personal, professional and social politics will be defined by the racist dynamic that exists between any individuals or groups of black and white. All activities during the working day have to be seen in this context.

The primary unit of black organization within social work must be an autonomous office group forming part of a larger divisional, departmental and regional structure. The right to participate in electing representatives and delegates must be structured into the constitution of the organization. The decision-making process of the organization must be democratic if it is to survive and be effective. Traditional fears that such groups provide the power bases and career vehicles for individuals must be overcome and rank-and-file participation acknowledged. The centralizing and consolidation of control by cliques has to be avoided. Despite the undemocratic environment in which black workers have to function, the responsibility is on black workers to organize and function in a democratic manner.

Most social work offices do not have procedural guidelines on which decisions can be made collectively and which are the sole responsibility of management. This can be used to highlight the inconsistencies of a system where workers have no defined rights to make decisions affecting their work.

Paradoxically, the struggle for workplace democracy may be counter-productive. It may result in a situation where black workers and progressive supporters find themselves a voting minority, which only serves to reinforce the status quo in the legitimacy of democratic procedures. However, office voting may force reactionaries to reveal their hand, exposing their real interests. This in itself can be a tactical victory. As an example, if workers can draft a proposal and force it to a vote without amendment, then the meeting will have only two options, to capitulate or totally reject a 'progressive' proposal in an obviously reactionary response. To successfully achieve such manipulation, coordinating and debating skills will have to be developed. The organization and structure of formal meetings will have to be studied and practised in preparation for such tactics.

In relation to this aspect of black organization, there must be a thorough and proper assessment of whom to ally with and with what objective in mind. Most black social workers will be employed by urban councils, the majority of which will be controlled by the Labour Party. Even so, black workers in Conservative councils may not find circumstances much different. In this situation black workers will often find themselves in opposition to their employers or sometimes in alliance with them against other groups such as trade unions. Whatever the combination of alliances, the method should always be strategic.

In order to short-circuit obstruction, black workers should enlist sources of support from outside the workplace. Black workers should look for support amongst black community groups and black councillors. The personal dilemmas faced by individual black representatives working within white institutions are often embarrassingly obvious. An objective of any organized group should be to support them in maintaining their commitment to the black cause. This may mean convincing them that they have more to lose by colluding with white patronage than in making a stand. Trade unions and other organizations need to be involved by black social workers as part of a political campaign around social work issues. Local government policies and procedures are accessible to black workers prepared to campaign and lobby to develop or change them. In order to do this effectively, workers will have to constantly assess in which direction it is most advantageous to apply pressure or elicit support. Such a degree of political calculation will require some skill. Black workers will also need to have a realistic appreciation of their influence in order to avoid selling themselves short in any transaction. Alternatively, they should avoid aiming unrealistically high.

Most social work agencies conform to a hierarchical structure within a larger organization such as a local council. The highest level of decision-making is the council committees controlled by a political grouping within the council. Considerable power is invested in the leader and deputy leader of the council and the various chairs of committees. Below this political level of policy formulation and decision-making are the officers of the council, from the top of the pyramid, the Chief Executive, and departmental directors, assistant directors, principal officers, area officers and so on, down to individual basic grade workers. In social services departments, policy and procedures can be formulated locally at the lowest level of organization, e.g. area offices and 'patch teams'.

Theoretically, decisions on policy and procedures at this lower level should not conflict or contradict general departmental or council policy made higher up the structure.

However, despite the purpose of the organizational structure being to facilitate power and decisions from the top downwards, the system can be reversed. For instance, a black workers' group based in an area office can initiate policy within the immediate workplace. This can provoke a confrontation with management and council, which will serve to illustrate the inconsistencies the group wish to expose. This can in turn lead to modification of policy at departmental and council level. As has been stated earlier, reform will never be a satisfactory solution. However, reform can push liberalism to its limits, beyond which the fundamental conflict of interests will be exposed. Only at this point does the possibility of a radical and effective resolution of the struggle become attainable.

Workers can stretch the boundaries of their professional tasks to include more overtly political issues. Where social workers have the power and responsibility to define the problem and recommend a solution, black issues can be introduced. Social enquiry reports presented to courts and other agencies should contain a black perspective where appropriate. The need for black workers to campaign around practice issues will require an individual commitment to professional study and above-average standards of practice. Black workers should also not confine themselves to those areas considered related to black problems such as youth work, the juvenile justice system, fostering and adoption and mental health. Black interests include all aspects of social policy and we should not allow ourselves to be marginalized in such a way.

Conclusion

When first approached to write this paper I was asked to include something for the white reader. I would ask that you respect the right of black colleagues to state their position separately. Do not feel threatened by this, but perhaps meet separately yourselves to discuss the issue of racism and what you can do to end it. Racism is an exploitive and oppressive system that you yourselves operate. This is not a reason to be overcome by guilt, followed by liberal good intentions. White social workers do have a positive part to play in combating racism, as well as other forms of oppression. To do this will require positive action. If you fail to do so, you may find yourselves marginal to profound developments in society.

And for those of us who are black? Can we as black people afford to wait until the oppressor develops an awareness of his injustice? Enough to lift the boot off our face?

Bibliography

J. Cheetham, *Social Work and Ethnicity* (National Institute of Social Work, Allen & Unwin, 1982).

A. Davis, *Women, Race and Class* (The Women's Press, 1982).

P. Fryer, *Staying Power, the history of black people in Britain* (Pluto Press, 1984).

A. Gibson, *Social Services: a bane to the West Indian Community* (West Indian Press, London, 1980).

M. Hutchinson-Rcis, 'After the uprisings – social work on Broadwater Farm', *Critical Social Policy*, Issue 17 (1986).

C. L. R. James, *Beyond a Boundary* (Stanley Paul, 1963).

A. Sivanandan, 'Racism awareness training and the development of the black struggle', *Race and Class*, vol. 26, no. 4 (1985).

P. Stubbs, 'The employment of black social workers', *Critical Social Policy*, Issue 12 (1985).

9 It's up to you sisters: black women and radical social work

NASEEM SHAH

What does 'radical social work' mean for black women? Because only part of the answer can be provided from the perspective of white feminism, radical social work must come to terms with the issue of racism. This chapter focuses on the role of racism in social work and especially its consequences for black women. We will also summarize the various criticisms of white feminist analyses from an anti-racist perspective.[1]

The following argument assumes that readers share a basic grasp of the consequences of class and racial inequalities in British society and the social welfare system.[2] However, mere recognition of these inequalities is not enough. Those committed to radical social work must grasp the far-reaching effects of racism on social policy. This is a difficult demand for many white radical social workers to accept, partly because, although much has been written on race and racism in Britain, little has been written on race and social work, despite some recent contributions.[3] Because black people in Britain experience racism every day of their lives, they are better informed about prejudice and discrimination. It is high time that radical social work recognized racism as a concept of central significance and reorganized its theory and practice accordingly.

When white women write about women they often write only about themselves. When they occasionally write about black women they usually just incorporate them in a racist and ethno-centric way. Although recently white women have been keen to include black women in their writing, it is clear to black women that white feminists have made the same sort of mistake that they in the past accused male radicals of making; that is, white women have made black women mere appendages to the perspectives of white feminists. Until recently there has been no acknowledgement from white society that not only are black women facing the triple oppression of race, class and gender, but their experience of sexism is also different from that of white women and they face racism in a different way than black men.[4]

Racism and sexism work in similar ways by discriminating against people and by reinforcing stereotyping. For example, both women and black people are excluded from power structures in education and in the employment market. However, as Bell Hooks insists, the idea that all women experience similar oppression oversimplifies reality: 'The idea of "common oppression" was a false and corrupt platform disguising and mystifying the true nature of women's varied and complex social reality.'[5] Let's look at the distinctive experience of black women more closely.

Smith and Stewart[6] point out that black people and white women are labelled as 'childlike' and incapable of taking responsibility. This stereotype is often used to explain the failure of black people and white women to achieve in education or in their careers. On the other hand, there are other stereotypes of black people and white women. White women are often seen as warm and caring but as people who need protection. Black people are often depicted as angry, violent, or aggressive, but there are also contradictory stereotypes. For example, Asian women are often viewed as weak, passive, prisoners of their cultures, while Afro-Caribbean women are looked on as people without a culture, unmarried mothers, or as 'big mamas'.

According to Smith and Stewart, researchers have not until recently looked into how sexism affects black and white women differently and how racism is experienced differently by black men and black women. One of the reasons for this is that the dominant white culture does not accept the unique experiences of minorities and continues to impose its standards and values. However, black people are now challenging white definitions of sexism and racism. From their own research Smith and Stewart conclude that white women and black men are very eager to achieve and compete in education and they are strongly motivated by the fear of failure. The history of black women and their experience of living and working in non-competitive third world agricultural communities with other women means that the notion of failure has a different significance for them. That is not to say that black women do not have high expectations in life. Although both black and white women are able to reveal their feelings of fear and anxiety openly, as this is more acceptable for women, black women are seen as strong while white women and black men are seen as weak; on the other hand, black men are seen as dangerous.

Why, given the distinctive experience of black women, has white feminism failed to apply its principle of acknowledging the value of autonomous organizations? Although the mechanisms used to exclude white women and black people from participation in society are the same, it would be simplistic to view the effects of discrimination in the same way. As Hazel Carby points out:

> We would agree that the construction of such parallels is fruitless and often proves to be little more than a mere academic exercise; but there are other reasons for our dismissal of these kinds of debate. The experience of black women does not enter the parameters of parallelism. The fact that black women are subject to the *simultaneous* oppression of patriarchy, class and 'race' is the prime reason for not employing parallels that render their position and experience not only marginal but also invisible. (Original emphasis).[7]

As a result of the invisibility of the particular oppression of black women, the white feminist movement has ignored the urgent need for autonomous organization by black women.

Jenny Bourne[8] notes that radicals and white feminists have a tendency to play down the importance of the anti-racist struggle because this often does not fit into the traditional politics of the left. Feminists, although recognizing that there are people on the left who will not support a cause unless it is a white and male dispute, fail to acknowledge and support black women, falling into the same trap for which they have blamed white men over the past two decades. She gives the example of the 1977–8 Grunwick strike, where black women stood on picket lines for months confronting strike breakers, employers' thugs and the police. Yet the white women's movement did not offer solidarity to the Grunwick strikers until the issue became one of lack of union support rather than racial discrimination.

The exclusion of black women from feminist theory and practice has helped to marginalize black women in every aspect of life – including social work. This exclusion puts white social workers in an even more powerful position to interfere in black people's lives, a position that is reinforced by white institutions and white-controlled management.

Chris Jones has linked the strength of white liberal prejudices among social workers with the emergence of modern social work out of the philanthropic and paternalistic traditions of the Victorian Charity Organisation Society.[9] It was liberalism that produced a *same for all* treatment of clients, which did not recognize that different needs are produced by unequal power structures. As a consequence, white ethno-centric views have remained unchallenged in social work and at best, even among radicals, a focus on black cultures has become the way of dealing with black people. As Stubbs points out:

> It is interesting that, among social workers in Ayeborough, the most 'progressive' or 'radical' appeared to limit their understanding of the differences black social workers could make to precisely this 'ethnic sensitivity' conceptualisation of the filling of a cultural gap.[10]

Denney has also identified the preoccupation with black people's culture that leads radical social workers to avoid challenging racism and racist practices.[11] Although some social work educationalists, for example Leonard, Pearson and Jones,[12] have attempted to link radical social work and structural inequalities, even they have neglected the issue of race. As a result the structural, political and economic needs of black people have been at worst ignored or at best seen in terms of language and culture. Nobody would deny that an understanding of culture, racial background and ethnicity is important for a social worker in multi-racial Britain. But there is little acknowledgement of the central importance of power relationships and their implications for black people in the 1980s. Most social work education and practice, for instance, chooses to ignore the exploitive relationship between Britain and the countries of origin of black people. Yet it is difficult to understand how radical social work can escape the racist historical record and contemporary practice of British society. How can a social worker make an accurate assessment of black families and individuals without a full appreciation of everyday racial experiences in housing and employment, education and recreation? Charles Husband has emphasized the need to examine the position of black people in Britain in its specificity: '[only with] an appreciation of the structural position of black communities can social work begin to comprehend the specific consciousness of the black client.'[13] He further emphasizes this point, by stating:

> I am not here speaking of the awareness of cultural variation in an ethnographic sense between say Hindu, Muslim and West Indian families. The 'Isn't it fascinating' travelogue anthropology which abstracts the cultures of ethnic minorities from their location in Britain as a class society is positively racist in effect since it denies the unique experience of black minorities in a racist society.

The day-to-day practice of social work illustrates the need to confront the specific experiences of black people. For example, a social worker may be required to take on the case of a family with young children in bad housing conditions which is suffering the effects of parental illness or social isolation. Such problems often beset poor white families. In inner-city areas they increasingly affect black families, where they may well be caused or exacerbated by racial harassment, or family separation due to immigration laws. Social workers often feel that these problems are beyond their capacity or competence and they refer the families to voluntary organizations, or projects set up by black people themselves. When this approach becomes standard policy it amounts to a systematic evasion of racism and its effects by (radical) social workers.

In practice, radical social workers have avoided racism and structural inequalities to focus on ethnicity and culture. It is also the case that their notion of ethnicity and culture is employed in a narrow sense because social workers (like others in British society) have a history of looking negatively at the cultures of slaves and former colonial peoples. If radical social workers are serious about tackling racism, they must accept that this means questioning not only their own practices but also those of their departments, their local authorities and, indeed, the whole fabric of British society. If a white social worker fails to take up the challenge, then he or she will inevitably continue oppressive practices as a social worker and as a powerful white person. The point can be highlighted by a number of examples from social work practice in relation to black people.

A client may need to prove a need for assistance from the social work agency. Black women have to show that they are inadequate mothers or that they cannot cope with life in general. They have to demonstrate these 'failures' to a white bureaucracy that is part of a pattern of racial discrimination. A young Asian mother may be depressed, but very reluctant to join the mother and toddler group organized by the social services department. This may be for a variety of reasons, some of which could be common to white women. But it might be because the Asian mother is afraid of racist vandalism to her home, or racial harassment on her way to the centre, or racism in the centre. She might not identify with the mother and toddler group, as her needs will not be catered for unless the organizers fully appreciate the needs of Asian women. A white social worker might easily conclude that the Asian woman is shy and unsociable, lazy and apathetic, or that her husband does not allow her to leave home.

Radical white social workers tend to regard the family as an agency of oppression – a notion that is rejected by most black

women. Black feminists also reject the white feminist condemnation of domesticity, arranged marriages and extended families. The
major forces of oppression for most black women in this country
are institutional, personal and cultural racism. For black women,
the family can be a source of support and comfort in the struggle
against the problems of racism and depression.[14] British immigration laws divide black families and place enormous obstacles in the
way of relatives who want to join or even visit their families in
Britain. Immigration to Britain has the effect of disrupting traditional support networks for women, particularly in the Asian
community.[15] Black women have a long history of working and
supporting other women in their countries of origin.[16] The statutory and voluntary services in Britain provide little to replace these
networks, or what they provide tends to be based on a white family
model. However, black women themselves have taken the initiative and challenged the authorities to respond to their particular
needs. Unless social workers take a decisive anti-racist stand they
will respond to the needs of black women by confirming and
reinforcing racist stereotypes. Whenever white people (whether
working for institutions or not) have attempted assessments of
black people they have come out with a distorted analysis. Because
black people's ways are different, and white people cannot be
bothered to work at a proper understanding, black experience is
distorted and dismissed. Radicals are not exempt from this process:
there are many examples of white feminists visiting Africa or Asia
and trying to impose Euro-centric values. The result is research
studies that either romanticize black women or 'label them as
deviant':[17]

> I have visited villages where, at a time when village women are
> asking for better health facilities and lower infant mortality rates,
> they are presented with questionnaires on family planning. In
> some instances, when the women would like to have piped water
> in the village, they may be at the same time faced with a
> researcher interested in investigating power and powerlessness in
> the household.

Anthropological studies have been used against black people in
Britain. A range of examples could be drawn from evidence of
black children in care or from the experiences of black people
exposed to the mental health services and the criminal justice
system.

The stereotyping and pathologizing of black people operate in
two ways. Women are seen either as dependent and pathetic or as

aggressive and domineering. The first stereotype is characteristic of Asian women and the latter is generally reserved for Afro-Caribbean women. These stereotypes guide white social workers in making crucial decisions about black families. For example, if an Asian woman is not willing to leave a violent husband then she will be branded a typical Asian female who is incapable of independence. It is also worth observing that if an Asian woman can speak English and in her appearance does not seem to be poor then she might be refused help because she does not fit into the unwritten rules of stereotyping! On the other hand, social workers might decide that the only problem with an Asian woman is that she can't speak English, or is unable to free herself from the 'shackle' of her culture. In this case it is quite possible that she might be viewed as someone who is not in genuine need of welfare services. Such attitudes pervade the housing and social security services and even confront black women in mixed refuges for battered women.

Hazel Carby challenges the stereotype of the 'dependency' of black women on 'dominant' black men:

> How then can we account for situations in which black women may be heads of households, or where, because of an economic system which structures high black male unemployment, they are not financially dependent on black men? This condition exists in both colonial and metropolitan situations. . . . How then, in view of all this, can it be argued that black male dominance exists in the same forms as white male dominance? Systems of slavery, colonialism, imperialism, have systematically denied position in the white male hierarchy to black men and have used specific forms of terror to oppress them.[18]

The racist concepts of female dependency and aggression follow black women into employment. The pressures on black people to conform include the threat of being seen as 'disruptive' or 'dependent'; either way, the threat is particularly powerful when used against black women already marginalized through a racism underpinned by white feminist acquiescence.

Some social work authorities, including many 'radical' practitioners, argue that employing more black social workers may alleviate the problems of dealing with black clients. Opening up the social services labour market to black workers is important, but the terms on which people are employed are also crucial if a serious challenge to racism is to take place. The presence of black psychiatrists or black police officers will not of itself solve the problems of black people in relation to the mental health services or the administration of criminal justice. Pre-employment or in-service training is also a crucial area. Black people have to go through the same social work education and training system as their white colleagues and often have to prove in examinations and other assessment procedures that they have absorbed the ideologies – including the social 'blindness' towards racism – of the training institutions. Black social work students, in effect, have to prove that they can work with white people; there is no such criterion for white students. This is not to say that black social workers, once trained, automatically 'mirror' the outlook of their white colleagues. In reality, many black workers use their own experience of racism to perceive disadvantages common to black people.[19]

Black people, as workers and consumers within social work, could testify to many more specific instances of racism. It is a picture that is not easy for white radicals to accept, as several recent incidents in both social services departments and CQSW courses have demonstrated. In some situations, the response of white feminists to allegations of racism has been one of outrage and personal recrimination, leading to destructive ways of solving conflicts. The challenge facing radical social work is whether it can devise methods of fighting racism that are of real use to black people and at the same time ensure that white and black people can jointly overcome the structural inequalities of wealth and power that imprison both groups in a society that is not of their making. But can black people and white radicals work together?

Black and white people working together

There are examples of black and white people working together. Bhavnani and Coulson[20] have shown that it is not impossible. However, it is vital to define the terms of collaboration. White definitions of integration or assimilation are unacceptable because they mean exercising control over black people at the expense of black identity and independence. Recognizing the importance of black people coming together is an essential starting point. Black people experience all sorts of oppression in white society in the course of their personal or professional lives, including the crass dismissal of their thoughts and ideas. This is why it is imperative that black people should be able to meet and work together to reinforce their thinking and confidence. White feminists have a long history of operating separate groups to build self-confidence and coordinate forces. The black sections movement in the Labour Party is one attempt to organize black people autonomously.

The black population is not evenly spread throughout Britain, and in some cities with small black communities individuals may be very isolated. The pressures on individuals in such circumstances can be intense as they face the awkward alternatives of being used in a tokenist manner, being labelled 'disruptive', or being made totally invisible. If these individuals are identified with unpopular causes then they are labelled from all directions. In these circumstances, the question of allies becomes crucial for black women. White allies have to be found, not only to preserve sanity but also to get things done in practical terms.

Strategies of working together require genuine effort on the part of white people to listen to what black people are saying. One of the main complaints put forward by black people is that they are ignored. Another is that ideas are taken up but are used primarily to the advantage of white people. These are not clichés but real life experiences for people who have been marginalized in every sphere of their lives. White people who wish to work with black women must be prepared to listen, and accept that they have power that is not available to black people in a racist society. This is not to say that in specific settings the motives of black people should not be questioned, or that healthy discussion should not take place, or that ideas should not be challenged openly. However, a condition of successful collaboration is that white people should not set themselves up as the experts or set agendas which exclude black people. It has to be accepted that black women are not just the consumers of social services but are also people with ideas and identities and skills in their own right. White women have managed to work successfully with black women, but only where they have been willing sincerely to acknowledge their own racism and power together with their intention to share power.

For black and white women to work together on sensitive issues, it is essential to construct an environment that is trusting and not one in which white women exercise power over black women by making judgements and imposing values. Here are three examples from my own experience: the first was as a member of a management committee of a law centre which sponsored the establishment of an Asian Women's centre; the second was as a foundation member of a black women's support group; the third involved organizing an access course in higher education.

Asian women's centre

The first problem was that the centre was expected to serve a variety of Asian women who had conflicting needs. Because the dominant culture does not allow individuality to the minority cultures, it is often assumed that all black people have the same needs. Thus nurseries or refuges are set up where all black children or all black women are expected to 'get on with it' despite enormous language and cultural differences. In the context of the centre this also meant that different groups of women were competing for the few available resources, a situation that put a lot of pressure on Asian women. Local white women had the administrative expertise and the knowledge of resources, but they were unable to grasp the internal politics of the Asian community in that particular area of the city. Some Asian women took advantage of this situation by deliberately confusing the white women further. Other Asian women looked to the white women for solutions to complex problems. This did not just undermine the confidence of the Asian women but also placed white women in the position where they were making judgements and decisions about the Asian women and their work in the centre. This was a classic situation where white women were not just articulating the needs of Asian women, they were also defining reality for them.

Some of the more assertive Asian women got together and canvassed local politicians and other influential members of the community to persuade the council to find posts and activities at the centre. Meanwhile an Asian woman was employed to work with the centre, but she was accountable to the white women with whom she was based – an arrangement that was less than helpful. The process of obtaining city council recognition and funding for the centre took over a year of demonstrations and arguments by the Asian women. While a significant number of white feminists promoted 'womens issues' in the city they took no active role in supporting the Asian women's campaign. Other white women did help with organizing and lobbying work, sometimes on the terms of Asian women but sometimes too on the terms of their own agencies. In the end the determination of the Asian women won funding from the council for two part-time posts. However, the delivery of funding became the focus of power politics within the white local government structure and among white feminists.

A real improvement took place when full-time Asian women workers were employed at the centre and the management committee was composed of Asian women. White women have continued to play an important part in raising funds for the Asian women's centre and in helping with the activities. This is not to say that there are no problems in running the centre – just as all similar community organizations have problems. But, now that the Asian

women themselves have control, less time and energy are spent on
seeking approval from white women.

The centre for Asian women provides a common meeting place
where women can discuss issues and identify with other common
struggles. As the centre is situated in the middle of the Asian
community it is convenient for most Asian women as a place to
spend their free time.

A black women's support group

The second example concerns a group of black women who
responded to the local council's policies of racial equality by
organizing a group. They applied for funding and resources (i.e.
stationery and accommodation) from the city council. White
women saw this as an opportunity to learn about black women and
their communities, so they could work more effectively with black
people, though this aim was never discussed openly. White women
assumed control over the group as they were more accustomed
to taking minutes and negotiating resources with white men.
A background in administrative skills and familiarity with local
authority systems are themselves significant sources of power.
Although the group was termed a black women's support group,
the reality was that black women were enabling white women to
work with black communities. Black women found that their
involvement with the group provided the white women with
information and skills that enhanced their careers. Again, there was
extra pressure on black women to be seen to agree with each other,
while the differences among black women were exploited and used
against them. A good example was when the Asian women were
put in the position of being experts on every form of Asian culture,
and inevitably contradicted each other. Failure to agree was somehow viewed as a fault in Asian women. Black women were
viewed, admittedly mostly by the white men in the Civic Centre,
as middle class and not 'proper' Asian women because they were
not seen to be interested in sewing and cooking, but preferred
meetings and 'talking'. This was yet another problem that had to be
overcome.

The problem of 'social colonialism' was resolved when black
women decided to engage in a struggle to take control of the
group. After taking control and redefining the aims of the group in
accordance with the needs of black women, they exchanged
expertise with white women but on new terms. These new terms
stipulated that black women should form the agenda, write the

minutes, and make all the major decisions as a core group which met without white women in separate meetings.

An access course for black people

The third example deals with setting up an access course in higher education to provide a route for black people onto courses in a social sciences faculty. In this case it was important that black and white women worked together to achieve agreed objectives. As white women are often in relatively powerful positions inside white institutions, *they* need to push the ideas forward. However, this does not mean that white women should exclude black women from decision-making processes or undermine their expertise and views. Instead, white women holding positions of influence need to recognize that they have power and that they should place this power at the disposal of black women. They should do this by acting as the agents of black women who are excluded from influence in institutions. In this establishment of higher education, standard recruitment procedures were clearly inappropriate to attract black people from the community. An approach to recruitment rooted in 'reaching out' to people in the community was needed, and proposals for such (including an 'open day' in a community centre) were put forward by black people. In order for the new approach to be adopted by the polytechnic it was necessary for white academic staff to listen to what black women were saying and then support a new policy. Given the controversial nature of the proposed new approach to recruitment, the role of those white women who lent support became crucial, especially in encouraging black women who were facing criticism of their ideas from other white women who claimed to be anti-racist.

These three examples reveal a number of common features, and offer lessons for the development of successful partnerships between black and white women. The key issue is one of *power*. It is vital that black women retain control over ways of meeting the needs that they identify. White women, who do have power, must understand and acknowledge their power. They can use it either to give real support to black women, or to sabotage black projects, often by taking control away from black women. In this context, it is also important that white women clarify their own motives for wishing to support black women, and that they firmly reject any temptation to 'use' black people as a means of winning enhanced status or career advancement. The fact that white women may be acting as agents on behalf of black women is not due to any inability on the part of black women to determine their own needs and articulate their own ideas. The point is that black women lack power whereas most white women are relatively powerful and are therefore in a position to make change feasible. Finally, white women acting as agents in partnership with black people should not see themselves as social missionaries.

Conclusion

White women will often ask how can they help without patronizing. Men have asked similar questions of women. The answers are similar too. It is not our responsibility to provide solutions for white women; they must find genuine ways of support by examining their own practice, ideas and motives. All over the world black women organize themselves effectively and powerfully (the history of anti-colonialism ought to have demonstrated this by now to white feminism). White sisters should make a conscious and serious effort to understand the history and experience of black women. It's up to you sisters!

Notes and references

1   See, for example, Hazel V. Carby, 'White women listen! Black feminism and boundaries of sisterhood', and P. Parmar, 'Gender, race and class: Asian women in resistance', in Centre of Contemporary Cultural Studies, *The Empire Strikes Back. Race and racism in 70s Britain* (Hutchinson, 1982); B. Hooks, *Ain't I a women, Black women and feminism* (Pluto Press, 1981); Valerie Amos, Gail Lewis, Amina Mama, Pratibha Parmar, 'Many voices, one chant: Black feminist perspectives', *Feminist Review*, no. 17 (autumn 1984); F. Williams, 'Racism and the discipline of social policy: A critique of welfare theory', *Critical Social Policy*, Issue 20 (autumn 1987).
2   Williams, op. cit. (n1).
3   D. Denney, 'Race and crisis management', in N. Manning (ed.), *Social Problems and Welfare Ideology* (Gower, 1985); also D. Denney, 'Some dominant perspectives in the literature relating to multiracial social work', *British Journal of Social Work*, vol. 13 (1983). C. Husband, 'Culture, context and practice: racism in social work', in R. Bailey and M. Brake (eds), *Radical Social Work and Practice* (Edward Arnold, 1980); V. Coombe and A. Little (eds), *Race and Social Work – A Guide to Training* (Tavistock, 1986); L. Domenelli, *Anti-Racist Social Work* (Macmillan, 1989).

4   A. Smith and A. Stewart, 'Approaches to studying racism and sexism in black women's lives', *Journal of Social Issues*, vol. 39 (1983).

5   B. Hooks, *Feminist Theory: From margin to center* (South End Press, 1984).

6   Smith and Stewart, op. cit. (n4).

7   Carby, op. cit. (n1), p. 213.

8   J. Bourne, 'Towards an anti-racist feminism', *Race and Class*, vol. 25 (1983).

9   C. Jones, *State Social Work and the Working Class* (Macmillan, 1983).

10 P. Stubbs, 'The employment of black social workers', *Critical Social Policy*, Issue 12 (spring 1985), p. 15.

11 Denney (1983), op. cit. (n3).

12 See, for example, P. Leonard, 'Towards a paradigm for radical social work practice', and G. Pearson, 'Making social workers', in R. Bailey and M. Brake, *Radical Social Work* (Edward Arnold 1975); Jones op. cit. (n9).

13 Husband, op. cit. (n3), p. 72.

14 Carby, op. cit. (n1), pp. 215–17.

15 K. K. Bhavnani, 'Racist acts', *Spare Rib*, no. 115 (1982); A. Wilson, *Finding a Voice* (Virago, 1978).

16 Parmar, op. cit. (n1).

17 A. O. Pala, 'Definitions of women and development: an African perspective', *Signs, Journal of Women in Culture and Society*, vol. 3, no. 1 (autumn 1977) p. 10; also quoted by Carby, op. cit. (n1) on p. 227.

18 Carby, op. cit. (n1), p. 215.

19 Michael Hutchinson–Reis also takes up this issue of racism and social work education in his contribution to this book (Chapter 8).

20 K. K. Bhavnani and M. Coulson, 'Transforming socialist feminism: the challenge of racism', *Feminist Review*, no. 23 (summer 1986).

10 Challenging dependency: towards a new social work with older people

CHRIS PHILLIPSON

It is both appropriate and significant that a book on radical social work should include a chapter on older people – appropriate in that it acts as a corrective to the limited discussion about this group in other relevant texts[1]; significant in that the crisis faced by social work during the 1980s has been deepened by the pace of demographic change. Social work has faced a crisis over the past ten years in terms of the resources at its disposal and the environment facing its clientele. At the same time, it has also experienced a fundamental change in the type of services being demanded and the nature of the group making the demands. This chapter will try to identify some of the issues for radical social work emerging from the ageing of Britain's population.[2] It will review the pressures on social services departments and consider how these are affecting older people. Finally, it will examine the basis for a radical social work practice with older people, drawing upon both a political economy and a feminist perspective.

Ideology and old age

Whilst it would be wrong to exaggerate the impact of population changes on social work, there can be little doubt that these have played an important role in intensifying the pressure facing workers in the community. The welfare state, as John Myles[3] reminds us, is predominantly a welfare state for older people. Between 1931 and 1981 the number of people in Great Britain aged 65 and over more than doubled (from just over 3¼ million to nearly 8 million); for those aged 75 plus the rise was from 920,000 to just over 3 million. Apart from a slight decline between 1991 and 2001, current forecasts suggest a steady increase in the population aged 65 and over – by one-fifth overall – between 1983 and 2021, with significant increases in those aged 75 and 85 and over.[4]

The problem for social work has been how to develop a positive and constructive response to these changes, in the light of a political climate focusing on older people as a burden and cost to society.[5] Examples of this view came in a series of speeches, during 1983 and early 1984, from the Prime Minister. Thus, in explaining the rationale for re-examination of the welfare state she argued:

> . . . there will be a substantial increase in the number of old people relying on pensions and welfare benefits in the coming years, as well as an increase in the number of young people seeking further education. The working population now [have] to consider how much of their incomes must be allocated to this kind of expenditure . . .[6]

This argument was rehearsed two years earlier by the then Chancellor of the Exchequer, Sir Geoffrey Howe, when he questioned the readiness of today's workers 'to provide for the retired, sick and disabled'. Using the phrase 'nothing is for nothing', he was reported as saying: '. . . working people may have reached the point beyond which they would not be prepared to increase their contributions to the pensions of the retired.' There was, he suggested, a new 'affordability' factor to be weighed in the pensions debate.[7]

Phrases such as 'the growing burden of elderly people' or 'the rising tide of elderly mentally frail people' have themselves entered into the theory and practice of social work, distorting both the nature of the social work response and the worker's relationship with older people. Functional incapacity and mental disability in old age *are* a significant problem. Altogether some 900,000 severely disabled people live in their own homes, together with an additional 1,900,000 who are moderately disabled. But the fact remains that the vast majority of older people are *not* in need of care and are able to support themselves without assistance from either relatives or the social services. Even among those aged 75 and over nearly half experience no or only slight disablement.

But for those who do need help with a disability or for those facing a crisis following bereavement, the resources and forms of assistance available remain severely limited. This is due to a combination of changes in income support received by older people, and the nature of the social work response.

Support for older people

The question of resources has already been discussed at some length in Chapter 2. Here, we shall just summarize some of the most important elements in the current situation. The first point of note is that since 1945 there has been a deterioration in the economic position of older people (particularly those from the working class), with a steady decline in their financial resources when compared with the non-aged. Using the *Family Expenditure Surveys* as his standard of measurement, Thomson reports a decline from 83 per cent to 68 per cent between the early 1950s and the late 1970s in the average weekly resources of the elderly when compared with the non-elderly.[8]

This decline has been accelerated by a number of measures taken by the Thatcher government during the 1980s. One change alone – the substitution of a prices for an earnings index in the uprating of pensions – has resulted in a substantial loss of income for older people. A single pensioner who retired in 1981 is now £9 a week worse off (1988 figures) and a couple £14.40 poorer. Astonishingly, £750 a year has been taken from the incomes of married people with hardly any public protest.

The benefit changes introduced in April 1988 have been especially damaging to older people: first, because of the loss of additional allowances payable under the supplementary benefit system to those with a disability; secondly, because of cuts in housing benefits and the abolition of housing benefit supplement. Overall, around 2 million pensioners found their income substantially reduced as a consequence of the social security changes.

Finally, older women have been particularly disadvantaged by changes in social policy. The clearest examples are in the fields of housing and pensions. Tory housing policy has been to make decent housing more and more dependent on ability to pay. The break-up of the public sector is particularly serious for older women, with 40 per cent of female-headed households over 60 being either local authority or new town tenants.[9]

The government has also made a significant challenge to the rights of private tenants – many of whom are elderly. The Housing Bill, debated in the 1987/8 parliamentary session, proposed altera-tions to the rights of succession for private tenants. This will have a major impact on older women, as one in five of them over the age of 40 is caring for a sick, disabled or elderly person. Thousands will be faced with either homelessness or a new assured tenancy at a higher rent as the Bill reduces their rights to take over a tenancy when someone dies or goes into institutional care.

In the field of pensions, the changes to the state earnings-related pensions (SERPS) will have a considerable impact on the pension rights of women. Most important is the abolition of the rule under which 'twenty best years of earnings are used to calculate the pension'. Instead, it will now be based on the whole lifetime's earnings, including years of low pay or no pay. The exceptions are years in which a person has home responsibilities defined as bringing up children or looking after a person with disabilities, and people with disabilities themselves. This protection is weaker than the twenty best years' rule and penalizes mothers and carers who take part-time work paying above the national insurance threshold. Combined with a reduction of SERPS from 25 per cent to 20 per cent of earnings, it will on average cut the earnings-related component of women's pensions by around one-half.

In the light of the changes described above, it is clear that social workers are likely to be seeing both more and poorer older people. Two out of nine pensioners, in fact, live at supplementary benefit level, while a further one in nine exists on an income below this level. At the same time, the resources available to social workers to challenge poverty in old age are being cut back by central government.

The extent of public expenditure cuts was highlighted in the fourth report of the House of Commons Social Services Committee (1986).[10] Reviewing spending on the personal social services over the period 1980–5, the report noted that in real terms expenditure grew by only 5 per cent compared with the 8 per cent necessary to meet population pressures. The report showed that, over the period analysed, fifty-two social services departments had failed to increase real spending by the 2 per cent per annum traditional demographic growth allocation.

The attempt by some local authorities to protect social services has come under intense scrutiny from central government, particularly through the operation of the social services element in grant-related expenditure (GRE). Walker notes that GRE is now established as the main arbiter of local needs and services, and that older people are crucially affected by its operation. Yet he suggests that the GRE for the elderly suffers from five serious deficiencies: first, failure to allow for variation between local circumstances and local needs; secondly, the setting of GRE assessments below, in many cases, actual spending patterns; thirdly, the use of static assessments of need in situations of rapid change, fourthly, the failure to allow for the impact on local services of the government's own policy changes; fifthly, the use of inaccurate and inadequate data.[11] Walker concludes that, on the basis of this analysis, GRE methodology was adopted as a means of reducing spending in targeted local authorities, and that the GRE for elderly persons is *below* actual spending in a majority of all authorities.

The long-term consequences of reduced spending on the personal social services are many and various: reductions in home helps and meals-on-wheels, fewer local authority homes for the very frail and confused, limited budgets to modernize existing homes, and restrictions on social work time allocated to developing new social work methods and techniques for working with older people.

Alongside the restrictions on central and local government spending there has, of course, been a powerful drive towards privatizing aspects of care for older people. This is most apparent in the residential sector, which expanded from providing 18,000 registered places in 1975 to around 78,000 in 1986. It is likely, in fact, that the private sector will soon have outstripped local authorities in the supply of places for older people. This exponential growth has been fuelled both by demographic change and through the role of supplementary benefits. Government expenditure on social security payments for the private and voluntary sector rose from just over £6 million in 1978 to £460 million in 1985. Bradshaw and Gibbs note that, of this 400 per cent increase in expenditure, only about 70 per cent can be accounted for by inflation. The rest has been due to a 700 per cent increase in the number of people in homes claiming supplementary benefit, and a 200 per cent increase in the average payment.[12]

This expansion in private care poses a significant challenge for social work. First, it draws resources away from supporting people in their own homes, even though this remains a central theme in official government policy. Secondly, entry into private care is based not on any assessment of need but merely on the individual's ability to secure supplementary benefit. Thirdly, the pace of growth in a highly stratified commercial area (ranging from individual owners to large corporations) raises problems of control for individual local authorities. The resources available to social services departments and registration officers are, however, extremely limited – the latter invariably being untrained in the area of work and facing the additional pressure of interpreting relatively new legislation and a somewhat limited code of practice.[13]

Confronting structured dependency

Taken overall, the changes affecting older people amount to a strengthening of those processes leading to what Townsend describes as the 'structured dependency of the elderly'.[14] These include: the experience of poverty, the impact of compulsory retirement, the negative effects of residential care, and passive forms of community care. At the same time, it must also be acknowledged that social work has itself had limited success in challenging dependency in old age. Indeed, some would argue that its ambivalent stance towards older people is itself a factor in the creation of dependent status. Bowl finds a 'depressingly similar pattern of social work with old people'. He comments:

> . . . even in areas where most requests for help involve old people, these receive more superficial attention that those from other client groups . . . Assessment is frequently scanty and limited to consideration for a particularly scarce resource rather than of the all-round needs of the individual, whether it be assessment for aids and adaptations, meals-on-wheels . . . residential accommodation or day care.[15]

It could be argued that social workers are simply responding to events and influences outside their control. It is commonly argued, for example, that political and legislative factors invariably give precedence to work with children. Social work training will itself have supported this and conveyed a clear sense of how priorities need to be structured in the field.[16] However, there is a more fundamental reason why social work has had such a limited impact in challenging the dependent status of older people. This relates to the fact that the beliefs held and relationships developed with older people are invariably built around an element of dependency and marginality. This insight was explored by Carroll Estes in her study *The Ageing Enterprise*. In this book she describes the relationship between older people and service providers as follows:

> Public funded social services are more than systems for distributing services; they are systems of social relationships that reflect and bolster power inequalities between experts and lay persons, as well as between providers and recipients of service . . . [Moreover] services strategies in general, and those for the aged in particular, tend to stigmatize their clients as recipients in need, creating the impression that they have somehow failed to assume responsibility for their lives. The needs of older persons are reconceptualized as deficiencies by the professionals charged with treating them, regardless of whether the origins of these needs lie in social conditions over which the individual has little or no control, in the failings of the individual, or in some policy-maker's decision that a need exists.[17]

These characteristics are presently being highlighted in strategies for the social and health care of older people. First old age is being represented as a cluster of physiological and biological problems – the construction of dependency through economic and social inequality usually being ignored. Secondly, terms such as 'frailty' and 'disability' are being used to stigmatize particular groups of older people and are being used to define service eligibility. Thirdly, references to a so-called 'age explosion' are being used to justify restrictions in social expenditure (most noticeably in relation to pensions) and to suggest that an ageing population is both unnatural and undesirable.

Social work has, in general, found it difficult to challenge these perspectives. It remains to be seen whether organizational changes such as patch social work or specialist teams seriously alter this picture. However, the evidence from early research on patch[18] would question this. As regards specialist teams, these may themselves 'ghettoize' work with an already stigmatized client group, particularly where such teams receive fewer qualified workers (than, say, specialist teams concerned with children) and where there is insufficient training relating to work with older people.

In the light of the difficulties and problems described, what are the alternatives that might be developed by social workers? In the following section, some perspectives are analysed that might form the basis for a radical social work with older people.

Developing a radical social work with older people

Developing a different kind of social work will first depend on a clearer understanding of how dependency is maintained. In this respect it is important to understand how marginal status is imposed by older people being outside the major arena of capitalist productive and reproductive activity.[19] From a political economy perspective, this marginality will be differentially experienced according to labour market conditions. At the present time, older people are defined both as an expendable group in a context of high unemployment and as a potential economic burden given competing claims on public expenditure.

Marginality is also created through the inequalities generated by particular class, gender and race experiences. For the working-class elderly, for example, old age may be experienced not only as a period of extended poverty, but also as a time when, in comparison with those from middle-class professional occupations, there may be fewer opportunities for self-development. Old age, therefore, reproduces (and may indeed widen) class divisions created at earlier periods in the life cycle.[20]

How do these general points relate to developing a different kind of social work practice? First, they suggest that a challenge must be made to those ideological forces that help to justify and maintain marginal status. For example, older people are deeply affected (as indeed are social workers) by ageism, i.e. discrimination against the old (and young) on the basis of their age. Ageism finds institutionalized expression through job discrimination, loss of status, stereotyping and dehumanization. A starting point for radical practice is, therefore, the development of a non-ageist social work practice. One possibility might be for social work departments to develop in-service training programmes that reassess the assumptions and values underlying work with older people. This would comprise both an analysis of services and an examination of the attitudes held by social workers. Catherine Itzin's development of ageism awareness training provides a framework for such activity.[21] Itzin has devised a model where individuals, working within small groups, examine particular questions about the internalization of ageist attitudes, about relationships with older people and about how ageist practices can be challenged within the workplace. In terms of changing attitudes at work, Itzin writes:

> The goal of any 'oppression awareness' work *must* be to change policy and practice. Changing oppressive structures and assisting others to change the oppressive conditions of their lives is inter-dependent on changing attitudes. Ageism awareness work can and should be used as the basis for deciding on different, less oppressive ways of working. And, as eliminating internalised ageism is an essential [complement to] eliminating institutionalised ageism . . . awareness work should also be used as the basis for deciding on goals, working out strategies and then acting on them, individually and collectively.[22]

This work might be extended to examine how ageism is reproduced in different ways across the range of social work settings (e.g. residential homes, private households, luncheon clubs, day centres). Some of the principles that might need to be observed in developing a non-ageist practice include:

(1) the idea of ageing as a period of normal development;
(2) the positive social and economic functions performed by older people;

(3) the importance of using the term *older people* not 'the elderly';
(4) the importance of talking about the rights and responsibilities of older people;
(5) the importance of *listening* to what older people have to say about their experiences and emotions;
(6) the necessity of standing alongside older people, in some cases, where there is conflict with GPs, relatives or staff in residential homes.

A second element for a radical practice can be drawn from feminist literature and practice. The application of a feminist perspective to work with older people is particularly appropriate in the context of demographic realities. Amongst the population aged 75 plus, for example, women outnumber men by 2:1 and women are invariably the dominant group in many of the contexts in which social workers meet older people (this is particularly true of the residential sector). Yet it is noticeable how this important characteristic is often ignored or underplayed within social work practice. That practice is often about women caring for other women is surely significant. Indeed, as the work of Helen Evers suggests (in relation to the work of nurses), gender may be an important element in the strategies used by professional carers when managing their relationships with patients. She argues that:

> . . . in some ways women patients posed a greater threat to nurses' professional control of care work in the ward. The bulk of such work is so-called 'basic' care, a field in which elderly women patients have themselves often been great experts. The nurses' work is therefore open to criticism and sabotage by women patients of quite a different order than a potential male critique. Part of the nurses' control strategies included depersonalizing and devaluing the women to a far greater extent than men, whose identities were so often tied up with their pre-retirement work roles. The nurses often simply knew far less about the women, or ascribed to them the status of 'just housewives' or 'just widows'.[23]

Evers also argues that the deprivation of freedom of choice in hospital and residential settings is differentially experienced by men and women. Women are reduced to non-persons through the lack of control over the domestic round, an area that may have been a crucial part of their identity before entry into hospital or a residential home. Awareness of the importance of gender may thus help clarify sources of tension between the worker and older women and may also stimulate a more creative approach when designing environments to be used by older people.

At another level, ideas from the women's health movement might offer some important perspectives for working with older women. Central to this movement has been a concern to 're-define women as healthy [and] to replace the medical view of women as sickly and inferior creatures'.[24] The main themes of campaigns in the area of women's health (e.g. the struggle against sexist beliefs and practices in health care, the attempts to demystify medical knowledge, and the idea of women being in control of their bodies) have considerable relevance to all kinds of work with older women.[25] These ideas suggest that feminist approaches to social work with older people might accomplish the following things: first, focus on the naturalness of growing old as a physical and mental process; secondly, explore with older women the knowledge they need to manage their lives in an affirmative and positive way;[26] thirdly, explore new approaches to issues such as sexuality and intimacy for people adapting to living alone[27] or adapting to life in residential settings; fourthly, identify collective solutions to some of the problems women cope with in isolation from other women. These problems can vary from the transitions faced in middle age;[28] in the period around retirement;[29] and in the period of late old age, with the possibility of adjustment to a chronic illness such as osteoporosis. In all these areas, a feminist perspective might stimulate the application of alternative or complementary therapies to assist older people. For example, massage,[30] yoga[31] and relaxation therapy[32] can assist in helping women cope with a problem such as osteoarthritis, and the social worker may be able to play a useful role (along with other paid carers) in ensuring that older women have access to these non-pharmacological methods of treatment.

A third major area of social work practice must concern itself with the material life of older people. One aspect of this is the 1 million pensioners who fail to claim benefits to which they are entitled. Other key issues for social workers include the annual crisis over hypothermia and the impact of poor housing. On the former, it should be noted that Britain has the highest winter death rate among the elderly in northern Europe and north America, this reflecting both the high cost of fuel and the lack of effective insulation in homes. On the question of housing, findings from the 1981 English House Condition Survey show 41 per cent of elderly owner-occupiers living in 'poor' or 'unsatisfactory' houses (classified as unfit or in need of more than £2,500 of repairs) compared to 22 per cent of owner-occupier households with a younger head.[33] A minority of older people also experience deprivation of basic housing amenities. The 1981 census, for example, recorded 163,250 houses in which a pensioner was living which lacked both a bath and an inside WC; nearly 5 per cent of households with elderly people in them do not have an inside lavatory.[34]

An effective social work practice with older people needs to support campaigns on all the above areas. Some examples of good practice in relation to welfare rights include the work of the Wandsworth Pensioners Rights Project Association[35] and the take-up campaign mounted by the Greater London Council.[36] In relation to hypothermia, some authorities have mounted mass campaigns with visits to private households in search of older people at risk.[37] The London-based Pensioners Link organization has established a special unit to focus on the issue of hypothermia. Finally, right-to-fuel campaigns have been successfully mounted in a number of areas, these demanding: an end to fuel disconnections; a warmer and healthier home for everyone; increases in benefits and incomes so that people can afford sufficient fuel for their needs; and an end to wastage of natural resources.[38]

Such campaigns on hypothermia, whether led or given support by social workers, need to be part of a more general awareness of the way in which housing and living conditions relate to community care policies. As Rose Wheeler[39] argues, warmer and more suitable housing for older people will greatly strengthen the effectiveness of policies aimed at helping older people remain in their own homes. The implication of this is that a radical programme for older people would need to develop closer ties between areas such as housing and social work. Social work, as well as acting as an important source for referring people for help with housing improvements, might also provide counselling support during the process of housing repair, a period that can itself be stressful for older people.

A final area for action concerns the needs of elders from ethnic minority groups. This is an area that has at last begun to receive attention from academic researchers and, to a lesser extent, from policy providers. The findings from research suggest that black people face a number of problems in their old age. These include: first, increased susceptibility to physical ill-health because of past experiences such as heavy manual work and poor housing; secondly, great vulnerability to mental health problems, a product of racism and cultural pressures; thirdly, low uptake of health and social services, in part because providers are perceived as being unable or unwilling to respond to the needs of ethnic groups; fourthly, acute financial problems, with elderly Asians being at a particular disadvantage. The problems faced by ethnic elders have been defined as representing a form of 'triple jeopardy'. This refers to the fact that ethnic elders not only face discrimination because they are old; in addition, many of them live in disadvantaged physical and economic circumstances; finally, they are likely to face discrimination because of their culture, language, skin colour or religious affiliation.[40]

Social workers can play an important role in responding to the problems faced by ethnic elders. A starting point must be that black elders must be brought into the planning and development of services; this will be essential if questions such as the low take-up and rejection of services are to be resolved. Social workers must also look at the issue of developing services that respond in a more flexible and sensitive way to social and cultural differences. Specific work must be done to improve the nature and take-up of domiciliary services. Policies relating to the provision of day care and residential care also need to be examined. In relation to day care, Glendenning and Pearson[41] suggest that local authorities should consider the need to set up, in collaboration with local community groups, specialized day centres that take account of major ethnic and religious differences. As regards residential care, the same authors make the following points:

- The allocation of places in residential care should be reviewed, to ensure that black and ethnic minority elders are not isolated in a potentially alienating environment.
- The provision of recreational material and activities, food, sittingroom arrangements and religious arrangements should be reviewed to ensure that they are equally appropriate for all residents.
- Consideration should be given to the staff in residential homes to reflect the composition of local black and ethnic minority communities.

Finally, Vivienne Coombe[42] has identified a number of important questions to be raised about black elders on racism-awareness programmes. She lists the following:

- 'What percentage of ethnic minority elderly do you have on your caseload?'
- 'From which countries do they originate?'
- 'What provision exists for black elderly in terms of luncheon clubs, pre-retirement groups, or day centres?'

- 'Does your authority have a policy regarding the housing of ethnic minorities in sheltered housing? If "yes", what is it?'
- 'What would you like to see your local authority do in respect of residential accommodation, home help, meals-on-wheels for ethnic minorities?'
- 'Having determined which minority group has the largest number of elderly in your area, can you ascertain from that group what their needs are and how they feel they would best be met?'

Conclusion: dependency and interdependency in old age

In this chapter, I have tried to outline some of the issues that a radical social work with older people will need to tackle. In particular, I have argued that it will need to be non-ageist and non-sexist, that it will need to draw upon a broad range of therapies, that it will need to support or initiate anti-poverty strategies (in relation to both income and fuel), and that it will need to develop a range of services for and with black and ethnic minority elders. In terms of its core values and assumptions, much of this work must be around challenging those social, professional and political forces that contribute to dependency in old age. Principally, this will be achieved through the worker developing a partnership with older people in the organization and delivery of services[43] and in playing an advocacy role in situations where, for example, the older person is housebound with no surviving partner, relative or close friend.

This kind of social work should challenge the labels currently used to describe older people and question the type of resources made available to them. In essence, what is being proposed here is a new basis and set of assumptions in work with older people. At present, either social work operates through what are often dependency-creating relationships; alternatively, it pursues an ideal of independence that may be neither possible nor desirable for an older person to attain. The alternative proposed by Maggie Kuhn,[44] convenor of the American Gray Panthers, is relevant to this dilemma:

. . . we in the Gray Panthers are trying to promote the idea of interdependence instead of independence and dependence for older (and younger) people. We say that we cannot be human all by ourselves; we need each other. I have arthritis and I have failing vision and the two conditions are very complicated; they complicate my life and they could make me a housebound cripple. But I try to conquer my fears. I say to people: 'Help me, may I take your hand up this step or down this kerb.' I have learnt not to feel diminished by asking for help. Instead, I feel a new kind of reward from human love. I touch your arm and something happens, something that is warming and affirming. The person who helps you feels good and the person who is helped also draws strength and encouragement. We need to develop this interdependency in all our services.

Fostering the idea of interdependency needs, then, to become part of a new radical philosophy for work with older people. It provides recognition of the help older people need from us, as well as the rewards to be gained from giving this help. It also reminds us of the skills possessed by older people and the resources these might provide for activities and campaigns within the community. Most important of all, the idea of mutuality between young and old, worker and older person, might offer social work practice the basis for a new vision of how work with older people might be developed. This, given the pressures currently facing social workers, would seem worth exploring.

Notes and references

1   R. Bailey and M. Brake, *Radical Social Work* (Edward Arnold, 1975); S. Bolger, P. Corrigan, J. Docking and N. Frost, *Towards Socialist Welfare Work* (Macmillan, 1981).
2   For a review of the main trends, see C. Phillipson and A. Walker, *Ageing and Social Policy: A Critical Assessment* (Gower Books, 1986).
3   J. Myles, *Old Age in the Welfare State* (Little, Brown, 1983).
4   For an analysis of the impact of these trends on informal carers, see M. Henwood and M. Wicks, *The Forgotten Army: family care and elderly people* (Family Policy Studies Centre, 1984).
5   J. Bornat, C. Phillipson and S. Ward, *A Manifesto for Old Age* (Pluto Books, 1985).
6   Cited in the *Guardian*, 29 July 1983.
7   Cited in the *Guardian*, 10 June 1984.
8   D. Thomson, 'The overpaid elderly?', *New Society*, 7 March 1986, pp. 408–9.
9   J. Morris, 'A place of their own?', *New Society*, 25 March 1988, pp. 26–7.
10 House of Commons Social Services Committee, *Fourth Report* (HMSO, 1986).

11   A. Walker, *The Care Gap: How can local authorities meet the needs of the elderly* (Local Government Information Unit, 1986).

12   J. Bradshaw and I. Gibbs, 'Value for money?', *Community Care*, 27 August 1987, pp. 26–7.

13   L. Kellaher, S. Peace, T. Weaver and D. Willcocks, *Coming to Terms with the Private Sector* (PNL Press, 1988).

14   P. Townsend, 'The structured dependency of the elderly', *Ageing and Society*, vol. 1, part 1 (March 1981), pp. 5–28.

15   R. Bowl, 'Social work with older people', in Phillipson and Walker, op. cit. (n2), pp. 128–45.

16   C. Phillipson and P. Strang, *Training and Education for an Ageing Society* (Health Education Council in association with the University of Keele, 1986).

17   C. Estes, *The Ageing Enterprise* (Jossey-Bass, 1979), p. 235.

18   P. Beresford and S. Croft, *Whose Welfare?: Private care or public services* (Lewis Cohen Urban Studies Centre, 1986).

19   P. Leonard, *Personality and Ideology* (Macmillan, 1984).

20   C. Phillipson, 'The transition to retirement', in G. Cohen (ed.), *Social Change and the Life Course* (Tavistock, 1987).

21   C. Itzin, 'Ageism awareness training: a model for groupwork', in C. Phillipson, M. Bernard and P. Strang, *Dependency and Interdependency in Later Life* (Croom Helm, 1986).

22   ibid., p. 125.

23   H. Evers, 'The frail elderly woman: emergent questions in ageing and women's health', in E. Lewin and V. Oleson, *Women, Health and Healing* (Tavistock, 1985), p. 105.

24   L. Doyal, 'Women's health and the sexual division of labour', *Critical Social Policy*, Issue 7 (1983), pp. 21–33.

25   B. Burns and C. Phillipson, *Drugs, Ageing and Society* (Croom Helm, 1986).

26   J. Porcino, *Growing Older, Getting Better: A handbook for women in the second half of life* (Addison-Wesley, 1983).

27   R. Butler and M. Lewis, *Sex after 60* (Harper & Row, 1976).

28   I. Starr, 'Tackling the problems of adjustment to middle age', *Social Work Today*, 18 August 1986, pp. 14–15.

29   G. Fennell, C. Phillipson and H. Evers, *The Sociology of Old Age* (Open University Press, 1988).

30   G. Downing, *The Massage Book* (Random House, 1972).

31   'Yoga for all', *Nursing Times*, 4 January 1984.

32   H. Benson, *The Relaxation Response* (Avon, 1975).

33   Great Britain Department of Environment English House Condition Survey 1981.

34   Census 1981/Office of Population, Censuses and Surveys Household and Family Composition, England and Wales 1984.

35   Wandsworth Pensioners Rights Project, *Old, Proud and Poor* (Pensioners Rights Project Association, 1978).

36   C. Victor, 'How effective are benefits take-up campaigns with elderly people?', in Phillipson, Bernard and Strang, op. cit. (n21), pp. 198–216.

37 *Community Care,* 3 July 1986.

38 See, for example, the work of the Merseyside Right to Fuel Campaign, *Energy Action Bulletin* (May 1986).

39 R. Wheeler, 'Housing policy and elderly people', in Phillipson and Walker, op. cit. (n2).

40 A. Norman, *Triple Jeopardy: Growing Old in a Second Homeland* (Centre for Policy on Ageing, 1985).

41 F. Glendenning and M. Pearson, *The Black and Ethnic Minority Elders: Health Needs and Access to Services* (Health Education Authority in association with the University of Keele, 1987).

42 V. Coombe, 'Ethnic minority elderly', in V. Coombe and A. Little (eds), *Race and Social Work: A guide to training* (Tavistock Publications, 1986).

43 This is an important theme both in reviews of residential care and in general discussions of consumer perspectives in the social services. For examples see G. Wagner (Chairperson), *Residential Care: A Positive Choice* (HMSO, 1988); and P. Beresford, 'Consumers' views: data collection or democracy?', in I. Allen (ed.), *Hearing the Voice of the Consumer* (Policy Studies Institute, 1988).

44 M. Kuhn, 'Social and political goals for an ageing society', in Phillipson, Bernard and Strang, op. cit. (n21).

11 Health issues, social services and democracy: steps towards a radical reintegration

MIKE SIMPKIN

For radicals in the social services to take an active interest in the NHS may, to say the least, seem somewhat quixotic. It could be said that we have enough to occupy us without forcing our attentions into an arena in which we have not usually been particularly welcome. My purpose is to argue that such professional and political isolationism on either side, based on the traditional, defensive barriers between medical and social care, can no longer reasonably be sustained if there is to be any genuine attempt at meeting people's needs. Health and social services staff can no longer avoid working together either in institutions or in the community. Referrals and responsibilities have to be negotiated; agreements have to be reached about agency priorities that take account, not only of local, regional or national resources and needs, but also of legitimate conflicts of interest. The process demands that social workers cease the habit of regarding health care delivery as part of a separate, narrow and monolithic system.

Breaking down the barriers between health and social services cannot simply be a matter of internal restructuring of professional orientations. The NHS, and indeed local government, have been forced by Mrs Thatcher's Conservative government into a series of fiscal, structural and ideological crises in which any attempt to overcome historical divisions must also involve a political response. But the fundamental crisis has not been caused, only exacerbated, by Thatcherite policies. In Conservative terms it is represented by the fear, voiced in the early 1950s, that, contrary to Labour's expectations in setting up the NHS, the demand for health care could never be satisfied; its scope and costs would inevitably increase as standards rose.[1] For others it is not the concept of the NHS but its structure that is at fault. In 1979, Dingwall forecast an end to the fundamentally unstable social democratic compromise of providing free health care on a collective basis, while abdicating collective responsibility for the causes of disease.[2] The public has remained loyal to the NHS to an extent that was, by 1986, beginning to worry the Tories. Yet even the most blinkered professional has had to acknowledge both the increase and the incoherence of public awareness over health care issues. Those claiming a right to health also form a new market to be exploited by the commercial interests of private medicine and by the new health and leisure industries. This is the context in which new forms of health care have to be developed.

Both right and left acknowledge the need for basic change. The socialist case is that initiatives for a newly viable health service, committed both to preventive care and to negotiated priorities, demand political and economic change. They also depend for their legitimation and success on a changed relationship with those who use the health service. This entails a shift in the social relations of health care.[3] Such a restructuring of the NHS must allow for public support not only to be mobilized but to be involved in the re-creation of a service that is defined not by professional, budgetary and administrative constraints but by the people who need health, by all of us. This is neither just a piece of fashionable political rhetoric, nor the threat to the NHS that Conservatives would have us believe; new forms of individual and collective responsibility for health may well be the only way of laying the spectre of infinite demand.

Efforts to increase participation face the hostility of those in power and the labyrinthine information and decision processes of the NHS. They also have to confront that old bulwark of conservatism, alleged public apathy. Appreciation of the NHS can also be conveniently interpreted as satisfaction. But survey answers have to be seen in context; in general it seems that people are grateful for what they have got and are reluctant to give ammunition to critics unless they have strong individual grievances. Until they are drawn into deeper discussion, with the opportunity to articulate experiences that may be ill defined and to gain knowledge of alternatives, the availability of help may be a more prominent issue than its form or content.[4] Without taking such care to build up confidence, reforms that challenge people's accepted mode of thought will meet strong resistance.

Thinking about health and illness is clouded by elements of irrationality, fed by the processes of mystification and information control on which professionals often rely. For reasons that have complex roots, doctors remain the most highly esteemed in public mythology of all the professions; it is safer to mock than to

challenge them. The demedicalization of society may sound attractive in the seminar room, but will not be welcomed by those whose
interests appear, whether permanently or temporarily, to depend
on medicalization, as a gateway to such social benefits as exist for
the sick.[5] This is the nub of the matter. It has been politically and
commercially convenient to channel the upsurge of health awareness over topics like diet, exercise, smoking and general stress into
the realm of individual choice. But choice is partially determined
by the opportunities afforded by income and education. In addition, people often prefer not to think of illness unless it occurs, and
sometimes not even then; the positive promotion of health has a
worthy ring to it that many find unappealing. This is especially true
of those who are drawn to activities that risk their health as an
escape from an ever-harsher reality. Everybody faces social and
emotional difficulties in taking responsibility for health.

Changes in practice and in attitude should be stimulated and
consolidated by the development of theory. Doyal and Gough,
who identify health rather than survival as the basic human need,
have recently argued for the rehabilitation of 'needs theory' as the
only way of articulating people's often inchoate and contradictory
experiences and harnessing them in the direction of change; Croft
sees needs as changing concepts whose definitions are developed
through dialogue.[6] It is on this sort of basis that the barriers
between medical and social care should be dismantled and new
definitions drawn. Theorizing itself should become in some respects a democratic enterprise involving discussion and dialogue
over our changing ideas about health, illness and disease, so that
both roles and expectations can be adjusted. This is indubitably a
task with which social workers should be concerned and for which
radical social work, with its emphasis both on the social and
political context of services and on the limits of professionalism,
should be well suited.

Collaboration – a series of failed blueprints

Much of the history of the NHS is characterized by the tension
between a growing realization of the need for change and the
inadequacy of administrative measures to meet it. Government
strategy, dominated, through electoral fate, by the Conservatives,
has combined a series of rationalizing assaults on NHS organization
with an ideological offensive against 'unrealistic' public expectations. The government has shifted the duty of preventing illness
onto the population as individuals, and the onus of care onto the

community (in effect onto unpaid women). For a time in the 1970s considerations of effectiveness and equalization were given some priority (the Labour influence) but, both before and since, the predominant criterion has been efficiency. The evaluation of efficiency has been by economic and managerial criteria, though latterly the Tories have shown an interest in consumerism, again related to their boosting of private practice. Thus, despite a general recognition that the NHS needed to be flexible enough to respond to local demands, the tendency has been to centralize.[7]

Commonsense would nominate local authorities as the obvious candidates for partnership in the care the NHS cannot provide. Calls for increased coordination, first to provide continuity of care and then to promote community care, are nothing new.[8] Nevertheless, the services have until recently moved away from each other and it is essential for practitioners to realize how directly the resentment between disciplines often felt in the field is directly related to structural issues. The compromises built into the 1948 National Health Act confirmed medical power in a service whose structure and ideology have fettered and intimidated efforts to bring integrated health care into being. This is hardly surprising given the priorities of a society for which the comprehensive inclusion of health into social and economic planning would pose far too great a threat to vested interests and to profit levels.[9] Navarro has demonstrated how standards and services in the NHS are dominated by class interests,[10] and the definitional problem is further highlighted by the pervasion of ideas of normality originating from the nineteenth century that clearly depend on 'male-dominated cultural values and forms, which viewed female bio-logical processes as deviations'.[11] Issues of racism in service delivery as well as in NHS employment have largely been ignored. The achievements of the NHS are considerably offset by increasing evidence of its failure to make significant inroads into health inequalities as well as a wider recognition of the effects of iatrogenic illness.[12] The domination of curative hospital-based medicine appears increasingly inappropriate given the demands of longer-term care for the chronically infirm and the aged, and the unsuita-bility, even indifference, of the medical process and NHS organiza-tion both for these people and for those needing short-term care in normal life crises like the birth process.

Power struggles over professional interests and financial control have effectively scuppered most efforts at collaboration between health and local authorities, their fate mostly being determined, as Bill Davis has put it, in committees filled with senior officers who have reached their positions through paths that have often not involved collaboration at all.[13] This failure at strategic level has been matched by difficulties at the other two levels of collaboration distinguished by Sargeant – operational and case levels.[14] Much effort went into the *planning* of health and welfare services during the 1960s, only to be overtaken by the unilateral reorganization of social services in 1971, which, by separating social work from medical or para-medical skills, prepared the ground for the transfer of many community-based health services to the NHS in 1974. Furthermore, there was little to show that local authorities had either the interest or the capacity to respond to health problems, the failure to develop community resources under the 1959 Mental Health Act being one conspicuous example. Then as now the authorities were underfunded, but when in 1976 the International Monetary Fund demanded that the Labour government reduce public expenditure, it was precisely those services most needed by the short- or long-term dependent populations that were the first to be cut by local authorities.[15]

The 1974 NHS reorganization made collaboration a statutory duty in England and Wales. However studies of the health care planning teams and their successors, the joint consultative committees, have shown that, although there was eventually an increase in mutual understanding, especially at officer level, assistance and coordination were barely improved. This was partly because of incompatible structures and partly because of conflicts of interest. Councillors were seen as politically opportunist, while they themselves felt powerless.[16] The introduction of joint financing after 1976 did act as an incentive to some pioneering work, but the available cash was never more than 1 per cent of the NHS budget, and, despite changes to the structure in 1983, it could not compensate for the cash limit squeeze on local authorities. More disturbingly, there was frequently a dearth of new project ideas at senior level as social services departments failed to address the issues involved. The result is that funding has started to flow towards NHS-based activities. Radicals are likely to be disturbed at such extensions of the medical model, but more worrying still is the implication, as Wistow has noted, of community projects under the NHS umbrella coming ultimately under the control of the health authorities. These are bodies that, in Allsop's words, at present lack both visibility and legitimacy.[17] However, seen from the other side, scepticism in the NHS about local authorities is based not just on history but on current experience. The power of this hostility should not be underestimated as the *Nursing Mirror* 'No way Mrs Jay' campaign against the 1979 Jay Report on mental handicap services clearly showed.[18]

In the context of an under-resourced, inflexible and unaccountable service, the community health councils, intended by Sir Keith Joseph to be toothless watchdogs, have often stepped bravely into the accountability vacuum. It is a tribute to the campaigning power of their full-time secretaries both that the 1979 Green Paper *Patients First* proposed their abolition and that this was subsequently retracted because of their 'surprising popularity'. However, their funds are limited and they are almost always the domain of the concerned middle classes. Despite the successful activism of CHCs such as Brent, they are too often tied to issues of patient comfort, rather than mounting more fundamental challenges.[19]

To overcome the divide between health and social services, some critics advocate a full-scale integration. However, experience in Northern Ireland, where services have been integrated at control level since 1971 (in a brutalist process of 'banging heads together'),[20] has also failed to produce any model of success. Little more progress, if any, has been made in achieving collaboration.[21] There may be a theoretical reason for this overall failure. Tibbitt, using a general typology of collaboration suggested by Davidson, has argued that agencies have often approached each other using strategies of exchange. These are usually suitable only between equal partners and Tibbitt proposes that strategies of penetration may work better,[22] thus building on existing links. Local authorities have long relied on nursing staff, particularly in residential and day facilities. In recent years, more clinical psychologists have been finding local authority work. Conversely, hospital social work team leaders are generally accepted as members of the multi-disciplinary management teams and there is a growing interest in different types of social work attachment. It is at this level that collaboration needs to be effective, a goal that depends in part on the relations between the various professions and occupations.

Professionalism: cut-throat competition and blinkered isolation?

Although individual doctors sometimes complain of powerlessness, there can be no doubt about the extent to which their collective power is enshrined in the NHS, because ultimately they set the rules.[23] Medical power is buttressed by claims to exclusive scientific knowledge, the doctrine of clinical freedom, and most of all by the knowledge that every one of their critics will at some point be dependent on them. All these justifications are being undermined by new critiques and the documentation of the limited impact of medicine in effecting major changes in public health.[24] These pressures are beginning to render doctors' traditional relationship with other professions untenable. Huntington has aptly characterized the circumscription of social work practice in medical settings as 'the exercise of traditional, chauvinistic and rational–legal authority by a male and intensely powerful occupation over a predominantly female and relatively powerless one'.[25] When challenged, doctors have appeared hurt, resentful and hostile, often choosing to abandon the relationship entirely rather than adapt.

The result has been the attempts by different groups to develop alternative power structures. Social work broke away in 1971 and the power that it derives from its independence is still an important element in building up a network of alternative resources. But other groups like nurses, psychologists and occupational therapists are still trying to loosen the medical yoke and protect themselves by building separate spheres of activity defined either by location (away from hospital) or by quantifiable expertise administered by a separate management and professional structure. Nursing aspirations have been recognized by a succession of reports, the latest of which recommends a new generic training and a limited right to prescribe.[26] But each group has to struggle not just against medicine, but also to find an acceptable role vis-à-vis each other. This necessitates drawing new boundaries just at the time when the move towards a more humane social care is increasing the overlap of job content. Here we enter a looking-glass world as the interpenetration I referred to above becomes more prevalent. For example, as psychology shifts from the behaviourism that dominated it in the 1960s to extolling the virtues of 'non-specific' factors in therapy, it begins to sound rather like old-fashioned casework. Hence psychologists cross paths with social workers whose training has become increasingly based on task rather than skill. They also encounter an increasingly assertive nursing body, whose practitioners are often behaviourally oriented. As Wilding put it: 'Services are organised around professional skills rather than around client needs – because of professional needs.'[27]

Some change has also taken place in the medical profession itself. While some doctors have sought to regulate their responsibilities by a clear distinction between social and medical matters, the best and most humane have always practised beyond the restrictions of a biological model. The numbers of the latter are now increasing, as the profession attempts to respond to change; a minority are prepared openly to take up feminist or other radical positions. However, it is sometimes difficult for social workers to know which sort of doctor is easier to cope with. The first group leave us freer in our own sphere, but at the cost of a distinction that rarely matches patients' needs, and that can lead to destructive conflict. The second group are undoubtedly more sympathetic, both as colleagues and as doctors, but the spread of their interests means that medical power intrudes into spheres claimed by the newer groups, and can allow them to retain control. A professional training that emphasizes that full independence is the lynchpin of their status and self-esteem blocks adjustment to a collegial role;[28] eclecticism tempts them to claim leadership. In fact, as Baruch and Treacher comment, such eclecticism is often imbued with the very woolliness often criticized in social workers and does not entitle them to much more than keeping diagnostic or treatment options open.[29] On the other hand, those few doctors who genuinely attempt to let power go face real hostility and pressure. Animosity comes from colleagues who feel that they are letting the side down, and from patients, public and even co-workers who may shrink from the responsibility demanded of equals. The social position of the doctor, attained through education and class, reinforces this tendency, so that the doctor who surrenders the defences of professionalism without adequate support remains even more vulnerable to overload.

These discomforts demonstrate that the role of doctors in changing the balance of care should more generally be one of enabling rather than leadership. The wide-ranging capacity of medicine to determine and control health care can no longer be justified. As Wilding puts it:

> Doctors have persuaded us of two things – one of which is clearly not true and the other of which is dubious. They have persuaded an ever gullible public that they are the crucial factor in preserving our health – when they are clearly not. Secondly they have led us to see them as the crucial group in the provision of health services.[30]

If doctors were to abandon these claims, they might see their decrease in power compensated for by an increase in genuine rather than ritual appreciation. A less gullible public may make more appropriate demands on them, removing at least some of the unnecessary stress of the occupation. But subversion within the medical camp must be accompanied by a significant growth in the non-medical understanding of health and of non-medical practitioners bold enough to take on some of the responsibilities of health care without mystification or quackery.

Demedicalizing health care practice

Social workers have been prone to a narrow anti-medicalism that overstates our own resources and alienates potential allies. Nurses, on the other hand, have found that the sickness orientation instilled in training cannot be eradicated simply by verbal commitment to other models and goals.[31] If radical change is to be effected, it must be by a dual process both of redefinition and of creating a network that includes not just these groups but also others like home support workers, psychologists and therapists, and that is open to lay participation.

An American writer has suggested recently that the active seriousness with which social workers treat health issues can be gauged by how far they accept the (somewhat notorious) World Health Organization definition of health as 'a state of complete physical and emotional well-being', or whether, like traditional medicine, they see health as the mere presence or absence of illness.[32] Social work understanding of the Parsonian 'sick role' tends to be applied mostly in the 'specialist' fields of mental health and physical or mental disability. In the former, social workers have been keen to challenge the biochemical and organic models but, as Huxley argues, have often come unstuck, not least by treating mental illness as if it were distinct from physical ill health.[33] Not many are aware of the extent to which these models do not work for physical illness either, if the social context of illness and socio-cultural components in causation, presentation and treatment are taken into account. The way in which a society or culture is organized will not only heavily determine illness behaviour, it will do so in ways that maintain that organization; different conditions will have a different status; syndromes may be ignored when it is economically or commercially convenient. Contrast, for example, the glorificatory attitude to non-severe (and non-psychiatric) war wounds with the foot-dragging over asbestosis, leukaemia clusters near nuclear power stations, alcohol or lead poisoning, and race-related conditions like thalassaemia or sickle cell disease. Prevalent attitudes lead to a considerable understating of health problems. Studies of both physical and mental disorder repeatedly confirm the extent to which aspects of disease are simply accepted by their bearers, whether or not they regard their experiences as symptoms; this is particularly so among the working class.[34]

For an individual, the medicalization of health problems only comes at the end of a process that begins with an awareness of pain, discomfort or change; may include phases of denial, alternative explanation, seeking support and advice within the family or social circle; and may or may not involve adopting a sick role before seeking medical advice and negotiating an illness status with the doctor. Each phase is influenced not just by physiological events or individual decision, but also by social norms and expectations. Illness can therefore be seen as a social fact.[35] From this insight, the radical task involves developing the implications of health as a moral, not a medical concept,[36] and validating theories of health and illness as social, not biological constructs.[37] In doing so, it will be important to avoid two errors. The first is the fallacy, much attacked by organizations like the Schizophrenia Fellowship, of reducing illness to insignificance; to talk of social constructs carries the same risk of denigration as the phrase 'psychosomatic disorder'. This line of thought was responsible for discrediting much of the anti-psychiatry movement and undermining the trenchant criticisms of medicine mounted by Illich and others. The second possible mistake is to delineate health too closely. The WHO definition has the value both of legitimating social and political concern with health and of serving as an ideal. But we also risk creating an ideology of 'healthism', which could subject all our activities to a medicalized labelling process.[38] Moreover, positive notions of health can easily be associated with socially imposed criteria, and are characteristic of totalitarian politics. Health is the product of social, economic and biological conditions, and the concept can be used to evaluate them. But it is the conditions that produce health or illness, rather than health itself, that should be the object of struggle.

Beginning to radicalize health care practice

It is appropriate for radicals to focus on perceived inequalities in the availability and effectiveness of health care. Measures to reduce inequalities may achieve a broad consensus, in theory if not in practice. Thus Daniels has recently argued that it is fundamental to any concept of the just society that health care institutions should be governed by a principle that guarantees equality of access and opportunity.[39] However, the Working Group on Inequalities in Health, which produced the Black Report, split between the doctors and the social scientists on the question whether, in times of relative scarcity, the resources to achieve equality should come from the acute medical sector or from elsewhere.[40] It is also part of the radical argument that the persistence of inequalities in health is not unrelated to inequalities of working relationships within the NHS.

The Black Report suggested that there were three priority areas for collaborative action: for children to have a better start in life; the elderly and disabled who have to bear the brunt of cumulative ill health; and preventive and educational action to encourage good health. Most social service workers and managers, while agreeing in principle, might see only the second of these as being in any way relevant to their own priorities. Despite resource constraints, it is in the sphere of services for the elderly and disabled that some innovative work can be found. But collaboration is easily thwarted by conflicts of interest and the remoteness of strategic planning from operational reality. Thus in Calderdale the principal motive for medical participation in joint planning was 'to tackle social services about the elderly'.[41] There is generally a complete misunderstanding on the medical side about the possibilities and limitations of social care, whether residential or domiciliary. This is reciprocated by bitterness not just from social workers, but from home helps and residential workers, at the increasing number of medical problems they are left to deal with. These often result from medical inflexibility or deteriorating nursing capacity in the hospitals, as expenditure cuts take effect. The hospital 'Newspeak' that now calls discharges 'transfers to the community' adds insult to neglect. Only when the workers who are in direct contact with service users are enabled to play some part in the planning of home support, day care and respite, in conjunction with patients and carers, is there likely to be sufficient stimulus for change to halt such double-dealing.

Mental health and mental handicap are other areas that, in terms of crisis intervention, counselling provision, family and marital therapy, day care and normalization projects, probably have most to show in collaborative ventures. But even here there are major difficulties, for instance over the nature and resourcing of community care or the role of the Approved Social Worker. Again it is significant that many of the most successful ventures have been initiated from practitioner level, and offer very different formats. For example, the two mental health day centres cited by Huxley as examples of good practice have contrasting histories and emphases.[42] Brindle House in Tameside owes its existence to the support that a radical psychiatrist was able to find from social services and elsewhere in shifting his outpatient and day care facilities to a large house in his catchment area. From the start, the centre was jointly staffed and financed, with the social workers acting as a specialist sub-team with line accountability back to the area office. The workers – who included nurses, a drama therapist and a nursery nurse – were able to find ways of sharing, developing and differentiating skills that enabled them to carry out their conventional duties both accessibly and effectively. The project also drew sufficient commitment from them to overcome major hurdles such as the different pay and conditions that prevailed among different authorities and disciplines. But at Chesterfield's Tontine Road Centre – a social services venture in community-based day care, which was backed by the consultant psychiatrist – Derbyshire Health Authority pulled out just before it opened. Despite the initial trauma, social services staff were thereby freed to develop a democratically run facility with a genuine community base and in which user groups have a significant degree of control. They were freed to pioneer a fresh approach to mental illness work without having to cope with medicalism.

In the other two priority areas it does not take much thought to envisage possible contributions from social services departments, well within their remit, which might reduce pressure in some of their ordinary work. Some departments are already creating flexible day care and support schemes for parents of young children, although there are politicians and even practitioners who still cannot accept that such facilities underpin family relationships and do not undermine them. Under-fives work needs to be taken far more seriously: little more than lip service is usually paid to the support of childminders and playgroups, even though these are statutory tasks with a major role in the prevention of abuse and even in rehabilitation. In health care, such developments could range from resourcing (with workers, materials or money) improved forms of antenatal support and well-baby clinics, to introducing health care programmes in all establishments, for users and for staff. Another possibility is for social services departments to share or resource child health care for minority or stigmatized groups for whom access is a problem. Infant mortality rates for the travelling population are well above average, but in Sheffield a gypsy support group including health visitors, GPs and local authority social and community workers has succeeded in improving the figures through a concerted campaign both among the travellers and in the official agencies, which has resulted not just in a specialist health visitor but also in a jointly funded mobile clinic.

Many departments, especially since Jasmine Beckford's death, feel so deluged with child abuse referrals that they cannot even consider such work. Many staff feel discouraged from multi-disciplinary approaches by the unpleasant nature of many case conferences. These have often become processes by which the human needs of children and parents are transmuted, through the anxieties of frontline workers, into organizational bartering between agencies. Both parents and their closest workers often end up less recognized and more isolated than they were before.[43] Yet it is only by learning to work together at this level that appropriate, adaptable and flexible child-oriented services can be developed. Significantly it appears that authorities like Merton, which allow access by parents to case conferences, have been able to attend better to the group and power dynamics involved, making the whole process easier for those concerned and more realistic.

Working together in service delivery: advantages and difficulties

It would be both naive and rash to pretend that collaboration at practitioner level is easy; differing professional interests hold sway here as well and even successful joint work is often attributed by doctors to personality.[44] There are few precedents to encourage optimism about the impact of administrative change on practice: even committed critics of the present system such as Dingwall admit to pessimism about multi-disciplinary team work.[45] Hunt has suggested five common barriers to effective interdisciplinary functioning: educational preparation of team members; role ambiguity and incongruent expectations; status differentials; authority and power structures; and leadership styles.[46] This list is not exhaustive, but it is worth noting how in each of her categories there is a conflation of organizational demands, professional attributes and personal traits. Gilbert Smith has offered an analysis of the organizational and individual processes through which social policy is translated into action, with an emphasis on the corresponding stress of reconciling ideology and reality both within organizations and in the encounters between them.[47]

It is only too easy to get drawn into boundary disputes over such matters as admission criteria, confidentiality, or key worker responsibility. These quickly escalate far beyond the immediate issue, not to mention the client. The mismatch of expectations about roles, skills and resources often exacerbates conflicts. The result is that the received stereotypes of each profession become reinforced; health and social service workers become more convinced that their own security depends on separation, despite the fact that it is separation that either causes problems or makes them worse.

Yet, within a generally grim picture, there are more and more examples of schemes and projects, albeit mostly on a small scale and outside the mainstream, that involve social workers and community nurses or health visitors working together; many do not involve doctors at all.[48] If multi-disciplinary work is to be attempted, it may at first feel safer to remain within firmly negotiated and separate roles which allow some degree of independence to the different practitioners. However, an understanding of the changing pattern of health needs suggests that it will be hard to avoid some overlap of roles, a factor that sets the team the much harder task of sharing. In this context we should not be operating within our professional and organizational boundaries but at and beyond them. Our ability to undertake this and our security in doing so will depend not just on agency support but on issues such as gender or race, as well as ideology, skills and personality. This is the more radical agenda for collaboration, involving a subversion of the accustomed power structures. It can work successfully only where team members are willing to give some degree of personal as well as professional commitment to casting off their professional cloaks, and are ready to understand each others' vulnerability in doing so.

Some steps towards team collaboration

We have to start from a shared recognition that no one occupation or method holds all the solutions and that each member has much to learn from the others. Traditional strengths of the different disciplines – for example, the practical and observational skills of good nursing and the dynamic understanding of relationships and change on which social work prides itself – can produce complementarity rather than antagonism. Differences in intervention styles can be discussed, together with techniques and capacities for dealing with the anxieties they produce. Social workers can perhaps learn more of behavioural techniques in exchange for sharing the listening skills of which there is such a dearth in medicine and nursing. They may also be surprised to find out the extent of local knowledge among good health visitors or district nurses, who, like home helps in their own departments, often feel overlooked by social workers. Communicating through a loose team association is also helpful at bypassing the generally less than helpful NHS hierarchies. A sharing approach can help team members develop skills they feel comfortable with, as opposed to the limitations imposed by the occupation that they happen to have entered.

Furthermore, this form of work allows a team much more flexibility in dealing with demand.

Teamwork also depends on mutual trust, an essential protection for both teams and individuals against the stress that competing interests and unmeetable demands continually impose. In shared work, especially when a patient may be seeing more than one member of the team, there is a degree to which one's work is under continual scrutiny. It is important to recognize both competitive urges on the part of team members, and the ways in which patients or clients may consciously or unconsciously play on them. Such situations demand that respect is maintained within a context where discussion, criticism and disagreement are possible. Where work does overlap, there may be a need for clear contracts to be involved. For example, if counselling is taking place, the GP should not feel an unfettered right to prescribe anxiolytics without consulting the counsellor. Perhaps paradoxically, the team also needs to recognize that this kind of sharing and working out of role can be a lonely business. This does not matter too much when the team is working well, but it may be important for workers not to feel they have lost all contact with their professional peers, however orthodox.

A shared location is certainly desirable and probably essential for this form of teamwork, but in practice there are several difficulties. If, in the last analysis, control of the accommodation belongs to one group alone, any tendency for that group to dominate will be reinforced. Numerical balance will also affect dynamics between disciplines. A few general practices have tried to develop ways of collective working, but have been hindered by the fact that the collective cannot be recognized as such by the Family Practitioner Committee, and so the doctors remain formally as employers.[49] There are difficulties in integrating administrative workers or those attached from other agencies. Furthermore, the outside pressure against radicalism can easily drive collectives and cooperatives into introversion as they struggle to maintain themselves. Less ambitious attempts at ensuring regular multi-disciplinary liaison, particularly outside hospital, can sometimes provide a firmer base for collaboration by reducing the stress imposed by closer links: it helps not to have made too many enemies at once! But though proximity between workers can accentuate both formal and informal difficulties, it also provides both incentive and opportunity to work them out. Convenience, informal contact, growing familiarity with people and procedures, and speed of reaction are all strong arguments in favour of shared accommodation if the circumstances are right. Much can be learnt by having to answer the phones of colleagues from other disciplines. Moreover, for the service user, it is generally far better to have a range of services under one roof, provided that travelling distance is not unreasonably extended. If the building can also be used as a resource centre, so much the better.

To function well, the team needs a reasonably clear decision-making structure that compensates for inherent inequalities. This will be more complicated if the team has additional administrative or management responsibilities. Time must also be given to aspects of organizational maintenance, dealing with problems on the team and providing support. Patient care cannot be improved if the workers themselves become depersonalized, a major occupational hazard given the propensity of this sector of the welfare state for turning its beneficiaries (in terms of wage earners) into casualties. There should be joint training programmes, whether skill centred (e.g. counselling or assertion skills) or problem oriented (e.g. looking at how the team deals with alcoholism). Some qualifying courses already contain elements of multi-disciplinary familiarization, and there have been various successful efforts to bring local practitioners together. A simple model for such workshops was described in 1976, aimed at increasing familiarity between workers and services.[50] A second stop might be to use local educational resources to provide either topic- or area-centred training for workers in overlapping agencies, perhaps building on such in-course initiatives as described by Brake in his advocacy of topic-centred learning.[51] On a more radical level, such workshops could examine worker and agency responses in a critical and political manner, looking in particular at questions of power: experiments of this nature have been described by Banton and her colleagues.[52]

However critics are right to warn of a new multi-disciplinary 'conspiracy against the laity', in which the professionals tidy things up comfortably and exclusively between them. It would be heartening to believe that the very process of working together for the public health would inspire wider political alliances, campaigns and innovations that were genuinely patient centred. But it remains possible that such a realignment would take up so much time and energy that a concentration on internal demedicalization would still involve health workers in structures whose secondary purpose was to defend them against public pressure. Health is a public affair, and the public must be directly involved, if possible in training programmes as well. We thus return to the theme of a new form of dialogue around need between workers, users and planners and to democratic involvement as the key issue for radicals.

Democracy and participation

Despite the importance of health to each and every one of us, it is an area of our lives over which we have little effective control, especially in the treatment process. While there are real problems in reaching a fair balance of interests in the decision-making process, professionals and politicians have found it too easy to arrogate the relevant powers to themselves without any adequate justification. Even the exercise of the basic formal right of consent to treatment can depend on a right to information that is still not commonly conceded. Ironically perhaps, the greatest powers that people have are the negative ones of staying away or not complying with treatment, a defiance or neglect that follows about one-third of GP consultations.[53]

Such 'irresponsibility' is only one factor in the general collusion that limits public participation in the NHS. Health services, runs the dogma, are too important to be ruled by the vagaries of public opinion. Patients are seen as a stage army being wheeled on and off by shroud-waving consultants or populist politicians. For the Tories, participation is through consumerism, a model that is inappropriate and that bypasses issues of control. Labour favours direct elections to health authorities, although any such reform would need a great deal of groundwork to be effective. Nevertheless, the vast area where social and medical care overlap, and to which no profession has an unchallengeable claim, is territory that should be capable of definition through public and user representation. Here social work, while in the general sense being part of the problem rather than of the solution, does have both opportunity and some legitimation in terms of traditional roles and values to enable the development of such representation without trying to capture the dominant position for itself. This can be initiated in social services units by moving beyond the supportive role usually reserved for patients, relatives and carers towards some form of power sharing. This could span the range from open records to a democratic structure that takes account of the different interests involved.

There has already been some pioneering work, both with the physically disabled and in the field of mental illness, challenging the traditional definition of sufferers as incapable of responsibility. The inherently political nature of such an enterprise is illustrated in Italy by the Psychiatrica Democratica movement, which has even entered the electoral process. But the inaccessibility of NHS institutions to outsiders has meant that struggles about democratic control have largely taken place within and between the staff groups, rarely reaching public awareness. Industrial disputes, whether over pay, conditions or principles, highlight the lack of channels for communicating with patients. Hospital closures have provoked strong reactions and bitter protest from both workers and public but, with one or two exceptions, have generally been completed by the health authorities either through *force majeure* or by attrition. Links forged during such struggles have weakened for lack of any legitimate form in which they can be maintained.

Services in the community are generally also run from hospitals or some other central point. GPs are independent and self-employed, accountable principally to their local Family Practitioner Committees, which are perhaps even more remote from public scrutiny. Some GP practices have set up participation committees, but in 1983 there were only about eighty in the UK and about half of them fail for lack of commitment. Where they exist they often seem to have been helpful in improving conditions for patients, but they are also justified for their contribution to public relations and information flow – in other words, to practice management. This may be necessary to sell a difficult idea to GPs but hardly suggests a significant transfer of power.[54]

There are a few other isolated models, notably the Lambeth Community Care Centre, which involved local residents early enough to take part in the architectural consultations; some community health projects campaign around local issues.[55] But professionals tend to fall into perplexing tangles when trying to open up participation, the more so when users are geographically scattered and when their involvement with the services varies over time. In Sheffield, the Labour Council initiated an open Health Care Strategy Group, now an official sub-committee, which sought to rouse public interest in different areas of the city by convening local discussion groups. Despite limitations of finance and energy, these produced a good deal of useful information and acted as a forum for hearing perspectives about health that are not often expressed. Professionals also gained a chance to participate in the areas where they lived, freed from immediate work issues. With better resourcing, such groups (under whatever aegis) could provide a much more effective stimulus to activism. However, the authority did collate the information as well as commissioning an influential survey on health inequalities, which revealed some startling disparities and has provoked the refocusing of some services.[56] More recently, the WHO 'Health for all by the year 2000' campaign has helped to stimulate interest within local authorities in the new public health movement and over sixty are now affiliated to a national network. Liverpool and Oxford are prominent in the

'Healthy Cities' initiative, working on the three WHO principles: tackling inequalities, participation and collaboration. Here the health authorities are also involved; Oxford has developed both a charter and the basis of a local health audit.

Through developing an awareness of health issues, social workers of whatever description might be able to encourage and support the creation and work of local health interest groups at various levels. Women's health and the health experience of black people are two possible issues. Croft and Beresford, in their extended and realistic discussion of participation in social services, warn against trying initially to mix campaigning groups with those that are intended primarily to give users the confidence of their experiences.[57] The first stage would be to encourage the formation of such groups; the second, which could well overlap, would be to find a structure in which they could communicate with each other. Progress will inevitably be slow and uneven. Many people will only be interested at a specific time or for a particular issue; for the disabled, the chronically sick, the elderly, and their carers, isolation will be more of a problem than lack of interest. Local health groups will have all the problems of development and disunity that will be familiar to community workers; in particular they may be prone to promoting specific or sectional interests. But this will matter less if they can be woven into a wider network in which they and we can come to grips with some of the conflicts of practice, principle and priority involved, sharing the goal of promoting collective, democratic, positive and effective health care.

Probably the greatest public participation in health care consists of charity campaigns; socialists have often steered clear of these, arguing both that their goals are often inappropriate and that they detract from government responsibility to fund essential facilities. While it is correct to argue that such campaigns subsidize an already unequal distribution of resources, this stance risks a pusillanimous purism which isolates the left from public motivation. An alternative might be for labour organizations to assist in promoting schemes that offered the chance of building in some form of democratic control.

Social workers are well placed to promote democratic health care within their authorities, but they can also do so within trade unions. The unions must face up to a reassessment of their positions as care priorities change. Nalgo and COHSE have tried separately to develop positions on health and social policy, as has the Medical Practitioners Union (part of ASTMS). Given that resource problems are also likely to increase, there is a case for the unions, and perhaps the TUC through its Health Services Committee, to give more priority to the stimulation of discussion, both local and national, around the differing perspectives on health among their membership.

Conclusion

Health and illness concern us all, but I have tried to show how the concepts, the conditions that give rise to them and the services set up for them deserve more rational attention and involvement from social workers than we have often allowed. We can no longer keep our distance; the woolly thinking that, as Berry has recently pointed out, has let four competing models of mental health and illness go unrecognized as such among the left, must be shaken out.[58] I have tried to make the case that these issues can be resolved only by the development of a new practice at the level where health and care have precedence over economics and professionalization and where the problem of dependence is most acute. Such a practice cannot be achieved without beginning to overcome the formidable socio-structural and psychological obstacles to participative involvement, and there are signs that, with very different purposes, both Tories and Labour are attempting to diminish them. It is hard to fight for change when NHS expenditure is being so devastatingly reduced, but struggles against cuts, which I have here had to take too much for granted, are essential to the process, especially if longer-term goals can be kept in mind.

Lesley Doyal rightly states that the issue of health is one that can be used to draw people together. She goes on to argue that, because health objectives will not be pursued if they conflict with profit, as they ultimately must, the demand for health is in itself a revolutionary demand.[59] Again I would agree, but with a note of caution. The emotions and conflicts aroused over health are powerful and confusing, and render people prey to exploitation. Opening up the ideological aspects of health care is one thing; politicizing its delivery is rather different. Our aim is to enable people, perhaps for the first time in history, to own knowledge, understanding and control of their own health. The process will be slow, careful and often unambitious, probably reaching its goal only as part of a major social upheaval. None the less, in so far as it bestows power and dignity, sufficient to resist the forces that seek to blind us with complexity and to divide us, those who take part have the opportunity to make a more considerable contribution to change than may at first appear.

Notes and references

1 Infinite demand was forecast by Dr F. Roberts in *The Cost of Health* (Turnstile, 1952) and, although research by Townsend and Abel-Smith for the *Guillebaud Report*, (Cmnd 9663, HMSO, 1956) refuted the claim that costs had escalated in real terms, the dilemmas and tensions remain. See Lesley Garner, *The NHS: Your Money or Your Life* (Penguin, 1979).

2 R. Dingwall, 'Inequality and the NHS', in P. Atkinson, R. Dingwall and A. Murcott (eds), *Prospects for the National Health* (Croom Helm, 1979).

3 Lesley Doyal, *The Political Economy of Health* (Pluto, 1979); Bob Deacon, *Social Policy and Socialism* (Pluto, 1983).

4 e.g. Jeanette Mitchell, *What Is to Be Done about Illness and Health?* (Penguin, 1984), esp. ch. 2. Power over definition is central to Paul Wilding's critique, *Professional Power and Social Welfare* (Routledge & Kegan Paul, 1982).

5 Eda Topliss, 'Common concerns in health care', in P. Brearley *et al.*, *The Social Context of Health Care* (Martin Robertson and Blackwell, 1978).

6 Len Doyal and Ian Gough, 'A theory of human needs', *Critical Social Policy*, Issue 10 (summer 1984); Suzy Croft, 'Women, caring and the recasting of need – a feminist reappraisal', *Critical Social Policy*, Issue 16 (summer 1986), n. 30; G. Smith, *Social Need* (Routledge & Kegan Paul, 1980) demonstrates the problems of defining need independently of organizational context.

7 There is a mass of literature on policy development in the NHS. An easily accessible general book, with a good bibliography, is C. Ham, *Health Policy in Britain*, 2nd edn (Macmillan, 1985). Judy Allsop, *Health Policy and the NHS* (Longman, 1984) concisely summarizes various perspectives. Localization is the specific topic of S. Haywood and A. Alaszewski, *Crisis in the Health Service* (Croom Helm, 1980).

8 e.g. *The Guillebaud Report* (1956); *Health and Welfare: the development of Community Care* (HMSO, 1963); House of Commons Social Services Committee, *Primary Health Care* (1987). Alan Walker (ed.), *Community Care* (Blackwell and Martin Robertson, 1982), p. 16ff. Sir Roy Griffiths' *Community Care: an agenda for action* (HMSO, 1988) was published after this paper was written and continues the trend, albeit from a different perspective.

9 Colin Thunhurst, *It Makes You Sick* (Pluto, 1982).

10 V. Navarro, *Class Struggle, the State and Medicine* (Martin Robertson, 1978).

11 E. G. Mishler, 'The health care system', in Mishler *et al.*, *Social Contexts of Health, Illness and Patient Care* (Cambridge University Press, 1981), based on B. Ehrenreich and D. English, *The Sexual Politics of Sickness* (Feminist Press, 1973). See also Ehrenreich and English, *'For Her Own Good': 50 years of experts' advice to women* (Pluto, 1979).

12 M. Whitehead, *The Health Divide* (Health Education Council, 1987). Ham, op. cit. (n7), ch. 6. I. Illich, *Medical Nemesis* (Boyars, 1976); *Limits to Medicine* (Boyars, 1977); 'Medicalisation and primary care', *Journal of the Royal College of General Practitioners* (August 1982).

13 In M. Marshall *et al.* (eds), *Teamwork, for and against* (BASW, 1979). See also M. Hill, 'Professionals in community care', in Walker, op. cit. (n8).

14 Tony Sargeant, 'Joint care planning', in T. A. Booth (ed.), *Planning for Welfare* (Blackwell and Martin Robertson, 1979).

15 Tom Heller, *Restructuring the NHS* (Croom Helm, 1978).

16 e.g. Tim Booth, 'Collaboration between health and social services', *Policy and Politics*, vol 9, nos 1 and 2 (1981); J. Wright and F. Sheldon, 'Health and social services planning', *Social Policy and Administration*, vol. 19, no. 3 (autumn 1985); G. Wistow, 'Collaboration between health and local authorities: why is it necessary?', *Social Policy and Administration*, vol. 16, no. 1 (spring 1982).

17 G. Wistow, 'Keeping it in the health service', *Social Services Insight*, vol. 1, no. 15, 12–19 April 1986; Allsop, op. cit. (n7), p. 140.

18 *Report of the Committee of Enquiry into Mental Handicap Nursing and Care*, (Cmnd 7468, HMSO, 1979). *Nursing Mirror*, 15 March 1979, 7 June 1979.

19 Garner, op. cit. (n1), ch. 8.

20 J. Tibbitt, 'Health and personal social services in the UK: interorganisational behaviour and service development', in A. Williamson and G. Room (eds), *Health and Welfare States of Britain* (Heinemann, 1983).

21 D. Birrell and A. Williamson, 'Northern Ireland's integrated health and personal social services structure', in Williamson and Room, op. cit. (n20); M. Connolly, 'Has integration worked?', in *Health Care UK 1985* (Chartered Institute of Public Finance and Accountancy, 1985).

22 Tibbitt, op. cit. (n20); S. M. Davidson, 'Planning and coordination of social services in multi-organisational contexts', *Social Services Review* vol. 50, no. 1 (1976).

23 Haywood and Alaszewski, op. cit. (n7) ch. 7, using a definition of power from S. Lukes, *Power – a radical view* (Macmillan, 1974).

24 T. McKeown, *The Role of Medicine* (Blackwell, 1979); R. Dubos, *The Mirage of Health* (Anchor, 1959).

25 June Huntington, *Social Work and General Medical Practice* (Allen & Unwin, 1981), ch. 1.

26 *Cumberledge Report* (HMSO, 1986). For earlier reports (Salmon and Briggs), see B. Watkin, *Documents on Health and Social Services* (Methuen, 1975). P. Bywaters and T. Clay, 'The future for social work and nursing', *Social Work Today*, vol. 18, no. 28, 16 March 1987.

27 Wilding, op. cit. (n4), p. 26.

28 Paul Atkinson, 'The production of medical practitioners', in P. Atkinson *et al.*, op. cit. (n2), p. 82.

29 G. Baruch and A. Treacher, *Psychiatry Observed* (Routledge & Kegan Paul, 1978), pt 4.

30 Wilding, op. cit. (n4), p. 57.

31 A finding of the Jay Report, (Cmnd 7648, HMSO, 1979).
32 H. Pehr, 'Medical care organisation and the social services connection', *Health and Social Work*, vol. 10, no. 4 (Fall 1985).
33 P. Huxley, *Social Work Practice and Mental Health* (Community Care/Gower, 1985). See also P. Sedgwick, *Psychopolitics* (Pluto, 1982).
34 See, for example, Agnes Miles, 'The social content of health', in Brearley *et al.*, op. cit. (n5); Allsop, op. cit. (n7); M. Blaxter and E. Patterson, *Mothers and Daughters* (Heinemann Educational, 1982).
35 R. Fitzgerald *et al.*, *The Experience of Illness* (Tavistock, 1984). For the literature in and beyond the Parsonian tradition see Doyal, op. cit. (n3); See also D. Mechanic, *Medical Sociology* (Free Press, 1976); L. Eisenberg *et al.*, *The Relevance of Social Science for Medicine* (Reidel, 1981); Mishler, op. cit. (n11); A. L. Caplan *et al.*, *Concepts of Health and Disease* (Addison-Wesley, 1981); for a brief summary see Kate Robinson, 'What is health?', in J. Clark and J. Henderson (eds), *Community Health* (Churchill Livingstone, 1983).
36 R. Dingwall, *Aspects of Illness* (Martin Robertston, 1976) especially ch. 4.
37 Mishler, op. cit. (n11), ch. 6; R. Totman, *The Social Causes of Illness* (Souvenir, 1979).
38 H. Radder, 'Alternative medicine: analysis of a Dutch controversy', *Radical Philosophy*, vol. 41 (autumn 1985); R. Crawford, 'Healthism and the medicalisation of everyday life', *International Journal of Health Services*, vol. 10 (1980), pp. 365–88.
39 N. Daniels, *Just Health Care* (Cambridge University Press, 1985).
40 P. Townsend and N. Davison (eds), *Inequalities in Health: the Black Report* (Penguin, 1982), p. 29.
41 Booth, op. cit. (n16), p. 35.
42 Huxley, op. cit. (n33), Appendix.
43 I owe this point to Kath Butler.
44 M. Jefferys and H. Sachs, *Rethinking General Practice* (Tavistock, 1983), ch. 7. A. Clare and R. Corney (eds), *Social Work and Primary Health Care* (Academic Press, 1982) covers a wide field; a very basic introduction to collaborative work is given in A. Rushton and P. Davies, *Social Work and Health Care* (Heinemann/Community Care, 1984).
45 R. Dingwall, 'Problems of teamwork in primary care', in S. Lonsdale, A. Webb and T. L. Briggs (eds), *Teamwork in the Personal Social Services and Health Care* (Croom Helm, 1980), reprinted in Clare and Corney, op. cit. (n44).
46 M. Hunt 'Possibilities and problems of interdisciplinary teamwork', in Marshall *et al.*, op. cit. (n13); also in Clark and Henderson, op. cit. (n35).
47 Gilbert Smith, 'Professional ideology in social policy', *Sociological Review*, vol. 25, no. 4 (1977). It is worth speculating to what extent application of the unitary approach would be helpful: for developments in an FSU see D. Holdsworth and M. Wardle. *Teamwork and the Development of a Unitary Approach* (Routledge & Kegan Paul, 1981).

48 By chance, as I was writing this, a single non-specialized issue of *Community Care* (no. 610, 8 May 1986) contained descriptions of three such projects.

49 Difficulties at one such practice are described by B. Briggs, 'Abolishing a medical hierarchy', *Critical Social Policy*, Issue 12 (spring 1985).

50 L. Payne, 'Interdisciplinary experiment', *Social Work Today*, vol. 6l, no. 22, 5 February 1976.

51 M. Brake, 'Topic-centred curricula in social work education', in R. Bailey and P. Lee (eds), *Theory and Practice in Social Work* (Blackwell, 1982).

52 R. Banton, P. Clifford, S. Frosh, J. Lousada and J. Rosenthall, *The Politics of Mental Health* (Macmillan, 1985), ch. 4.

53 J. Thompson, 'Compliance', in Fitzgerald *et al.*, op. cit. (n35).

54 A. Hutton and S. Robins, 'What the patient wants from patient participation', *Journal of the Royal College of General Practitioners*, vol. 35, no. 2 (March 1985). R. Mann, *British Medical Journal*, no. 290 (1985), pp. 209–11.

55 *The Guardian*, 'Society Tomorrow', 9 April 1986. Liz McShane, 'Health services in working class areas', *Critical Social Policy*, Issue 14 (winter 1985). The Community Health Initiatives Resource Unit Newsletter is available from 26 Bedford Square, London WC1B 3HU.

56 People's Campaign for Health, *Sheffield's Health: could we care less?* (1985). Sheffield Council now advocates direct local authority control. See A. Wigfield, 'The case for reform', *Social Services Insight*, vol. 1, no. 34, 23 August 1986.

57 P. Beresford and S. Croft, *Whose Welfare?* (Lewis Cohen Urban Studies, 1986). The London Health Democratisation Campaign has prepared a charter supported by many organizations concerned with health and available from Health Rights, 344 South Lambeth Road, London SW8 1UQ.

58 D. Berry, 'Last days of the asylum', *New Statesman*, 10 January 1986.

59 Doyal, op. cit. (n3), p. 297.

12   *Residential care: what hope for the future?*

BRUCE SENIOR

This chapter has two main aims. One is to contribute to a further understanding of residential care and the key role it plays in the personal social services. The second is to argue that residential care can be a progressive activity. This is an unfashionable and minority view. As others have pointed out,[1] condemnation of residential care is one of the few issues on which all points of the political spectrum unite. Most critics discuss care as damaging and oppressive, regardless of whether these are contingent or necessary features of institutional life.

When the former Social Services Secretary Sir Keith Joseph rhetorically asked a conference on residential work: 'Your old people would rather not be in residential homes, wouldn't they?'[2] he appealed to a prejudice widely held among social service workers, commentators and the public at large. He could have referred to any client group and expected agreement. The well-known critiques by Goffman[3] and Townsend[4] have done much to establish this consensus on the negative effects of residential care. Studies attempting to assert the positive value of institutional care[5] have not won widespread popularity or approval. Why then is the place of residential care in the personal social services still worthy of debate? Is it not finally being crushed by the twin forces of government spending policies and the all-embracing enthusiasm for community care? Three reasons are suggested here for continuing the debate on residential care.

First, there are signs of cautious re-awakening of interest in the role residential care can play in relieving the heavy weight placed on women carers by community care policies.[6] Secondly, residential care remains a key construct in major social policy debates. Analysis of residential care can reveal much about more frequently discussed aspects of welfare. For instance, negative perceptions of institutional care have been central to the ideologies of familialism and community care. Finally, radical developments have taken place in local authority residential care over the past decade – developments that not only are valuable in themselves, but are also relevant to other forms of service delivery. For example, experiments with collective forms of organization in residential work may provide useful models for those engaged in decentralized community social work.

Although this chapter focuses on residential care of older people and of children and young people, the main areas of discussion are applicable to all client groups. Particular emphasis is placed on the organizational and managerial aspects of residential care; it is argued that these are neglected in the relevant literature and hold the key to progressive practice in this impoverished area of social work.

Before discussing these points in greater detail it is necessary to locate local authority residential provision in its historical and ideological context.

Roots of residential care

Histories of residential care often identify the Victorian workhouse system as the progenitor of contemporary residential provision.[7] The continuing relevance of the workhouse system lies not just in the buildings or in the memories of older people, but also in the administrative arrangements it established.

In his detailed study of the Victorian workhouse, Crowther argues that the system was based on the principles of deterrence and refuge.[8] The regime of the workhouse was harsh and unpleasant in order to deter all but the most desperate from entry. Townsend quotes an Assistant Commissioner of the Poor Law; 'Our object is to . . . establish therein a discipline so severe and repulsive as to make them a terror to the poor and prevent them from entering'.[9] At the same time, the workhouse provided refuge for the ailing and helpless.[10] This apparent contradiction at the heart of the workhouse system was in practice resolved by emphasizing the deterrent function.

The 1834 Poor Law Amendment Act, which established the deterrent workhouse, aimed to reduce the supposed drain on the wealth of property owners imposed by the system of outdoor relief. The Poor Law Commissioners concluded that the cost of misconduct, laziness and extravagance fell 'not on the guilty person or his family, but on the proprietors of the lands and houses encumbered by his settlement'.[11] The solution was to pay relief only on entry to the workhouse. The operation of the nineteenth-century poor law reveals the driving force of capital in shaping the nature of residential provision. Later in the century, it became more difficult to sustain the deterrent character of the workhouse. Massive unemployment and mass popular defiance, as well as growing reformist criticism, undermined the workhouse regime. Nevertheless it survived, not least because of the realization that 'any effort to make public institutions more comfortable was bound to be expensive'.[12]

According to neo–Marxist analysis, the capitalist state performs two basic and contradictory functions: 'the state must try to maintain or create the conditions in which profitable capital accumulation is possible. However, the state must also try to maintain or create the conditions for social harmony'.[13] The history of the workhouse system reveals the early signs of this contradiction between accumulation and legitimation. The deterrent regime, designed to rectify the drain on private capital by the system of outdoor relief, was implemented by a recognizably modern welfare bureaucracy: the Poor Law Commission. From this time on, residential institutions played an increasingly important role in the social control of the poor and of other unproductive groups. The residential institution became a crucial vehicle for pacifying and controlling those whom Offe describes as 'engaging in deviant, criminal, or other kinds of behaviour that are considered incompatible with the orderly pursuit of surplus-value production'.[14]

Residential institutions have often proclaimed their commitment to 'treatment' or 'rehabilitation', images that have facilitated the legitimation functions of the welfare state. The primary purpose of the residential institution, however, has been to contain potential threats and thus to enhance the pursuit of accumulation. This control function is not confined to those inside the institution: the central aim of the deterrent principle is to keep potential inmates out of residential care. The persistence of the deterrent principle partly explains the longevity of the 'poor law' character of much state residential care, despite the years of rhetoric and the goodwill and energy of thousands of workers.

Parents, carers in the community and social workers still use the spectre of public sector residential care as a warning to troublesome younger and older people of what might befall them. How many older people put up with miserable treatment by their relatives because of the fear of residential care as the alternative? There is a long-established class division in the use of residential services. Residential care is provided by the state for the working class and is thought generally to be shunned wherever possible; yet residential care in the private sector has been a highly prized resource (particularly in education) for people with large disposable incomes. Many poverty-stricken and harassed parents in the inner city would dearly love to have their children off their hands during term time, knowing they were receiving a useful education. The success of the British public school in producing generations of 'leaders' can in part be attributed to the efficiency of residential living.

One crucial difference between the private education system and local authority residential care is, of course, that the former represents the first choice of parents while the latter is thought to be no choice at all. In fact the dismissal of institutional care as the eternal second best is simplistic. Residential care provokes images of ageing and death, deprivation and poverty, and the disruption of idealized family life. So when social workers and others say, 'I would never want my child/mother to be in a home', they are often talking about the circumstances that might make residential care an option, rather than making a thoughtful appraisal of the potential of good residential care in very complex and often desperate circumstances. Residential care has been used as a deterrent and as a means of social control, but as with all forms of welfare it contains contradictory aspects. Residential workers can provide a progressive dimension to their particular area of expertise, just as much (or as little) as field social workers can in theirs.

One of the paradoxes of residential provision is that, even while few people would say they would want their friends or family to enter an institution, residential establishments became in the nineteenth century, and still remain, a tangible sign of doing good. As Crowther expresses the point: 'institutions had an inexhaustible sentimental appeal. They were visible signs that charity was "doing good"; the best of them were clean, orderly, fit for ladies to visit, and quite unlike the homes of the poor.'[15] This view remains today: local authority homes have minibuses provided by well-known charities, the name proudly emblazoned on the side to the acute embarrassment of all who ride within. Plaques are prominently displayed in the entrance halls commemorating the opening by some soon-forgotten local dignatory. Residential homes are monuments that prove to the world that the state cares for the poor, deprived and needy. Later we discuss whether this historic role of the local authority residential institution is changing.

The residential institution in welfare ideology

One of the central strands of welfare ideology is concerned with the family and the family's willingness and ability to care for its own.

Ann Davis argues that 'it is possible to trace a concern with reinforcing the family's responsibility for caring for its dependent and incapacitated members through almost four centuries of social legislation'.[16] She maintains that the deterrent regime of the workhouse was a major means 'of reinforcing the notion of family responsibility in nineteenth century England',[17] and that this deterrent aspect of residential care is a key aspect of contemporary provision.

The most recent manifestation of the concern of the state to reinforce the ideology of family care (for 'family' read 'women'[18]) is the much-heralded 'community care' debate. The deterrent function of residential care is a key construct in the ideologies of community care and family care. The vacuous nature of the notion of community is now widely accepted. Less frequently acknowledged is the centrality of residential provision to the notion of care in the community. Alan Walker defines community care as 'help and support given to individuals . . . in non-institutionalised settings'.[19] Community care is thus defined as the absence of residential care (and presumably day care as well). Even if residential homes are implicitly being distinguished here from institutions, the effect is the same: to make negative comparisons between residential care and community care. As Cohen writes, 'the contrast is between the good community – open, benevolent, accepting, – and the bad institution – damaging, rejecting, stigmatizing'.[20]

The stereotypical view of residential care as overwhelmingly negative fuels the mythology of community and community care. If local authority residential care was perceived as a positive resource, the ideologies of the family and community would be drastically weakened. Hence residential provision in the public sector cannot be improved without undermining these dominant ideologies. The state's emphasis on the family as the proper source and location of caring legitimizes both state inaction in terms of welfare provision and the actions of the state in 'punishing' recalcitrant families who do not adequately care for their members. Residential care, of course, has played a key role in stigmatizing the recipients of its services.

Having located residential provision in its historical and ideological context we can appreciate the dimensions of its negative image. Before considering how this might be replaced with a more constructive perspective, it will be useful to examine changes in the rhetoric and practice of residential provision in the era of Thatcherism. Two significant trends are immediately apparent: the great expansion of private residential care for older people and the decline in residential care for children and young people.

Private residential care for older people

In 1976, 2,561 local authority homes in England provided accommodation for just over 99,000 people aged over 65; in the same year, 1,769 private establishments provided for just over 21,000 residents. By 1980, 2,638 local authority homes provided for just over 102,000 people aged over 65; in the same year 2,278 private establishments provided for just under 29,000 people.[21] Local authority provision in terms of homes and people accommodated has remained remarkably static since 1976, and since 1982 the number of residents has actually declined. The number of people over 65 in voluntary homes is also fairly static. This rose from under 24,000 in 1976 to over 26,000 in the early 1980s, but in 1985 declined again to less than 26,000. This contrasts markedly with the private sector: between 1980 and 1985 provision more than doubled. In 1985, 5,200 homes accommodated more than 66,000 people over 65.[22] The forecast that private residential care will exceed that in the public sector by the end of the decade looks to be reliable.[23]

The predominance of the private sector has already arrived in certain areas of the country: the South-west and Southern local authority regions of England already had 65 per cent of their total beds provided by the private sector in 1984.[24] The detailed examination of changes between 1982 and 1984 by Larder, Day and Klein shows that, apart from inner and outer London, all regions of England showed increases in the private sector of over 30 per cent. The number of actual beds produced by such percentage increases of course varies widely: the 30 per cent increase in the Southern region represents 4,416 extra places, while the 80 per cent rise in the East Midlands produced 1,337 extra private beds.[25]

It is clear that, whatever the regional and local differences, private residential care has become an important feature of welfare provision, and that the balance between the public and private sectors has shifted dramatically. The private sector has absorbed all the pressure from increasing numbers of older people,[26] especially those in the 75+ age range, who are most likely to enter residential care. The predominance of women entering these institutions should also be emphasized. One private company catering for 'the top end of the market' (a market worth, in their estimation, over £500 million in the residential and nursing home field in 1985) reckons women account for 87 per cent of residents at an average age of 84.[27]

How has this dramatic growth in private residential care come about? The expansion is largely a result of government decision-making. Changes in the supplementary benefit rules 'provide a direct financial incentive for the elderly to move into a residential or nursing home'.[28] The National Council for Voluntary Organisations report detailing the crisis in voluntary homes charts the changes in supplementary benefits in the 1980s and the impact on residential homes.[29] The 1983 changes prompted the most significant shifts in private sector provision: owners and prospective owners realized that their market now extended beyond residents able to pay for themselves to people who could be funded by supplementary benefit, and that they could raise their charges to the DHSS maximum. Residential care was increasingly seen by older people, and significantly by their relatives, as a possible solution to their problems; and they were no longer reliant on the local authority for assessment and allocation of a place. Another factor in the explosion of private care was the realization by health and local authorities that they could shift their financial liability onto the supplementary benefit system.

How does one account for the government's decision to fuel this expansion of residential care, which at first sight seems to conflict with its much-heralded community care philosophy? Although there is a risk in overemphasizing the rationality of government policy and decision-making, the growth of private residential care fits very well with other aspects of Thatcherite philosophy. The welfare pluralist lobby advocates the need for private provision to meet welfare needs.[30] It is easier to open a residential home than to start a private domiciliary service, although that too could have been funded by the DHSS.

Residential care utilizes existing capital and personnel resources. A study of provision in Devon found fifteen homes (12.7 per cent of those studied) that had partners previously self-employed in the tourist trade, nine of whom had converted their premises to residential care.[31] Similarly, the study found significant numbers of builders, estate agents and architects involved in the burgeoning residential care business.

Another explanation for the expansion of private residential care is that it meets the needs of many older people and their relatives. The needs of parties other than the consumers themselves often take priority. Weaver *et al.* found that 'because people enter residential care under pressure and with a sense of urgency, the consumer's own wishes tend to be superseded by the immediate concerns of caring others'.[32] The rhetoric of choice surrounding private provision of residential care is a distortion of reality: in practice there is little choice as to which home one can enter.

Nevertheless, residential provision clearly meets an important need of people involved in the caring of others.

The state's promotion of private residential care rather than domiciliary services prevents a major increase in costs and the rupture of dominant welfare ideologies. Provision of the extra domiciliary services required to enable the more dependent older person to stay in their own home would open a flood of demand and therefore be extremely expensive. Residential care as the main form of state provision for those in need of the most expensive forms of welfare acts as a brake on demand, thereby keeping overall costs lower. Entry to residential care therefore remains the cost that must be paid for the highest levels of state support.

Standards of private care

As is true of the public sector, standards of private care vary enormously. The range of difference is probably greater in the private sector, where Johnson indicates that it provides some of the worst and best examples of residential care.[33] This is not surprising given the existence at one end of the market of a demand by very wealthy people for residential care. Research by Rosalind Brooke-Ross indicates how appalling private provision can be:

> old people . . . died because their physical care was of so low a standard they suffered from hypothermia or bed sores. Their houses were sold on behalf of the proprietor, their pensions and post office savings drawn by the proprietor, sometimes to pay for fees months in advance. Old people were locked in as the easiest ways to deal with their difficulties . . . rubbish bin plastic bags were used on incontinent elderly people.[34]

Brooke-Ross indicates how difficult it is to enforce statutory measures against excesses of ill treatment, let alone against general poor standards. Existing procedures of inspection and control of private homes are clearly inadequate. Local authority inspectors often face an impossible task in attempting to ensure that the profit-oriented sector provides a satisfactory service to older people.

Poor standards and ill treatment are also prevalent in the public sector. The growth of the private sector has, however, undermined and restricted positive developments in the public sector. For example, workers in local authority homes have been increasingly effective in challenging hurried and unnecessary admissions to care. Visits to the home in advance of making a decision, getting to know a key worker, attempting to make clear to all what a home may or may not offer – such practice has been developing in the local authority sector. The growing preponderance of profit-oriented facilities clearly undercuts such practices. Beds must be filled to ensure financial survival in the smaller homes and to ensure a return to investors in the larger concerns.

The organizational structure of an institution is a crucial factor in providing good residential care. Private sector enterprises seem unlikely to work in any other than a strictly hierarchical mode. Labour costs are the principal financial burden and must be kept as low as possible if there is to be a profit.[35] The smaller homes rely on family members, and part-time working is the norm in larger concerns.[36] The vast majority of workers in the private sector are women, as in the state establishments, but here there are not even the basic work rights of low-paid workers as found in the public sector. Nor do these private employees have ready access to the knowledge of improved standards and training to be found in some areas of the public sector. The private sector is reproducing the worst aspects of local authority residential care, but with less likelihood of effective democratic control and outside the progressive policy frameworks introduced by some local authorities. Even if such policies do not ensure good practice, they are an essential starting point.

If the government had deliberately set out to undermine improvements in public residential provision, while continuing to maintain the deterrent principle and conventional ideologies of welfare, then it could scarcely have found a more effective instrument of policy than the private residential sector.

Residential care for children and young people

The number of residential places for children and young people has declined significantly in the 1980s. In 1978, there were 34,400 young people in residential care in England (not including physically and mentally handicapped young people). By 1980, the corresponding figure was 32,500, and by 1984 the figure had dropped to 18,200.[37] The total number of children in care (not just residential care) in England has also fallen: from 95,300 in 1980 to 74,800 in 1984.[38]

The decline in residential care can be partly explained by demographic changes in the relevant age groups. However, since 1980 the proportion of the child population in care has also fallen,[39] a reduction that can only be explained by marked changes in policy and practice. Tunstill[40] has identified two key factors: the changing relationships between state, child and family; and the tensions between residential institutions and foster care.

Recent social service departments policy documents express a strong commitment to reducing the amount of residential provision and the time spent in it. There is every indication that these aims are being met. This trend can be explained by a variety of factors. Costs of residential care rose dramatically through the 1970s: overtime payments were introduced (to the dismay of those who savoured the 'vocational' nature of the work), there were significant salary increases, and a spate of new buildings left a legacy of high repayments. Today the residential care of children is no longer provided by unpoliticized houseparents. Although standards have not risen universally, residential child care has now to be recognized as a skilled and expensive business.

Changes in professional ideology have contributed to the drive to reduce residential provision. The influence of 'permanency' (the attempt to find longer-lasting substitute parents) has direct implications for residential provision. Residential care is rightly seen as inappropriate for long-term placements, but the viable role it could play in the child care planning process has been lost. The shift to permanency has contributed to the general failure to adequately consider constructive use of residential care, a point made by the Beckford Report.[41]

The shift to making permanent arrangements for children in care was prompted by the best of intentions, and was clearly based on an assumption of prior preventive work. However, the same policy documents that promote 'permanence' reveal that the essential preventive work is ill defined and receives low priority. Tunstill's account of the workings of the 1975 Act concludes that services to natural parents have further deteriorated and that this is accompanied by a swing from residential care to foster care.[42]

Residential provision could be used as an important component of social work aiming to prevent the permanent and unnecessary break-up of families. Residential placements are often more acceptable to parents and young people than fostering. Good residential social work, used as part of a coherent approach to child care planning, can play a key role in preventing long-term (and costly) disruption of family life.

A third reason for the swing away from residential care is the recognition by managers and policy-makers that residential workers were increasingly organizing themselves and articulating demands about working conditions and their own practice. Many traditionalists have bemoaned the demise of the dedicated vocational staff member, willing to work 80 hours a week or more for very low pay in return for accommodation. The Excellent residential child care can be provided by shift patterns and a working week of less than 40 hours, but this requires good organization and a willingness to implement democratic work structures; and it is expensive. Over the past decade many managers have become frustrated and angry with the growing cohesion of residential workers and their insistence on helping to shape the professional practice of the authority. One director reputedly said of one such staff group: 'They may do excellent child care, but let them put one foot wrong and I'll . . .' The sentence was not completed, either because this director did actually appreciate the high standards of care achieved, or because such was the cohesion and strength of the staff group that he may have found it difficult to know how to complete it!

It is important to note that the declining importance of residential care for children is not a uniform one. Sinclair has indicated how child care statistics vary across the country, and suggests that the level of resources available in any authority is a key factor in child care decision-making. [43] It has been generally accepted that there is a causal relationship between poverty and numbers of children in care. Yet, as Sinclair points out, 'in the 1980's the number of children in care has declined despite the growth in the number of unemployed and the number of families dependent on state benefit'. [44] Financial restraints on local government and changes in policy and practice have transformed this relationship.

The shift from residential care for younger people

In 1980, the National Children's Bureau warned against treating residential care as if it was already a small fraction of total provision. The bureau commented that 'even less attention than now might be paid to the detailed consideration of which kinds of residential care are required for which children for what purposes and at what time'. [45] There is a danger that, in all the debate about the decline of institutional care for young people, the fact that many remain in, and continue to be admitted to, residential provision may be forgotten. This is particularly the case for 13 year olds and over: the Social Services Inspectorate in a 1984 survey of 149 community homes in twenty-nine English authorities found that four out of five residents were aged 13 or over. [46]

Young people enter residential provision at a time when there is a marked lack of overall policy and detailed planning. The Inspectorate found that all twenty-nine authorities studied were reformulating (or had recently done so) their child care policies. Many of such policies paid scant attention to residential care, and in many 'policy for residential care could only be deduced by examining alternative provision'.[47] Very few authorities had examined the implications for residential workers of proposed changes in child care services. The Inspectorate noted that 'fear of closure was a factor in staff attitudes in many places, but disquiet arising from inadequately explained change was equally great'.[48]

The restructuring of social service departments has created a great deal of uncertainty for residential workers about the future. The result has been a decline in morale and subsequent threats to standards of practice. Low morale was noted in a 1983 study of staff turnover,[49] and continuing uncertainties about jobs and tasks can only have made matters worse. Long-running debates about decentralization, rate-capping, cuts and changes in services have simultaneously marginalized residential child care workers and undermined any sense of job security and satisfaction. Many social service managers appear to think that this is the fault of the workers themselves, and at times there will be some truth in this. Very often, however, residential workers are still isolated and in many ways treated as second-class citizens in social service departments.

Changes in residential provision for young people

Despite this bleak picture, there have been significant changes in the rhetoric and practice of residential child care. In 1980, the National Children's Bureau called for community-based residential care where 'reasonably small units offer their facilities in a variety of ways to meet the needs of children and their families as they arise in reasonably local areas'.[50] 'Family resource centres' and 'family centres' are some of the terms that indicate this shift. Some of these provide authentic community-based services, others merely reflect a change in name. One recently qualified student returned to his seconding authority to work in a 'family centre', only to find an unimaginative children's home where the officer in charge wouldn't admit girls (probably, for their sakes, just as well!).

As one research study pointed out, the concept of a family centre is ill defined and varies considerably.[51] As long ago as 1974 'The Family Day Centres Project' began as part of an EEC anti-poverty programme. A defining feature of these early family centres was that they were 'unofficial' and based on principles of flexibility, reciprocity and participation. As the research into the project

pointed out, such principles are generally considered to be antagonistic to those of social service departments.[52]

Local authorities have taken up the name 'family centre', often
using it to denote ex-nursery provision and making use of existing
buildings.[53] The term is also used to describe community or
children's homes for a much older age range, which often provide
some residential accommodation.

The emphasis on the family in the residential care of the 1980s
has in part grown out of the recognition by workers themselves of
the need to work with significant others in the lives of the children
in their care. The stereotypical isolated institution where the only
link with the outside world consists of infrequent visits by field
social workers undoubtedly still exists, but it is a far cry from the
reality of many residential establishments.

The notion of shared care has emerged to indicate a greater
flexibility in child care arrangements between state organizations
and the family. This may either produce social work practice where
the needs of the young person and family may be better met,
or it may lead to increased scope for surveillance of families
and neighbourhoods. Parton[54] has argued that shared care may
be decreasing in child care cases because of the overwhelming
concern about 'child abuse' and the growing emphasis on control. With other client groups, and with mentally and physically
handicapped children, there are increasing numbers of creative
schemes.

The development of community-based residential care is one
result of the restructuring of social service organizations and social
work practice. Residential workers were amongst the first to push
for this type of work, but when child care is increasingly dominated by concerns over child abuse it is an ambivalent development.
Cohen has indicated the changing nature of social control, from an
institutionally based form of control to a community-based one,
and it would be easy to characterize the new links of residential
workers with communities in this light. Yet, as Cohen also points
out: 'institutions with less visible margins would allow better
things to happen around the edges . . . [workers] might be able to
deploy more resources along those margins, create more opportunities, and provide more services to groups who need them
most.'[55]

Residential workers who have tapped the potential of collective
ways of working can make some of the rhetoric of community-
based and decentralized social services a reality. Optimism must,
however, be qualified with the insights of more traditional residential work. Community-based facilities serving a specific locality

will usually find themselves working with a wide range of young people, including some highly disturbed adolescents. In Packman's terms, there will be 'villains, victims and the volunteered'.[56] Sometimes attempting to work with such an extensive range of clients may be both naive and dangerous.

Residential workers have always been under pressure to work with all sorts of people, usually in a fairly undifferentiated way and at the behest of an often insensitive and uncomprehending management. The emphasis on locality adds an extra pressure: 'if this person lives in your patch you will work with them.' This will at times be inappropriate and potentially damaging for all concerned. Workers will need help and support from managers and outside consultants to work appropriately with the multi-faceted demands of their job, but also to enable them to refuse some tasks. In addition, some degree of specialization will continue to be necessary to provide appropriate help for a small minority of young people.

There is no doubt that the opening up of residential homes to more contact with a wider world was long overdue, as was the greater questioning of entry into residential care. In most workers' experience it is obvious that many people in the past were taken into care unnecessarily: the example of black children is the most striking one. Recent research into child care decisions reveals that poor practice is still alarmingly common. Part of the explanation for this lies in the failure to identify the strengths of institutional care. Such provision is appropriate for only a minority of young people, but they will always receive a second-rate service while insufficient attention is paid to the value of high-quality residential work. The image of the oppressive institution props up the progressive facade of 'community care'. Only by identifying the strengths and appropriate use of well-organized and effective residential care can the aspirations of care in the community become a reality.

Residential provision in the public sector has been a convenient scapegoat for the inadequacies and failures of other forms of welfare provision. For example, field social workers have been pleased to find a residential place for some of their most difficult and demanding clients. They have subsequently provided minimal if any support for clients or residential workers, and then held residential services accountable for the poor outcome. This is not to suggest that overall standards of residential care are satisfactory – visiting residential establishments often remains an all too depressing experience. To conclude however, that there is no place for residential care is mistaken.

It is popular to condemn large long-stay residential establishments in the depths of the countryside. Under Thatcherite principles these are being closed and sold off; it will be interesting to note who ends up living in these rural retreats. Will we see them turned into homes for the rich, while the former residents find a new life in the inner cities? Of course, unimaginative institutions should be condemned, and of course residential care has been used as an effective form of social control. Yet in the process of restructuring social and economic life it may be possible to create a new role and a new style for residential care – where it stands for communality and social living in an increasingly individualized and fragmented world. The next section discusses the possibility of progressive residential work.

Progressive residential care: the organizational context

The organizational dimension of residential care, which is generally overlooked, holds the key to progressive practice. Resnick and Patti refer to organizational context as the structural arrangements and organizational processes that collectively determine the nature and effectiveness of relationships between subordinates and superiors, and practitioners and clients, in social agencies. They argue that many of the 'problems that interfere with the delivery of services are not the result of individual choices and/or personal competencies, but rather grow out of and are perpetuated by systematic forces'.[57] Calls for more and better training litter policy debates on residential care, but this emphasis on individual skills is ill conceived without adequate acknowledgement of the organizational context of residential care. Many enthusiastic residential workers leave training courses to return to organizations and structures that prevent them implementing what they have learnt. Calls for 'sensitive management'[58] are not sufficient; a more rigorous examination of the organizational context of residential care is required.

Earlier it was argued that residential provision is connected to welfare ideologies of the family and community, and the requirement for social control of unproductive labour. Here we examine the linkages between the deterrent function of residential institutions and the organizational context. The hypothesis is that the usual and conventional forms of organization will produce practice that reinforces the negative perceptions of residential care and its deterrent effects.

The familiar model of organizational structure in local authority residential establishments is hierarchical and elitist. In his work on children's homes, Berridge concluded that in smaller homes the officer in charge is 'omnipresent and is responsible for all major decisions'.[59] In larger homes there may be a greater degree of delegation, but they still control major events like admissions and staff appointments – thus maintaining considerable power.

Booth found that, out of 178 homes for older people in four local authorities, less than half held regular staff meetings; a quarter of all homes held no staff meetings of any sort involving staff or residents.[60] Meetings do not by any means guarantee participation and democracy, but they are an essential prerequisite. Booth saw officers in charge as 'exercising undisputed personal authority within homes . . . in short, they are in a position to ensure that things are done as they want'.[61] The historical continuity of the role of the officer in charge is revealed by this comment from *The Workhouse Officer's Handbook* of 1907: 'The master of the workhouse is answerable for the general order of the whole establishment and minute personal attention on his part can alone detect and remedy defects in the discipline and cleanliness of the house.'[62] The continuing emphasis on the all-embracing power and influence of the officer in charge and a hierarchical organizational structure is a major means by which the poor standards of residential care, and their deterrent effects, are maintained.

There is ample evidence from organization theory to suggest that a hierarchical model is counter-productive to the supposed positive aims of residential care. For instance, in their classic work on organizational innovation, Burns and Stalker argue that where unpredictable and unstable conditions apply in an organization (a hallmark of residential work, although they were researching the electronics industry) the 'organic' model is much more effective. Two of the defining features of that model are a 'lateral rather than a vertical direction of communication through the organization . . . resembling consultation rather than demand' and 'omniscience no longer imputed to the head of the concern'.[63]

Similar points emerge from research directly into residential establishments. Heal and Cawson concluded that 'a hierarchical and bureaucratic style of organization is associated with a poorer quality of staff/child interaction'.[64] Tizard stresses that 'the organisational structure of a residential unit in a large part determines staff roles and their performance'.[65] The durability of the hierarchical and elitist mode of organization in the face of clear evidence of its negative effect needs to be explained. Organizational inertia and lack of awareness of research findings may be factors. Two more fundamental explanations, however, stand out.

Hierarchy is cheap: it keeps the largest number of employees at the bottom of the organization. The symbiotic relationship between hierarchical structure and a large proportion of untrained and low-paid workers has been clearly spelt out by Menzies.[66] Yet this link is overlooked by those who lament the low proportion of qualified residential workers.

Hierarchy acts as a means of control. Apart from imposing discipline from above, the hierarchical model produces poor and ineffectual communication in a situation of stress and instability. This in turn leads to vulnerable and isolated workers who, faced with painful and challenging work, are more easily disciplined and controlled. The very terms 'staff', 'officer' and 'establishment' indicate the type of control common in residential homes. Many complex organizations rely on self-regulation rather than hierarchical control from above, and the necessity of this for effective teamwork is clear.[67]

This control function extends to the recipients of residential care. As the Central Council for Education and Training in Social Work has clearly stated: 'what matters fundamentally is that the predominant staff values in the culture of residential care should be egalitarian rather than elitist, for an elitist system of values inevitably places residents at the bottom of the pile.'[68] Effective participation by residents is increasingly seen as a major goal of residential care.[69] This aim is not attainable while a hierarchical form of organization prevents residents and workers from engaging in the policy and decision-making of residential establishments.

Hierarchical structures do confer some advantages on basic grade workers. Menzies' analysis, for example, revealed how workers can be protected from overwhelming and anxiety-provoking situations by rigid work patterns.[70] Collective work structures can, paradoxically, reduce the discretion of individual workers and increase anxiety and pressures. Lipsky's concept of the street-level bureaucrat shows how the inability of management effectively to police frontline workers provides a degree of discretion.[71] Discretion is, of course, a two-edged sword: it is essential for responsible social work, yet at the same time it can result in abuse towards residents. In any case, Lipsky's work demonstrates that policing from above is ineffective. Far more effective is the control on poor practice produced by teamwork. Creating a culture where workers are responsible to each other and to residents produces far better practice than the usual policy of controlling through intermittent intervention from above.

Given the importance of the connections between organizational structure and standard of care, how can we move towards providing positive residential care in the local authority setting?

The culture of residential homes

One of the keys to successful residential care is the creation of a coherent culture that is directed to achieve stated and consistent aims. Local authority institutions seem often to be muddled about what exactly their purpose is and how to achieve it. The fundamental confusion arises from the conflict between a rhetorical intention to produce positive standards of care, and a structure that delivers a negative and deterrent effect. Establishments often reveal a host of contradictory beliefs and practices. A home for adolescents will have individual counselling on the psychotherapeutic model, talk of resident participation, yet keep the larder locked. A home for older people may be in an authority with a progressive policy on client choice and participation, yet the staff will not sit and eat with the residents.

The varied personal beliefs of workers about such aspects as caring, morality, social work, health and personal development, all play a part in creating what Wolins terms the 'powerful environment'.[72] It is clear that all the myriad influences that go to make up a residential home are not effectively channelled into a coherent and constructive culture in local authority establishments. This view gains support from recent research by Booth and his colleagues. Their study concluded that 'very often practices which increase the personal choice, privacy and participation and community integration of residents are counteracted by others in the same homes which reduce them'.[73] Booth argues that it is more accurate to see establishments as being composed of 'multiple regimes' rather than coherent wholes.[74]

This is an important and far-reaching conclusion. One of the main tenets of residential work theory is that the nature of the regime is fundamental to the quality of service. For example, Jones argues that 'the regime, in the sense of an overall pattern, has more importance than anything else for the impact an institution has on those who live in it'.[75] If Booth's findings are extended to all forms of local authority residential care, then the conclusion is that there is no overall pattern to be found. Instead there is a confusing and contradictory set of policies and practices.

There are two basic ways of creating a coherent culture in residential homes: either through imposition from above, necessitating a more effective version of top-down management than has been achieved so far; or through effective teamwork where staff themselves create an effective and positive culture, within guidelines provided by the employing agencies.

Managerialism

In her illuminating study of public sector agencies in the United States, Shan Martin identified 'the myth of management'.[76] The myth is that managers are so supremely important that only they can and should perform the functions necessary for organizational success and survival; furthermore, they must direct, control, monitor and discipline others. Martin identifies three assumptions that underpin the myth of management:

(1) The actual human labour applied in the creation of a product or service must be controlled by others not directly involved in the labour.
(2) Those who labour directly on this product or service are (and should be) paid less than those who control or manage them.
(3) Without this control, the work would not get done and organizations would fail.[77]

Martin's research led her to question these assumptions and the emphasis on management that they support. For instance, she argues that a reduction in the emphasis on, or elimination of, the conventional manager/subordinate relationship would allow workers to be more responsible and accountable to their goals or services, rather than to their bosses.[78] The conventional assumptions of management are an essential part of the way in which organizations control their workforce and the recipients of their services. It is not irrelevant that most managers in the social services are white males, and that the preponderance of men directors has increased since Seebohm as 'managerialism' has extended its grasp on the public sector.[79] 'Management' as a process that is essential for organizational survival and effectiveness should be distinguished from the cult of managerialism that Martin identifies. Different forms of 'management' and organizational structure are required in local authorities if the many promising policy documents are to be worth more than the paper they are written on. For example, it is difficult to imagine the often espoused equal opportunity policies being implemented from a managerialist framework.

Emphasis on the officer in charge in residential work is strongly influenced by the charismatic model. Much of the influential literature on residential practice concerns the work of charismatic pace-setters, often in the private sector: for instance, George Lyward, Barbara Dockar-Drysdale and Bruno Bettleheim.[80] Consciously or not, many officers in charge aspire to, or are encouraged to develop, this charismatic form of leadership: the all-knowing, totally sensitive and perceptive, born-leader approach, with an emphasis on qualities rather than skills.[81] Very few can achieve this superhuman position. The relevance of such a model of management and authority to anti-racist and anti-sexist policies needs to be seriously examined. The damaging effects of hierarchical elitism and the emphasis on the officer in charge sometimes permeate to influential policy-makers. A Social Care Association seminar at least got to the point of asking some relevant questions: 'Do we have to use hierarchical models of authority, with the officer in charge at the top? Is this simply a device to make line management in bureaucracies simpler? Does it create a tendency towards paternalistic care? Are there alternatives which are preferable?[82]

Although the criticism of managerialism and elitism has been presented here in terms of its unsuitability to implementing anti-racist and anti-sexist policies, there is nothing necessarily radical about such a position. Public sector organizations are merely lagging behind many parts of private enterprise where participative and democratic work forms have long been popular. The adoption of such techniques, coupled with effective utilization of information technology, could lead to more effective services in the public sector.

Progressive residential practice

The creation of a satisfactory residential environment takes years, a point that many managers and practitioners often appear to miss. Many agencies do not provide the support and nurture necessary for developing residential cultures. Coherent plans for change and the necessary time spans often seem alien to the ethos of local authorities. Many workers are wasted in residential work by having their initial enthusiasm squashed out of them by the inertia and rigidity of the local authority process. Some improvements in job conditions, salaries and unemployment have combined over the last ten years to contribute to a reduction in the turnover of workers. As Berry indicated, however, this does not of itself lead to improved standards of care.[83] Any consideration of the progressive possibilities of residential work must be prefaced by the realization that implementation of such ideas takes exhaustive struggle and time.

The most comprehensive account of progressive practice in the residential arena is the published work of the Harlesden Community Project.[84] Similar ways of working developed in Frogmore children's home from which the following example of progressive practice is taken.

Example: Frogmore children's home

This was a local authority residential centre for around twenty-five people between the ages of 5 and 17 which underwent a significant process of change between 1972 and 1980.

One particularly fruitful period of change was when there were separate groups for men and women workers. In a job that is traditionally seen as women's work, though with many men in better-paid positions, this approach can pay rich dividends. In Frogmore, it reinforced a policy of sharing jobs so that (for example) men cooked and cleaned while women drove and built. This sharing of jobs extended to those traditionally seen as the province of senior workers. A duty system was created so that, once workers were established within the home, they took it in turns to 'manage': taking referrals, coordinating and facilitating the work of the day, etc. One could then have a situation where the officer in charge would be preparing a meal with two or three children for thirty people, while a 'junior' worker took the details of a referral before consulting with others in the home on its suitability. This scenario may sound simple, but it takes time and hard work to bring about and can be threatening to many managers.

An excellent indication of the results for residents and workers of democratic work structures arose out of this development of the duty system and separate support groups for men and women. In this particular home, as in many others, the physical restraint of aggressive and panicky children was a common feature of the work. For a variety of reasons men felt more comfortable with this aspect of the work than women. When the duty system introduced more women into the 'managerial' role, it became clear that they tried to stop situations developing to the point where aggressive and violent behaviour needed physical restraint. Men, in contrast, felt able to take a more relaxed view and then step in with 'authority' to control the situation. This analysis of events was developed and talked through in separate groups and in staff meetings. A policy of early intervention and the development of ways of working that more successfully anticipated aggression were the productive results. In a matter of months, levels of aggression and threatening behaviour, which had hitherto been tolerated and taken for granted, fell dramatically.

This example clearly shows the benefits for residents and workers of collective ways of working. The sharing of tasks in a structured environment, where the need for exercise of authority is not denied, has great advantages for workers who would otherwise be restricted to low-status roles. At a time when some authorities are actively seeking to recruit more black workers, a collective work structure allows inexperienced recruits to gain experience in all the varied tasks of a residential establishment. Such working methods need to be developed if the domination of hierarchical local authority structures by white men is to be challenged effectively. Equal opportunity policies are only part of the struggle towards a more progressive practice in residential, or any other form of, social work. They are only a step on the way to transforming elitist and hierarchical organizational structures.

Summary and conclusions

This chapter has argued that residential work is a key construct in a contradictory set of ideologies of welfare, and that this needs to be recognized if the aspirations of care in the community are to be met. The pretence that residential care is now redundant helps maintain poor standards of care in both the private and public sectors. The fear of entering residential care helps perpetuate the acceptance of inadequate domiciliary services. The growth of private sector care of older people indicates the need for residential provision for a significant but growing minority. This, it is suggested, is the case no matter how good are the services to people in their own homes. An oppressive aspect to caring for very dependent people is inevitable; provision of a real choice about good-quality public sector residential care for all concerned is both necessary and possible.

Despite a decline in provision, many young people spend some time in residential care, time that can be welcomed and productive. The development of different forms of work structures can facilitate a progressive practice in local authority institutions. Those departments that aspire to the delivery of equal opportunities in the workplace, and the delivery of anti-racist and anti-sexist practice, need to implement democratic and collective ways of working. The organizational aspects of social work are generally neglected, apart from within an ethos of managerialism. Only by acting on this front can good practice be maintained, let alone opportunities for new and better practice be created.

Residential care has been used to reinforce ideologies of familialism and community care. This should not lead to the conclusion that residential provision has no place in progressive welfare services. It does, however, indicate the enormity of the task in creating high-quality residential care. Transformation of the usual organizational ethos of residential care does hold out some hope for the future.

Residential care means being dependent on others, a state of affairs that is viewed by most people as repugnant. Yet residential living could come to represent communal and social living, and the recognition of the ways in which we are all dependent on each other in some form or another. High-quality residential care is possible in the public sector and some people need it. Old prejudices from the past should not prevent a reassessment of the progressive possibilities of residential care.

Notes and references

1 Ann Davis, *The Residential Solution* (Tavistock, 1981), p. 127; Phil Lee and David Pithers, 'Radical residential child care: Trojan horse or non-runner?', in M. Brake and Roy Bailey, *Radical Social Work and Practice* (Arnold, 1980), p. 87.
2 R. Clough, *Old Age Homes* (Allen & Unwin, 1981), p. 4.
3 E. Goffman, *Asylums: Essays on the social situation of mental patients and other inmates* (Penguin, 1961).
4 Peter Townsend, *The Last Refuge* (Routledge & Kegan Paul, 1962).
5 M. Wolins and Y. Wozner, *Revitalizing Residential Settings* (Jossey-Bass, 1983); L. Davis, *Residential Care: A Community Resource* (Heinemann, 1982); Clough, op. cit.
6 Janet Finch, 'Community care: developing non-sexist alternatives', *Critical Social Policy*, Issue 9 (spring 1984), p. 16.
7 Davis, op. cit. (n1).
8 M. A. Crowther, *The Workhouse System 1834–1929* (Batsford, 1981).
9 Peter Townsend, 'The structured dependency of the elderly: a creation of social policy in the twentieth century', *Ageing and Society*, vol. 1, no. 1, p. 8.
10 Crowther, op. cit. (n8), p. 10.
11 ibid., p. 13.
12 ibid., p. 74.
13 J. O'Connor, *The Fiscal Crisis of the State* (St James Press, 1973), p. 6.
14 Claus Offe, 'The theory of the capitalist state and the problem of policy formation', in L. N. Lindberg *et al.* (eds), *Stress and Contradictions in Modern Capitalism* (Lexington, 1975), p. 126.

15 Crowther, op. cit. (n8), p. 63.
16 Davis, op. cit. (n1), p. 24.
17 ibid., p. 25.
18 Elizabeth Wilson, 'Women, the "community" and the "family"', in Alan Walker (ed.), *Community Care* (Basil Blackwell and Martin Robertson, 1982), p. 40.
19 Walker, ibid., p. 5.
20 Stanley Cohen, *Visions of Social Control* (Polity, 1985), p. 116.
21 Department of Health and Social Security Statistics, in W. Laing, *Private Health Care* (Office of Health Economics, 1985), p. 32.
22 Chartered Institute of Public Finance and Accountancy, *Personal Social Service Statistics* (CIPFA, 1987).
    See also Chapters 2 and 10 in this book by Phillipson and Frost and Stein.
23 M. Johnson, quoted in *The Health Service Journal*, 19 June 1986, p. 817.
24 Duncan Larder, Patricia Day and Rudolf Klein, *Institutional Care for the Elderly* (University of Bath, 1986).
25 ibid., p. 31.
26 Malcolm Wicks, 'Community care and elderly people', in Walker, op. cit. (n18), p. 97.
27 Residential and Care Services (UK) PLC, 'Offer for subscription', p. 6.
28 Linda Challis, Patricia Day and Rudolf Klein, 'Residential care on demand', *New Society*, 5 April 1984, p. 32.
29 Christine Peaker, *The Crisis In Residential Care* (National Council for Voluntary Organisations, 1986).
30 For a discussion of welfare pluralism see Peter Beresford and Suzy Croft, 'Welfare pluralism: the new face of Fabianism', *Critical Social Policy*, Issue 9 (spring 1984), pp. 19–39.
31 D. R. Phillips and J. A. Vincent, 'Petit bourgeois care: private residential care for the elderly', *Policy and Politics*, vol. 14, no. 2 (1986), pp. 189–208.
32 Tim Weaver, Dianna Willcocks and Leonie Kellaher, *The Pursuit of Profit and Care: Patterns and Processes in Private Residential Homes for Old People* (The Polytechnic of North London, 1985), p. 8.
33 Malcolm Johnson, 'Private lives', *Health and Social Services Journal*, 28 July 1983, pp. 901–3.
34 Rosalind Brooke-Ross, *Regulation and the Private Sector: The 1980 Residential Homes Act* (University of Bath, 1985), p. 11.
35 Weaver *et al.* op. cit. (n32), p. 36.
36 Phillips and Vincent, op. cit. (n31), pp. 197–202.
37 *The Government's Expenditure Plans 1986–87 to 1988–89 Vol. 2*, Cmnd 9702 (HMSO, 1986), p. 219.
38 *Health and Personal Social Services Statistics for England* (HMSO, 1986), p. 113.
39 Ruth Sinclair, 'Behind the numbers: an examination of child care statistics', *Policy and Politics*, vol. 15, no. 2 (1987), pp. 111–17.
40 Jane Tunstill, 'An overview of how the Children Act has affected child

care policy', in National Foster Care Association, *A Review of the Children Act 10 Years On* (NFCA, 1986), pp. 8–18.

41 The Report of the Inquiry into the Circumstances Surrounding the Death of Jasmine Beckford, *A Child in Trust* (London Borough of Brent, 1985), pp. 263–8.

42 Tunstill, op. cit. (n40), p. 17.

43 Sinclair, op. cit. (n39), pp. 114–5.

44 ibid., p. 115.

45 R. A. Parker, *Caring for Separated Children* (Macmillan, 1980), p. 78.

46 Social Services Inspectorate, *Inspection of Community Homes* (DHSS 1985), p. 11.

47 ibid., p. 5.

48 ibid., p. 6.

49 Martin Knapp, 'The turnover of care staff in children's homes', *Research Policy and Planning*, vol. 3, no. 2 (1985), pp. 19–25.

50 Parker, op. cit. (n45), p. 137.

51 Alan Tibbenham, 'The West Devon family centre', *Social Services Research* (1986–4+5), pp. 113–35.

52 Phyllis Willmott and Susan Mayne, *Families at the Centre* (Bedford Square Press, 1983), p. 147.

53 Tibbenham, op. cit. (n51), p. 114.

54 Nigel Parton, *The Politics of Child Abuse* (Macmillan, 1985), p. 191.

55 Cohen, op. cit. (n20), p. 257.

56 J. Packman, J. Randall and N. Jacques, *Who Needs Care?: Social Work Decisions about Children* (Basil Blackwell, 1986), pp. 59–70.

57 H. Resnick and R. J. Patti, *Change from Within* (Temple, 1980), p. 23.

58 B. Kahan, 'Issues in residential care', in T. Philpot (ed.), *A New Direction for Social Work* (IPC Business Press, 1982), p. 41.

59 David Berridge, *Children's Homes* (Basil Blackwell, 1985), p. 54.

60 Tim Booth, *Home Truths* (Gower, 1985), p. 158.

61 ibid., p. 188.

62 W. H. Dumsday, *The Workhouse Officer's Handbook* (Hadden, Best & Co., 1907), p. 10.

63 T. Burns and G. M. Stalker, *The Management of Innovation* (Tavistock, 1961), p. 121.

64 K. Heal and P. Cawson, 'Organisation and change in children's institutions', in J. Tizard, I. Sinclair and R. V. G. Clarke, *Varieties of Residential Experience* (Routledge & Kegan Paul, 1975), p. 86.

65 J. Tizard, 'Quality of residential care for retarded children', in Tizard, Sinclair and Clarke, ibid., p. 52.

66 Isabel Menzies, *The Functioning of Social Systems as a Defence against Anxiety* (The Tavistock Institute of Human Relations, 1970).

67 K. Vander Ven, 'Towards maximum effectiveness of the team unit approach in residential care: an agenda for team development', *Residential and Community Child Care Administration*, vol. 1, no. 3 (autumn 1979), pp. 287–98.

68 Central Council for Education and Training in Social Work, *Training for Residential Work* (CCETSW, 1973), p. 14.

69 P. M. Barclay, *Social Workers: Their Role and Tasks* (Bedford Square

Press, 1982), p. 64; National Institute for Social Work, *Residential Care: A Positive Choice* (HMSO, 1988).

70 Menzies, op. cit. (n6).
71 M. Lipsky, *Street-Level Bureaucracy* (Russell Sage, 1980).
72 M. Wolins, *Successful Group Care: The Powerful Environment* (Aldine, 1974).
73 Booth, op. cit. (n60), p. 169.
74 ibid., p. 170.
75 Howard Jones, *The Residential Community: A Setting for Social Work* (Routledge & Kegan Paul, 1979), p. 14.
76 Shan Martin, *Managing Without Managers: Alternative Work Arrangements in Public Organizations* (Sage, 1983), pp. 125–33.
77 ibid., pp. 129–30.
78 ibid., pp. 142–3.
79 David Howe, 'The segregation of women and their work in the personal social services', *Critical Social Policy*, Issue 15 (spring 1986), pp. 21–35. See also Annie Hudson in this volume (Chapter 4).
80 For example: M. Burn, *Mr. Lyward's Answer* (Hamish Hamilton, 1956); Barbara Dockar-Drysdale, *Consultation in Child Care* (Longman, 1973); B. Bettelheim, *Truants From Life* (Collier-Macmillan, 1955).
81 For a discussion of qualities and skills, see Hilary Barker, 'Recapturing sisterhood', *Critical Social Policy*, Issue 16 (summer 1986), pp. 80–9.
82 The Social Care Association, *The Bonnington Report* (SCA, 1984), p. 23.
83 Juliet Berry, *Daily Experience in Residential Life* (Routledge & Kegan Paul, 1975), p. 63.
84 Fatma Dharamsi *et al.*, *Community Work and Caring for Children* (Owen Wells, 1979).

13 Community work in recession: a practitioner's perspective

IAN SMITH

Between February 1976 and February 1983, I was employed as a community worker by local residents in Southwick, an inner-city neighbourhood in north Sunderland. Since February 1983, I have been employed by Sheffield City Council as a leader of a team of community workers covering a slice of north Sheffield. This chapter discusses six areas of community work:

- developing an anti-racist and anti-sexist practice;
- developing and sustaining advice and advocacy services in welfare rights;
- supporting community self-help projects and links with community social work;
- the effect of state-sponsored 'make-work' schemes as a response to increasing unemployment;
- responses to working 'in and against the state' in the context of threatened or actual privatization measures;
- the tension between those who see community work as facilitating a 'social movement', working on an agenda set by local community activists, and those who see community work as a profession, working on the state's agenda for community improvement.

While some of these concerns are not new, the current recession has given them increased urgency.

Anti-racist and anti-sexist community work practice

The interim report to Sheffield City Council's community work review group[1] gives high priority to anti-racism and anti-sexism.

The evidence given throughout the review has shown that black men and women and white women should have the highest priority in community work time and as community workers they are in need of greater and clearer support. It has also been demonstrated that men and white women need urgently to re-think their working practices to ensure that they (we) are agents of progress and not perpetuaters of some oppressions . . .

The evidence given to the review revealed some deep-seated problems. The definition of community work agreed by community workers in Sheffield in 1986 was drawn up by an exclusively white group of workers. All the community work managers in Sheffield are white and all but one of them are men. The black workers who are employed are funded by central, rather than local, government funds. Recognition is more readily given to community work that achieves 'hard results' – such as a campaign victory – than to 'soft' work, such as that required to support a group of women who are meeting together for its own sake.

As a white man who manages a team of community workers that contains four black women, one black man, two white women and one white man (apart from me) the development of an effective anti-racist and anti-sexist practice is urgent! I have serious reservations about the validity of a white male managing a team with this race and gender profile – a profile that has developed since I have been in post. I have little doubt that, if I left the job now, the post would qualify for an exemption under employment legislation which would allow for the recruitment of a black woman or man or a white woman.

An anti-racist practice[2]

An effective anti-racist community work practice must incorporate four distinct elements. First, we need *a definition of community work appropriate to black workers and black community groups*. This means acknowledging that existing definitions of community work are very much based on a white (and predominantly male) experience of community work. For example, a white community worker may refuse to be used as an all-purpose fieldworker – taking 'clients' to social security offices, running literacy classes, organizing youth activities, etc. The (white) community worker might argue that it would be more appropriate to assist the group with which she is working to make demands on the service providers – the local advice centre, the adult education service and the youth service – to provide an extended and improved service to meet local needs. A black community worker is usually not in a position to encourage black groups to make such demands simply because the service providers do not have the black staff to provide an acceptable service to the black community. As a result, the worker and the groups with which she is working understand that there is no alternative for the community worker but to meet the demand herself. Definitions of community work must be sensitive to the different positions into which racism pushes workers. The last thing they need is to have a white – and therefore racist – definition of their job that prevents them from properly facilitating a black response to community need.

Secondly, we need to ensure *appropriate consultation and support for black community work*. When black community workers find themselves supervised by white managers, an additional mechanism is required to assess the quality of work from a black perspective. I know from my own experience of supervising black workers that I am hesitant to challenge a particular course of action because I am aware of the fact that I am white and can legitimately be asked, 'Who are you to question?' This may be fair enough, but it denies the black worker the discipline of the sort of rigorous criticism received by white colleagues. In the absence of black supervisors, black colleagues encourage me to be as critical of their practice as is possible and I try to do this *while recognizing that this is a criticism from a white perspective.*

Thirdly, it is important to *defend the space of black colleagues*. Black colleagues are often asked to do something, not because they are community workers, but because they are black. They might be requested to advise on the development of day centre services to older black people, to provide translation services, or to sit on an interview panel. It is essential that black workers receive support when they decide to say no to such requests. I have known workers who have acquired a reputation for being 'awkward' and 'difficult' when they have refused a number of requests. White colleagues must be vigilant in their defence of black colleagues from such insidious institutional racism. This means developing a clear contract between black and white colleagues that acknowledges that racism targets black people as the victims, but that it is a white problem. In our team we have an agreement that, whenever a black colleague is victim to racism (conscious or unconscious) from the institution that employs her, then the problem is brought to the team. It is the task of the white team members to discuss and agree a course of action aimed at remedying the grievance.

For most black community workers, working with black community groups is of paramount importance. Sometimes they will find themselves working with groups that also include white people. In such situations the needs of the black members of the group may be ignored by the white members and the black community worker can find herself being asked by white members to work on their particular problems. This may lead to black members of mixed-race groups becoming alienated and leaving. In turn, this leaves them feeling bitter towards the black community worker who has been hijacked by white people. White workers need to be sensitive to this possibility and offer support to black colleagues to ensure that they have the time and space to spend with the black members within mixed-race groups. To ensure that this can happen, white workers need to 'reserve' some time so that they *do* respond when asked and not plead commitment elsewhere.

Fourthly, we need to develop *effective strategies for challenging white racism in community groups*. Most white community worker colleagues find it difficult to avoid colluding with racist remarks and behaviour within all-white community groups. At the same time they are concerned to find ways of challenging racism that are effective in developing positive attitudes and avoid pushing it 'underground'. Most agree that staying silent is unacceptable, not least because it misses the chance to let other group members who are offended know that support is at hand to offer a challenge. Silence suggests agreement.

One approach is to record a racist remark or racist behaviour and also to record the responses, if any, that were made by others present. If other white workers do the same, within a short space of time a supply of case studies will be available for discussion in a team or seminar setting. As people learn from each others' attempts at confronting racist incidents, their skills will develop and improve. Given that most people are intimidated by racism, it is important that a worker's confidence is developed so that intervention is less hesitant and clumsy. Another approach is to work in pairs with groups where it is known that racism is likely to manifest itself. If you know that a colleague is there as well, the chances of collusion are reduced!

There are no instant answers to the problem of white racism in community groups. Black colleagues are understandably impatient: 'We want you to stop talking about it and start doing something!', one told me. Once it is clear that white workers take the problem seriously, share their responses and develop their skills in tackling racism when it occurs, then their black colleagues will begin to feel a bit more comfortable about being colleagues.

An anti-sexist practice

There are similarities between the lessons that men need to learn to develop an anti-sexist community work practice and the lessons that white workers need to learn to be effectively anti-racist.

First, we must be *aware of who the consumers of community work are.* The evidence to Sheffield's community work review suggested that community work is increasingly with women. This may be work with women as women, or with women as people in need of better under-fives' provision, or with women as activists within a tenants' association, or with women as volunteers within an advice centre. When the work is with women as women, then male community workers have no part to play in delivering the community work service directly. They may have a role, negotiated and agreed with women colleagues, in providing back-up or administrative support to the women workers who are delivering the community work service directly. In working with groups that contain a significant proportion of women, male community workers need to develop skills that promote the women's ability to play a full part in the life of those groups. For example, a male community worker may collude with an organizational structure that grants power to male members of the group at the expense of the women – this is often the case in community groups that use formal constitutional structures that favour male members with experience of trade union or working men's club rulebooks and procedures. Male members may fail to question decisions to meet at times that are inconvenient for members who have child care commitments. A male worker may not devote as much energy to helping a group secure resources for child care at its meetings as a woman colleague. A male community worker may collude with sexist remarks and behaviour within a group with which he works. To fail to challenge traditional power relationships, to ignore the needs of women within groups, to fail to challenge sexist behaviour means practising community work on behalf of men – the minority consumers of community work!

Secondly, *the way people work together is as important as the task.* What one woman colleague described as 'hairy-chested' community work was, in the late 1960s and early 1970s particularly, about looking at the local council 'down the barrel of a gun'. In other words, it was about dramatic confrontations and, above all, it was about achieving results – the sort of things that 'boys' love. The great majority of community workers in those days were men, whose aggressive style rose partly from two things: the paternalism and 'we know best' attitudes of much of local government, and the fact that it was possible to win resources to finance change and improvements. This provided an irresistible combination for male community workers attracted by the prospect of leading the attack on 'out-of-touch bureaucrats' to secure change, followed by the chance of exercising influence over the distribution of resources in the local community. Today, resources are no longer available and this approach can no longer achieve results – unless the resources are secured at the expense of some other service. In Sheffield, for example, a campaign by people with disability to have improvements made to a local library to allow for access by people with disability has succeeded because the city council has shelved a road improvement plan. Yet this is regarded by many as a successful example of community action supported by community workers. However, it was the task that was all important. The campaign was encouraged by the City Libraries Department and without community worker input and leadership would not even have happened. The fact that people with disability really did not own, design or carry out the campaign – except to turn up at a media event/demonstration – was not seen as a problem by those who described the campaign as a success in community work/ community action terms. To collude with this description of the campaign is to undermine the importance that women workers wish to place on the *process of community work* – the way people learn, the way decisions are reached, the way people help each other, the way people develop an independence and confidence that empowers them for ever – not just for the duration of what happens to be the campaign of the moment. As a man and as a community work manager, it is imperative that I support this desire to keep the *process* of community work on the agenda.

Thirdly, we need to discover *an effective role for the male community worker*. If a male community worker is to resist the temptation to say 'There's no role for a bloke in community work these days!', it will be because he has been able to develop an effective male role within community work. This must start from an understanding of his strengths as a male community worker and develop through an alliance with other male community workers who wish to develop an anti-sexist community work practice. Together, male community workers can share concerns and develop skills. They can help each other to work out specific commitments to challenge sexism and male power either within their organizations or within community groups. They can offer each other support in refusing to collude with practices that reinforce traditional power relationships. If such mutual support by male workers leads to an improvement in their practice as community workers, there is a chance (although they have no right to expect it) that women colleagues will be interested in talking about ways in which men can support their work as women community workers.

Finally, we need to promote *anti-racism and anti-sexism as an underlying set of values*. There is a temptation to see work on anti-racism or anti-sexism as a separate or additional sphere of work. While there may be specific areas of anti-racist or anti-sexist activity, we must acknowledge the importance of anti-racism and anti-sexism as an underlying set of values that guides all our work. I believe that this is true in any workplace situation – but it is especially true of community work, which aims to offer support to the powerless and the oppressed within society.

Welfare rights

In the early 1970s a new welfare rights movement emerged including claimants' unions and local neighbourhood-controlled advice centres. An important reason for this was a growing awareness that state benefits were a *right* as opposed to *charity*. As a result of rising unemployment, a growing number of families were forced to negotiate the maze of state benefit regulations. They discovered – with encouragement from refugees from the 'alternative society' – that by collective action they could win a better deal from officials of the DHSS. It became good advice to 'never see the "nashy"[3] alone'.

The growth of modern community work in Britain coincided with the emergence of the welfare rights movement. Many claimants' unions enjoyed support from community workers, who discovered that it wasn't enough simply to support people when they were visiting the DHSS offices; they needed good advice close to home. Soon advice centres were being established in neighbourhoods where the number of claimants was rising, and these centres tended to be controlled by the neighbourhoods themselves. Community workers insisted that advice should be given in a supportive and welcoming atmosphere, which would not deprive claimants of their dignity in the name of traditional charitable 'good works'. These centres concentrated on getting the message across that to claim was a *right*.

Taking action to secure greater take-up of benefits proved an effective way of learning how to navigate the maze of welfare benefit regulations and laws. Experiential learning has never had a better advocate than the welfare rights movement – many of the best advisers and advocates are people who first became involved as claimants. Courses were offered to activists within the tenants' and labour movement and gradually the business of being a claimant became more and more acceptable, although many older people remained resistant to claiming their full entitlements. In recent years the renewed propaganda attack on 'scroungers' and the 'work-shy' has undermined a decade of growing confidence among claimants. The explicit aim of the 1986 Social Security Act[4] is to ensure that 'help is targeted at people who need it most' – implying that many people who receive benefit do not really need it.

In 1983, when the reviews of social security were first launched I moved from Sunderland to Sheffield and stopped undertaking welfare rights advice sessions. However, I have subsequently sat on the management committee of a local advice centre in Firth Park and have been in a good position to see the problems arising from the changes in benefit regulations at a time when increases in unemployment in Sheffield have tripled the demands on the advice centre's services.

One result of the increased burden of the work required to service the growing demand for advice and to keep abreast of regulation changes is that workers have had little time to do any campaigning work to alert the claimant and wider population to the significance of the Social Security Act. At the same time, the government has made it clear that it will not tolerate state funds being used for campaigning or anti-government propaganda work In the past, advice centres have always tried to develop a wider awareness of the needs of the poor – now they are frustrated in doing this at a time when a major reorganization of the whole security system is under way. In Sunderland, this threat from the government resulted in the Urban Programme funding[5] being removed from two advice centres. In Sheffield, it resulted in the Manpower Services Commission – the major funder of advice workers in the city – issuing an instruction that workers were not to become involved in campaigning work. The gradual introduction of changes in benefit regulations meant that campaigning against changes was difficult because it had to be organized over a long timescale. The fact that different groups of claimants were affected at different times made the task of establishing common cause among different groups of claimants very difficult. It takes a great deal of effort not to believe that all these factors were the result of a carefully calculated strategy by the Department of Health and Social Security to minimize opposition to the changes in social security provision.

Workers at the advice centre believe that the gains made in the 1970s in terms of increasing confidence and awareness amongst claimants have been lost. The conviction that community workers are helping to create a climate that empowers a claimant to do a great deal on their own behalf has given way to an equally clear belief that it is now *essential* to have strong 'professional' involvement in making a claim to ensure that the claimant doesn't unwittingly damage a good case.

The increased pressure on claimants to prove need has made the process of claiming more and more humiliating. For example, in the past it was accepted that from time to time a family in receipt of social security support would need to replace bedding. Now, claimants have to prove that bedding has worn out because of bed-wetting or incontinence. Hence, people are less and less willing to make claims and are turning elsewhere for help. Alternatives include borrowing from relatives, increased use of second-hand shops, clubs and mail order houses on costly credit, use of loan 'sharks' to pay off credit debt, and going without.

The amount of time that is now given to debt counselling is proof of the seriousness of the problem arising from the easy availability of credit. Perhaps the greatest irony is that, having prevented MSC–funded advice workers from getting involved in campaigns about the Social Security Act, the MSC is currently funding an expensive new service set up to deal with the effects of benefit changes – a fully fledged debt counselling service!

When the Social Security Act came into full effect in April 1988, Firth Park advice centre organised a take-up campaign to ensure that what can still be claimed is claimed. The first item on the agenda for the campaign organizers was to recruit more campaign organizers! The volunteers and workers at the centre remain at full stretch dealing with the (still) increasing work load.

Community self-help projects

Community work has always encouraged community self-help projects. It has done so in the belief that services could and should be controlled, as far as is possible, by the people who receive the service. Many people involved in community work believed that if services were designed by local communities they were much more likely to meet need effectively. Community workers and the groups that they supported would often have to battle hard to get reluctant town halls to release the resources needed to fund community-based initiatives. Many of these early initiatives have been copied by many local authorities and run as mainstream council services. Examples include advice centres, adventure play-grounds and refuges for women suffering from domestic violence.

When community activists were pioneering these initiatives there was no suggestion that they should be run on the 'cheap'. The only considerations were that they were effectively designed by the communities that needed them and that they ought to remain under community control. However, government pressures to cut social services costs by promoting care in the community has introduced a new element into proposals for community care projects or self-help initiatives. The fact that the government is keen to transfer the cost of care onto the family and the community means that we need to exercise greater caution in assessing proposals for new community initiatives.

A number of examples from my community work experience illustrate the differences between community projects designed by the users to satisfy real need and those promoted with the central objective of cutting costs.

A self-help group for people with disability. A small group of users of a council-run day centre for people with physical disability decided that the atmosphere within the day centre was too passive. They felt that their abilities were not being developed and that, despite many requests for changes in the day centre programme, the wishes of the majority to leave things as they were had prevailed. As a result, a group of five users in their late thirties and early forties broke away and formed a 'self-help group'. They received some community work support and a small grant from the social services department to pay for the rent of alternative premises.

The group decided that they needed their own transport: after a year's campaign they were successful in getting an ambulance/minibus from the city council. They tried to get the city council to provide drivers, but lack of finance meant that they were forced to do a deal with the MSC, which agreed to provide them with drivers under the Community Programme.

The group is very active and now has a membership of seventy, and has a varied programme of activities, including sports such as horse riding, bowls, archery and swimming. Users socialize together, going to pubs that have made them welcome, and participate fully in community activity in their area. The group has campaigned to get its style of operation accepted as a recognized alternative to day centres. To back up this campaign the group produced a booklet[6] describing its work and sent a copy to every member of the social services committee.

It is very likely that new funds will now be found to expand the services offered to people with physical disability to include support for self-determined groups modelled on the self-help group described above. This is an excellent example of the sort of self-help initiative that needs to be encouraged. The service is designed and controlled by the users. The users believed that the purpose of the exercise was to demonstrate an additional way of supporting people with disability and campaigned for the council to take it up. The users were not arguing for this initiative to be funded at the expense of traditional day centres, which they recognized were important to older, less active people.

A less encouraging example concerns a *care scheme for older people run by a tenants' association*. Members of this tenants' association, which services a large estate of 4,000 houses, had become increasingly concerned about the needs of the population of older people on the estate. The social services department was also concerned and was planning to establish a community support programme in the area to provide a more comprehensive service to older people in their own homes. The service would include an alarm link to wardens for all those older people requesting it, increased home help provision, additional lunch clubs and meals-on-wheels, a community laundry and support for community groups that wished to play a part in this 'new initiative in community care'. The social services department embarked on a comprehensive consultation programme with local residents and members of the tenants' association. While expectations were raised, the implementation of the scheme was delayed for three years pending the construction of some community buildings.

In the meantime, the MSC decided to increase the numbers of places on the Community Programme and sent their agents[7] off in search of suitable work. They visited the tenants' association and suggested that they could sponsor a care scheme for older people in the area. Given the delay in the council's plans, it was not surprising that the tenants' association agreed to sponsor the MSC's more limited care scheme, though local community workers tried to explain the disadvantages.

While local people agreed to participate in this care scheme, despite hearing the arguments against, it cannot be described as being a scheme that has been designed by the service users. It was easy for the self-help group for people with disability to ensure that the service was designed by the users because *they were the users*, and it was equally easy to ensure that the service remained in their control. It was always going to be much more difficult for the tenants' association to ensure that their care scheme was designed by the older people who were to be the users. Even though it would have taken time and care and a good deal of consultation around the estate, it would not have been impossible. Yet the MSC had no time for such an exercise.

The self-help group for people with disability was in a position to make the workers supplied by the MSC accountable to them as the service users. The workers employed by the tenants' association ought to have been accountable to the service users, but in practice they were accountable to officials of the tenants' association.

The tenants' association's 'initiative' happened because someone else needed it to happen – in this case the MSC. What were the MSC's motives? The MSC's main objective was to respond to political pressure to increase the number of Community Programme places for the long-term unemployed so that, in turn, there would be a corresponding decrease in the unemployment statistics. Is there perhaps another motive? There is a growing recognition that the current Conservative government, because of its antagonism to local government, aims to centralize control of local services. There is clear evidence, for example, that more and more centralized control is being exercised over the delivery of education services. Could the care scheme being run by the tenant's association be one of a number of trials being conducted for some future centralization of the provision of personal social services, perhaps even leading to privatization?

This is not simply a problem for community workers. Social workers are being encouraged to find and develop new ways of working: the Barclay Report[8] was full of encouragement for community social work. Social workers are developing new and imaginative links with the communities in which they work so that they can mobilize resources not previously available. The self-help group for people with disability provides a model that can be applied to other client groups. The growth of 'make-work' schemes looking in the same direction should alert us to the danger that is always present in self-help groups. This approach should only be embarked upon when it is clear that *additional* resources are being brought into play, not when it is in reality a *cheap and inadequate alternative* to traditional services.

From 'make-work' schemes to 'workfare' for the long-term unemployed

Various 'make-work' schemes have expanded in proportion with the growth of unemployment during the last decade. The scheme with which I have been most closely involved is the one aimed at the long-term unemployed over 18 years of age. In 1977, this scheme was called the Job Creation Programme (JCP). It was, at first, treated with some suspicion by community workers but it came to be accepted as a useful addition to the resources available to local communities. It was also seen by many as a way of offering working-class activists a chance to get some paid experience of community work, which could act as a springboard to permanent employment.

In Sunderland, the advice centre where I worked used JCP to expand its service in late 1977 and, as a result of the successful use of workers funded in this way, was able to make the case to Sunderland Council for two additional permanent advisers to be provided through the Urban Programme. Four people were employed under the JCP scheme – two local activists, one graduate of Sunderland Polytechnic's community and youth work course and one unemployed social worker. Both local activists are now employed full time by the advice centre – one straight away, the other after she successfully completed the Sunderland Polytechnic community and youth work course. The graduate of this same course went to work as a welfare rights adviser in Milton Keynes and the social worker also gained permanent employment with the advice centre. Similar experiences with JCP are reported from all over the country.

Late in 1978, JCP became STEP – the Special Temporary Employment Programme – and continued in much the same way as JCP had done. It still involved relatively small numbers of workers and, notwithstanding concerns about low pay and the limited twelve-month nature of the contract, was seen as a valuable resource in community work, especially for married women who were considering a return to work and for whom STEP was a convenient first move. Because the numbers involved in the STEP scheme were still limited and as full-time and permanent jobs in community work and community work-related fields were still increasing, it was possible for many people leaving STEP jobs to find permanent work in reasonable time.

When, a year later in 1979, STEP became CEP – the Community Enterprise Programme – things began to change. First, the Manpower Services Commission introduced stricter regulations about who was eligible for participation in the scheme. The MSC also became more interested in what the workers were doing – previously, the MSC had been fairly relaxed and left it up to scheme sponsors to interpret regulations liberally. Now schemes were visited regularly and deviations from the original contract, however small, were not permitted. However, the most serious problem with CEP was the fact that it was becoming larger and larger at a time when unemployment was more than 2 million and the numbers of long-term unemployed were steadily increasing. The MSC wanted the CEP scheme to be used much more for manual work schemes, which the MSC considered would be more appropriate for people in the pool of the long-term unemployed. As the CEP expanded, funding for permanent community work and related jobs declined. The Urban Programme, which had funded a steady increase in community work jobs, began to suggest, then insist, that people should look to CEP schemes for the resources to employ workers on community projects.

The replacement of CEP with the Community Programme (CP) in 1983 consolidated the MSC's influence over community work. While the number of places in the scheme soared – to over 6,000 in South Yorkshire in 1986 – Urban Programme support for employing workers virtually ceased. Local government finance was in such short supply that CP 'graduates' expected their next job to be anther CP job, when their eligibility of six months' unemployment came round again (twelve months' unemployment if over 25). Some people employed in advice centres in Sheffield 'enjoyed' three periods of employment on the scheme.

As employment opportunities following CP schemes deteriorated and as eligibility was tightened to the virtual exclusion of married women, more and more community organizations and local authorities withdrew from sponsoring the schemes. This meant that the MSC had to bring in 'incentives' to ensure that enough places were provided. The MSC introduced the concept of the 'managing agency', an intermediary between the MSC and the local project that employed the CP workers. In Sheffield, these managing agencies included the Council for Voluntary Service and a consortium of churches. The MSC paid these agencies a 'fee' of £100 for every place they managed to fill. This fee could be used by the agency in any way it wished – it was not obliged to spend it on administering or benefiting the project. In my experience, this encouraged agencies to play a 'numbers game' and consequently pay less attention than was necessary to the quality of the placements that were on offer to the long-term unemployed. Two examples confirm this view. A pensioners' lunch club that had previously relied on volunteers drawn from the neighbourhood to collect and serve lunch from the nearby school had these volunteers 'replaced' by CP workers. The CP scheme decided that, if the dinners were cooked by CP workers, then more CP workers could be employed – ignoring any threat to the school meals service that this might provoke. The decision to introduce the CP workers into this club was taken by the CP agency with little or no reference to the wishes of the volunteers or the lunch club users. The other example concerned the one referred to earlier – the tenants' association's care scheme for older people. Following the increases in the numbers of CP places required by the MSC, managing agencies were literally 'touting' their wares around local communities. The tenants' association eventually discovered some of the difficulties involved in managing, with little or no support from the managing agency, a complex home-care scheme for older people.

Following the Conservative victory in the 1987 general election, the government soon signalled its intention to change yet again the nature of 'make-work' schemes for the long-term unemployed. At the same time, changes in social security regulations made it more difficult for those 'eligible' for work to survive on benefit, and checks on 'availability' for work were intensified. The government's intention to crack down hard on the 'work-shy' was clearly apparent.

At the end of August 1988, the Community Programme was replaced by a new unified training scheme called Employment Training (ET). For the first time, the concept of 'community benefit' was dropped from these 'make-work' schemes. ET concentrates on getting 'trainees' fit for work through spending about two days a week in off-the-job training. After the first twelve months of the scheme, it remained unclear what off-the-job training would involve and to what extent 'hard skills' would be gained by the trainees. Three days a week are spent on employers' premises.

The high cost of the ET scheme to employers (expected to be £5 per week per trainee) seems calculated to undermine the role of schemes for the unemployed in local authority community work and shift the emphasis to the private sector. In Sheffield, for example, about half of the total of 4,000 CP workers were engaged on projects that benefited local communities, at a wages cost to the MSC of about £7 million in 1987/8. In addition, the MSC contributed over £1 million in project costs and fees to community and voluntary organizations in Sheffield. The total contribution amounted to over £8 million. When this is compared to the £1½ million spent by Sheffield City Council on community work, it is clear what a massive influence the MSC and its 'make-work' schemes have had on community work and related fields.

Before the Community Programme was replaced, many community workers were growing increasingly concerned that cheap MSC schemes were being used to run essential services. However, as long as these schemes were being run by voluntary and community groups, there was still an element of accountability to local people. Many local citizens' groups have recognized the attack on community services and accountability inherent in the shift from the Community Programme to Employment Training and have resisted the introduction of the new scheme. Both the Sheffield Advice Centres' Group and the Sheffield Churches Community Programme Agency refused to participate in ET. They objected to the facts that 'trainees' would not be paid a wage (instead they would receive a £10 top-up to their weekly benefit) and that they would be treated not as workers, but as trainees. It was also evident from government statements that the freedom of the unemployed to refuse to participate in ET was likely to be undermined by the more rigorous enforcement of availability for work tests. In short, both the advice centres and the Churches feared that ET would turn out to be compulsory.

More voluntary organizations that managed schemes under the Community Programme may refuse to do so under ET. While it is possible to hope that such 'defections' will make the MSC consider the wisdom of ET and 'workfare', it is perhaps more likely that the government had already anticipated that the 'wet' community and voluntary sector would shrink away. This would explain the MSC's wooing of the private sector and its decision to drop the prohibition on trainees being used to generate profit. With that restriction gone, £5 per week is a small price to pay for three days' labour.

Twelve years of 'make-work' for the unemployed have finally become 'workfare'. A creative and relatively caring scheme – JCP in 1976 – has been cynically corrupted into Employment Training in 1988. The damaging effect on local communities – especially those in the inner city – arises not only from the huge withdrawal of CP money. Many local networks of self-help and groups of volunteers have been disrupted by the arrival of make-work schemes. These took years to build up and cannot be replaced overnight. Meanwhile what will the private sector be doing with workfare? Will some private 'care' agency be knocking on a tenants' association door offering workers – three days a week – to cut grass for old people? Will local authority social services departments finally be replaced by new private 'care' agencies?

'In and against the State'

The publication in 1980 of *In and against the State*[9] by the London-Edinburgh Weekend Return Group provoked much thought among community workers about the role of state-employed workers. In the late 1960s and early 1970s, nobody questioned the existence of the welfare state. Thus it was not a problem for community workers to encourage local residents to launch critical campaigns on the standard of services provided.

Today, the situation is quite different. A tenants' association criticizing the quality of work undertaken by the direct labour organization (DLO) can be used as a justification for privatization. The same organization's campaign to get local authority management of their estate improved could now be used in a 'prospectus' for the selling of the estate to a private developer. Often a group's desire to establish a self-help initiative arises out of dissatisfaction with the quality of service that is provided by the local state. Whereas in the past such an action would be regarded as additional to the state-provided service there is now real anxiety that such an action could *replace* a local state service. The current political climate presents an enormous challenge to all workers employed by the state who are critical of the way the state provides its services.

In Sheffield, the Tenants' Federation has taken the initiative in establishing regular meetings between representatives of the tenants' movement and trade union members representing the direct labour organization. The objective is to enable the workers to hear the tenants' frustrations with the performance of the DLO and for the DLO workers to explain to tenants' representatives why the DLO performs in a certain way. Sometimes the DLO is obliged to recognize that the indefensible cannot be defended; sometimes the tenants are made aware of health and safety factors that are ignored by many building companies in the private sector.

I have recently had the difficult task of trying to defend the actions of the DLO to members of a neighbourhood centre who are frustrated at the way the DLO is carrying out alterations and improvements to their building. Part of the problem is that the DLO is accountable to building maintenance officials within the social services department and not directly to the service users. I have failed to provide that defence and am trying hard to get the DLO to negotiate directly with the neighbourhood centre members in the future. This is difficult because it is asking people to work in unfamiliar ways.

Similar problems are being experienced by users of day centres for people with physical disability. They have observed with envy the difference that control over mobility has made to members of the self-help group mentioned earlier. All that day centre members get from council-run ambulances is a trip from home to the day centre and back – they never get to go to the pub or to watch Sheffield Wednesday play football. When the council's transport manager came to a heated meeting of day centre members and failed to respond to their demands for a more flexible service capable of some control from them, he left the meeting in a highly agitated state saying that he wasn't accountable to them but to the Municipal Enterprise Committee.

The only effective way of criticizing local services when they need to be criticized, yet defending the very existence of those services, is through the development of new accountability arrangements for council and other workers providing public services. Genuine satisfaction with the quality of a local service – such as exists, for example, with the home help service in Sheffield – must be its best defence from privatization.

Community workers must challenge local authorities, often their employers, to develop such accountability arrangements. Community workers have the skills to work on establishing these new accountability arrangements and they shouldn't be afraid to offer them.

One feature of early attempts to establish accountability arrangements is the lack of a clear framework for the involvement of service users in service management. For example, day centre users involved in the local management committee thought, wrongly, that they had responsibility for hiring and firing staff. They arrived at this incorrect assumption because they had been invited to participate in some staff interviews and had been inadequately briefed about their role in the process. As their preferred choice was appointed they thought that they had been instrumental in the decision – in fact this was coincidence. The misunderstanding went on for months. Not surprisingly, when the truth dawned, there was some cynicism and bitterness. Community workers have a much clearer understanding of the need for explicit contracts.

Service managers wanting to involve users in management are disappointed at what they see as the limited view of service users and of their reluctance to change. Community workers have had experience of providing training and learning opportunities for activists that have included visiting other towns and cities to see how others do things. We recognize that people's own experience of how things are done is often their only view of what is possible. This experience can be shared with service managers who want to increase the awareness of service users involved in managing their services.

Clearly, such assistance can only be given on the basis of a *separate* contract. It would be impossible for a community worker to assist a group of service users to make demands on a particular day, and then on another day put on a different hat and advise the service manager on how to respond to user demand.

Community work: social movement or profession?

Over the last decade the debate has raged between those who want to see community work or community development establish itself firmly as a professional activity and those who insist that community work is simply a core of skills that aims to enable local community groups to achieve their own objectives. Those who emphasize the professional nature of the task want to establish a community work equivalent of the National Institute of Social Work. Such a national body would speak for the profession on community work, influence the training of community workers and exercise influence on government community development policies. It would also seek to influence the amount and type of resources available for community work and community development in the future. The proposed national body would commission and publish research into developing trends in community work/ community development. Against this, many community workers and community activists argue for support to be channelled into local and regional groupings of community workers and activists so that the field can have a chance of influencing national developments from the 'bottom up'.

The debate reached a climax when the Gulbenkian Foundation published a consultative document entitled *Making a Start*[10] in 1985. *Making a Start* argued the case for a national body to support the development of community work and community development along the lines of a community work equivalent of NISW. The proposition provoked a divided response. My view is that it would unhelpfully influence the development of community work and community development from the centre – from London. It would give the funders of community work, the trainers of community workers and probably the employers of community workers even more power to influence the direction of community work. I was invited to sit on the Gulbenkian Foundation's working party which produced *Making a Start*. I saw in the working party a vision of what a community work 'NISW' might look like. I was the only practising community worker present, and there were only one woman and only two black people. This predominantly white, male and middle-class working party was proposing to shape the direction of community work by arguing for the creation of a national body that had every chance of ending up as a mirror image of the working party trying to create it.

Community workers in the field, alarmed by the proposition for such a national body, managed to intervene to prevent it for the time being. They did this in two ways: first, they convinced the

Community Projects Foundation (a suggested home for the national body) that it was an inappropriate suggestion, thus denying an early and speedy opportunity of setting up a national body; secondly, the 'field' persuaded the Voluntary Service Unit within the Home Office (any national body's likely main funder)[11] to await a full consultation of the views of grass roots workers and activists. Accordingly, a consultation exercise took place during 1986, which resulted in a proposition for a different kind of 'national body' – one based on regional groupings of workers and activists but with space, as well, for representation of national organizations with an interest in community work and community development. In March 1986, an interim committee of the Standing Conference on Community Development was established at a conference in Birmingham called to hear the results of the consultation. This interim committee has twelve representatives of regional groupings and six representatives from national organizations. The interim committee received a modest amount of money from the Home Office so that it could work out in its 'interim year' a constitutional framework for the proposed Standing Conference.

During this same period another organization has been taking shape – Community Development UK. Its accommodation address is the National Institute of Social Work! Many of its founder members include the white men who wished to see the establishment of a community work equivalent of NISW as proposed in *Making a Start.* I hope that if any national organization is created to promote the interests of community work it will be an organization with its roots in the localities where community work is practised and that it will be an organization that can reflect the concerns of black women and men and white women. If it ends up looking like the working party, from which I resigned, then it will be yet another agency of oppression, not one of liberation. Community work needs resources that will enable local networks of workers and activists to flourish so that people can learn from each other and from shared experiences. Such networks will allow ideas and proposals for future directions to filter upwards to a 'national' Standing Conference, which can, in turn, attempt to influence the funders of community work, the makers of social policy, the trainers of community workers and the employers of community workers. Yet I fear the worst. Since when has anything as sensible and democratic as that happened?

Notes and references

1 Interim Report to the *Community Work Review* conducted by the Family and Community Services Department of Sheffield City Council in 1987.

2 This section draws on A. Ohri, B. Manning and P. Curno (eds), *Community Work and Racism* (Routledge & Kegan Paul, 1982), p. 12, Guidelines for white community workers.

3 A north-east England 'slang' term for the National Assistance Board, predecessor to the Department of Health and Social Security.

4 *The Social Security Act: A Brief Guide* (CPAG, 1988).

5 Additional assistance provided by the Department of the Environment to cities and towns with severe inner-city problems. DoE contributes 75 per cent of funds while local authority contributes 25 per cent.

6 North Sheffield Disabled Federation, '1982–1986: Four Years On' (photocopied report, 1986).

7 Community Programme managing agents appointed by the MSC to run the Community Programme – usually local authorities or large voluntary agencies.

8 Peter M. Barclay, *Social Workers: their role and tasks – Working Party Report* (Bedford Square Press, 1982).

9 London-Edinburgh Weekend Return Group, *In and against the State: Discussion Notes for Socialists* (Pluto Press, 1980).

10 Gulbenkian Foundation Working Party, *Making a Start – a consultative document on a national structure for community development* (Calouste Gulbenkian Foundation, 1983).

11 Major funder of national initiatives in community work and community development, the best example being the National Community Project of the late 1960s and early 1970s.

14 Towards a black perspective in social work: a transcultural exploration

JOHN SMALL

Introduction

Much of the debate about social work with black families has been rooted in constructs of social pathology in a Euro-centric framework that is permeated by racism at the institutional and individual levels.[1] Given the pervasiveness of institutionalized racism, it was inevitable that its constructs would influence social policies, predicated on the false assumption that the black family is inherently unstable. Given such assumptions, it is not surprising that the conclusion was reached that black families cannot provide the economic, social and psychological resources to enable their members to adapt and become productive participants in British society. This deficit model has entered social work practice as the conventional wisdom that guides the understanding of black families. It determines the ways in which social workers view black people in general and shapes the style of social work that is carried out with black families.[2]

The deficit model is not only racist but also systematically masks both the historical experience and the contemporary realities that shape the black family. It denies the strengths of black families by dismissing the networks of support and flexible structures that are the stabilizing factors for black families, in contra-distinction to Euro-centric conjugal forms of family relationships. Such false constructions provide no basis for understanding the objective conditions of black people today and fail to sensitize workers to the adoptive mechanisms used by black families to ward off the harmful effect of racism.

In this chapter I hope to demonstrate how those working with the deficit model of the black family can cause further disruption or even exacerbate the difficulties caused by racism. This may well explain how a significant number of black family members become casualities of the system and are relegated to mental institutions, the prisons, children's homes, or fostering and adoption arrangements.[3]

Conceptualizing and contextualizing the black family

This conceptual framework is constructed to provide a coherent and systematic understanding of the factors that intervene in the relationship between the white worker and the black family. My intention is to demonstrate how Euro-centric social work methods exert additional pressures on black families to conform to a pattern that is often alienating and disruptive. Such disruptions have serious consequences, not only for the immediate family, but for the family of the next generation.

Within the dynamics of the relationship between the worker and the black family two factors are of importance for this purpose. These two factors are analytically separate.

The phenomenon of primary identification

The first factor may be termed primary identification. It consists of all the constructs of black people. These constructs are derivative of the conditioning process that they had in their own societies and families. They include ideas, the construction of events based on experience, beliefs and practices. In short they represent total being. They constitute a social whole, embodying the basic fabric of character and personality, in an integrated and coherent structure.

Primary identification performs a number of essential functions. First, it provides continuity and predictability of behaviour for individuals within their families and societies. Second, it legitimizes a person's value system and gives it ultimate authority. Third, it provides people with a web of security. Fourth, it tells people who they are, where they should go, the direction to take, what they should do, how it should be done. Finally it integrates life and provides people with a sense of identity and purpose to life.

The phenomenon of secondary identification

The other factor may be termed secondary identification. It consists of the dominant constructs of ideas and modes of behaviour of the individual in society. However, the dominant construct excludes the black experience. It has little relevance to the lifestyle, values, behaviour, attitudes and aspirations of black people. Consequently, concepts, definitions of situations and descriptions of events are seen purely from a white perspective. Secondary identification fails to take account of the distinctive position of black people, our differential historical experience, differential level of economic activity, differential status in the community, differential opportunity and life chances and differential access to the use of power and authority. Operating within this framework, the social worker uses professional techniques to bring the individual or family into line with the built-in assumptions and values of the dominant constructs as they relate to secondary identification. It further implies a substitution principle, which operates at the deepest mental level.

Given certain conditions, primary and secondary identification may give the impression that they have merged but, on close examination, one will discover that they have not. If they do, the merging is often brittle and, even if it is not brittle, it is found within so few cases that they are statistically insignificant in relation to the number of blacks that workers encounter in carrying out their duties.

The origin of the substitution principle

In British colonies, the subject peoples were conditioned to believe that they shared a common loyalty with the English and other citizens of the Commonwealth to the Crown and the Mother Country. Thus it was easy to induce many people from these countries to travel to Britain to participate in rebuilding 'their' country after the war. The promise of material advancement which could not be achieved in the Caribbean, Africa and South Asia proved a powerful incentive. The subsequent parliamentary pressure to restrict the flow of people into England heightened fears of immigration controls among blacks already here. The fear of a clampdown led black people to bring over their young dependants from colonial and former colonial countries. At the same time, measures were taken to facilitate the assimilation of the 'Dark Strangers' into British society.

The postwar immigration and the climate of racism that accompanied it created the context for the whole debate about the black family and black family breakdown.[4] Movement from one society to another implies changes in personal relationships and alterations in the physical environment. It further implies psychological changes resulting from separation and disassociation from the familiar, which require the mobilization of inner and outer resources to enable adaptation to the new environment. For black people, immigration meant the disruption of the basic patterns of their original social and cultural experience. For many it meant greater cultural restriction and social isolation, experiences compounded by a system of oppression of which racism was the major element.

However thoroughly an individual prepares, he or she can never be adequately equipped for life in a new society. Indeed, society is dynamic and not static and the primary construct systems and subsystems of the individual cannot be changed in absolute terms. Settlement in the new society involves choices in reordering and redefining not only the new situation but roles and relationships. (It is within the arena of this transitory phase that black children are often caught). Frequently, the families do need help in the exercise and it appears to be at this point that social workers fail in their intervention.

A great deal of understanding and knowledge is required of the before, during and after experience to help people through the processes of separation from the original society and attachment to the new. The situation is often very fluid and the worker may well try to attempt to induce the individual to desocialize and resocialize into the dominant constructs of the new social milieu. Indeed, this has been the main approach of the white professionals.

The black person carries to the new world a residue of the old that is vital for maintaining the person's psychological system. This residue – 'memories of things past' – is indeed a significant source of strength for a black person, and one which is often passed on to family members. However, the white social worker's conceptualization of the situation fails to acknowledge the differential character of the black person's experience. Instead the social worker brings to the situation the dominant assumptions of his or her own experience, borne out of the conditioning process of white society and reinforced by social work education and training.[5]

The fallacy of the substitution principle

The main assumptions behind social work practice prevent the white worker from grasping the significance of the before and after experience of immigration for black people. In the first instance, social workers tend to assume that the black person will identify with the new or 'superior' social order. They expect that the old will be wiped out and substituted by the new. If it is not, then the residue can be attributed to 'assimilative lag'. The task of the social worker is therefore to help the black person to 'wipe it out' because the significant experience should be the present one. These attitudes may reflect the fact that the worker knows little about black people, that he has been subjected to a conditioning process, or it may be simply the manifestation of racist assumptions. If these factors are operating then the worker is prevented from recognizing the importance of the primary identification of black people. The strengths and values of this identification have not hitherto been recognized or appreciated.[6]

Primary identification is further consolidated by the experience of the black person in British society. The alienating feeling of not belonging to society, of having been let down and cheated, is further reinforced by racism, whether it is encountered personally or transferred from relatives or community members. It is finally cemented by the feeling of powerlessness and the rising level of social and political consciousness of racial identity in the black community. Here the substitution principle is doomed to fail.

An individual with a permeable or semi-permeable personality may attempt to wipe out the residue of primary identification as a response to pressure to reorder, to integrate and to achieve. The usually unspoken wish of the social worker and of society is that the black person will become like the social worker, thus enabling the worker to relate better and to assist with the assimilative aim.

The attempt at integration is unsuccessful primarily because the individual is required to substitute an experience that is not only alienating in content but negative and disruptive in process. The pressure to integrate thus generates internal struggles in the black person and provokes resistance to the substitution process. This saps the energy of the individual and creates a state of normlessness, the logical consequence being a state of psychopathology. The state of normlessness may result in family disruption and may go some way to explain the reception into care of some black children on the grounds that, or in the words of the social worker, their parents are 'unfit to cope'.

The phenomenon of primary identification is at variance with the thesis of the common shared value that lies behind the frame of reference of the social worker. This seems to be a misguided use of the Durkheimian[7] and Weberian[8] concepts that all societies depend upon normative consensus or should be analysed as if they did. That is to say, the majority of members of society obey the rules out of willing submission. Effectively this means that most individuals in the society obey the rules because it is right to do so. But this ignores those who are unwilling and are not constrained by the rules of their representatives. In fact, what social workers should see in their work with black people, or any clients for that matter, is the Hobbesian war of 'all against all' and at the same time be constantly aware of the fact that the profession and its authorities do not embody, enjoy or reflect the representative authority of their clients. There has never been that common normative consensus between the classes in society, therefore it is unrealistic to assume that it exists among the races, particularly with the state of race relations in the 1980s and the harmful effects of racism.

To start from the premise of a consensus between black people and the British state, to relate to black people as if consensus existed or to interpret aspects of behaviour in this way, is nothing short of utopianism or stark cultural imperialism. Workers should bring to their practice a perspective based on cultural pluralism and at the same time look for degrees or levels of stability and functional coherence in the structure of values within the specific cultural and ethnic group. They should then apply differential assessment techniques, thus adopting a transcultural mode of practice to their work with the black client.

Another false, yet 'domain assumption' that affects the way in which social workers practice with black families is the construct that the movement of black families from their original society is a deviant activity. The act of immigration is associated with all the elements of disorganization and is therefore regarded as a threat to the harmonious relationships that should exist within families. Again the influence of a functionalist approach to the analysis of society has bedevilled social work thinking and practice. Social workers often make reference to the number of children who have difficulties with their parents after lengthy separation and conclude that 'separation issues cannot be resolved within the framework of the family'. Consequently, the child is received into care. They substantiate their findings by research which has shown that in the United Kingdom if children remain in care for more than six months then rehabilitation becomes impossible. Yet if they looked at the total situation they would see that the number of children who experience so-called unresolved separation and attachment problems as a result of the immigration process is insignificant compared with the number of children who went through similar processes and nevertheless have been able to work through these issues in their own families without the help of outside agencies. Perhaps this reductionist approach makes it easier for social workers to rationalize their racism and their ignorance in an unfamiliar territory. These assumptions further prevent the worker from having to distinguish between separation and 'not in care' and separation and 'being in care'. Given the fact that immigration, particularly of people of Afro-Caribbean origin, has dried up since the early 1970s, social workers should not be dealing with these problems in the mid-1980s.

Yet another false assumption is that immigration is usually a once-and-for-all phenomenon. Or if it is not, then it ought to be. This view seems to arise from a confused parallel between black migrants and white people who migrate from Britain to Canada, Australia, New Zealand or the United States. It has been seen that distance has not been and will never be a barrier to black people, who are traditionally travellers. There is frequency of travel back and forth. Black children often spend many of their early years in their own country, then they set off to Britain. They return often to their homeland and then travel back to Britain, and there is never a final break. Some would say that a final break would be in the interests of mobilizing political action and would result in total involvement of the black community in the affairs of society. However, this could equally well be the catalyst for a mental breakdown by virtue of the feeling of not belonging to this society, a consequence of repeated negative experiences for individuals who have no foundation to fall back on, because these have been 'wiped out'. The English and the Jews who have migrated to other countries have held on to their primary experience because of its strength. It has preserved their identity and their psychological well-being and, of course, this does not necessarily affect their allegiance to the country in which they have settled.

The dynamics of the substitution principle

The substitution principle creates an environment that is not conducive to equitable communication between the white social worker and the black family. Consequently, communication channels are not clear enough to enable the worker to assess the strengths of black families and identify objectively the quality of the resources that are being offered. The task of establishing communication channels must first be successfully performed before the resources of the family can be identified. It is therefore of paramount importance that a free flow of information exists between the family and the worker if there is to be constructive work with black families. The worker has to use the tools provided first by his personality, and through the relationship, use the knowledge gained by his training to establish meaningful contact with the family. In the relationship there should be warmth and reciprocity. The worker must therefore be in a warm and understanding relationship with the black person.

It is the worker who is identifying, assessing, studying and evaluating the resources that the family have to offer. If information is not flowing then the assessment will necessarily be biased. Social workers are in a position to lay bare the foundations for basic trust, to clarify, to demystify and to reinforce the positive aspects of black family life. The worker is strategically placed to be the agent of change and to identify factors that inhibit communication. Although the worker is more appropriately placed than any other individual, nevertheless he is often unsuccessful, primarily because he tries to impose order on a situation that he does not understand and that appears to him chaotic. In fact, in the majority of cases, it is not chaotic. The only problem is that the worker cannot recognize the disjunction between primary identification and secondary identification, or escape the consequences of his latent wish to substitute in the black person the dominant constructs based on notions of black inferiority.

Respect for black culture. A precondition for good practice

Understanding, warmth and the ability to reciprocate are qualities that social workers are assumed to possess and that they strive to acquire and enhance. However, social workers are as much part of a class-ridden and race-conscious society as the rest of the population. The benefits of the stratification process, the colour/class dichotomy, the unlimited access to education, occupation, employment and housing of the white population in contra-distinction to what is available to blacks, the advantage of being white in a society where colour has been made into such an issue, necessarily create different constructs between the social worker and black people. Both have different social experiences so they operate from distinctly different social bases. The experiences differ not only in quality but also in style. Consequently, the background from which the social workers come, consciously or unconsciously, inculcates an attitude and approach that rejects the style and behaviour of blacks in general, except in the few instances where the substitution principle has been applied and has been effective. The structure of the society, the strata from which the vast majority of social workers are drawn and the subjective experiences of their training prevents them from connecting with black families. This in turn inhibits the development of familiarity and respect for black people. Understanding and respect for black culture are a prerequisite for the creation of an environment conducive to exercising empathy and reciprocity, which in turn is necessary for the assessment of black families and the implementation of any successful work with black families. Social workers therefore need to develop transcultural modes of analysing their interaction with black people through a comparative evaluation of the cultural pattern and values in the black community and the ways in which racism affects the black population.

The substitution effect

When primary and secondary identification fail to integrate, conflicts arise. These conflicts are often interpreted as failure of the family or individual to adjust to or incorporate the dominant constructs.

Some individuals may achieve some sort of equilibrium between primary and secondary identification; the degree varies with their intellectual capacity and their ability to work out strategies to manipulate institutional structures. The dominant construct prescribes certain institutional procedures for advancement, which the worker has been conditioned to accept as legitimate and desirable. But this may not be the construction of the black person and consequently these arrangements have no relation to the black person's experience. Even when the constructions are similar for a black person the avenues of advancement are often blocked. The choice available and the life chances of the black person are therefore limited. While a black person is constantly aware of this, the white social worker may not even conceive that the avenues could be partially or totally blocked. The construct of the white social worker and of the black person are sometimes diametrically opposed.

What about blacks who were born in Britain? It could be said that they are outside this experience since they have been socialized in the dominant constructs and therefore have the phenomenon of secondary identification in their cultural and psychological system. Hence it is argued that they are different and analytically separate. I would suggest that in practice the two categories of black people merge imperceptibly as a result of racism and alienation. An absolute rejection of the dominant culture has taken place among British-born blacks accompanied by a total internalization of the primary identification. This substitution creates a close affinity between the blacks who were born in other countries and the blacks who were born in Britain. This is often reinforced by racial tension and the subjective experience of racism at the individual or institutional level.

Within the relationship between the black person and the white social worker there is often an inordinate pressure to incorporate the dominant culture without recognizing the barriers that confront black people generally. Blacks cannot exist without interaction with the wider society. Yet blacks are forced to restrict their interaction in an attempt to protect their personality from constant assault. This undoubtedly causes further difficulties.

The disintegrative function of the reordering process

In adjusting to the world that is constructed by the white social worker, black people have to attempt to alter their entire outlook and these alterations must become a part of their construction system. Consequently, they defend two psychological systems: the relatively constant and familiar, which is at the nub of existence, and the acquired, which is internalized, maintained and protected in order to advance in this society. It is indeed within the interplay between primary and secondary identification that equilibrium must be established. It is therefore with this nucleus of duality that the worker should be equipped to work.

In the original society this process is non-existent, and even if it were not it would not have assumed such a measure of importance, since all other things are familiar. In British society, however, the repeated experience of black people is that of alienation and consequently the objective of a total adjustment to the demands of the worker and society in the majority of cases is almost impossible. The most important ingredients that contribute to a full integration of people are all those ways and habits that unify their world and give them a sense of who they are. If this is clear, then a constant picture of what they are and what they ought to be provides guidelines for conduct and behavior. However the conception of self by black people and the conception by white society is generally contradictory. In response to the pressure to integrate, black people may temporarily 'forget themselves' – or at least think they have. In such instances the powerful defence of repression is brought into operation, but the constant confrontation with negative experience in society undermines the defence, and the individual remembers what s/he is. This in turn disrupts equilibrium. People therefore engage in a desperate reordering of old habits in an effort to create a connection between themselves and reality. Family members are frequently caught up in this web, which may well result in social disorganization. If black people feel they have failed, and indeed they may have, it is not surprising that their subsequent actions and reactions indicate tendencies towards social pathology. Society is constantly reminding black people of their position in daily life and through the media. When they face this confrontation, their perception of themselves and of others and their definition of their situation will inevitably change.

A significant number of 'fall-outs' of blacks from mainstream society and of observed psychiatric disorders, particularly among West Indian women, I would suggest are a direct result of the failure of individuals to live up to the ambivalent demands of the white social worker and society.[9] My impression is that these disorders are more prevalent among West Indian women probably because they are manifestly more conscientious, so the internal drive to reorder and achieve is more powerful. Success depends not only on one social worker acknowledging the social worth of the black person but on this acceptance being generalized to the level of society as a whole. Acceptance at both levels essentially requires self-transformation on the part of the black person. Primary identification must give way to the 'superior social order' – that is, the world of the white society which is considered to be the minimum requirement for acceptance. If the transformation takes place, the subsequent behaviour is generally the projected construct of the white worker and of society. If this reordering process occurs it often means that black people have lost the internal battle. Their whole personality has been conquered. In such instances a very rigid pattern of behaviour must be established to maintain that image of the self. If this is not possible or a further disruption of the equilibrium takes place, the person is transformed into an actor of confused roles. It is at this point that labels are placed on the black person and the generally accepted psychiatric procedures are brought into operation.[10]

In their own community, parents may have had ambitions for a child to become a lawyer, doctor, nurse, or teacher. In some instances these parents are illiterate, a direct result of colonialism. However, the children who show such aspirations are praised and encouraged by relatives, clergy, teachers and all with whom the child interacts. In their original society it is quite normal for a child from such a family background to aspire to a position outside the social sphere of his parents and grandparents. In Britain, however, black people's aspirations are controlled and limited to specific roles. If their ambitions or aspirations are outside of what is ascribed to their rightful position, the authorities and society regard this as regression to infantile fantasies. If these ambitions are maintained, the child and the family may well be labelled as psychologically ill. A disproportionate number of the psychiatric disorders found among blacks have their roots in the struggle of the world constructed by white society.[11]

In their own society, the roles are clearly defined. Ambitions and aspirations are limited only by the quantity of opportunities and the keenness of the competition that exists in the social world. There are no limits to aspirations and ambitions, except those set by self and objective circumstances. The ingredients of the social world are easily understood. Personality is not threatened in such a manner as it is in Britain. Even if it was threatened, there are built-in protective mechanisms in the system. There are social symbols and actions that cushion the effect. There is not a constant assault on personality. In Britain, however, failure leaves black people between 'the devil and the deep blue sea'. They cannot return to their own country and yet would rather not be living here.

Conclusion

The desire to wipe out, reorder and achieve is a real one since the process should logically lead to qualification, higher social status, authority, power, and a sense of achievement. The drive to achieve is often greater among blacks because of the 'push' and 'pull' factors and the drive is even greater among young adults than black people of middle age. Older blacks have been able to rationalize the pressures because they have already adapted to the secure world embedded in primary identification. Here lies the locus of the credibility gap between black children and their parents. The young blacks see the process in terms of reordering for achievement and social prestige. The older blacks see the process as resisting and maintaining their primary meaning systems.

Notes and references

1 D. Bannister and C. F. Fransilla, *Inquiring Man, The Theory of Personal Constructs* (Penguin, 1971) pp. 15–41.
2 S. Ahmed, J. Cheetham and J. Small, *Social Work with Black Children and their Families* (B. T. Batsford, 1986) pp. 1–50.
3 J. W. Small, 'New black families in adoption and fostering', *British Agencies for Adoption and Fostering*, vol. 6, no. 3 (1982).

4 J. Rex, *Race Relations in Sociological Theory* (Routledge & Kegan Paul, 1983), pp. 116–35.

5 K. Fitzherbert, 'West Indian children in London', *Occasional Papers in Social Administration*, no. 19 (1967) pp. 15–33.

6 The report of the 'Soul Kid Campaign' in 1976 to find black families for black children brought these issues to the foreground for the first time, and this gave statutory and voluntary agencies a glimpse of the processes at work.

7 E. Durkheim, *Professional Ethics and Civic Morals*, trans. Cornelia Brookfield (Routledge & Kegan Paul, 1957), p. 61.

8 M. Weber, *The Theory of Social and Economic Organisation*, trans. A. R. Henderson and Talcott Parsons (William Hodge, 1947), p. 289.

9 R. Littlewood and M. Lipsedge, *Aliens and Alienists: Ethnic Minorities and Psychiatry* (Penguin, 1982), pp. 87–106.

10 L. Carpenter and I. F. Brockington, 'A study of mental illness in Asians, West Indians and Africans living in Manchester', *British Journal of Psychiatry*, vol. 137 (1980), pp. 201–5.

11 R. Littlewood, 'Ethnic minorities and the Mental Health Act', *Bulletin of Royal College of Psychiatry*, vol. 10 (November 1986), pp. 306–8.

J. Small, 'The crisis in adoption', *International Journal of Social Psychiatry*, vol. 30, nos 1 & 2 (spring 1984).

The Report of the Committee of Inquiry into the Education of Children of Ethnic Minorities, Cmnd 9453 (HMSO, 1986).

Interim Report of the Committee of Inquiry into Education of Children from Ethnic Minority Groups, Cmnd 8273 (HMSO, 1984).

15 Radical probation: surviving in a hostile climate

PAUL SENIOR

Introduction

When I became a probation officer in the mid-1970s the service was in uneasy transition between a secure past and an uncertain future. The probation service had become an accepted part of the criminal justice system, with a growing faith in the use of social work methods to rehabilitate offenders. This sense of purpose was subject to new and challenging ideologies which competed to influence practice. Over the past decade the insecurity of the probation service has intensified as a result of the pressures of economic recession and the authoritarian populist penal policies pursued by the successive Thatcher governments since 1979. It has always been an uphill battle to spread the influence of socialist ideas in the probation service, and the climate of the last few years has made it more difficult than ever. This chapter will examine the progress of socialist ideas in probation in the new political climate and discuss how socialist practice can be sustained.

Socialist probation: the seeds of optimism

What was it like entering the probation service in the mid-1970s? The service pursued a casework approach focusing on individuals or their families. This meant using individual social enquiry reports to process offenders through courts, the organization of casework through statutory court orders and the use of diverse casework techniques. The goal of rehabilitation was underpinned by positivistic theories of criminology. The commonsense assumption that probation officers using their skills can directly reduce criminal behaviour remains influential today.

The unspoken assumption behind the widespread faith in rehabilitation was that offenders were responsible for their criminal behaviour. Any apparent lack of a sense of responsibility was interpreted as a deficiency of insight into the nature of their deviance. Deviant behaviour was incompatible with accepted societal norms and thus needed treatment. The incorporation of the 'medical model' into the criminal justice system promised to give expert status to the fledgling professional probation officer who applied the new techniques. Early casework theories used Freudian methods but not all such techniques were imbued by psychodynamic approaches. However, although behaviourial forms of casework came from a different school of thought, they carried the same underlying assumptions. The probation officer was expected to work within a framework of consensual values. Societal goals were assumed to be shared by all and the pursuit of individual betterment was by definition in accordance with what society desired. As I learned about the probation order, I noted how its basic conditions sought to uphold and inculcate the work ethic, legitimate leisure pursuits, respect for law and order, social discipline and the sanctity of family life.

Probation officers were held in high esteem by those in authority, particularly compared with social workers. The concern expressed by magistrates when local authorities assumed responsibility for juvenile offenders following the 1969 Children and Young Persons Act indicated something of the symbiotic relationship that the probation service had established with the courts. The probation officer's job was to promote harmony and conformity in society by encouraging non-offending lifestyles. This occupational value system stemmed originally from Christian or military conviction. By the 1960s and 1970s the professionalization of the probation service was closely linked to the development of a pseudo-scientific justification for promoting conventional values in society.

Given that such values were regarded as universal, probation officers could believe that their work was apolitical. As a worker you could concentrate on improving technical competence. The expertise, when applied, could justify major interventions – including imprisonment – on the grounds that it was necessary to achieve the desired change. The supervisory role of the probation officer could be likened to that of the good parent; care and control were opposite poles of essentially similiar objectives: the professional determined what was best for the client.[1]

It was not hard as a worker in the 1970s to believe that you were doing good. Much of the work of the probation officer in assisting the offender in terms of accommodation, employment, marital and relationship problems, social and life skills and benefits advice, etc.

did humanize the criminal justice system. It was and is worthwhile. While the overall system remained punitive, it seemed appropriate to have a caring adjunct. As the probation service took on bigger and more diverse tasks, its positive contribution was never seriously questioned. As Raynor recalls, 'social work in the late sixties and early seventies reflected the optimism of the times, in which good intentions, faith and commitment were more important than tedious detail'.[2] Starting with prison welfare tasks in 1962, followed by parole in 1967 and community service, day training centres and hostels amongst other measures in 1972, the probation service was expanding and diversifying. Probation benefited from being part of an expanding criminal justice network. Belief in its effectiveness encouraged probation managers to wield their skills in increasingly diverse ways. They rarely gave much consideration to the wider policy or political dimensions.

Yet the very growth of the probation service in the 1970s pushed a number of awkward questions to the fore. The first signs of uncertainty appeared over the Younger Report in 1974, which suggested a more coercive role for probation officers. Policy concerns arose around what activities constituted probation work. Social work questions concerning method and approach emerged. Probation officers felt increasingly uncomfortable with the dichotomy between their official role as officers of the court and their day-to-day practice as social workers. Raynor points to three broad challenges to the complacency of this period: the interactionist critique; the empirical critique; and the structural critique.[3]

The interactionist critique emerged out of the revolution in deviancy theory. It questioned the role of agents of social control such as the police, the sentencers and probation officers in the administration of justice. These new sociological approaches to crime and deviance exposed the problems of working uncritically from official definitions of the criminal. Nagging questions emerged. What was it about the process of becoming deviant that brought certain social classes and groups more to the fore?

The second challenge to conventional practice followed the publication of a number of empirical surveys which revealed the ineffectiveness of established treatment and rehabilitation methods. These findings shattered the confidence of those who had faith in the philosophy of rehabilitation.[4] This crisis has dogged the probation service ever since, despite various attempts to rejuvenate treatment or seek an alternative unifying philosophy.

In response to the interactionist and empirical critiques, some authorities reasserted the virtues of an approach that focused on the individual as the object of practice and sought to make methods more client-centred and effective. McWilliams terms this approach 'personalist', which he defines as a strategy for 'the enhancement of the person in existing society'.[5] The personalist is fatalistic about political developments and substantive policy change, but optimistic about the potential of intervention at an individual level.[6] This approach has dominated probation practice and has encouraged much experimentation in useful client-centred methods. However, there is no substantive evidence of much real impact on offending. In isolation, the personalist approach appears close to Davies' maintenance role for social workers, in which they ameliorate rather than fundamentally attack the problems they encounter.[7]

Without a wider understanding of the political and economic processes that underscore the activity of any public sector welfare agency, the interactionist and empirical critiques could indicate problems with probation practice but could not provide a direction adequate to the task of overcoming them. If the early radical critique simply did not make enough sense, the structural critique, the third challenge to conventional practice identified by Raynor, did.

The magazine *Case Con* (1970–77) was the voice of much early radical thinking. It articulated the views of the consumers of services; it exposed the elitism and sexism of casework and the professionalism that mystified many clients. It pointed out that clients were overwhelmingly working class in origin and it began to develop an analysis of social work action, albeit from a rather deterministic Marxist perspective.

During the heyday of *Case Con*, probation was often on the sidelines. It was regarded by many radicals as being too closely integrated into the criminal justice system. However, the radical movement did become influential amongst small numbers of probation officers, and in the process of challenging the professional association, NAPO, it eventually created something of a revolution in the service. Meeting with colleagues in the socialist pressure group NAPO Members' Action Group (NMAG) helped me to make sense of the discomfort of working as a state employee and helped me to construct an alternative basis for practice.

There were two aspects of the socialist critique of probation. First, it explained the place of probation in a capitalist state and, second, it indicated a direction for practice. It has been a frequent criticism of socialist thinking on probation that it is stronger on critique than on prescription. However, it is the synthesis of the two elements that gives the socialist critique such relevance.

Like other operational ideologies, socialist probation practice has developed piecemeal. Attempts to fashion a particular socialist agenda began as the collective endeavour of NMAG. It was, at times, crude and deterministic. It certainly failed to give sufficient recognition to the relative autonomy of the practitioners' operational ideologies or to the dynamic relationship of these to other ideologies. The most developed account did not appear until 1981,[8] when Walker and Beaumont published their influential account, which still forms the best statement of the role and function of the probation service in the criminal justice system.

Walker and Beaumont's critique of probation was less deterministic than previous attempts. They emphasized the limitations within which the probation service operated: individualization; amelioration; consensual values; correctionalism; the beneficence of care; reinforcement of sex role stereotyping and legitimization.

Casework had long been under attack because of its psychodynamic focus. However, Walker and Beaumont argued that individualizing problems was mistaken not only from a methodological point of view, but also on the grounds that it inappropriately ascribed problems engendered by state action to individual or family pathology. An awareness of the structural character of unemployment, inadequate housing and restricted educational opportunities, etc., threw a different light on the plight of individuals caught up in the system. Given that opportunities for probation intervention were constructed around individual contact, which circumscribed the sphere of influence, any help that officers could offer would at best only patch up difficulties.

The ameliorative function of probation fitted well with the prevailing social democratic orthodoxy of the 1960s in which societal goals and personal goals were held to be compatible. Inherent in this belief in shared values was the assumption that failure to meet such standards was a failure of the individual. Criminal activity was one manifestation of the inability of people to conform to conventional values. It followed that intervention should adopt the correctional approach of rehabilitating offenders. A socialist analysis begins from different assumptions. In a society based on antagonistic social classes, values are inherently in conflict; the state promotes the values of the dominant class as universal. These values are often rejected by certain groups because of the alternative reality present in the conflict of their everyday lives. Thus during economic recession the unemployed offender finds the promulgation of the work ethic somewhat incongruous!

Walker and Beaumont suggested that the probation service, although part of the welfare state, was in fact situated within the legal apparatus: 'While connections and parallels with welfare services can be seen, we think it is more useful and consistent to locate the probation service primarily in the general context of the juridical system.'⁹ Recognizing the position of the probation service in the criminal justice system, and the contradictory nature of the welfare state, meant understanding that care could at the same time be both benevolent and controlling. Walker and Beaumont grappled with this dichotomy, arguing that probation officers often felt that they were being used to patch up problems that required more fundamental solutions. They stated,

> In this way the Probation Service plays an important ideological role – by acting as the benevolent face of the penal system it reasserts the image of the 'caring' society, extending welfare from 'the cradle to the grave' even to the Court and the prison cell . . . [but] . . . the common image of the Probation Service as an independent, professional social work agency gives way to an understanding that it is a marginal and incorporated adjunct to the State's coercive machinery, the Criminal Justice system.¹⁰

Maintaining and developing forms of progressive practice that are consistent with a socialist perspective is an inherently difficult task. In a society in which any apparent improvements are mediated through the interests of the dominant class and the organization of a capitalist economy, it may render the reform functional to that dominant class only. Beaumont recognizes the dangers:

> These difficulties are heightened for socialists by the contradictory nature of reform within the capitalist system. . . . Reforms will be mediated in the interests of capital, affecting both the form and delivery of provision. Often reform will be partial . . .¹¹

Whilst some have condemned Walker and Beaumont's analysis as pessimistic, it has the distinct merit of being realistic. The ability of any state employee to undertake action against the state is limited. Alliance with other workers, the ability to overcome individualization or not to be a legitimator of consensual attitudes, is limited by the history, organization and structural position of the probation service. It is difficult, though not impossible, to produce a positive socialist agenda. All socialists will find such difficulties working 'in and against the state', but oppositional action can be conceived as a positive and appropriate response that works with the contradictions whilst creating space for progressive work with clients.

As the 1970s drew to a close, many radical workers were grappling with the problems of developing a progressive probation practice. Much useful work was achieved in union activity and this was a natural, if limited avenue for progressive change. My own involvement in the union as a member of NAPO's Probation Practice Committee tried to make sense of daily events within a socialist orientation. A practice handbook edited by Walker and Beaumont[12] looked at the limitations and potential for socialist practice. Although published in 1985, this approach originated from practice in the 1970s and gained a foothold before the New Right set about changing the direction of penal policy. Before turning to these issues it seems relevant to outline how I used the critique in practice.

Towards the development of a socialist style

Critics often complain that socialist writers fail to specify what a socialist strategy for probation work means in practice. 'Long term' becomes reinterpreted as idealistic and impossibilistic. McWilliams argues that the socialist practice prescriptions of Walker and Beaumont turn out to be 'more cautious and less "radical" than might have been expected from their apparently uncompromising theoretical stance'.[13] And Raynor contends that many non-Marxists can follow socialist practice prescriptions without sharing their analysis.[14]

Given that socialist probation officers work alongside colleagues who are guided by diverse and often sharply conflicting beliefs and values, it can be easy to lose focus. A socialist practice must also understand developments in feminist and anti-racist thinking, as well as a community focus that may not necessarily coincide with a socialist orientation. A majority of probation officers do share the same concerns: the critique of rehabilitation and treatment; a recognition of the need for greater organizational democracy; a concern for the rights and civil liberties of clients, including notions of social justice; support for decarceration and moves towards community; scepticism regarding control functions; identification with the interests of victims. The roots of such practice imperatives can originate from different ideological stances, from Christianity, feminism or liberalism, as well as from socialism. However, the incorporation of such diverse radical ideas into the mainstream of probation practice acts as a unifying force.

The translation of ideology into practice is a complex process. Ideologies are mediated through a complex range of influences, which include personal background, political beliefs, allegiance to agency objectives, theoretical commitments, as well as geographical, race, class and gender factors. However, workers with different ideological views often can work together towards common objectives. Indeed, in a recent contribution McWilliams argues that, despite the differences among what he terms the managerial, radical and personalist schools of thought, they come together in three crucial respects: 'each of the schools is pragmatic, each sees the offender as bounded by a framework of policy, and each says that the service should be *providing alternatives to custody*.'[15] (Emphasis added)

The way ideologies are employed in policy development and practice often appears at odds with the original ideal. This is noted by Cohen in his analysis of the decarceration ideal: 'consequences so different from intentions; policies carried out for reasons opposite to their stated ideologies; the same ideologies supporting different policies; the same policy supported for quite different ideological reasons.'[16] Cohen argues that the apparent non-correspondence between ideologies and operational practices should not be misconstrued:

> the contrast is false, because each side is obsessed with the same quixotic search for fit, congruence and consistency. Everything we know about the way social control ideologies originate and function, should warn us about the delusion of ever expecting a syncronization of words and deeds.[17]

In this morass it is vitally important not to lose sight of one's own socialist agenda. What crucially distinguishes socialist from personalist practice is a difference in the theorization of long-term goals and their relationship to short-term activity. Many of the changes in the 1970s occurred at an individual and organizational level without necessarily being linked more clearly and directly to wider structural change. Personalist solutions are based on a superficial analysis that ignores or seeks to diminish the importance of fundamental reorganization.

In describing the personalist approach McWilliams confirms the essential difference between a personalist and a socialist ideology: 'In the last analysis personalists, as probation officers, see their central task as the enhancement of the offender as a person within society as it exists.'[18] Yet for a socialist a commitment to challenge consensus and its consequential individualization of problems is fundamental. Maintaining an awareness of long-term goals in probation, which concentrates so heavily on work with individuals, is a difficult but necessary task. To lose sight of this vision may risk being incorporated into the system, a factor that Powell and Stone elaborate in relation to courts and prisons respectively. It is also important to recognize that there are realistic limits.[19] To attempt change too far beyond the acceptability of the organization or the wider system risks exclusion.

As Walker and Beaumont recognize, there are no easy answers:

> We have rejected the search for 'the radical method' and instead suggest that a more fruitful way ahead is to concentrate on approach and orientation. It is more useful to aim for clarity about the possibilities and limitations of the job, to look for ways of exploiting potential and minimizing negatives.[20]

By emphasizing certain elements of practice it is possible to develop an approach I would term a *socialist style* which can enhance the potential for achieving worthwhile practice.

Tackling oppression

Fundamental to a perspective informed by considerations of class, race and gender is a commitment to understanding the roots of oppression experienced by the working class, black people, women and communities. Not only does criminal justice bear down most forcefully upon certain sections of society, these same groups are also more frequently the victims of crime. Contrast, for example, the scale of domestic violence and racist attacks with the moral panic around mugging! The structural disadvantage experienced by offenders makes such issues of central importance to a radical practice. For example, this might mean taking into account the structural nature of unemployment in reports and thus sentencing. It could mean considering the relevance of community action on housing, education or health as crime prevention activity. It might also mean being careful when developing helpful services not to emphasize other forms of oppression – for example, prisoners' wives' groups run the risk of defining women in terms of their relationships with men, and groups for victims of crime may heighten the blameworthiness of offenders.

The personal and the political

One key practice orientation to emerge from the collective on *Working with Offenders* was the important feminist theme that personal feelings, attitudes, circumstances and understanding cannot be comprehended outside the political dimension of social experience. There are a number of levels on which such an orientation can operate: making sense of the social construction of disadvantage (unemployment is not an individual's fault); helping offenders understand racism by listening to the personal experience of black people; working for change on a collective level, through, for instance, community action. Conceptualizing individual and group problems in this way does not reduce or preclude attention to private concerns, but makes explicit (where it is feasible and appropriate) wider structural and political dimensions, which are then viewed as part of the way in which personal problems are actually formed and defined. Kirwin notes the importance of this strategy:

> Another pressure . . . I try to avoid when talking to clients is individualisation, so that they don't see their situation and the problems they face as unique to them. It is important they can understand their difficulties are shared – both with offenders and other working class people.[21]

Short and long-term goals

The connection between short-term goals and longer-term strategies is central to a socialist agenda. Many mainstream probation officers have failed to recognize any connection at all. In the rush to embrace parole or community service, value issues have often been secondary to pragmatism and spurious notions of credibility.

In *The Politics of Abolition*,[22] Mathieson distinguished between 'positive' and 'negative' reforms, suggesting that the former ultimately buttress the system rather than producing substantive change, whilst the latter have the potential to change the context of operation fundamentally. Penal lobby groups and NAPO face this problem in relation to campaigning activity. The apparent success of the removal of imprisonment for drunkenness (Criminal Law Act 1977) and soliciting (Criminal Justice Act 1982) offences has been offset by the use of heavy fines and imprisonment for fine default, which has maintained the numbers of prostitutes and vagrants in prison.

Mathieson's conceptualization of positive and negative reforms can be applied within a practice context, an area he eschews. A radical practice must understand how short-term action can enhance moves towards or away from longer-term goals. Given that the grounds of the debate will shift according to the issue, there are times when short-term goals appear in conflict to longer-term strategies. Is it right to abandon a reductionist ideology in considering the sentencing of rapists or perpetrators of racist attacks? Only through explicit discussion can such dilemmas be worked through. Socialist practice is a dynamic process.

Collective action

Reducing individualization in probation practice entails extending a collective approach through to work with colleagues. Looking at teamwork, co-working within groups, campaigning action and a willingness to challenge the working practices of colleagues must be part of this orientation. In certain areas such as anti-racist and anti-sexist practice this process is long overdue. It is often harder to be self-critical but it can help avoid some of the pitfalls of incorporation and exclusion. A fully integrated radical agenda embraces structural changes, campaigning action, organizational developments and a practice orientation simultaneously.

Empowerment and community involvement

Any claims that there can be equality in the relationship between worker and client must be treated with some scepticism. Whilst attempts can be made to diminish the use of such power, it cannot be ignored. An added dimension, given the way society is constructed, relates to the power that men hold over women and white people over black people. By reaching out to the community, these issues can be faced.

The Probation Rules 1984 legitimized forms of 'wider work in the community', although there are differing interpretations of the consequences of the state giving permission to this approach. Pinder in his work on black offenders has challenged probation practice to take a more contested view of who is the client:

> The tendency for the behaviour of black offenders to emerge as corporate behaviour, its logic determined by the social processes in which offenders were caught up: again, a central convention of the criminal justice system, individuation, militates against a response which recognises these qualities of offending behaviour.[23]

A community orientation is a risky strategy for the state even if its rhetorical power can lend practice an aura of democracy. A radical practice must grasp this potential to develop a more thorough-going community-based practice. Despite strong NAPO support, it is still unusual to encounter grass roots community work within probation. There are examples that must be developed and promoted.[24]

Educational developments

I have argued elsewhere[25] a view of education as a potentially liberating experience, utilizing the radical analysis of Freire and his idea of conscientization: 'A permanent critical approach to reality in order to discover the myths that deceive us and help to maintain the oppressing dehumanising structures.'[26]

Schooling has often been perceived in negative terms by offenders. Yet this is clearly not a product of education itself, but a result of the form and content of conventional schooling. It is not surprising that prisoners find some release from the oppression of incarceration through the discovery of study, which helps to integrate and make sense of their own experience. Probation officers can in their daily work encourage this critical awareness for offenders, and perhaps with colleagues too!

Maintaining relevance

The ultimate test of the potential of radical probation practice rests on its ability to influence the consciousness and actions of individual offenders and other key stakeholders in the criminal justice system. Walker and Beaumont emphasized that probation practice should provide 'useful services' for offenders and this may of course not always appear as useful services for the state. The probation service should be relevant to the communities within which it operates. But before suggesting ways forward, we need to consider the devastating impact of the Thatcher regime on the consciousness of probation generally and socialist practice in particular.

The advent of a law and order society

The Conservative Party made 'law and order' a central theme of the 1979 general election. Mrs Thatcher and her colleagues appealed to public concerns about crime and disorder with a powerful rhetoric to which the opposition had no ready response. In terms of policy development, the climate of reaction encouraged a growing harshness in the operation of criminal justice, which had already become evident in the 1970s. The key features of the coercive trend are the differential impact of fiscal prudence on welfare and coercive aspects of public spending; the shift from a 'restorative' to a 'repressive' approach to offenders; the criminalization of protest and social disturbance; and the systematic deployment of law and order propaganda to legitimize repressive laws and methods.

Since the late 1970s, pressures to curb public expenditure at a time of growing social instability had led to sharp cuts in welfare services at the same time as spending on the state's repressive apparatus has steadily increased. The cuts begun by Labour in 1976 and intensified by the Tory government after 1979 created increased poverty, homelessness, unemployment and disadvantage. Yet in the financial year 1987–8 the law and order budget exceeded £6 billion for the first time. Between 1979 and 1986 there was a 50 per cent increase in that budget while, for instance, there was a 60 per cent decrease in housing finance.[27] The law and order budget has been distributed disproportionately to the prison service and, to a lesser extent, the police. There still seems to be little public objection to the prison building programme, despite the obvious need for new hospitals and other social necessities. While nurses and teachers drift out of their low-paid vocations in thousands every year, the police or prison service offer a secure future.

The climate of austerity has encouraged a drive to economize and raise efficiency throughout the public sector. But efficiency in prison in practice means tighter security and control, not more effective rehabilitation! Current interest in the privatization of prisons is consistent with the general government drive to open up the public sector to private enterprise. Furthermore, the *Fresh Start* proposals for restructuring prison service working practices are regarded by the Home Office as 'searching for ways of improving the opportunities for staff and increasing the *efficiency* of the Service . . . because of the present inefficient working systems' (emphasis added).[28] Because offenders do not have an effective political voice, it is more likely that prison workshops and prison education will be cut than prison staff overtime!

The current overuse of prison is a striking indication of the growing emphasis upon the repressive aspect of penal law, an emphasis that creates more and more difficulties for the probation service. In an important commentary on the probation service, Downes has drawn on Durkheim's distinction between *repressive* and *restitutive* law.[29] Whereas repressive sentences aim to punish by inflicting suffering on the offender, the aim of restitutive measures is not to stigmatize but to restore the normal relationship between the offender and society which has been disturbed through the criminal act. While repressive sentencing places unconditional blame on the individual perpetrator, the restitutive approach implies that the problem lies in the social structure rather than in individual pathology.

While there are examples of restitutive law within the modern penal system, they are mainly of an individualistic kind: compensation, elements of community service, and of probation. However, the clear tendency in recent years has been towards repressive sentencing. Such sentencing has tended to target certain groups labelled as troublesome, a designation that reflects political judgement. Consider, for example, the unequal treatment of tax evasion and social security fraud, or student frolics compared with football violence. While 'victims' may have been neglected in the past, the zeal with which many authorities now pursue reparation makes offenders themselves the major victim of an unjust system. Speaking to the probation service, Downes focused on the socially discriminatory character of the penal system: 'the operation of the principles of repressive, retributive and punitive justice are at their most severe in dealing with the general run of "street" crimes against property whose perpetrators are disproportionately working class.'[30] I would stress too that the victims of a repressive justice are also increasingly black.

At a time of deepening recession, the Tory government has criminalized any protest or disturbance as a way of depriving it of legitimacy and popular approval. Inner-city 'rioters', football 'hooligans', 'violent pickets' in the miners' strike have all been identified by politicians and the media as a menace to all decent people: the police and the courts have enjoyed a free hand in clamping down on those engaged in these activities. Sociologists have helped by describing these groups as 'problem populations',[31] 'surplus populations',[32] or 'unproductive elements'.[33]

Spitzer has noted the differential treatment meted out to those he described as 'social junk' and those he calls 'social dynamite'. The former, he argues, can be decarcerated as they are little more than a nuisance which can be managed in the community. The category 'social junk' includes the elderly, the mentally ill and handicapped and, I would add, most petty offenders. By contrast, those identified as 'social dynamite' are a threat that must be contained by state repression. In Britain in the 1980s, the category 'social dynamite' includes the young unemployed, black people in the inner cities and working-class offenders.

Box and Hale have analysed the role of law and order propaganda in preparing the way for state repression:

As far as the criminal justice system is concerned, the state's preferred solution to this legitimacy problem takes both an ideological and control form. Ideologically, it propagates the view that crime, particularly 'street crime' has dramatically increased and that only a 'law and order' campaign, pursued with determination and vigour, has any chance of dealing with this problem and hence protecting the people. This prepares the path for strengthening the forces of social control, particularly police powers and resources, the judiciary's sentencing armoury, and the prison estate's capacity to absorb an enlarged number of prisoners in an even harsher regime of punishment and deprivation.[34]

To buttress the repressive arm of the state, new laws have been implemented often to justify actions already taken. Thus the outcry against the 'Sus' law may have led to its repeal, but the Criminal Attempts Act (1981) and the Public Order Act (1986) have more than compensated. The powers that the police and the courts made up as they went along in the miners' strike have now been institutionalized in the Police and Criminal Evidence Act (1984). The tougher action demanded by the Tory hawks has led to restrictions on parole eligibility and life licences, new powers in the Criminal Justice Acts of 1982 and 1987 and the approval of continuous prison building programmes. The 1980s appear to have brought a legislative ratification of trends towards repressive practice clearly under way in the 1970s.

The increasing use of custodial sentences and a growing prison population are the inevitable result of the clamour for harsh measures against offenders. However, it is clear that custody falls unequally upon certain groups – the unemployed, young working-class people and in particular black offenders, and to some extent women. Indeed, decisions about who are appropriate for inclusion in the category hard-core are essentially political ones and represent decisions by the powerful in an atmosphere of moral panic.

The latest degrading and dehumanizing punishment to be proposed as an alternative to prison and as a way of relieving overcrowding is the electronic tag. For some time technology has demonstrated the capacity for instituting house arrest and surveillance of an offender's movements (and for registering variations in emotional states!). Yet, when it first emerged only a few years ago, the Offender Tag Association was widely regarded as a marginal extremist grouping comparable with those demanding a return to birching. What once seemed an extremist fantasy is now welcomed in some circles.[35] Three experimental schemes were approved by government in 1989. The dogma of fiscal prudence provides a powerful argument for tagging, which is demonstrably efficient and economical, whilst providing effective surveillance. Proponents of tagging argue that it would serve to defuse the social dynamite!

Trying to stand still

The clamour for tougher state repression dominates the climate within which the probation service operates. Whatever their individual motivation, probation officers cannot escape the consequences for their work of this increasingly coercive penal climate. As Downes asserts, the probation service is placed in a contradictory position between the repressive and restitutive approaches to dealing with offenders:

> Probation work . . . is sited at the most sensitive juncture of the repressive/restitutive divide in criminal justice. Though most evidence suggests its practices are more restitutive than repressive, there are strong pressures for tougher and more controlling strategies to be adopted.[36]

It is not difficult to discern the impact of Tory penal philosophy within the probation service. As a former chief probation officer has stated: 'Containment should become the unambiguous objective of supervision'.[37] 'Control units', 'tracking', 'intensive supervision', 'close support' (*sic*) and 'curfews' – these expressions of the terminology of repression are commonly heard within the probation service.

As part of the law and order budget the probation service has been relatively protected from the cuts that have hit the personal social services. The service may not be expanding as it was in the early 1970s, but nevertheless job loss has not occurred. Indeed, as Shaw suggests, the very interconnectedness of the criminal justice system means that a growing crime rate or prison population will enable the probation service to benefit. Prisons need welfare officers; offenders about to be sent to prison need reports: 'In this sense anyway, probation is carried along on the shirt-tails of the boom in law and order'.[38]

Financial control is linked however with the repressive imperative, signposted by Walker and Beaumont in 1981 as the 'coercive tilt' of the service:

> The drift into a law and order society has also produced proposals for change. These are characterized by the use of more,

and tougher, conditions in probation orders, suggestions for increased use of breach proceedings and that probation officers should act as 'surveillance' agents, devoid of any social work role. The general trend is towards the use of more coercive measures and greater restrictions on clients. The coercive tilt is likely to produce a harder probation service, servicing a harsher penal system.[39]

The publication of the Home Office document *Statement of National Objectives and Priorities for the Probation Service* (SNOP) in 1984 indicated central government's priorities for the locally run service. It was a departure from the loose accountability of the past. Accompanying this there have been two attempts to quantify the work of the probation service through Financial Management Initiative (FMI) exercises. Both SNOP and FMI are bureaucratic initiatives that seek to minimize the social work aspects of probation work.

SNOP emphasized that work with the high-tariff, serious or persistent offender was the priority and charged the service with ensuring rigorous standards of supervision. 'It must be made clear that in every case those under supervision will meet real demands on their time, effort and adherence to the terms of supervision and that non-compliance will be dealt with firmly . . .'[40] When high-tariff offenders were sent to prison and recategorized as prisoners they became low priority, as SNOP grudgingly proposed 'sufficient resources for through-care to enable statutory duties to be undertaken but made scant provision for social work support in prison or for social work with offenders' families through the various stages leading up to resettlement'.[41] The aim of SNOP was to reorient the probation service along the ideological path approved by the Thatcher regime. Local areas were required to demonstrate how their area responded to the broad directives of national policy.

The repressive direction of government policy is potentially disastrous for the probation service and for radical practice. Instead of seeing a confident service charting more progressive policies and practice, we have seen a service struggling to stand still.[42] Defensive strategies have been adopted throughout the personal social services and must be the starting point for radical probation officers in the present climate. Fortunately, given the traditional autonomy associated with the probation service, there has been some resistance to the prescriptions of SNOP, especially at grass roots level. There are also some signs of resistance to the repressive trends in the joint statement of the service organizations (employers, management and union), *Probation – The Next Five Years*.[43]

A defensive strategy means being acutely aware of the structural position of probation work. Believing simply that the congruence of our personal practice and an historical mission to 'do good' can transcend the wider repressive climate, not only is it naive, it ignores the history of good intentions being subverted by the structure of the probation service. The problem is that there is no simple dichotomy between prison and community alternatives, with the former corresponding to a repressive strategy and the latter to a restitutive approach. Because the recent proliferation of non-custodial alternatives is a component of a more general drift towards coercion, it is vital that radical probation workers recognize that such alternatives are not necessarily progressive.

The fact that many offenders now put on non-custodial orders would not previously have been sent to prison reflects the process of *net-widening* that has taken place. The fact that the numbers of people involved in community schemes and day centres has increased in parallel with an increase in the prison population confirms that these options are not so much an alternative to prison as another arm of the state's controlling apparatus. Most research work which has looked at the populations on probation, intermediate treatment, community service orders and suspended sentences acknowledges that at best only 50 per cent are diverted from custody.[44] Clients for such alternatives come from previously untouched populations now dragged into the system for more intensive intervention.

Mathieson has warned of the danger of radical approaches to probation being subverted within the wider repressive framework: 'the control system as a totality may *expand rather than shrink* as a consequence of "progressive" political initiatives'.[45] Another danger in the promotion of non-custodial alternatives is that these are obliged to assume a more coercive character to maintain 'credibility'. This has resulted in what Hudson describes as *net-strengthening*[46] as 'the principle of incarceration' is transferred to community programmes. This approach is apparent in tracking and intensive intermediate treatment schemes for young offenders and in day centres and hostels for adult offenders, especially those with alcohol problems. However, NAPO and many individual officers have refused to cooperate with such schemes and have prevented a greater intrusion of repressive measures.[47]

The 'controllism' highlighted by developing alternatives has been the focus of an internal battle within the service and within NAPO. This is a key point of conflict between socialist and some progressive personalist thinking on the one hand and on the other those who occupy the terrain of the New Right. The socialist approach recognises the limitations of working within a control system such as probation. Resistance to the further imposition of conditions and support for the rights and dignity of individuals under supervision is a prerequisite for any form of socialist practice. For the Inner London Probation Service Demonstration Unit,[48] reluctance to use coercion is not merely an expression of socialist commitment; it shows that the probation service can defend its traditional welfare role and avoid both net-widening and net-strengthening.

The third danger of non-custodial alternatives is what I would term *net exclusion*. The unemployed, women and black people are three groups which are more likely to secure sentences and thus experience exclusion from even the limited progressive scope of community alternatives.

Box has shown how the unemployed generally receive harsher sentences:

> Taking the evidence as a whole, it supports the hypothesis that sentencing severity is related to the defendant's employment status. It is also related to the defendant's race. Since blacks suffer from much higher rates of unemployment, sentencing severity is probably related to the fact that they are both black and unemployed.[49]

It is the responsibility of radical probation officers to consider how social enquiry reports are constructed and how they can be used to challenge stereotyped responses to the unemployed among sentencers.[50] 'Leading an industrious life' cannot seriously be an expectation of offenders under supervision.

While community service has expanded dramatically over the past ten years, it has only recently become apparent that it systematically discriminates against women. Assumptions about the 'appropriateness' of work, the lack of child care facilities and inflexibility about hours of working contribute to a principle of less eligibility for women offenders. Women end up in prison for less serious and less frequent offending at an early stage in their criminal career.[51]

By far the most serious exclusion from alternatives has been that suffered by black people in their access to probation, community service, intermediate treatment, hostels and probation provision more generally. The beneficiaries of community options are predominantly white. Black offenders are over-represented in prison and under-represented on most non-custodial options. The 1978 NACRO report *Black People and the Criminal Justice System* noted that:

> A cumulative process of radical disadvantage in available options for black defendants was at work, first at the stage of being referred for a report or not, secondly in the proportion recommended for probation and lastly in the frequency with which the court accepted recommendations for probation.[52]

There is no evidence that the situation has improved over the past decade. The NACRO Report provides detailed evidence of the complicity of probation officers in the differential treatment of black offenders; its conclusions were summed up in the *Guardian* headline – 'Longer sentences for blacks blamed on Probation Officers'.[53]

The endemic nature of net exclusion should alert the radical worker to the dangers of presuming a unified approach to problems experienced differentially.

Women have begun to receive more attention in criminological study. Hilary Walker has challenged some of the practice assumptions of traditional probation work. She questions the notion that the justice system exhibits a paternalistic benevolence towards women, citing numbers on remand, women in custody with children, the petty nature of offending that puts women in prison and the differential experience of probation and community service. She also critically appraises the stereotypes that have informed sentencing. These view women as unbalanced or mad; at mercy of their biology; evil; or make excessive inferences from their sexuality or personal circumstances.[54]

These concerns need to be reflected in an anti-sexist practice that is centred on the need to change attitudes and institutional practices. Key issues include attitudes to the family; recognition of and challenge to existing power relationships in society; the avoidance of 'double jeopardy' – a key feature of women's experience of the criminal justice systems;[55] and acknowledging that conflicts exist between general attitudes to sentencing and short-term measures designed to reduce inequality and discrimination, e.g. the sentencing of rapists. There is evidence that the impact of such groups as Women in NAPO are having a beneficial effect upon attitudes and provision, although progress is halting.

While Walker has incorporated a feminist critique into a radical framework, until recently the particular concerns of black people have largely been ignored in the socialist analysis of probation. A radical socialist practice has to address ways of improving service delivery to black offenders, as Walker has begun to do for women.

Towards anti-racist probation practice

There has been no shortage of criticism of key organizations in the criminal justice system such as the police, prison service and courts. Yet until recently there has been a marked reluctance by white probation officers to look inwardly at their own work. It is important for white workers not to abdicate responsibility for developing strategies through dialogue with black people and it is in that spirit that I offer these suggestions.

Emergent practice in anti-racist social work has followed similar routes to the debate within education. In broad terms the debate has progressed from discussion of policies of assimilation through multi-culturalism towards an anti-racist strategy. The view that different ethnic groups should merely be assimilated into white society is rightly criticized by Green[56] as ethno-centric. The liberal assumption that differing cultures simply need time to adjust to the British way of life is both paternalistic and doomed to failure. Such an integrationist stance fails to recognize that theories of criminal behaviour applicable to white, male offenders are not simply transferable to black offenders. As Green writes: 'this kind of colour-blind approach fails to recognize that the black life experience is fundamentally different from white experience in our society, and that the difference is due to racism.'[57] Green goes on to elaborate: 'To try to reintegrate black offenders with society as it is currently structured is to try to persuade them to accept a position of disadvantage on the basis of their ethnicity.'[58] This colour-blind approach is congruent with the consensus model and its spurious claims of universality. Green suggests: 'probation officers regularly meet examples of racial disadvantage which properly ought not to lend themselves to offender-centred explanations. Nevertheless, their socialization into Probation Service culture leads them to conclusions drawn from family or individual pathology.'[59]

This neatly locates the 'problems' as those of black offenders themselves, not those of the white criminal justice system. As Pinder notes: 'Put more pointedly the behaviour of the courts – and of those who work in and for them – become problematic.'[60]

A multi-cultural approach, by which I mean attempts by white workers to familiarize themselves with different black cultures, has limited impact on the ethos and practice of the agency as a whole. It is important to have greater awareness of cultural differences, to acknowledge the impact this can have on personal interactions with offenders and to use such knowledge to improve outcomes for those offenders within the system. Clearly much training needs to be undertaken to enable workers to be able to adapt white social work practice to the cultural diversity of different black groups. For instance, the service in general has been slow to consider the need for the provision of interpreters; the changes in hostel ethos that would make them more viable for black offenders; the development of day care that responds to different needs; the significance of language, tradition, family practices, and the role of local community leaders in civil as well as criminal work.

Yet multi-cultural sensitivity is clearly insufficient on its own if it fails to generate wider change in the structure of the organization. It may even be diversionary. A greater awareness, which ensures that client status is maintained and therefore avoids a transfer of power and influence, may simply buy off some dissent. Without empowerment, lip-service to change is achieved but outcomes remain unaltered. Pinder noted in his research how black offenders appeared to resist client status and it was this that represented a threat to the professional culture of the service: 'Put somewhat elliptically, black offenders differ not so much from white offenders, as from the model of offenders and offending behaviour with which probation officers operate.'[61]

Training has to be undertaken, although here there is so much to learn from the experience of the past decade. The belated recognition that race awareness training has failed to affect service delivery in the agency as a whole despite greater personal awareness and sensitivity reveals the limitations of a multi-cultural approach. The fate of Pinder's research – which suffered loss of funding from the Home Office – may indicate the threat it appeared to pose to the operational culture of the service as a whole. Safe, non-threatening accommodation is often the hidden ideological agenda.

An anti-racist practice must understand the centrality of structural factors that give power to white decision-makers at all points in the criminal justice system, including the probation service. An anti-racist practice must seek to clarify the connections between racist ideology, bureaucratic procedures and institutional practices in order to create a practice that challenges white power and effectively eliminates discriminatory outcomes. Anti-racist practice is distinct from but consonant with a socialist analysis. Again as Pinder asserts in his critique of conventional social work:

> Such a perception is only possible if social work is held, and held to be, separate from the struggles between groups variously

defined in class, religious and ethnic terms, that are social history. Release that hold and it becomes obvious that social work is at the centre of a highly political process, in which workers are called upon to mediate between a variety of interests.[62]

There are clear connections in this analysis that distinguish a socialist practice from a personalist approach. Any radical departure must spring from a structural analysis that raises uncomfortable questions for conventional probation work about the social construction of crime and the significance of criminal behaviour, and thus questions the relevance of a practice that individualizes and allocates blame for collectively experienced problems.

An anti-racist strategy should include: information gathering; development of an ethnically sensitive service; acknowledging and challenging racism; changing attitudes; effective gatekeeping; the involvement of black people; creating a positive environment; and restructuring the management of the service.[63] A growing awareness of the racism that operates in the criminal justice system has emerged from limited exercises in monitoring, survey work and research. Although it is important to understand national trends, it is vital to use small-scale local monitoring to inform grass roots practice. We need to test out the extent to which black people do not take up probation options, asking why, and understanding what strategies can be developed. This will involve a greater willingness on the part of probation staff to acknowledge racist actions, to seek to alter behaviour and at the same time to be prepared to challenge racist behaviour amongst colleagues and other key personnel in the criminal justice system. It is important to listen to the experience of black staff and to work to change the attitudes and practice of staff through anti-racist training as well as confronting white racist clients in our practice.

Personal commitment to anti-racism is rarely enough to achieve substantial institutional change. Management needs to be encouraged to develop effective policies that check on individual practice. This can be organized on a team, district or support group basis. This implies the capacity of management to understand better what the black community wants (if anything) from the probation service. It is crucial to open an effective dialogue with black people and to promote greater accountability to the community. Pinder argues: 'the skills most appropriate to the development of work with black offenders might be said to be those which serve to identify and take up, not the special "needs" of a new, minority "client" group, but rather the interests of black citizens.'[64]

Green discusses the problems of developing specialist services, giving examples in Birmingham where facilities have been set up outside the probation system to give a more effective service to black offenders. He is concerned that such projects give black people a 'special' status, which might be unhelpful in the long run. He points to three difficulties:

> One of the most difficult is that they ghetto-ize black people, diverting them into projects primarily designed for a single racial category . . . there is a risk of developing a two-tier probation system, with black people receiving a second class service . . . a third area of concern is the danger of the Cultural Centre and CHAS raising the expectations of the black people they serve with little hope of their expectations being fulfilled . . .[65]

Green leaves the uncertainty unresolved. Yet here a radical framework may be most useful in showing how short-term goals can be seen as working towards a more productive future.

Future prospects: resistance to Thatcherism

Given the economic, political and ideological context for social work with offenders in the 1980s, any attempt to refashion the system along socialist lines might appear doomed from the start. Probation officers have been confronted with a growing burden of social problems, compounded by mass unemployment and deepening poverty. For offenders, a job has become a rarity, and housing the alcoholic, the drug abuser, the rootless, the mentally ill has become increasingly difficult. Access to health services, education, jobs and adequate means is everywhere reduced and is particularly restricted for the offender. There is growing evidence[66] of more intense discrimination against black people in all these areas, with a direct parallel within the criminal justice system.

The problems are not simply material and economic. Since the heyday of rehabilitation the probation service has exhibited an ideological incoherence with a number of negative consequences. Two probation commentators[67] have shown how differing approaches to probation have co-existed. One of the strengths of the service in its early years was its apparent clarity of task and purpose. However, the service has become increasingly complex: it now serves both courts and the prison executive; it has increasing numbers of staff not trained in social work; it has a range of orders to service including licences. The probation service is, in short, a highly differentiated service, which has developed in 'hotchpotch fashion'.[68] Defence of the principles of humane social work to offenders has not been negligible in its effect.[69] Defensive action, in alliance with other workers, must necessarily be strategic and focused. The government will not worry about having to take on the probation service – a more real threat may be that of exclusion. Leaks concerning privatization of the probation service, the expansionism of NACRO, and the drift to 'controllism', combined with the difficulty of effectively engaging in community and black politics, makes the probation service more vulnerable than it has ever been.

Paradoxically, the beleagured position of the service has in some ways enabled a radical perspective to be sustained. Walker and Beaumont[70] point to the fact that the probation service may on the one hand be acting as a form of soft coercion for the state but on the other it remains the human face of that system, offering some compensatory services to the powerless. Although a small and perhaps marginal part of the criminal justice system as a whole, the probation service appears to express the ambivalence that accompanies penal sentencing along the repressive/restitutive divide. Perhaps it holds one significant key to a more positive future. In the balance between consent and coercion that Walker and Beaumont discuss, they suggest how important it is for any government not to so tip the scales towards coercion that it delegitimizes its practices. Probation officers can engage radically in this space. This degree of autonomy and room for manoeuvre means that a radical socialist-oriented probation service can still develop on the strengths of the analysis fashioned in the more open climate of the early 1970s. By firmly asserting a progressive practice, the dissonance socialist practitioners have always felt can be reduced and the risk of incorporation avoided.

Notes and references

1 See R. Foren and R. Bailey, *Authority in Social Casework* (Pergamon Press, 1968).
2 P. Raynor, *Social Work, Justice and Control* (Blackwell, 1985), p. 3.
3 ibid., ch. 2, 'Labels, structures and results: three critiques of social work'.
4 See R. Martinson, 'What works?' in *The Public Interest* (New York, March 1974) and S. R. Brody *The Effectiveness of Sentencing* (HMSO, 1976).
5 W. McWilliams, 'Probation, pragmatism and policy', *Howard Journal of Criminal Justice*, vol. 26, no. 2 (May 1986), p. 98.

6   For examples of such an approach see B. Jordan, *Helping in Social
    Work* (Routledge & Kegan Paul, 1979) and B. Hugman, 'Radical
    practice in probation', in M. Brake and R. Bailey (eds), *Radical Social
    Work and Practice* (Edward Arnold, 1980).
7   M. Davies, *The Essential Social Worker* (Heinemann, 1981).
8   H. Walker and B. Beaumont, *Probation Work: Critical Theory and
    Socialist Practice* (Blackwell, 1981).
9   ibid., p. 141.
10 H. Walker and B. Beaumont (eds), *Working with Offenders* (BASW/
    Macmillan, 1985), pp. 2–3.
11 Beaumont in Walker and Beaumont, ibid., pp. 93–4.
12 Walker and Beaumont, op. cit. (n10).
13 McWilliams, op. cit. (n5), p. 108.
14 Raynor, op. cit. (n2), p. 57.
15 McWilliams, op. cit. (n5), p. 111.
16 S. Cohen, *Visions of Social Control* (Polity Press, 1985), p. 158.
17 ibid., p. 155.
18 McWilliams, op. cit. (n5), p. 114.
19 See M. Powell, 'Court work' and N. Stone, 'Prison-based work', in
    Walker and Beaumont, op. cit. (n10).
20 Walker and Beaumont, op. cit. (n8), p. 174.
21 K. Kirwin, 'Probation and supervision', in Walker and Beaumont, op.
    cit. (n10), p. 40.
22 T. Mathieson, *The Politics of Abolition* (Martin Robertson, 1974).
23 R. Pinder, *Probation and Ethnic Diversity* (University of Leeds, October
    1984), p. 192.
24 D. Scott et al., *Going Local in Probation* (University of East Anglia,
    1986).
25 See P. Senior, 'Groupwork with offenders', in Walker and Beaumont,
    op. cit. (n10).
26 P. Freire, 'A few notions about the word "Conscientisation"', in
    Schooling and Capitalism (Routledge & Kegan Paul in association with
    Open University), p. 225.
27 The *Guardian*, 15 January 1987.
28 Home Office Prison Service, *A Fresh Start*, Bulletin No. 7, p. 2.
29 D. Downes, 'Probation and criminal justice in the 1980s', in NAPO,
    Probation: Direction, Innovation and Change in the 1980s (NAPO, 1984),
    p. 6.
30 ibid., p. 7.
31 S. Spitzer, 'Towards a Marxian theory of crime', *Social Problems*,
    vol. 22.
32 R. Quinney, *Class, State and Crime*, 2nd edn (New York, Longman,
    1980).
33 Mathieson, op. cit. (n22).
34 S. Box and C. Hale, 'Unemployment, crime and imprisonment, and
    the enduring problem of prison overcrowding', in R. Matthews and
    J. Young (eds), *Confronting Crime* (Sage, 1986), p. 73.
35 J. McVicar, 'The Damocles detective', *Criminal Justice* (May 1987).

36 Downes, op. cit. (n29), p. 10.
37 B. Griffiths, 'Supervision in the community', *Justice of the Peace*, 21 August 1982.
38 S. Shaw, 'An uncertain future for the probation service', *Public Money* (December 1985), p. 41.
39 Walker and Beaumont, op. cit. (n8), p. 152.
40 L. Brittan quoted in Walker and Beaumont, op. cit. (n10), p. 13.
41 Home Office, *Statement of National Objectives and Priorities for the Probation Service* (April 1984).
42 B. Williams, 'The "coercive tilt" in probation practice: one step forward, two steps back', *Critical Social Policy*, Issue 18 (winter 1986/7).
43 Central Council for Probation Committees, Association of Chief Officers of Probation and National Association of Probation Officers, *Probation – The Next Five Years* (1987).
44 A. E. Bottoms, 'Limiting prison use: experience in England and Wales', *Howard Journal of Criminal Justice*, vol. 26, no. 3 (August 1987).
45 T. Mathieson, 'The future of control systems – the case of Norway', in D. Garland and Peter Young (eds), *The Power to Punish* (Heinemann Educational, 1983), p. 140.
46 B. Hudson in NAPO, *Probation: Engaging with Custody* (October 1986).
47 Beaumont and Walker, op. cit. (n10), pp. 89–90.
48 Inner London Probation Service Demonstration Unit, 'Increasing the use of probation', *Probation Journal*, vol. 33, no. 3 (September 1986).
49 S. Box, *Recession, Crime and Punishment* (Macmillan, 1987), p. 183.
50 See P. James, 'Day centres', in Walker and Beaumont, op. cit. (n10).
51 L. Dominelli, 'Differential justice: domestic labour, community service and female offenders', *Probation Journal*, vol. 31, no. 3 (September 1984).
52 NACRO, *Black People and the Criminal Justice System* (NACRO, July 1986), p. 15.
53 The *Guardian*, 30 September 1986.
54 H. Walker, 'Women's issues in probation practice', in Walker and Beaumont, op. cit. (n10).
55 F. Heidensohn, *Women and Crime* (Macmillan, 1985).
56 R. Green 'Racism and the offender: a probation response', in J. Harding (ed.), *Probation and the Community* (Tavistock, 1987).
57 ibid., p. 188.
58 ibid., p. 188.
59 ibid., p. 187.
60 Pinder, op. cit. (n23), p. 2.
61 ibid., p. 167.
62 ibid., p. 168.
63 See NAPO, *Manifesto for Action: developing an anti-racist probation practice* (NAPO, 1987).
64 Pinder, op. cit. (n23), pp. 187–8.

65 Green, op. cit. (n56), p. 191.
66 See NACRO, op. cit. (n52) and I. Crow, 'Black people and criminal justice in the UK', *Howard Journal of Criminal Justice*, vol. 26, no. 4 (November 1987).
67 Consider P. Senior, 'The probation order: a vehicle of social work or social control', *Probation Journal* (June 1984) and Raynor, op. cit. (n2), pp. 41–69.
68 Shaw, op. cit. (n38), p. 37.
69 See Beaumont in Walker and Beaumont, op. cit. (n10).
70 Walker and Beaumont, op. cit (n8).

Index